THE PRINTS OF JAPAN

THE
PRINTS OF JAPAN

Dr. F. A. Turk

OCTOBER HOUSE INC. NEW YORK

First published in the United States of America, 1966 by
October House Inc.
134 East 22nd Street, New York, N.Y. 10010
Copyright © 1966 by Frank A. Turk
Library of Congress catalog card no. 66–25524
Manufactured in Great Britain

TO SIGNORINA
ADRIANA BOSCARO
MEMBER OF THE ROYAL ASIATIC SOCIETY

MEMBER OF THE JAPAN SOCIETY

VENEZIA–CORNWALL

1963

'Noi non potemo avere perfetta vita senza amici'

DANTE

CONTENTS

Contents

III. *The Print Productions of Cities other than Edo*

IV. *A Miscellany of Notes on Prints and Printed Books*

ILLUSTRATIONS

Illustrations

PREFACE

THE three quotations that stand at the head of this book isolate three of the several attitudes to—as indeed aspects of—the prints of Japan. Almost all the illustrative or fine art printing in Japan has, for many western connoisseurs, an extraordinarily winning and powerful aesthetic appeal which has developed in more than a few admirers of the *ukiyo-e* print something not far removed from monomania. During the last decade several well written and sumptuously illustrated books have catered for this public; mercifully so, since the colour prints themselves become more difficult to obtain as more and more of the necessarily limited supply find their way into museum collections and the prices of those remaining continue to rise.

But also there is a growing interest in the thought, ways and attitudes of the Far East and for many people those of Japan will seem more accessible to our age than those of China or Korea. This turning to a superficial exoticism is no new thing in an affluent society but such interests in things Japanese often go deeper today. As the values of our society become lost in confusion or fail altogether, it is often felt that a new understanding—perhaps, sometimes, only a welcome relief—can be found in the contemplation of the many motivations of Edo society which, in a manner, seems curiously modern and able spontaneously to call up our sympathies. It is probable, I think, that the post-war western interest in the Japanese print has a very strong admixture of this need and if so, it is no doubt the main reason why much of the appeal these prints have for the present generation of collectors and students has, mixed with it, a seriousness of purpose which demands, far more than formerly, new perspectives in historical and even sociological analysis. For many, it is not as a spectacle and from the outside that they wish to view these colour prints but as appropriate illustrations of what they can experience in their own thoughts and emotions. Such adds a new dimension to their art appreciation.

For the collector who is still in his apprenticeship, as for the student of this art who lacks special knowledge of Japanese arts and literature, there are many difficulties in the way of his informed enjoyment of these prints and, although there have been books published in the past that were designed to help him to the knowledge he required, these are mostly out of print and costly besides being in several ways out of date. There are, it is true, several available monographs of the highest standard of scholarship and the most informed sensibility on individual artists, but for the most part these go no further than the single artist whose work forms their subject matter. In addition, there is Binyon and Sexton's *Japanese Colour Prints* which is probably still the best one-volume work on the Japanese Print available and which, if supplemented by Mr J. Hillier's *The Japanese Print*, will give rather more than the fundamentals of the *history* of the *ukiyo-e* school. Although, of course, the collector and student want this, they want also something more. Mr B. W. Robinson, probably Britain's foremost expert on Japanese art, reviewing Mr Hillier's earlier book, *Japanese Masters of the Colour Print* in *The Listener* (March 11th, 1954) calls attention to the 'correct' view of the subject which entails a predilection for the Primitives and a decline after 1800 and continues 'But the new collector to whom, as well as to the general art lover, the book is dedicated . . . will find that for every eighteenth-century print he encounters in real life there will be at least a dozen from the nineteenth'. The purposes of the present book are to enable the student to place correctly the majority of the prints he comes across, to read signatures and seals, to identify the subject matter with understanding, to satisfy himself of the reasons for changes of style and technique and especially to be able to do these things for the less well-known prints and artists, which have a way of turning up with a surprising frequency, leaving the connoisseur powerless to identify the subject, the artist or even the approximate date. It is for those who have known these frustrations and have suffered the attendant dilemmas that this book has been made.

Finally, there is the vast and even more frequently bewildering subject of the Japanese illustrated book: closely related as it is in technique and to some extent history to the better documented Japanese Colour Print it offers more opportunity to the collector of restricted means to find those satisfactions which I have indicated above. Mr Holloway, in the wholly excellent and quite indispensable work from which my third quotation is drawn, has provided the only modern account in English of the *oeuvre* which he has called, the Classic School. However, it is not part of that book's purpose, to aid the student in the task of reading titles, dates or artists', publishers' and engravers' names. Nor does it deal with the more arcane matters of editions, reprints or the technical aspects of book production in Japan as a whole. These needs have also been in mind in the making of the present book, and within the necessarily restricted limits available, at least a preliminary attempt has been made to meet them.

In no sense therefore is this a picture-book. In a modest way it looks to have what would be best thought of as the material, partly of a technical handbook, partly of a study complementary to works currently available and partly of an *aide-mémoire*.

F. A. TURK

INTRODUCTORY NOTE

THE transliteration of Japanese names for the English-speaking reader has always been a matter of contention and disagreement. It is made more difficult when the purposes to be served are those of the general reader who will not readily recognize, for example, 'Fuji' in 'Huzi' or 'Jujutsu' in 'Zyuzutu'. More than one student of the Japanese print has searched vainly in a book on the subject for, say, Enkyo and, failing to find it has concluded that the work in question is incomplete when the explanation is that it treats this artist under Yenkyo or even Yenkio.

Whatever system an author adopts he lays himself open to one of two serious charges; on the one hand, that of inexact scholarship, on the other, pedantry. The more kindly and tolerant critic may perhaps demand only that there should be consistency in whatever system is used: yet if the author adopts this view, there must surely be many readers with little knowledge of either phonetics or Japanese and these will have to seek long and diligently for many matters on which they require information. They would hardly be human if they did not experience a certain exasperation when ultimately they find that the word which they sought under 'K' is, in fact, listed under 'G' and that even this discovery leaves them with a small residual uncertainty.

In the view of the present author there is no adequate answer to this at all. Some consistency has been attempted in this book but it has been varied here and there in favour of those transliterations which, it was believed, would be more easily recognized by the average collector of Japanese prints. In a few instances too, this consistency has been waived when a name has been taken from old French and German sale catalogues. The former of these two languages is notoriously uncertain in its rendering of Japanese names and, in the absence of the native characters, it was often impossible to be certain of the exact transliteration of such a name in the English Hepburn system or its later modifications.

In a general way, the following are considered to be interchangeable: Ye/E, Gwa/Ga, Kwa/Ka, Kwō/Kō, Wō/Ō and, in some few instances, fu/hu whilst the *nigōri* K/G is not entirely

15

consistent. It is believed however that the change of 'n' to 'm' before 'b', 'm' or 'p' has been generally adhered to since, in any event, it is more euphonious to English as to Japanese ears.

It remains to state that all the prints illustrated are in my own collection with the exception of those on Plate 8 which are the property of my friend, Mr Cyril Staal of Cotehele, Cornwall, to whom I owe also the photographs from which the plate was made. For all other photographs I am indebted to Mr Kay Larsen, B.Sc., whilst to Mr Norman Hall, A.R.C.A. I owe much for considerable help in the production of some of the material from which the line blocks have been made. To all three gentlemen must be given my grateful thanks.

'I find in the art of this astonishing people nothing strained, a calm, a grandeur, an extraordinary unity—a rather subdued radiance which is nevertheless brilliant.' *From a letter from Camille to Lucien Pissarro,* dated 3 February 1893.

'Japanese Colour Prints should not be collected solely as works of art; an intelligent study of the subjects and scenes they illustrate will tell us more of the life, history, and character of Japan in the days when it was a closed book to the rest of the world than any number of pages of print.' *Basil Stewart in the preface to* Subjects Portrayed in Japanese Colour Prints: *London 1922.*

'. . . there are also the masters called . . . the Classical School. Their work is found not in sheet prints but in printed albums of illustrations done for the most part in a completely different part of Japan.' *Owen E. Holloway in the preface to* Graphic Art of Japan, the Classical School: *London 1957.*

Part 1

The Origins and Production of the Prints

CHAPTER I

The Origins of Picture Prints in the Far East

THE INFLUENCES which shaped Japanese prints in all their variety are many and various and the origins of some of the basic techniques are very far off in time, so distant that we cannot now be sure just how much was borrowed, how much was invented anew, and how much was vaguely remembered from an earlier time and more distant place, hanging in the air of history like thin smoke, to be kindled into a new flame by the breath of necessity.

Certainly the beginnings were in China and the earliest woodcuts of which we have any knowledge are all of Buddhist deities. Sir Aurel Stein found several in the Tun-huang caves and one, showing an especially highly evolved technique, is dated A.D. 868. Binyon and Sexton mention two others dated 947 and 983 respectively. Some examples delineate not only figures but architecture, details of costume and other such things showing that the art had already passed beyond the stage of crude outlines. Animals are rare but do occur, e.g. one in the Central Asian Antiquities Museum of New Delhi No. KK II 0227a, shows a well drawn elephant. Occasionally little genre vignettes appear as in KK II 0230b which shows a man running through a storm of hail and is distantly reminiscent of the treatment given to this theme centuries later by Hokusai. Many of these prints in style and subject matter show a close similarity with the painted silk banners used in early Buddhist ceremonies. Stein found fragments of these at Karakhoto and, since some of them contain portions of landscapes, it might well be that the wood-block prints also depicted such themes although few have come down to us that can be said to show pure landscape treatment. A matter of further interest is that the British Museum has one of these prints produced with the aid of two blocks, these being used to print in two shades of blue on a design otherwise coloured by hand. Most of such prints have accompanying texts in Chinese and Hsi-hsia, a very complicated script in which the Tangut language was written and which in some ways looks not unlike Chinese, having decided decorative possibilities.

The theories purporting to demonstrate that printing began in China in the Sui dynasty (589–618) have all been refuted in recent years. It is almost certain that the printed book came into existence in late T'ang times but it was probably not in common use until the Five Dynasties period (907–960). Several works survive from this early time but the two most important are probably the copy of the Diamond Sutra, the blocks for which were cut by a Wang Chieh in 868, and an almanac for 882, both of which are in the British Museum. In view of the part played by the illegal, privately printed almanac in the development of the Japanese *nishiki-e* in the eighteenth century it is of interest to note that there is a record from the T'ang dynasty that Fēng Ssū (? 836) suggested that the imperial court should place a ban on the privately printed almanacs which were produced at that time in the provinces of Chien-nan, Liang-chuan and Huai-nan. Copperplate engraving was introduced in the period of the Five Dynasties and unspecified improvements were made in the process during the Sung (960–1279) but, as in Japan, the craft seems to have died out.

Most of the earliest books are printed in scroll form but single sheets are very common and when these are illustrated, the text and illustrations are sometimes—but not always—printed from separate blocks: not uncommonly the illustrations are coloured by hand. Bound books appear first in the Five Dynasties period.

Probably the techniques used to produce these works were not very different from these used in China in much later times. Texts, with or without illustrations, were engraved on small blocks of pear or plum wood of varying sizes but often around 26 cm × 7·5 cm[1] and of a thickness of 2 cm or less. (See Plate 1.) These blocks were soaked in water before the engraving commenced and then the text, which had been written out by hand, was pasted down on to the wood and engraved to a depth of perhaps 3 to 5 mm. After the blocks had been inked with the use of two brushes, one to transfer and one to work up the ink, the paper to be printed was placed face down on the printing surface and pressed with a coir pad. According to the late Dyer Ball some 16,000 copies could be taken before the blocks began to wear badly and even then it was often possible to run off a further

10,000. This is certainly far in excess of the number of copies possible of a Japanese colour print. However, allowing for the very generalized estimate, perhaps somewhat inflated, it is doubtful, judging by the great numbers of these Buddhist writings known to have been produced by this method, whether such numbers are really gross exaggerations on the part of Ball's informant. Nevertheless, once colour printing came into existence the difficulty of keying very worn blocks would have very greatly reduced the output that was reasonably possible.

In Korea wood-block printing never seems to have attained the eminence that it did in China or Japan. However, here too, early Buddhist works, often handwritten in silver or gold on purple coloured grounds, were embellished with woodcut designs. Several Buddhist wood-blocks with text and pictures have survived from the Koryo period (A.D. 935–1392) and the monastery of Pong-un-sa in Kyong-ki is said to have possessed an engraved block 40 cm × 70 cm. Many large maps were similarly engraved and one in the household library of Prince I was over one metre long and nearly 80 cm broad. Movable type is said to have been first used in Korea in 1403 in the reign of king Tha-tjong (1401–1418)[2] and texts with engraved illustrations become fairly common from the mid-fifteenth century onwards.

As the result of this short survey, it is interesting to note that almost all the ingredients of Japanese wood-block printing were in existence already in the earlier development in China and that this included not only the basic technique but also all the motifs which were later to develop more or less separately in Japan. Almost certainly Buddhism would have transported these to that country from the continent but for many of the later developments the connecting thread is very tenuous, some being, no doubt, suggested anew by the very limitations of the techniques used. Moreover, as other authors have said, it is not enough merely to say that this or that thing was borrowed; we must inquire as to the purpose of the borrowing. In all these countries the first purpose was the dissemination, rapidly and in quantity, of Buddhist texts and it would be worth considering at another time why Buddhism at such an early date should have felt this need more acutely than Confucianism.

The production of coloured woodcuts was a much later development in all countries of the Far East. But here too the technique appeared in China a little before it did in Japan. Printed books with coloured plates made from engraved blocks were being produced in some numbers in the Ming dynasty. The earliest known work of this kind is the *Ch'eng shih mo yuan* by Ting Yun-p'eng, a work on ink cakes. It was printed in five colours and published in 1606. K. T. Wu in his article on Ming printing and printers, published in 1943, has corrected many previous statements on this subject. He tells us that only two copies of this early coloured woodcut book are in existence, one in China and the other in Japan. Two other more famous works are the *Shih-chu-chai Shu-hua-p'u* (The Ten Bamboo Hall painting book) published, according to R. Paine, in 1633 although other authorities give variously 1625 or 1643, and, even more famous and certainly better known, the *Chieh-tzu Yuan hua chuan* (Hand-book of the Paintings of the Mustard Seed Garden) which is said to have been printed between Spring 1677 and Winter 1679. This, incidentally, shows something of the extreme care taken in these productions and indicates that they were made for the richer classes since they were necessarily expensive.

The papers on which these Chinese works were printed are rather variable, especially in the later editions, but most usually they are on a fine, white, very tough and durable paper. Some of the prints show a careful and tasteful blind or *gauffrage* printing and Professor Kurth came to the conclusion that wood-blocks, metal plates, engraved stones and hand colouring were all used to produce some of these prints. Up to twelve colours, often graded by wiping the block, were produced at a single printing and ten more by superimposition. Few if any sheet prints of this altitude of refinement were produced in China and it is safe to say that generally the Chinese had nothing at all comparable with the finer *nishiki-e* of Japan.

However, China did originate a form of fine printing, often in colour, which has lasted down to the present day. This was the art of the printed, decorative letter papers. Some authors have claimed that designs printed in two colours on plain or tinted paper and produced as fine writing paper, were in being soon after the end of the sixteenth century A.D. but this seems largely conjecture based on possibilities only. The singer Hsieh T'ao (768–831) seems to have been the first to sketch a little design—bare branches and pine needles—on the paper which she used for writing her poems. This practice was quickly followed by other poets and calligraphers and the standard poetry paper became one having a suitable but very simple design sketched lightly in a single colour contrasting or harmonizing with the black pine soot ink of the writing. Such papers came to be called Hsieh-T'ao's poetry paper (*Hsieh-T'ao chien*). So widespread did this practice become and so much the vogue, that it was inevitable that it should be followed by Heian society in Japan.[3] Perhaps it was brought back by some of those who travelled with such scholar priests as Enchin or Ennin in the ninth century. True polychrome woodcuts, *t'ao-pan*, are said to have been used in China for poetry papers as early as the twelfth century but these seem to have been extremely crude productions and were probably not used for more than the common antithetical couplets which decorated all but the meanest homes. So far as can be told at present the final and definite form of such writing papers was established by Hu Cheng-yen's *Shih-chu-chai Shu-hua-p'u* of 1633. It was not long before the employment of such designs for letter writing papers was common practice among the Chinese literati and the few presses, mostly at Pekin and Soochow, which produced such work, had a large output and were prolific in new designs. Printed stationery, for those able to afford it, became *à la mode* in Japan in Tokugawa times and several of the *Ukiyo-e* artists designed for it whilst, a development of this, printed envelopes (*futō*) became an added refinement. Those decorated with polychrome wood-block prints by Hiroshige have become famous in recent years and are amongst the treasures of the few western collections that have been fortunate enough to acquire them.

China produced yet another class of woodcut print, often polychrome but perhaps more commonly with at least some of the colours added by hand. This class includes the rather crude popular prints of gods (*ma chang*) and other heavenly personages (see Plate 2), New Year Prints (*nien hua*) and the rather rarer, but equally crude, theatrical prints. The origin of the first class of prints is uncertain but they are unlikely to be earlier than the Ming dynasty and it is extremely doubtful if any later than the latter part of the eighteenth century are to be found in western collections. This kind of print usually shows either the gods of wealth, healing, longevity or some other of the pantheon that minister to an all too material happiness, or else the so called 'door gods'. Others again represent the 'ancestors of the last three generations' (*san-tai tsong-ts'in*) which are used in the

New Year ritual of their cult. Some of these wood-block prints, and strangely enough not always the crudest, show either the fifty-four or the sixty groups of divinities—a mixture of Buddhist and Taoist worthies—and are designed to be burned. Many other celestial beings of somewhat confused iconography are to be found depicted in this class of print.[4] Such prints may be produced from an outline block only or have in addition five or six colour blocks. Many are partially or wholly coloured by hand and often, in the better kind of print, this is very delicately done. Rather curious are those prints which have the faces of the various personages reproduced by polychrome wood-blocks whilst the remainder of the picture is coloured by hand. All prints of this class await detailed investigation especially as to provenance, dating and technique but from the evidence so far available it would seem that differences in the latter are most likely to be conditioned more by the local custom of the region of their production than by the date of it. These regions were several and as yet are probably not fully known; Shanghai, Peking, Soochow, and, most famous of all, Yang-liu-ch'ing near Tientsin, all had their distinct local forms. Large prints, and some were as much as 4 ft. by 2 ft., were printed from several blocks and then placed side by side, a matter calling for quite exact register as did the very effective technique, seemingly never undertaken by the Japanese, of printing in grey by the side of the black outline to give the effect of the nuances of the ink tones in the calligraphic line of the original drawing.

The theatrical polychrome woodcuts of China are usually, if not cruder than the others, then certainly in more garish and decidedly less pleasing colours. Nowhere, and at no time do these prints seem to have evolved anything at all comparable to the theatrical print in Japan. Always an ephemeral thing, no study seems to have been made of the dates when the different forms have been in production nor do we know when the use of them was first started. Most of the dramatic forms had their origin in the musical dramas of the Yuan dynasty (1260–1368) and early illustrated wood-block texts of these dramas are known which date from the Ming (1368–1644).[5]

Binyon and Sexton in their standard work *Japanese Colour Prints* say 'in all essentials the history of the Japanese colour print is independent of that of China'. This is somewhat equivocal if by 'history' is meant the origins as well as the development. From what has been said above it will be clear that the Japanese print probably owed much to China and the beginning of almost every development in the history of the Japanese print was antedated on the continent. More detailed study may well show that even the actor print, perhaps that most characteristic of the ukiyo-e school, had its far off genesis in the illustrated texts of the Ming and Yuan dramas. Certainly there is a parallel development in both countries: for example, both utilized the religious print designed to further the cause of Buddhism; both were bound up to some extent with folk-art, that is, if we include the Japanese Ōtsu-e (see below); both used on occasion similar techniques of printing and somewhat similar materials. Although there were differences in the papers used for printing, these were each relatively absorbent despite what has been stated to the contrary elsewhere. Lastly, as we have seen, both were put to the usages of the theatre. Of course, there were even greater differences in the development of printing in China and Japan—to cite but one such we may note that neither fashion-plate prints nor those of courtesans appeared in China—and it seems certain that these differences are to be ascribed to the fact that the Chinese wood-block prints were produced either for the scholar class or for one or other of the domestic cults, not far removed from a folk religion and accepted alike, with various degrees of seriousness, by scholars, nobility, semi-literates and illiterates. In Japan, the Edo and some of the Ōsaka sheet prints were produced for a more or less literate, highly sophisticated and intensely urban society whilst many of the books printed in Ōsaka and Kyōto were designed for the small society of court nobles and the older generations of connoisseurs and scholars. Other differences in the social background and *milieu* there were too, both economic and historical, but even more important, were the different moral values which Confucianism and Shintō respectively, emphasized. In the course of time there came to be differences in materials and techniques as well and hence, if a small re-statement is made, we may agree that the *development* 'of the Japanese colour print is independent of that of China'.

In Japan as in China wood-block printing was used to spread the teachings of Buddhism and the art probably came to Japan with the first Chinese and Korean priests. Curiously enough the first engraving seems to have been on copper plates (*bōshimei*) and these have been found in tombs of the sixth and seventh centuries A.D. with epitaphs engraved on them. A similar plate of gilt bronze in the

Nara museum commemorates the setting up of a Buddhist statue and is dated A.D. 694; printings from it, as with rubbings of engraved stones, show the white text on a black ground. The earliest Japanese pictorial wood-block print is of lions and is dated A.D. 740 being printed not on paper but on leather. In 764 the Empress Shōken ordered the four Buddhist *dharani* (talismanic words or spells), the *Kompon*, *Jishinin*, *Sōrin*, and *Rokudo*, to be engraved on slips about eighteen inches by two inches and each was enclosed in one of a million tiny wood pagodas. It is interesting that these are still common enough for one to have been sold in the Hayashi sale of 1902. Not all of them are of the same date nor indeed are they all printed on the same paper. As one would expect from a predominantly religious art the same designs, probably even the same blocks on occasion, were issued again and again over the centuries without change. From the standpoint of the later colour prints we can assign little more than the techniques basic to printing as being derived from these early Buddhist prints—that, and possibly the first move towards certain general pictorial themes.

Not very much later there came into existence woodcut portraits of priests which were designed to serve as souvenirs for pilgrims that visited their temples. There are indeed records of priests having themselves engraved these early woodcuts, e.g. the priest Gyōgi Bosatsu (670–749). Representations of deities were early added to the repertoire of such productions and one of the most interesting is that of Bato Kwannon at the Honga shrine, Nikkō which measures thirty-one inches by twelve inches and is actually dated A.D. Jan./ Feb. 844. The fact that some scholars have seen in this a product of the much later Muromachi period (1398–1573) serves only to stress the fact that the whole design, even including the original date, might be copied again and again over the centuries.

More important are the well known and often reproduced prints of the Hokke-kyo, many sheets of which are preserved in the Shitennōji temple at Ōsaka. This work, known as the Senmen Kosha-kyō, is written on a background of Tosa style designs, all of which are on fan-shaped leaves and some of which have the outlines printed. The backgrounds are covered variously with mica, silver and gold dust (the first and second of which are used in the more expensive and sumptuous of the prints of the much later Edo period). Still more important as showing the antiquity of the subject matter of the *ukiyo-e* output, is the fact that the themes of these paintings have no connection with the matter of the sacred text which has been written over them. They show scenes of everyday life in Japan at the time of their production i.e. twelfth century and depict all classes of the people; besides these there are scenes from old romances of the Heian era (794–1184), pictures of birds and flowers and similar decorative motifs. The technique and, in part, the themes, both follow the old practice of decorating poetry paper (*shikishi*) and it may well be that colour printing in Japan, as in a more restricted way in China, came into existence originally for the production of this kind of paper. The papers used at this period for printing are of the kind known as *senka*, thick, somewhat toned, very durable, and were produced at Iyo.

That Chinese printing was already reaching Japan and no doubt influencing the practice there, is shown by the fact that a Chinese printed paper roll in green and brown, with deep *gauffrage* printing, exists in the Daigō-ji treasury. Written on it is the text of the Tenchō Inshin and there is good evidence that it dates from the reign of Go-Daigō (1319–1339).

As early as the first quarter of the fifteenth century there is evidence of a considerable growth in the complexity of techniques and of a new mastery. Of about this time there exists a history of the Nembutsu sect of Buddhism (*Yudzu Nembutsu Engi*) by Ryōnin, written originally in 1125. It is engraved, with many illustrations, on two long scrolls each $11\frac{1}{2}$ inches high and the two scrolls together when placed end to end, have a total length of $96\frac{1}{2}$ feet. Many of the individual wood engravings are several feet in length, the average being 3 feet 6 inches long. Mrs L. N. Brown who apparently saw these scrolls at about the time of the first world war, describes them as being on a soft heavy paper somewhat like kid leather. The cutting of the text blocks began in 1389 and was finished in 1390, at which date the engraving of the illustrations was commenced and not finished until 1414. All this is evidence of the existence of skilled engravers at this time as well as of the maintenance of a high standard of technique and a belief that the final product was worthy of having an immense amount of care, and no doubt of wealth, expended on it. So, by the first quarter of the fifteenth century the wood-block print had evolved from the primitive mass-produced piece of religious propaganda, the rough talisman or the ephemeral souvenir that for the most part it had been in earlier times, and it might now be considered in its own right, a fine art.

Moreover, it would seem that we can see in this and other scrolls of the period a drift away from the old Yamato-e style of the Hokke-kyō engravings mentioned above. In them, as in the older school of painting as a whole, the viewpoint is obliquely from above, the picture plane being divided horizontally by cloud-scrolls; the draperies are stiff and represented by a medley of angles whilst for the most part faces are drawn in the *hikime-kagihana* style, i.e. with one side of the face bordered by a mass of hair and the other by a simple curve, the features being shown by a line for the eye and another angle for the nose. In the Yudzu Nembutsu Engi scroll, some of these characteristics are the same but some have already changed. The eyes, for the most part are more fully drawn and individually shaped and in some faces the nose is given individual contours whilst here and there are figures having the draperies drawn with curves reminiscent of the older Buddhist paintings and not in the stiff angles of the *yamato-e* style although these still persist in many figures. Much of the outline too is in a more modulated line which reminds us that the Tosa school of painting was coming into being during this same period. All in all, it is perhaps not too much to see in this scroll and in one or two others, not only that the wood-block illustration was moving now out of the domain of purely religious art and incorporating genre subjects but that it was acquiring a new refinement of technique, very probably the outcome of a special class of lay engravers who were ready to profit from the Chinese and Korean books and the ideas that came with them when they were imported from the continent during the period of increased trade that began during the fifteenth century and which was inaugurated as a government policy by the Ashikaga shogunate.

The period which we now enter is one extremely difficult of interpretation since there is an almost complete absence of illustrated, non-Buddhist engraved works of this time. One is tempted to think that such must have existed and for one reason or another have been destroyed. The great civil wars—the wars of Ōnin—delayed the continued evolution of most of the arts; peasant revolts, fire and pestilence contributed their quota of destruction. For the most part the times were unpropitious. Yet it is not unreasonable to suppose that letter-papers decorated with woodcuts continued in production and there is a high probability that certain illustrated works of a non-religious nature would have been printed at this time. As an example of such, mention might be made of the works on medicine; the texts of medical works are known from as early as the ninth century and generally contain a few simple illustrations. Most of them have been lost and only their titles remain, e.g. the *Kinran-hō* ('Prescriptions of the Orchid Door'—evidently a work on gynaecology and most probably Korean in origin). Besides medical works there were also military ones such as the *Bijin-gusa* ('A Collection of Beautiful Women')—an unlikely title for such a work since it is a collection of notes on military matters collected over some 170 years from 1256 and published privately with four woodcuts in 1464. These woodcuts are said to be very simple and it must be admitted that what little material there is in existence for the study of non-religious woodcut illustrations during these centuries does show only extremely crude and simple techniques—in most respects falling far short of those of the Heian era—moreover when material does become a little more plentiful, in the sixteenth century, the woodblock prints are still really very primitive. Nothing indeed equals the earlier religious illustrative work and with the destruction of many of the monasteries which had been publishing 'houses' (e.g. *Shōkoku-ji*) this too seems to have come to an end. We certainly cannot at present see that continuity in history which must have prepared the way for the new flowering of the old tree of the woodcut in the very early seventeenth century and a few years before.

Nor are we able to estimate what was the effect of the coming of the Portuguese and Spaniards to Japan and the introduction of Christian icons in the form of copperplate engravings. The first Portuguese came in 1548 and in the last decade of the sixteenth century several of these Christian prints are known to have been published at Kazusa and Ariie (in 1591 and 1596 respectively, and in 1607 in Kyushu). With the banning of Christianity in 1637 all further production of these copper engravings ceased and most of those which had been published in previous years were destroyed, so that there is now very little evidence from which we may deduce the effect of these imported techniques on the native arts of book illustration and production. That there was in fact still a tradition of fine wood engraving is shown by the publication in 1565 of the '*Kōbo-Daishi gyōjo zue*' on ten scrolls—an anecdotal history of the life of the priest Kukai who had been in China in the early ninth century and had introduced Shingon Buddhism to Japan.

This, in brief, is the known background of wood-block printing in Japan at the commencement of the 'modern' period of its production which may be said to have begun in the Keichō era (1596–1615). Through most of this early period, engravings had been produced by the monasteries for purely religious purposes but evidently a few private presses had been in operation both for the production of poetry and letter papers and, most probably, for a few books such as the *Bijin-gusa* mentioned above: of the names of designers and engravers—if indeed they were not at this time one and the same person—we know nothing whatsoever although it is to be supposed that such private presses as then existed would have been at Nara, Kamakura and Kyōto. This thread, tenuous as it is, running through the history of the centuries, cannot by any means be discounted but neither can the effects of the devastating civil wars, since wood-engraving seems to have sunk to a low ebb by the middle of the sixteenth century. We must look for some outside influence that could cause it to have the sudden re-awakening at the end of the century which was to produce within seventy-five years what was almost a new art, destined soon to burst into the full glories of the *ukiyo-e* colour print.

This influence was certainly the effect of the spoils brought to Japan after Hideyoshi's two successful expeditions against Korea. Among the loot were Chinese and Korean books and whole 'founts' of printing types; it was these last which enabled the *daimyō*—the great feudal lords—to set up private presses of their own. Moreover it is known that Hideyoshi's generals brought back with them many Korean artists and artisans—potters particularly are known by name —and it might well be that engravers and printers were among them. It is not without significance, considering that Hideyoshi's two campaigns were conducted in 1592 and 1597, that it was in the Bunrōku era (1592–1595) that the first book printed from movable type appeared in Japan. Later, Kōetsu designed a fount of movable wooden type of considerable beauty and it was with this that many of his books were printed.

NOTES ON CHAPTER I

[1] The names of some of the engravers have come down to us, e.g. a print of the *Diamond Sutra*, chapters 30–32, in the Bibliothèque Nationale, Paris, has the name Lei Yen-mei as engraver and is dated the 14th June, A.D. 949. A very useful reference is *The Evolution of Chinese Books* by Lo Chin-tang, published by the Nat. Hist. Museum, Taipei 1959, in English, and Chinese.

[2] A recent work on the subject, 'Early Movable Type in Korea', by Wong-yong Kim; *Publ. Nat. Mus. Korea*, Series A, vol. 1, Seoul, 1954, which has just come to my attention, makes it necessary to modify this statement. There seems to be evidence that movable metal type was actually a Korean invention of the late twelfth or early thirteenth centuries. In view of Japan's relationship with Korea, it is curious that the use of such movable type in Japan was not more prevalent in early times. Some of the illustrated Japanese books of the sixteenth and seventeenth centuries had the text printed with such type although this was apparently not made of metal. As demand for books became wider and, to a certain extent, more frivolous, metal types became less common. The Japanese love of cursive script would have made it difficult to fit that form of calligraphy to movable type. According to the author of the work quoted above, the Koreans used fixed type to print a complete version of the Buddhist Tripitaka soon after the Mongol invasion of their country in 1231. It is said that these blocks are still stored in the Haein-sa monastery in South Korea.

[3] A fine example of an extremely intricate and delicately printed floral design of circular composition, repeated over the face of the paper, is to be seen on that which served as writing paper for Fujiwara Yukinari (971–1027). A piece of fine calligraphy, written on such paper and ascribed to his hand, is in the Household Museum collection and is illustrated in the *Annual Report* of the Imperial Household Museum at Tōkyō and Nara for 1936.

[4] The best account of all these gods will be found in *Exposition d'Iconographie Populaire: images rituelles du nouvel an*; Centre Franco–Chinois d'études sinologiques, Pekin, July 1942. Notes on the Gods of Wealth with some very good illustrations of the better kind of these prints are to be found in Alexeiev, B.: *The Chinese Gods of Wealth*; School of Oriental Studies and China Society, London, 1928, and an extremely interesting further article is Gan Tjiang-tek: 'Some Chinese Popular Block Prints' in *The Wonder of Man's Ingenuity*, Rijksmuseum, Leiden; 1962, pages 26–36.

3

Two essential texts for the specialist student are *Yang-liu ch'ing Pan-hua* and Pommeranz-Liedtke, G.: *Chinesische Neujahrsbilder*, Dresden, 1961.

[5] An example is the illustrated Ming edition of the Yuan drama, 'The Western Chamber' (*Hsi hsiang chi*), by Wang Shih-Fu and Kuan Han Ch'ing. There is some reason to date the origins of later drama back to the Sung dynasty (960–1279) and perhaps earlier but there is also some doubt as to whether this really comprised anything more than comic sketches and miming dances performed to music. The earliest known representation of a Chinese theatrical stage is in a mural painting dated 1324 in a temple in Shansi and the earliest mention of theatrical posters—most probably printed from wood-blocks—is in a fourteenth-century text. Early printed texts of the Yuan dramas show an illustration printed from one block on the top half of the page and the text, printed from a separate block, on the bottom half.

CHAPTER II

The Illustrative Arts in Japan in the Seventeenth Century

CULTURES, like organisms, develop their distinctive forms from the interplay of many factors: there are those that inaugurate this process of civilization and determine the main lines of its development; there are those that modify this process of unfolding and give the characteristic and individual form in time and place; and finally there are those that accelerate or retard its evolution as a whole. So it is with the Japanese print. Those factors of the first and second kind which were discussed in the last chapter continue to operate during the century with which we are now concerned but those of the first group are less prominent whilst the second and third categories are much more in evidence.

Previous to 1590, Edo (Tōkyō as it now is) was no more than an undistinguished village of fisher folk dominated by the nearby castle which had been built by Ota Dōkwan in 1456. At the former date the shōgun Ieyasu determined to make this the virtual capital of Japan (it did not become the legal capital until 1868) and with that end in view allowed a certain Mori Magoemon, who had come from Ōsaka, with the thirty tradesmen who had accompanied him, to open a market on a nearby sandbank forming the isle of Tsukada-jima. In the light of subsequent history this seems to have been an act almost symbolic in its significance. Certainly it was to have great consequences for the later *ukiyo-e* colour prints of Edo. It recognized the important role of the merchant class and laid the basis of the commercial nature of Edo society in later years; in addition it shows the influence of Ōsaka in this process and represents the gradual winning of Ōsaka from the cultural sphere of the mikado's capital at Kyōto. Every aspect of these processes is to be found mirrored in the later history of the colour print in Japan.

Kyōto, the old capital, had for centuries and with varying fortunes, been the home of a small and restricted cultural group of court nobles (*kuge*) who, to a large extent, speaking a special language, lived in the aura of superlative refinement that had characterized their society in Heian days and in some ways looked still further back to the golden age of Nara. Many factors during the former three centuries—and among them the rise of Nobunaga (1533–1582)— had caused a blurring of the boundaries of this society and certain features of its cultural life had percolated downwards and outwards to the small merchant and banking classes that had grown up locally in Ōsaka, the great grain exchange city on the coast. These people were wealthy, leisured, and because of the increase in education that had come in the last quarter of the century, literate. Economic factors too were speeding this change. A monetary economy was taking the place of the local subsistence economy of former times and the bankers were favoured by the fact that all official salaries were paid in terms of so many *koku* of rice which had to be exchanged for money. This monopoly was much exacerbated later in the seventeenth century by the laws of Ieyasu.

It is not difficult to imagine that one of the most persistent demands of such a society was for books and the more easily available aesthetic pleasures of all kinds. Several events played a part in deciding what form this should take. Firstly, there was the coming of Christianity. The Jesuits set up a press at Asakusa and to meet the demand for simple stories had printed a translation of Aesop's Fables (*Esopo no Fabulas*) in 1593. But such productions had a relatively minor role. More important were the illustrated books written and illustrated at Nara, the so called *nara-ehon*. The general view of native scholars is that these had originated about a century before and had taken the place of the picture scrolls of the Kamakura age (1185–1333). Bound as a folding book, each illustration in the *Nara-ehon* occupied only one page and the illustrations were intermingled with the text. After the wars of Ōnin many of these artists, who were previously attached to temples, had lost their home with the destruction of these same temples and to a large extent their employment. It seems likely that they settled in a special quarter of the town of Nara and gave much of their time, not so much to Buddhist painting, but to the production of these *Nara-ehon*, a product that found a steady sale among the richer families of that centre of the '*ancien régime*', Kyōto. The subjects of these works were *otogi-zōshi* (servants' entertainments), *kōwaka-mai* (texts of the *kōwaka*, a dance-like dramatic performance) and shortened and simplified versions of the great Heian romances like the *Genji-Monogatari*. Besides these main classes of subject matter there were others, some of which are of especial interest. For instance, apart from some Buddhist and moralistic works (e.g. *Handbook of Moral Lessons for Women*) there were serious and prized literary works like Yoshida Kenkō's *Tsurezure Gusa* ('The Weeds of Idleness'). But even more significant are titles such as *Kasama Chōja Tsurukame mono-gatari* ('Tale of Two Millionaires at Kasama') which were most likely the forerunners of that literature called *ukiyo-e zōshi* to which the Edo colour prints were to owe so much.[1]

This relationship is well shown in a passage from Yumikiko Mizuntani's *Kohan Shōsetsu Sashie Shi* ('History of Illustrations in Early Novels'): 1935. '. . . picture scrolls painstakingly drawn and brilliantly coloured were in great favour among the noble and upper classes, but as they were quite out of reach of the less exalted, a simpler and cheaper substitute was evolved in the form of the illustrated books. The latter grew in popularity as objects of pro-duction and sale and, because they were first made and distributed in Nara, they came to be called "Nara" art.' But there is yet a reference of even greater import in involving the Nara books and their producers in the origins of *Ukiyo-e art*; this occurs in Mr Futaba Higuchi's *Tanryokubon* (Red and Green Books), Rare Book Reprint Society of Japan, series IV. In discussing the artists of the Kasuga shrine at Nara, he says, 'With the decline of Nara, the Kasuga school declined also, and the later artists were employed in painting reproductions on picture scrolls or in making colour wood-block prints.' If this can be substantiated we have here a possible clue to the origins of some at least of the early engravers.

But, the *Nara-ehon* apart, there was coming about another method of meeting this new demand. As was shown in the last chapter, after Hideyoshi's campaigns private presses began to come into being. Some of the most important were set up at Fushimi, Saga and Takagamine, villages on the outskirts of Kyōto. The moving spirit in this movement was Honami Kōetsu (1558–1637), potter, painter—he was especially noted for his bird and flower studies—calligrapher, and chief arbiter of the taste of his day; he turned in his middle age to book production. Fritz Rumpf, the German scholar—in his inaugural dissertation in 1931[2]—argued that the originator of the Japanese wood-block print was the illustrator of the *Ise Monogatari* published in 1608, in two volumes with forty-nine illustrations on *doromaniai* paper, i.e. a *maniai* paper (thick paper made at Najie in Arima) prepared with chalk-white. It is of some further significance that this paper is the one most commonly used in the *Nara-ehon*:[3] the work was published by the rich connoisseur, son of a ship-builder, Suminokura Soan who was at one time a pupil of Kōetsu's and who founded a famous press at Saga which has given its name to the whole group of such works which are thus called *Saga-bon*. It is in keeping with what we know of Kyōto society at this time that the work should have appeared in two editions, a luxury one for the nobility and a 'small paper' one for the less well-to-do. Possibly as an excuse for the production of a lighter, more frivolous literature, in an age ostensibly interested only in religious, moral and historical works, the *Ise Monogatari* pretended to be for women and actually has a postface by Yasokuso dedicating it to women. It is of interest to learn that the two editions were produced from two sets of almost identical blocks and we know the engraver of both to have been a certain Shimonura Tukifusa. The illustrations have been said by many scholars to have been in the *yamato-e* style but as we have seen in Chapter I, there were signs of changes in this style of wood-block illustration, far back in the fifteenth century, and it is not without good grounds that other scholars (e.g. Dr Lubor Hajek) have seen obvious connections with the Tosa school. Mr J. Hillier in his recent book, *The Japanese Print— a new approach* (London, n.d.), says '. . . these are, at best, only careful translations of designs from the Tosa school which, at that period, was suffering from marked debility, and the prints, though decorative in the books they adorn, look thin and meagre when detached from them.' That there is point in this argument is true and no doubt such a characteristic will be enlarged in the eye of a pro-fessional wood-engraver like Mr Hillier, but it is also true that, in their setting, they were not only well adapted to the techniques then at the command of the engraver but were also beautifully harmonized with the calligraphy of the text—a calligraphy moreover that had been written by Kōetsu himself.

Popular books now began to fall from these presses at an ever-increasing rate. Among the *Saga-bon*, printed with movable type on a characteristic embossed paper, were poetry books like the *Waka sanju-rokkasen* and the text of the *jōruri*, a kind of ballad drama chanted by professional reciters and named after the tragic figure of the Princesss Jōruri. Some of the latter had illustrations, e.g. the *Jōruri-hime Monogatari* but most were cheaper productions without these plates. Some of these works announce openly that the illustrations are taken from old Chinese works and the press at Fushimi seems to have specialized in reprinting continental books. One of these, *Bai-ju*, a Chinese work on acupuncture, was printed from movable type. In 1625–1626 appeared the first of the *meisho-ki* (popular guide books for pilgrims and others) called *Kumano-no-honji*, dealing with places and events in the province of Kii. Possibly a little later than 1630 the *Soga Monogatari*, a long historical drama, was published which was later to circulate in theatrical versions—the first of a type that was to remain popular until the end of the nineteenth century.

Until about 1625 the illustrations to these books were in *sumi-e*, i.e. in black and white only but then a red (*tan*) and, more rarely, a green, were added by hand, after printing. In a very few books the beautiful pinkish-red, *beni*, seems to have been used but this was distinctly rare. In the following years other colours appeared in the prints, added to the *tan* and blue-green (*roku*) which were the characteristic colours of the books that became known as *tan-ryokubon*: these colours were deeper blue, yellow, ochre and mauve, all applied by hand.

Typical of the men producing these books was Hinaya Nonoguchi Ryuho (1599–1669) a painter, a *Haikai* poet (he had studied under Teitoku), and possibly a maker of netsuke and dolls who is known as the designer of the *Osana Genji* of 1661 in ten large volumes. As doubtless many another whose name is no longer known to us but whose books remain, he was a gifted, wealthy and leisured amateur and no doubt designed for others like himself in the old Kyōto society. The small edition of the *Ise Monogatari* published by Hayashi Izumi-no-jō of Kyōto in 1661 is sometimes attributed to him. Nearly all these productions are, in greater or lesser degree, sumptuous and the total effect is that of small, personally produced, luxury editions; such a one is the *Hyakushō-den* or 'The Hundred Generals', published in 1656 in two large paper volumes and bound in heavily gauffraged covers bearing a design of dragonflies on a ground of small intersecting circles.

Such were the books of the Kyōto publishers and their public but in the still new city of Edo a new art had grown up, in an idiom in which quite different men were designing; the art of *ukiyo-e*. The founder of this school is traditionally said to have been Iwasa Matabei (1578–1650). An ancestor of this school he certainly may have been but equally certainly he is not the originator. He appears to have studied in the Kanō, Tosa and Unkoku schools and in his period of full activity he seems to have produced *genre* pictures but not ones of contemporary scenes and manners but rather those drawn from Chinese history and legend as well as of classical times in Japan. A legend grew up that also attributed to him the origin of *Ōtsu-e* (this derived from a fictional character in a play by Chika-matsu) which seems to have been quite unfounded on fact although there may have been some connection in his life with Ōtsu since one of his most famous pictures—or at least one attributed to him from early times although very likely wrongly—'An Outing', has, for some centuries, been in the *shinden* hall of the Emman-in monastery at Ōtsu. Mr James Michiner in his work *The Floating World* does this painter scant justice when he says, rather lukewarmly, '. . . he is shown to be a gifted painter who experimented modestly in colour but not in line or content.' This is not true of his great work, 'Honshōbo's Gigantic Strength',[4] in the Imperial Museum collections which, in its immensely powerful line and convulsive composition, recalls the terror which can be echoed from the scrolls of the old *yamato-e* painter, Keinin, (thirteenth century). Yet, in a different way, it recalls too the most powerful representation of pictures of sheer horror and intense terror which are found in the album of Edo woodcuts of 1657 called *Musashi Abumi*. This book deals with the terrible fire of 1657 in which much of Edo was burned down and 100,000 lives were lost. The designer of this book is unknown but one cannot help thinking that he had been influenced by some of the work of Matabei or of a relatively unformed tradition in which that painter shared.

Ukiyo-e began as a school of painting and most of the masters of the school, throughout its entire history, were certainly painters first and foremost (see Plate 24). Their designing for prints was often, not secondary perhaps, but was at least a participation in a different and corporate activity. Yet a new style of painting, more especially decorating screens, is found to be one of the threads which, passed by Time through the warp of history, becomes a major element of the fully evolved *ukiyo-e* design. Earliest of these screen paintings is certainly that of a party of well-to-do folk viewing maples at Takao. It is by the rather obscure Kyōto painter Hideyori, a member of the Kanō school, and is now in the Fuku-oka collection; it is certainly earlier than the dates given by Mr Hillier (1565–1570) since Hideyori himself died in 1557. Beautifully dressed people move sedately through a calm golden-lighted landscape or stand statuesquely on a great sweep of bridge which passes from the bank of a river to an island in the central mid-distance; the roofs of a monastery and a pagoda nestle among pines on the peaks of the mountains which rise above the billows of mist dividing the scene horizontally. It is very strongly reminiscent of those contemporary Ming paintings in China which had for their theme the 'Earthly Paradise'—yet another reminder of the part played by China in the development of the *ukiyo-e* style in Japan. Since a good account of these screens is easily available in English in Chapter fifteen of R. T. Paine's book,[5] it is unnecessary to describe more of such works here except to draw attention to the fact that, most commonly, they show people dressed in the contemporary fashion enjoying themselves on festival occasions and seemingly with no more purpose in life than to be superbly decorative. It only remains to add that over the following century there is to be perceived a tendency for the figures to grow larger, to come forward away from the background and ultimately to be isolated from it except perhaps for a few accessories.[6]

Two other types of screen are evidence of the shift to the contemporary scene shown by painters in the period 1560–1650. The first is that which recorded festivals or happenings of other public interest, e.g. the visit of the retired emperor Go-Shirakawa Hō-Ō to the Jako-in temple near Kyōto painted by Hasegawa Kyuzō (1568–1593) of that city. The other type of screen painting is that in the so-called Namban (Southern Barbarian) style which depicted the Portuguese, when they first arrived in Japan, in various occupations and quite often with wild animals, such as tigers and elephants. To a large extent this was a new subject matter for art although there were earlier paintings depicting such foreigners as Korean envoys but it is likely that these screens of Westerners played a part in turning men's minds to the possibilities for painting in the contemporary scene.

Another theme for illustration which was certainly a precursor of *ukiyo-e* is that of the *shokunin zukushi-e* (pictures of artisans and craftsmen). In these, different types of craftsmen are shown at their work either against a landscape background—the earliest type—or in front of their premises. Both types are painted on scrolls and screens in the old *yamato-e* style and perhaps they first appeared in the late fourteenth century. Like *ukiyo-e* they use the *mitate* or analogue (see page 126) for it is not uncommon to find them based on the *Uta Awase* theme in which the kinds of craftsmen take the place of the Thirty Six Poets.

Most of these art activities were centred upon Kyōto and intended for the wealthier rising merchant-banker class in Ōsaka. These were arts inaugurated by artistic amateurs or the small class of the professional painter of older times. Not far from the surface is always a *récherché* refinement; many of the productions are *shibui* (to use a Japanese adjective) that is to say, in a broad sense 'astringent', as befitted a society where the tea-ceremony was still a major recreation. Certainly in some of the works there is a hint of a new voluptuousness under the luxurious surface but it is a very different thing from the raffish, frank sexuality to be seen in many of the Edo works of art.

For Edo was a new town—a town without a past, without any really deep traditions, and from the tradesmen that had removed hither from Ōsaka, together with others coming in from elsewhere in the empire, new viewpoints and new evaluations were being quickly formed. The *edoko*, the typical inhabitant of Edo, in some ways very similar to the London cockney, was in fact busy forging a new culture. To control the turbulent territorial nobles the shōgun Ieyasu compelled them to spend a large part of each year in his new capital. Nor were they alone; each kept up an enforced, splendid but costly ceremonial and had perforce to live in a great palace with an enormous retinue of retainers who, the wars being ended and they forbidden to engage in trade, found themselves with almost limitless leisure. Moreover, Ieyasu's grandson Iyemitsu compelled the wives and children of the *daimyōs* to be left behind in Edo as hostages when their lords went to their country estates. Thus was the wealth of the nobles drained yearly away and prevented from financing a mischief to the shōgunate family of the Tokugawa itself.

With money in abundance flowing in one direction, into the

pockets of the petit *bourgeoisie*, the small shopkeeper, the master craftsman and the more highly skilled of the artisans found them-selves suddenly transported to an affluent society such as Japan had not seen before. The sons of these people, well taught and often well endowed, together with the *samurai* (gentry) and the *rōnin* (*samurai* who, voluntarily or not, had left the service of their masters, the *daimyō*) all had expensive tastes and a leisure that demanded ever new entertainment.

Dr Howard Hibbett[7] has surely given us the best short description of this society—an *élite* at once prosperous, creative and illegitimate. He says, 'With money, a fishmonger's son could be a social lion. Careers of beauty were never more accessible. An obscure shop or tea-shop might blossom into splendid profit; whereupon its owner would 'train an epicure's palate, renew his wardrobe and yearn for the exquisite in all things'. And his parties would begin to include celebrated actors and courtesans, with expensive tastes. It was this society that created a new literature, the *ukiyo-zōshi*, idle narratives of a floating world. It was these books that were illustrated with woodcuts of the new art, *ukiyo-e*. The *rōnin* and *samurai* in need of more money, forbidden to trade, set up everywhere as teachers and accepted an eager patronage from families anxious to rise socially. Quickly, in this way, did the aestheticism of the older aristocratic society filter down to the fishmonger and his son—and daughter. Yet in the tensions between a gentry jealous of privilege and a *bourgeoisie* envious of it but impotent politically, there was en-gendered, firstly a general irreverence and secondly an absolute devotion to aesthetic and sensual pleasure, none the less prized because it was known to be ephemeral. The prints, like the tales, caught the fleeting, floating moment; laughter and beauty were the only things worth cultivation in a world which even its devotees felt to be rotten-ripe. The solitary, contemplative world of aristo-cratic culture gave way in Edo to the gregarious, hilarious, colour craving one of the young, brash, middle class. Yet one feels, both in the tales and the prints, writers and artists in their more inward and lonely moments were but echoing Waller's lines:

'How small a part of time they share
That are so wondrous sweet and fair.'

There are two characters with which a Japanese may write the word '*uki*'. So, '*ukiyo*' 浮 世 means 'the floating world' and the other '*ukiyo*' 憂 世 means 'the world of sorrows'. The designation of the Buddhist's unreal world as floating—floating even in a sea of dreams, and to the Edoite the world would often seem dreamlike—was not new. Indeed, the Chinese poet Li Po (701–762) wrote:

> '*In this dream-like, floating life*
> *How often are we happy?*'

and no doubt such deeper sentiments were at the back of the minds of those almost too exquisite young fops—sons maybe of wealthy small traders and shopkeepers, their too indulgent fathers,—who in a summer's falling dusk, sang along the banks of the Sumidagawa the popular song of the day:

> '*In this dream-like life, take your joy in wine.*
> *When Tomorrow's come, this too will be among the dear dead days.*'

But these were not the only implications of the word. Other overtones would have occurred to the Japanese mind: '*uki*' is a native reading of the character (*kun*) i.e. the meaning of the character; but it can also be given its '*on*' reading, i.e. the old Chinese pronunciation as imitated by a Japanese, and if we use the *on* readings of the two characters 浮 世 we obtain the word *fusei* which means 'the world'. Hence the *ukiyo-e* 浮 世 繪 are also pictures of *fusei*, i.e. 'worldly pictures'; in fact, exactly what they were.

Half way through the century there occurred, by chance, something that was to hasten on these cultural processes—these particular interpretations of life—and to give an irresistible impetus to the production of *ukiyo-e* prints and to all that they mirrored, the tales, the theatre, the fast life of the Yoshiwara, the poetry clubs and so much else. This was the great fire of 1657 which Professor Takahashi has put forward as perhaps the most powerful of all the formative factors that made for the popularity of the print and the printed book. Previous to this, as the wealthier classes moved into Edo from Kyōto and more particularly from Ōsaka, which of course had been closely linked to the former city culturally, they brought with them multitudinous works of art over the greater part of the preceding century. In the fire almost all of these were destroyed.

It is known as the Fire of Meireki or the fire of the long-sleeved *kimono.* The fire occurred in February 1657, but tradition has it that more than two years before, a sixteen-year-old girl went to pray at the Hommyō-ji temple of Hōnga. Pining of love for a young man she had seen there, her mother gave her a long-sleeved *kimono* to attract his attention but for some reason the girl died at the beginning of 1655. The *kimono* was given to the temple and later sold by the monks to a secondhand clothes dealer and he gave it to his daughter Kinuko who died on the anniversary of the death of the first young woman. Given again to the temple it was acquired by a man named Kiemon who gave it to his daughter Ikuko. She too died and the abbot now decided to burn it in the presence of the three fathers. As it was burning a fierce wind arose blowing the flames to a conflagration and, changing direction twice in three days, burned three-quarters of Edo. In that fire perished 100,000 people and three hundred temples disappeared: the palaces of five hundred daimyōs, nine thousand shops and sixty-one bridges were destroyed. Following this, in a period of sharply rising prices, Edo was rebuilt. It is an interesting sidelight on history that Zacharias Wagenaar, who was then the Dutch factor at Deshima, gave 14,000 Dutch florins for the succour of the homeless.[8]

Nor was this the only catastrophe to strike Edo during the seventeenth century. For example, in 1680 a great typhoon struck the town and here again the damage was of incredible extent. Before the populace had fully recovered from this, in fact in December 1681, an even greater fire, called that of Ō-shichi after the young girl who caused it, again devastated the city. The girl being eventually put to death for incendiarism, left her story as one of the most popular tales of the years immediately following, a version of it being given at the puppet theatre at Ōsaka in 1682. Not only by the destruction of antiques and works of art, so essential to the cultural life of the new society, did these disasters encourage the great increase in prints and so much else besides. The new art was poured into what was virtually a vacuum uncluttered by the art attitudes of centuries: but the society that had suffered such destruction of the world around it, that saw only too clearly the injustice that was done 'under the sun', the whole frailty of the human world and the blind chance that swept away even the surest success, such a society may well have sought out madder pleasures and have been whirled away in a still more fevered pursuit of beauty. Every sensual aspect of life was to be explored to the uttermost even whilst it was passing away. It is not surprising that with such a clientele the print, for the next century and a quarter, went from triumph to triumph in the technical fields of production and resources.

It remains to consider only one more formative influence on the evolution of the Japanese print and particularly the *ukiyo-e* print; that is the Ōtsu-e picture.[9] Opinions on this matter are sharply divided among scholars and writers. Mr Hillier (*The Japanese Print*) goes so far as to say, 'Another old notion—still repeated by quite serious students even in the present decade—is that a forerunner of the Japanese prints was the Ōtsu-e.' Mr Michener (*The Floating World*) says, 'the safest conclusion is that during this period there was consistent cross-fertilization of artistic ideas, spurred by a very popular and vital theatre'. It is difficult to be sure at this remove in time and especially since one has to deal with a relatively undocumented folk-art. Yet Ōtsu-e certainly became famous in the early seventeenth century after Bashō had written a poem about them. Sold to the poorer classes of the towns when they were on pilgrimage and bought by them partly as a souvenir and partly as a talisman, they may well have done much to create a taste for a hanging picture (they were sold with a bamboo stick top and bottom) or one to be pasted on a screen or wall. Such a taste becoming widespread, did something to bring the print from the page of the book to the decoration of the home and in fact created the greater demand for the single sheet print (*ichimai-e*) the origin of which has been variously ascribed to Moronobu and, by Mr Hillier with much cogency, Sugimura Jihei. The date of the first production of these large prints is a little uncertain but it cannot have been more than a year or so from 1680. It is no doubt symptomatic of the new demand for cheap secular pictures to hang upon a wall that the Ōtsu-e at about the same date turned from Buddhist to secular art and, for the most part, satirical themes.

With the creation of the single sheet print and the printing of an increasing number of books illustrated with woodcuts coloured by hand with various pigments, the Japanese print proper had been brought into being. With the evolution of only a very few minor inventions, mostly of smaller scope, there remained only the introduction of the colour printed woodcut to be added and the whole historical development was, in consideration of technique alone and excluding the totally different colour prints of the twentieth century, complete. The true colour print, *nishiki-e*, was not to appear until the spring of 1765. This will be discussed in more detail in the chapter on technique.

NOTES ON CHAPTER II

[1] The most easily accessible account of the Nara-ehon is Yutaka Shimizu's *Nara Picture Books*, Dawson Book Shop, Los Angeles, 1960. However, some views expressed there should be considered in the light of Ashio Hotta's *Study of the Nara Picture Books* (*Shoshigaku*), 'Bibliography', Vol. 5, No. 4 of October 1935.

[2] Rumpf, F.: *Das Ise-Monogatari von 1606 unter sein Einfluss auf die Buchillustration des XVII Jahrhunderts in Japan*; Inaugural Dissertation: Berlin 1931.

[3] This paper is used in all the so-called *Koetsu-bon*.

[4] Reproduced in the *Annual Report* of the Imperial Household Museum at Tōkyō and Nara for 1932.

[5] Paine, R. T., and Soper, A.: *The Art and Architecture of Japan*, Penguin Books, 1955, where there is also a small reproduction of this screen. Mr Hillier, in his work, *The Japanese Print* (l.c.), has a good short account of them on pages 12–13 and there are a few excellent coloured reproductions in Dr Lubor Hajek's *Japanese Woodcuts; early periods*, London, n.d. (1955?).

[6] Compare 'Dancing under the Cherry Trees' by Kano Kyuhaku (1574–1654) in the Hara collection and some of the figures on the Hikone screen and the scrolls of dancers or seated ladies which are usually catalogued as 'School of Matabei'—if only because no better attribution can be attempted. It seems that certainly two, and possibly three painters were responsible for these. It is surprising that this type of 'primitive' *ukiyo-e* painting continued for nearly a century and a half, being found almost unchanged in the work of Hishikawa Wao who worked in Edo about 1710–20.

[7] Hibbett, H.: *The Floating World in Japanese Fiction*, Oxford University Press, 1959. The first chapter of this book must indeed be one of the best evocations of Genroku society in a western language.

[8] Yet another great fire, that of Meiwa 9 (1772), which destroyed the business centre of the city, did much to alter Edo again in the eighteenth century. Fashions in the city changed rapidly after this catastrophe; *geisha* of several kinds appeared on the streets and in the gay quarters and Tsutaya Jusaburō, the publisher, inaugurated some new styles and

formats in his wood-block prints. This trend can be clearly seen in the prints by Kiyonaga which he issued in the years following the fire. Fires indeed have been a major formative influence in the history of the capital and in the history of its wood engraving.

[9] These pictures have largely come into prominence in Europe as a result of the Japanese Folk Art movement, led by Professor Yanagi and also as a result of the treatment afforded them by James A. Michener in his book *The Floating World*, published in 1954. They are true folk-art and were produced in Otani and Oiwake, suburbs of Otsu on the southern shore of Lake Biwa. When they are first met with in history at about 1630, they were bought as souvenirs by pilgrims and travellers to Kyōto. The artists were peasantry who painted them for sale to the common people. Most of the earliest ones were crude representations of deities like Fudō which served as talismans and were no doubt in earlier times bought by the credulous and the half-credulous for their amuletic virtues. They were quickly executed on a rough brown paper covered with a yellow liquid clay called *ōdo*. Only certain shops acted as retailers and these at first bought but later seem to have commissioned them—perhaps in imitation of the production of the *ukiyo-e*. Round about 1680 satirical themes took the place of the religious ones and at about the same time blocks were used to stamp the outline of the faces on to the design, the rest of the figures being put in by hand. According to Michener, the blocks seem to have been the property of the individual retailer who would sell the output of three or four families. The prophylactic properties were publicised much more vehemently again in their later days and possibly we can see in this a piece of 'sales-talk' designed to bolster sales that were dwindling in the face of the increased competition of the wood-block print.

For the information of collectors the following list is added as being that of some of the subjects commonly met with in the *Ōtsu-e*. A few of these sometimes bear signatures but none have been identified. A seal is not very uncommon, the most usual reading of which is 'Tokaido Otsueki Sekisenen'. Dates are those believed to be that of the first introduction of the design and some indication is given, where known, of the period over which its production was carried on. The early seventeenth century ones were all Buddhist, showing divinities such as Amida, Fudō and Shōnen Kongō: in the late seventeenth century appear Daruma and Jizō as well as scenes from Kabuki.

Tayu, the highest rank of courtesan. 63 cm × 25 cm: seventeenth to early eighteenth centuries. A rare and highly interesting subject which may have influenced early one-sheet wood-block prints.

Geho Hashigozuri: in several versions. The god of good fortune is seated whilst Daikoku, the god of riches, climbs a ladder to scratch his head;

1. An early example of a Chinese engraved text on a whole block without the use of movable type (see page 22). The sixty-fifth block for printing the *Ta pei hsin Tsan fa yi chih* (The Great Compassionate's, i.e. *Kuan Yin's*, Laws and Ceremonies for Subduing the Mind). Text in Manchu: the character used here is the old unpointed form of Manchu invented by Engeddi in 1599 and superseded by the newer form with diacritical marks in 1632. The block therefore dates from the first quarter of the seventeenth century; it demonstrates clearly that the Chinese, like the Japanese, continued to print books by engraving a complete page long after the introduction of movable type.

2. Chinese popular print of the nineteenth century. Hui Hsing seated on an *Ao yü* (Ao fish); he was the god of learning and as such worshipped by schoolboys. (See page 25.)

usually 52 cm × 24·5 cm. In another version he is arranging his hair; 61 cm × 23 cm. Seventeenth to early eighteenth centuries.

Oni-no-Samisen: a devil playing a samisen. Seventeenth to early eighteenth centuries.

Oni-no-Nembutsu. Many versions of this are known. The devil is dressed as a monk and carries the attributes of umbrella, gong and hammer. The seventeenth-century versions of this are usually 61·5 cm × 25 cm. An even larger seventeenth-century one (96 cm × 30 cm) has a poem at top right signed Yofu Dōjin and the seal 'Seigai': another large kind (80 cm × 29 cm) is on textile material and is probably of the eighteenth century. Another version shows the devil enraged, beating with his hammer on a gong: eighteenth century. There is also one of very small format (11 cm × 11 cm) of the eighteenth century.

Yarimoshi Yakko: a hired porter carrying a staff; several versions of this but it seems commonest in *Kakemono* format. Eighteenth to the end of the nineteenth centuries.

Sake-nomi-Yakko: a servant drinking from a cup larger than himself. Seventeenth century to the end of the first half of the eighteenth century.

Sumo: two large wrestlers in action; seventeenth century. A rare subject that does not seem to have been in production for many years.

Fuji musume: a young woman with *Glycina* foliage; with a poem signed Yofu Dōjin and sealed 'Seigai'. Eighteenth and nineteenth centuries.

Shōki: the demon compeller. Commonest in size 33·5 cm × 24 cm: nineteenth century.

Tsurigane Benkei. The giant Benkei carrying the bell of Miidera: eighteenth and nineteenth centuries.

Rai-jin: one of the gods of thunder (Kaminari San). It became quite common, especially in small format, at the beginning of the nineteenth century.

Naginata Benkei. The giant Benkei clad in armour and carrying a halberd; usually in *kakemono* format and rather rare in later centuries. Seventeenth century.

Zatō: a blind man attacked by a little dog. Eighteenth and nineteenth centuries.

Takashō: a falconer. This probably only exists in a small format. Eighteenth and nineteenth centuries.

Hyōtan Namzue: a monkey fishing for a catfish with a gourd. Probably seventeenth to nineteenth centuries.

Various Buddhist gods: probably seventeenth to nineteenth centuries.

Boy Actors in Female Roles: various versions exist of this but all seem to be in a small format. Eighteenth and nineteenth centuries.

Peasant Women Dancing: always small format: eighteenth century.

Yanone Gorō. One of the Soga brothers; Gorō sharpening his arrow. A theme also found in early prints of the Torii school. Eighteenth and nineteenth centuries.

A Young Woman lighting a Lamp. Small format; eighteenth century.

A Young Woman carrying a Present. Small format; eighteenth century.

A Young Woman in her Best Clothes. Usually about 21 cm × 16·5 cm: eighteenth century.

A Nun Playing a Flute in Order to Collect Alms. Seventeenth and eighteenth centuries.

Cock, Hen and other Animals. Seventeenth to nineteenth centuries.

See: Yanagi, S.: *Ōtsu-e zuroku* (A catalogue of primitive Ōtsu-e folk paintings); Japan Folk Art Museum, Tōkyō, 1960. With explanatory text, introduction and list of plates.

CHAPTER III

The Organization and Techniques of Print Production, Distribution and Commissioning

MOST people interested in Japanese colour prints have, since the publication of Dr Tys Volker's justly celebrated essay,[1] been aware that the colour prints, whether as single sheets or as books, were not the sole production of artist, engraver and printer working together but that the publisher was the conductor of this small orchestra and occasionally even a performer. Singularly little accurate factual information seems to be on record as to how the earliest illustrated wood-block books were distributed. The *Kōetsubon* may well have been dispersed among the friends of the artist himself and almost all the very early works must probably be thought of as privately printed editions. By 1625 at the latest, but probably for some time before this, the publisher-bookseller must have been a well established business since, with the coming of the first hand-coloured prints and the first *meisho-ki*, the more complex techniques of production and the greater public demand would obviously necessitate a professional approach founded upon sound economic principles.

The first publishing houses were certainly those of Kyōto and Ōsaka, towns of the Kamigata or 'home counties'. Such businesses have remained down to the present day although readers of some of the books on the Japanese print which appeared early in the present century no doubt believed that all publishing—or perhaps all of any account—centred on Edo. Some of the most desirable of all Japanese printed productions came from publishers at the two former cities although it is true that Kyōto, in the century approximately dating from 1750 to 1850, produced for that older, somewhat aristocratic culture, many reproductions of Kanō school painters which are dull in the extreme.

Somewhat later other publishing houses arose at Nagasaki and elsewhere but it was the new, brash city of Edo that showed the greatest growth of this trade and that, no doubt, because it was the publishing houses there that developed the single sheet print in all its popular glory. Dr Volker has given us an estimate of the numbers of these publishers in Edo at different periods, based on the lists given in the work of Binyon and O'Brien Sexton. From 1670 to 1700 there were four; in 1730 there were thirty, a figure which showed little increase for many years perhaps because it seems to have been in this period that the wholesale publishers' association, the *Jihondoiya no nakama* was formed with many of those innovations which today we call restrictive practices. By 1810 there were forty-seven and, after the government veto on this monopoly in 1840, the number fell from fifty-eight in that year to only thirteen in 1860, falling again over the next twenty years to three only. As Dr Volker has pointed out, however, our knowledge of these firms in the West is little short of chaotic. Many have never been recorded at all in western books, little information is available in western languages on the identity or lives of the men who traded as publishers and many of the houses in Kyōto and Ōsaka were branches of the Edo establishments although, no doubt, in earlier times, the Edo houses were branches of the older established Ōsaka businesses. To add to the confusion both books and prints might be published simultaneously by two or more publishers and these sometimes from the same blocks or from different and separately cut blocks. For example, a volume of humorous drawings by Suzuki Rinshō was published jointly in 1778 by Zenya Shōbei of Kyōto, Kashiwaraya Yozayemon at Ōsaka and Yamazakiya Kimbei of Edo. Even in Japan, such information as is available about men in the publishing trade, the dates and history of their commercial enterprises and their notable productions, is almost all in the form of short notes in somewhat obscure journals of but very limited issue or circulation and it is almost impossible to consult these in the West.

It seems to have been the general practice throughout the whole of the earlier period of the colour-print for the firm who published the work to be the same as that which retailed it to the public but there were certainly some purely retail book and print shops in Edo although there is very little information recorded about them. However, the colophon to Toyokuni's well-known book, *Yakusha*

Sangai Kyo ('The Third Floor Amusements—i.e. in the Green-room—of Actors') published in Kansei 13 (1801) says, 'published by Shinshōken Nishimiya Shinroku; bookseller, Yorozuya Tajiemon.' Possibly in such instances, where the bookseller's name appears, we have either an associated house of the publishers or evidence of a bookseller giving an exclusive commission to the publisher.[2]

Commissions were certainly no new thing and to this practice it seems we owe, in part, the origin of the polychrome print, the *nishiki-e*. Clubs of amateurs in art (*renju*) existed, in the later seventeenth century, in Kyōto and Ōsaka and the custom soon spread to Edo but in some respects their activities, although often similar in all these cities were, on balance, of a more antiquarian kind in the two former towns and indeed remained so throughout most of the Tokugawa period. Certain of these clubs existed for the examination of antiquities and works of art and sometimes published short accounts of their 'Proceedings', e.g. the Tanki club to which the celebrated novelist Bakin (1767–1848) belonged, published the *Tanki Manroku* ('Miscellaneous Notes on Rare Books') which illustrated certain paintings on old pictorial manuscripts and which recorded several of the artistic and literary curiosities which members of the club had exhibited and commented upon. On the whole, however, the Edo clubs put more considerable emphasis on contemporary art and literature: poems were read and capped, fine prints compared, paintings shown and even fashions formed: such clubs were an important part of the life of the plebeian intellectual élite of the times. In Edo these clubs became centres to which bearers of the prized Kamigata culture naturally tended to gravitate and it was such clubs that played the major part in bringing into being the polychrome print. Woodcuts were much cultivated by their members and several prints bear a list of names in which we find that of the painter (*gwakō*), the engraver (*chokō*) and the printer (*senkō*) as well as another name to which the suffix '*kō*' has been added. It is now certain that this refers to the designer of the print and quite often he will be found to be a poet cultivating either the comico-satyrical verse called *kyōka* or the well known seventeen-syllable form called *haiku*. If the print is one of a series it bears only this one name, the others occurring on the cover or title page. The finely printed '*de luxe*' first editions of these prints were for club members only and were undoubtedly commissioned by them but the publishers would often issue from the same blocks second and third editions for the general public. This probably accounts for the differences in the refinement of the printing which may be noticed in certain prints.

Most of these prints were in fact illicit calendar leaves, *ryakureki* or *daishō Hō-surimono*. Illicit because the publication of pictorial almanacs *e-goyomi* was the monopoly of certain publishers who produced them under licence from the government. Professor Y. Takekoshi[3] tells us that in the Genroku period eighty-one such licences (*kabu*) were issued by the government and usually some eleven publishers shared this monopoly. The year 1765 was the nine hundredth anniversary of the victory of the great statesman Sugawara no Michizane and in celebration, a very large number of these calendar leaves were issued among them being, for the first time, several printed with the full polychrome technique including some signed by the artist Suzuki Harunobu and one by a certain Hakusei as well. Scholarly opinion now generally accepts the views of the Japanese writer Tomita, that it was to this man, as to others signing as '*kō*', that the whole conception of the print was owed.

These secret calendar prints were so designed that they showed, to those who knew how to read them, the long and short months of the year. This might be done by drawing long and short hairs on the chest of a saint, by rendering the design on a kimono in such a way that it was broken at certain points, by showing the long and short nodes on a chrysanthemum stem, and by other such means. In effect, this can be used for dating these prints since, for example, the long months in 1765 were 2, 3, 5, 6, 8, 10 whereas in 1766 they were 1, 3, 5, 6, 8, 9 and 11. Thus one of these calendar prints for any particular year must show a unique pattern in this respect. However, when the year had passed, it would seem to have been customary for these marks to have been erased from the blocks and new prints taken off with a view to public sale: these last are obviously much more commonly found. One club which played a large part in this kind of activity was the Kikurensha art group made up, for the most part, of more or less gifted dilettanti.

However, although 1765 seems to be the year when the full polychrome print first appeared, nevertheless the technique of printing in more than one colour antedates this by many years as may well be supposed. The German scholar Rumpf, in 1931, recorded a

Japanese work on astronomy, the *Temmon dzue*, published in 1593 and described it as having a colour-printed illustration. Mr Waterhouse (1964) gives an admirably detailed account of a mathematical work of 1627, the *Jinkō-ki* which was published in a black and white, four-volume edition in that year but which was reissued with colour printed illustrations in a three-volume edition in 1631. The same author also makes the important point that the *Semmyō reki* (a Chinese calendar) published at the beginning of 1644, had colour printed illustrations, two of which show *kentō* marks. Stencilled colour illustrations occur in books published in Ōsaka about 1730: these all seem to have been collections of moral precepts for women. A little earlier than this were books of *haiku* poems with decorations in the Chinese taste, some of which were printed in colour. Colour printing is, by tradition, a process ascribed to the invention of a printer Takekawa Minosuke, active in the Manji era (1658–1660) but although a few books are known, of a date not far removed from this, which are printed in colour, yet these show only one colour to each page and it is most likely that this printer was really responsible, if at all, for the introduction of some of the colours themselves, or rather of the form that they must take to be transferred successfully from the surface of a wood-block. Certainly at the end of the seventeenth century books printed with each design in several colours were appearing on the market but these were in imitation of Chinese illustrated books which did not necessitate fitting the colours into a black outline and so allowed a considerable latitude in the register of the blocks. A few other books used this method including the *Furyu Gionzakura*, an erotic book by the artist Sukenobu, published in 1715.

In 1740 appeared some coloured Japanese woodcuts employing two colours in a black outline; these were printed on fans and are variously said to have been the invention of the owner of the fan-selling business, Daimonji-ya or of the fan-maker Iba-ya Kanemon. In the first year of Enkyō, 1744, single sheet prints in two colours, appeared for the first time, these last being applied by wood-blocks within a black outline. This had been made possible by the re-invention or re-introduction of the device of the 'kentō' (see below) which is usually attributed to Kichiemon Kamimura, a wholesale book publisher, trading under the name of Emiya in Shiba. The colours used in these early colour prints were rose and green, some notable artists who designed for them being Masanobu, Toyonobu, Shigemasa and Mangetsudō. A third colour was added a few years later by the engraver Yoshida Kyōsen who also applied to prints more refined methods of gauffrage printing although a simple kind of embossed effect had been used for many years—even if rarely—being sometimes found in the *Saga-bon*. Yet two more colours were added by the block-cutter, Kinroku (died August 1804) who also seems to have perfected in some way the aids used to obtain perfect register.[4] This appears to have taken place about 1750 and several prints and illustrated books, printed in up to five colours with black outlines, appeared between then and the coming of Harunobu's 'brocade prints' in all their glory in 1765. The scholar, Hiraga Gennai (1729–1780)[5] played a very great part in this; he had issued two books with coloured woodcuts in 1762 and it is said to have been another coloured print of his, of chrysanthemums, which inspired Harunobu to produce the first *nishiki-e* or, as they were proudly called, *azuma-nishiki-e* (brocade prints from the eastern provinces)—a sure sign that these same eastern provinces, whose centre was Edo, had thrown off their cultural allegiance to the Kamigata.

Before the era of polychromatic printing, there had been, of course, a period of production of prints coloured by hand. Soon after the establishment of the first Edo publishers about 1659, Hishikawa Moronobu, whose early books had been published in Kyōto, began to issue albums which bore instructions for colouring the prints and we can only suppose that the customers either coloured their own albums or paid to have the work done by more skilful artisan colourists. None of the single sheet prints seem to have carried such instructions but there is little doubt but that they were occasionally coloured in the same way and some few very carefully and intricately hand-coloured prints are known. These make use of brilliant orange-red, yellow, green, slate-blue and pink, besides areas of printed black. Such prints were no doubt tinted by artistic amateurs and represent the achievements of unknown individuals of the public. But contemporary with these the publishers issued coloured prints, the colours being applied by hand and rather haphazardly in that they do not define natural areas of colour but serve merely to demarcate clothes and flesh or one garment from another. These are the so-called *tan-e* or vermilion prints named after the predominant colour, a brilliant orange-vermilion. Green and yellow were often added but fulfil only a minor role yet the whole ensemble is extremely bold and effective and reminds one of the coloured designs on folk-art pottery or the Ōtsu-e pictures.

Close inspection reveals more than a little skill to have been requisite to this work of colouration and so reminiscent is it of folk-art subtleties that one wonders if the workers could have been peasant craftsmen who had come to the city. There had been much to cause them to do so. In 1703 earthquakes and fires had caused widespread ruin and in the following year there were disastrous floods that spread over the countryside for miles around the capital. These floods were followed by very serious epidemics of smallpox, cholera, and influenza and thousands of people died as a result. Finally, and most disastrous of all for the country people, Fujiyama had its last eruption between the 16th December 1707 and the 22nd January 1708. Even fifty miles from the mountain, town gardens in Edo were covered with white ashes and all public life came to an end for the time being. Certainly country folk with the traditional skills could have been employed in some numbers on the hand colouring of these prints for Professor Takahashi tells us that the printers produced about two hundred outline prints a day. Perhaps one can gain a small glimpse of one of these unknown workers from a passage in a work by the same authority in which he says that 'an old woman at Suzaki, Fukagawa is reported to have been very skilful' at this work.

These *tan-e* remained popular for some three decades but about the year 1715 pictures, hand coloured with an extremely attractive, soft pinkish red (*beni*), were sold on the streets. This innovation is generally credited to Izumi-ya Gonshirō of Bōbō-chō, a publisher. The first of such prints seem to have been of *kabuki* actors and, as an especial product of Edo, they had a wide popularity in Ōsaka and Kyōto where they served as children's playthings. These prints, in which the new colour was applied by hand, are known as *beni-e*.

Around 1720 yet another innovation appeared; this was the lacquer print *urushi-e*. The so-called 'lacquer' was really a black pigment mixed with a glue which, when dry, took on a high varnish-like gloss. Such prints often have, in addition to the striking, pitchy-black blobs of colour, areas of metallic gold surface formed by mixing powdered brass with glue. Much more rarely, copper dust was

used in place of brass. Among the artists responsible for both
urushi-e and *beni-e* were Masanobu, Toshinobu, Kiyonobu, Kiyomasa, Kiyotada, Kiyotoma, Shigenobu, Kiyoshige and Shigenaga.
Some of these artists worked long enough to take part in the next
technical innovation before the true polychrome brocade print,
namely that of printing the *beni* colour from blocks—soon followed
by other colours as we have seen—such prints being referred to as
benizuri-e as distinct from the *beni-e* in which the colour was applied
by hand. To summarize the development of the single sheet print
(*ichimai-e*) the following dates can be set out:

Black and white single sheets (and it is to be noted that Mr
Hillier thinks Sugimura Jihei is to be credited with the invention
of these rather than Moronobu who is traditionally said to be
their inventor): soon after 1680 to about 1743.

Tan-e with this cinnabar colour applied by hand by jobbing
colourists employed by the publisher himself, the prints being
issued in their coloured state. Green and yellow were later used in
subsidiary positions on the same prints: probably about 1698,
perhaps to as late as 1725.

Beni-e prints with a soft rose red applied by hand. 1715 to about
the year 1745.

Benizuri-e with the *beni* printed from blocks and a little later the
subsidiary colours also produced from blocks. Soon after 1740
and, for the most part, to around the year 1770.

Nishiki-e (Brocade Prints) printed from many blocks in full
polychromatic colours. From the spring of 1765 onwards.

It must be made clear that the above dates are approximate only
and that they apply only to single sheet prints and of those, only to
such as have a black outline printed from a key block.

Having said a word about the publisher, the prints he issued and
something of the system of making commissions and retailing—a
system that lasted throughout the whole history of the *ukiyo-e*, since
it is not uncommon to find later prints with the inscription *ōju* or
ōjite 'to order' or *monotome ni ōzu* 'by special order'—the other
members of the quartet have briefly to be considered.

Certainly less is known about the engraver than the publisher or
artist nor is it even known from whence these engravers were re-
cruited in the early days of book and print publishing and much

research remains to be done on this subject. We have many more names of engravers recorded on prints than we have those of printers and this was an occasional practice from very early days of print production: as an example the name of the block-cutter Tsusen is recorded on a print by Torii Kiyomitsu, published by Maruko; this shows the actor Kikumojō as a woman. Why some prints have such names recorded and most others do not is quite unknown but since it is certain that some engraving was undertaken by families who worked in their own *ateliers* and contracted with individual publishers, these engravers often being among the most skilful, it may be that such names are in fact those of just such a family business or perhaps that of a master engraver. However, it may be argued against this that in some series the engraver's name appears only on some of the prints and not others, e.g. Yoshitoshi's series, *Tsuki Hiakkushi* ('The Hundred Moons'). Most of the block-cutters seem to have been employed directly by the publishers and often they lived in the home of their employer as little more than a paid assistant. Volker has cited one or two instances where the engraver and publisher are the same person and this may have been more common than is at present believed but the evidence is very scanty. The engravers were sometimes responsible for publishing on their own account and Binyon and O'Brien Sexton (l.c.) have cited an instance where the Guild of Wholesale Publishers had to take proceedings in the Appeal Court to stop this practice.

The engraver did not merely 'copy' the design of the artist. That is to say, it is not a facsimile copy. Lines were fined down and sometimes, as we know from Hokusai's letters to his publishers, various features, such as the nose, redrawn. Such letters also show us that the artist had no direct means of communication with the block-cutter but that he could only make his wishes known through the publisher himself. Whether the engravers ever had a guild or not seems to be unknown although it is very likely that they would have done so. Certainly these wood-engravers had such a guild in the present century and indeed the guild has sometimes arranged Buddhist memorial services for the many cherry trees that had to be cut down for the making of wood-blocks. Michener[6] (presumably drawing on the information given by Chie Hirano)[7] has stressed the fact that the skill of the engraver must have been greater than that of any other member of the quartet and says that it took four years to become an artist, three years apprenticeship to be a printer but ten years to be a first class engraver. Although these figures are not to be pressed to too great a degree of exactitude they may well represent approximately the time necessary to master the different techniques. There were a smaller number of engravers than printers and since it is said that three engravers could keep ten printers fully and continuously employed this seemingly did not cause any bottlenecks in the production.

The printer is, still more often than the others who laboured at the creation of the Japanese print, anonymous. Less is known of him than of any other craftsman. There is no doubt but that he always worked on the premises of the publisher where the latter could supervise every stage of the printing. More frequently than with the engravers, printers became publishers themselves and quite a few instances of this are known. Usually, however, it is not from prints that one may find this kind of information but from the colophons of books and a closer study of these may well give us more information about the printer than we have at present. No doubt many publishers were able to print and doubtless did so when personal supervision was necessary. Perhaps originally this had something to do with a curious practice which is sometimes found in relation to the publisher's name as it appears on prints. In such cases the name of the publisher is followed by the character 板 reading *'ita'* meaning 'a board or plank' and by extension 'a printing block', i.e. one on which the design was engraved. This character is, by common usage, often made to do duty for the character 版 which recalls the characters 版 元, read *'hammoto'* and meaning 'publisher'; originally *han* seems to have implied ownership of the printing blocks, the owners usually being the publishers.

Dr Volker (l.c.) has called attention to the effect that any differences in the performances of these various craftsmen could make to the final print. If printers and engravers were bad but designers good, then the result would always be disastrous; if painter and engraver were good but the printer bad the whole intention was ruined but the print might gain with age since the more garish colours would fade. Should the designers be poor but the engravers good—really good—then a fine print might still result if good printing was employed as well. Likewise if the engraver were bad, a skilful printer might still produce a pleasing print but age—and fading—would inevitably show up its faults: Just as this shows us the importance of the printer it also indubitably points to the supreme importance of the publisher as a kind of 'maestro' of print production. The leading publishers were often men of learning, cultured refinement and aesthetic sensibility and it is of much importance that more research be done on this aspect of the Japanese print. It is not uncommonly found that where a series of some single artist has been issued by two or perhaps even three publishers at once, one will consistently produce prints of each design that are obviously superior to those of the others and, in the last analysis, this can only be due to the publisher. Nor were the Edo publishers superior in cultural refinements and erudition to those of Kyōto and Ōsaka; indeed, ones such as Masayoshi Ōzaki (pseud. Ragetsuan, d. 1827) of the latter place, reached considerable eminence as bibliographers (as with him) or literary and art critics.

There is yet one more figure who features in the production of books and prints and who seems as yet to have received little or no attention from western scholars and collectors and indeed little more from those of Japan; this is the calligrapher. On most prints—almost all in fact—the artist seems to have been the calligrapher but with a few *surimono* and quite a number of the finer illustrated books this was not so; specially famed and prized calligraphers were retained for the writing of the text. As an example, the postface to Volume Two of Toyokuni's *Yakusha Sangai Kyo* (1801), mentioned above, cites the calligrapher Chikwa Tōryu as having written the text. A very short survey of some of the recorded names of these very special and highly prized artists shows that a surprising proportion seem to have been women although further and more prolonged research may show that this is not really so at all. Moreover we cannot be sure that the writing is in fact always by those to whom it is credited: for example, Tsune Isome was a lady famed for her calligraphy in the periods spanned by the years 1684–1704 and in 1688 appeared the two volumes of the *Onna Gohyku Isshu* ('Five Hundred Verses by Women Poets') with model calligraphy by her. In 1738 was published the *Onna Bunrin Takara bukuro* ('A Treasury of Literary Pieces by Women') which claimed to be written by her but it seems most unlikely that she would have been still active at this date. Sometimes these calligraphists were noted also as painters: such a one was a Miss Yamazaki Ryu who was active at the end of the last quarter of the eighteenth century.

It is obvious that an almost unworked field of research is here for the collector and student who should record in their catalogues and notes all particulars of publishers, engravers, printers and calligraphers that can be found on the prints and books that they come across. Where these can be dated we may well begin to understand more of the relationship of them all.

Whenever printing was first done in colour—and Japanese traditions point to Takekawa Minosuke (flourished 1658–1660) as the first to introduce it—it is certainly true that some of the first books with this colour printing had but one colour per page; Strange,[8] in fact, mentions a volume of costume designs of 1667 with each plate in a single colour and it is indeed not improbable that the idea arose from the practice of colour printing fabrics in such a manner. Polychrome xylography, the origins of which have been discussed in part above, was obviously dependent on a reliable system of register. In the explanation of this matter it may be as well to give here a short survey of the technique of print making.

The artist first drew his design on thin *mino* or *gampi* paper. The first of these was made in the province of Mino, hence the name *minogami*; it is made from *kōzo* (*Broussonetia papyrifera*) and has been manufactured since the late twelfth century. The mucilage of *Hibiscus manihot* is used as a glue and gives rise to a paper that is lustreless, relatively uncrushable, very thin, firm and translucent. *Gampi* paper was made from the pure fibre of *Wickstroemia gampi* and the best qualities came from the villages of Makidanimura in Mino. It is smoother, softer, thinner and a little more transparent than *minogami*. Parts of the artist's drawing might be altered by pasting pieces of paper over the first drawing or sometimes by redrawing over parts of the first design in red. Mr Robinson[9] has reproduced an example of this in a drawing of Kuniyoshi's.

When completed the design was placed face downwards on the block and the paper was sometimes oiled to make it more transparent. The wood-block was cut from the mountain cherry (*Yamazakura*) seasoned in the shade (not the sun as some writers suggest, e.g. Mr Michener l.c., p. 155) and sectioned along the grain and not across the grain as is the European practice. From this was cut the *daiban* or key-block which reproduced all the outlines of the drawing and on this key-block means were made for obtaining correct register (*kentō*) for printing from the subsequent blocks that carried the colour. This was done by means of two pieces left upstanding on the block; the first of these was a right angle (*kaji*) in the lower right-hand corner and the second was a short straight edge placed about two thirds the distance along one of the sides enclosing the corner in which the *kaji* was placed. This line was called the *hikitsuki* or 'draw close line'. In printing, each sheet of paper was placed to fit exactly into the angle and with one of the edges touching the *hikitsuki*; as far as is known no other means were used for obtaining the register of anything up to twenty or more colours such as were not uncommonly used in the production of *nishiki-e*. Each colour to be printed required a separate block except only that two very small areas of different colour might be cut on the same block. For all these cherry wood was used except that, as in some *surimono*, where very fine lines were needed and the edition was to be a small one, willow wood obtained from the Japanese willow of the species *Tokachiyanagi* (*Salix urbaniana* Seemen) was utilized. This is a wood of very fine texture and grain with a reddish yellow heart wood of considerable extent. In modern Japanese wood-engraving box wood has sometimes been used, obtained from the *Tsuge* (*Buxus japonica* Mull.) but the difficulty of engraving on Japanese box has always been its marked tendency to warp.[10]

The printing was done by transferring the ink or colour to a printer's board and, after mixing, using it to ink the block. The paper was then placed downwards on the block and the impression taken off by rubbing with the *baren*. This was a rubber made by coiling a cord of bamboo fibre around a card centre and fixing it with paper, string and paste, the whole then being enclosed in a large, pliable bamboo sheath kept soft with a little oil. It was used with a circular motion but sometimes the point of the elbow might be used to take the impression and indeed no doubt many other means were resorted to in order to create some of the finer effects. As an example, gauffrage printing was effected by putting the print back downwards on the block and going over the design with a boar's tooth. All the impressions necessary were taken from each block in turn, each impression taking, it is said, from fifteen to twenty-five seconds. The colour scheme to be used was generally indicated by the artist on the first pull from the outline block and this frequently had subsidiary instructions such as that on a theatrical print by Toyokuni in the Victoria and Albert Museum which says, 'Please gradate the colour thus'. It is perhaps possible that some 'de luxe' *surimono* would have been printed by completing all the colours on each sheet at one time and under the eye of the publisher or designer. The printers were often extremely expert in obtaining beautiful effects; for example, even in the blacks it was often possible to give a grained texture to the ink suggesting actual brush-work or even colour. Lighter ink tones were sometimes achieved by wiping the block or by exerting lighter pressure and this often effectively gave the impression of distance as did some of the very beautiful greys that were occasionally used on prints (especially of the Ōsaka school) and more often in some of the albums of the so-called 'Classical School'.

In general, warping of the wood-blocks, a matter which would obviously interfere with the register, was prevented by framing them on two sides and those likely to be used again were stored in this way. Carving of the blocks was done with knives (*kogatana*), gouges (*kamazarai*), chisels (*nomi*), saws (*kushigi*) and a mallet (*saizuchi*). Before printing, the block was washed and dried and stood upon a sloping stand ready for the operation of printing itself.

The early prints, i.e. those produced before the true *nishiki-e*, were printed on a thick white paper properly called *masame-gami* which is classified as a *shiro-kōzo* or white *kōzo* which term is used for papers made from the bark of *Broussonetia kajinoki* and related species. It was a cheaper paper than *hōsho* and because of this was re-introduced after 1842 as a direct result of the sumptuary laws of the Bakufu. Even after this date *hōsho* seems to have been very occasionally used for colour prints and even more commonly for *surimono*. The paper used for most of the colour prints was *hōsho*, a *nori-gami* paper, i.e. one which uses rice paste as a glue. *Hōsho*, a most beautiful, soft, rather absorbent, long-fibred paper, was made in enormous quantities in the villages of Goka-mura in the province of Echizen. It was the heaviest of the *kōzo* papers being marketed in a *jō* or quire of forty-eight sheets weighing some 850 grammes. This paper was one of the most expensive in ordinary production and sometimes, especially in later prints, it was adulterated with *mitsumata*, i.e. a fibre obtained from *Edgeworthia papyrifera*, a practice which is said to have reduced the cost by over 50 per cent when only two parts

3. *Kwa-Cho* print by Hiroshige: the male Hondo Copper Pheasant (*Yamadori*; Syrmaticus scintillans) on a snow-covered mountain pine, with a *senryu* poem above. Signed: Hiroshige fude. *Chu-tanzaku*. (See page 191.)

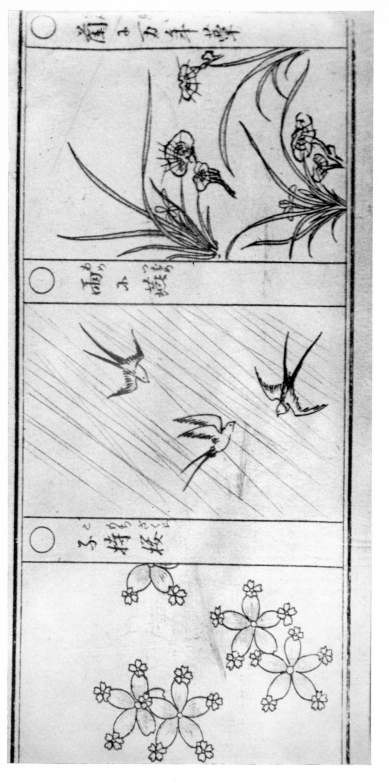

4. an example of the later copper engraving of Japan: a page from the Book of Designs (*Karakusa Moyo hinagata*) by Takizawa Sei. Publisher: Matsuzaki Nakaba: engraver; Yasudo Yanagi Taro. Dated 1885, the work consists of 432 etched designs, almost all with charm and ingenuity and a few of great beauty: the engraving shows incredible mastery of technique, some plates even reproducing the watermark effect in certain silks. (See page 245.)

of the latter were added to the *kōzo*. This paper did very much for the development of the Japanese print and its great toughness has preserved many prints and books of early times right down to the present day, even although many that appear in the salerooms show signs of having been subjected to considerable wear and tear.

These were not the only papers used in Japanese printing although from 1770 to 1840 single sheet prints were almost always on *hōsho*. A few illustrated albums used the fine *tōshi* paper from China which was presumably imported. Such paper seems to have been similar, if not identical, to that made of bamboo pulp and called by the Chinese, *hsüan chih*. Obviously such papers would have been extremely expensive and, except for very limited printings, were never a commercial proposition. They were used, however, for some *Nagasaki-e* single sheet prints. Of Japanese papers, some *ehon* used *hanshi* papers and that most favoured seems to have been *Ōsu hanshi* from Iyo. These were *mitsumata* papers and after 1785 even the dark toned *Suruga hanshi*, which was invented in that year, was very occasionally used.

The colours employed were the following: orange red (*tan*) made from red lead, a soft pinkish carmine (*beni*) made from the Safflower *Carthamus tinctorius*, blue (*Ao*) made either from indigo (*airō*)—a practice which may have been learned from China—or else an ultramarine which appears to have been imported from Europe in the form called *herō* but which may have come in earlier times in small quantities from China in the natural amorphous form called *ruri*. The older indigo was frequently produced by extracting the colour from rags that had been so dyed, the pigment always being in somewhat short supply and big demand. A yellow colour (*ki*) was produced most commonly from the yellow dye called *zumi* (extracted from the bark of *Pyrus toringo*) which is also used on *Ōtsu-e* and from orpiment (*kiwō*), whilst the best prints, some of those of the Ōsaka school and many *surimono*, used gamboge (*shiwō*). Purple (*murasaki*) was produced by mixing blue (*aigomi*, i.e. a reddish-brown purple) and *beni* whilst, in a few fine prints, e.g. some of young actors by Bunchō, it seems to have been the purple extracted from *shikon*, the name given to the roots of the borage, *Lithospermum erythrorhizon* S. and Z. Prints produced in the 1870s often made use of an imported German aniline colour. Green (*midori*) was either a mixture of *herō* and *kiwō* or of *zumi* and *airō*. An orange yellow colour (*Tō-ō*) was produced either by mixing *zumi* and *benigara* (an iron-red derived from colcothar manufactured from the treatment of iron pyrites) or from *zumi* and rouge (*yenji*) mixed. The blacks (*sumi*) had various origins: in some of the earlier books it seems possible that pine soot (*susu*) ink mixed with a suitable glue was used but in most prints and books the black is derived from lampblack (*yu-yen*) made by burning *dokuye-no-abura*, an oil obtained from the nuts of the tree spurge *Elaeococca cordata*; however, for hair and the other brilliant blacks that play so large a part in print designs, *tsuya-zumi* or brilliant black was used. It was made by mixing lampblack with a medium called *dōsa*, itself made from glue and alum; this was printed from a separate block. Silver (*gin-rō*), a beautiful colour used lavishly yet with incredibly delicate effect on certain *surimono* (e.g. Hokkei's series, 'Kai zukushi' (c. 1820) where the surf-line above the shells is done in silver), is made from brass powder with glue as a medium and the very rare copper colour (*akegane-irō*) from powdered metallic copper and glue. Mica (*kira*) was used in the form of minute flakes evenly sprinkled over a ground prepared with a mixture of rice paste and alum; at least for single sheet prints. This was very probably an invention, as Mr Hillier suggests, of the publisher Tsutaya (*c.* 1790).[11] White (*shiro*) was produced either with a mixture of powdered white clay (*jōfun*) mixed with a little glue or, for a more lively white and in more luxurious prints, clamshell powder (*namaguriko*) and glue.

It will be seen from the above that the producers of prints had many technical means and materials on which they could draw but these were often surprisingly dear and only large demand and, as a rule, large production could have made possible the comparatively small prices at which they originally sold. In this connection Michener in his work, *The Floating World*, page 359, has an extremely interesting table of the range of prices at which certain prints sold between the years 1677 and 1954. Anyone interested in the economics of print production would be well advised to consult this reference.

NOTES ON CHAPTER III

[1] Volker, T.: *Ukiyo-e Quartet, Publisher, Designer, Engraver and Printer*, Leiden, 1949.

² Besides this means of retailing books and prints, there were those that were disposed of by itinerant hawkers. Professor Takahashi tells us that it was after the fire of Meireki that the government issued peddlers' licences, selling these things as relief measures (January 1659) but they were restricted to those over fifty and under fifteen years of age and to the physically handicapped. However, by 9th April of the same year, books were exempted from this order—probably under pressure from the retailers. These peddlers of prints seem to have continued their business until about 1795 when finally the shop proprietors gained a monopoly for the distribution of books and prints. Books were first published for sale to the public in the Muromachi period (1338–1602) and were produced from wood-blocks until after 1887 when the first modern industrial printing machinery was introduced into Japan. Throughout the whole period the publishing firms were probably very small and it is said that, even today, there are 656 of these firms employing less than ten people. It is a matter of interest that there still survive seven publishers who were in business in the days of wood-block printing.

³ Takekoshi, Y.: *The Economic Aspects of the History of the Civilization of Japan*, London, 1930.

⁴ A short but very complete and reliable account of the known Japanese traditions and records relating to the craft of colour printing will be found in Waterhouse, D. B.: *Harunobu and his Age: the Development of Colour Printing in Japan*, London, British Museum, 1964.

⁵ This man was one of Japan's most illustrious minds. His interests were almost endless. He had studied western painting at Nagasaki in 1753 and ten years later he met Shiba Kokan. He acquired a knowledge of Dutch— he was indeed one of the foremost *rangakusa* or students of western learning—and became a notable botanist and zoologist in his own country. Later he turned his attention to physics and chemistry and obtained a knowledge of electricity and mining and was the discoverer of asbestos in Japan. Painter, potter and a fertile writer on political economy, a novelist and writer of some highly obscene books, he was possessed of phenomenal energy and countless suggestions from his teeming brain inspired others to triumphs in many fields. He founded a club in Edo which collected and designed almanac leaves and it was this club which later had as its chairman the *hatamoto* Kyosen who took a large part in the creation of the brocade prints of 1765. The whole debt of the colour print to Hiraga's indirect influence will probably never be known.

⁶ Michener, J. A.: *The Floating World*, 1954, page 154.

⁷ Chio Hirano: *Kiyonaga*, Boston, 1939.

⁸ Strange, E. F.: *Tools and Materials illustrating the Japanese Method of Colour Printing*, London, 1924.

[9] Robinson, B.W.: *Drawings of Utagawa Kuniyoshi in the collection of Ferdinand Lieftinck*, Gröningen, 1953. Privately published in an edition of 350 copies none of which were for sale.

[10] Dr Richard Lane (*Masters of the Japanese Print*) says: '. . . formerly catalpa wood had often been used for the blocks . . .' (page 152). This is certainly true and is, I think, a discovery first made by Dr S. Fujikake, but, so far as I remember, no other European author has noted it. The reasons why this wood was chosen are obscure. The Japanese species is *Catalpa ovata* (= *C. Kaempferi*) the wood of which is not at all strong, very brittle and, for the most part, coarse grained. It is, however, durable and soft and it may be the combination of these qualities which caused the very poor execution of much of the engraving of the sixteenth and early seventeenth centuries. A poem in the *Manyōshu* anthology (dating *circa* late seventh century) speaks of bows made of *catalpa* wood and one would not expect such wood as that successfully used for this purpose to have much value for the wood-engraver. The use of this wood was common even during the first half of the eighteenth century and obviously the engravers had learned to overcome many of its difficulties and perhaps they made use of the slower growing and denser varieties of the south island. More research needs to be carried out on the oldest surviving wood-blocks and if this is done it may be found that this wood was a significant factor in determining the evolution of some of the characteristics of the early wood-block prints.

[11] Mica was used for the cover designs of Japanese books long before this. Indeed, one of the private press editions of the *Saga-bon*—a volume of Nō plays (the *Nōka densho*) which deals also with their accessories—dating from about 1610, has its thick, coloured, paper cases decorated with mica-covered designs. Book covers and the techniques used in their production may well have influenced print techniques but western scholarship at least has hitherto neglected the subject of Japanese book-bindings.

ADDENDUM

Lists of Engravers, Printers, Calligraphers and Publishers engaged in the Production of Japanese Prints and Printed Books with Illustrations

THE FOLLOWING lists are obviously far from exhaustive but are believed to be the most complete yet published. Every name that appears in them is given with an indication of the approximate period in which the person or firm was in active production. This is done by giving the century in figures and the first, second, third or fourth quarter-century is designated by the letters a, b, c or d. Thus '18d–19b' indicates a period of activity between the approximate dates 1775 and 1850 but it might well be that the actual dates, if known—which indeed they seldom are—would stretch from 1782 to 1836. It is because of the uncertainty of most 'exact' dates and the fact that they are always subject to revision that it has been thought best to use this method rather than to give an air of spurious exactitude and finality to the dating.

Some of the names, especially of publishers, are not in the standard Hepburn system of transliteration. This is generally because they have been taken, in this or that instance, from old continental sale catalogues or other such sources and the manner of transliteration has involved some uncertainty; a few, however, are given in a form which, although possibly incorrect, is the one under which they appear in one or other of the major works of reference.

Wholesale publishers were organized into a guild, the *Jihondoiya no Nakama*. Each member of this carried on business under three names, the *dō-gō*, the *ya-gō* and his own personal name. Best known perhaps of all publishers is thus Kōshodō Tsutaya Jusaburō. Very occasionally the family name may appear instead, e.g. Uyemura, but this is perhaps more commonly found in books than on sheet prints.

69

Binyon and Sexton mention a single instance of the name used by a publisher being his *gō* as a comic poet, namely, Karamaro, which was used by Tsutaya Jusaburō in this connection. The *ya-gō* or name of the firm might be used by different men for several generations but the *dō-gō* was nearly always restricted to one person. In comparatively few instances do we know the synonymy, as it were, of *dō-gō* and *ya-gō* and much more needs to be done on this important aspect of the subject. Finally, each publisher had his own trademark or shop sign (*iye no shirushi*) and this is often stamped on the artist's original design, with or without one or more of the publishers' names. A list of such signs is also given. (See Appendix VIII).

Where the name of a firm of publishers, e.g. Wakasaya, is found in colophons of books without any other designation to identify individuals of the firm, the name is listed separately since it may, in certain instances, refer to some other individual than those that appear in the list, e.g. Wakasaya Yoichi. In most instances of this the *ya-gō* is listed alone when at least two different works have come to light bearing only this name in the colophon; thus, even if it proves to be the production of one or other of the listed individuals with this same *ya-gō*, it may be taken as an indication that books or prints are known to have been issued, during the period shown, without any indication of the publisher's personal name.

In the present state of knowledge and working, as I have done, far from the great libraries of Japanese books, it is quite impossible that this list will be found free from errors and omissions. However, it is hoped that it will form a basis for the further researches of others.

LIST OF ENGRAVERS

Akamatsu Senkicki
Akigama Naokadzu
Akiyama Kenkichi
Andō Nabejirō 19a
Andō Yasubei 18b
Andō Yenchi 18d
Aoyagi Takao
Asahina ?
Asai Renjiya
Asakura Gompachi 18d

Asakura Hachiyemon 19a
Asakura Ihachi 19a
Asakura Sakurao 19b
Asakura Shirōbei 19b
Asakura Tadaya (four of this name) 18?–19
Asakura Uachi 19a
Asano Hiroji
Atakubei 18d

Egawa Jokichi 19c
Egawa Hachizayemon 18d–19a
Egawa Sentarō 19c
Egawa Tomekichi, sealed
 'Gojotei' 19ab
Endō Gōroku 18c
Endō Matsugoro 18cd
Eshikawa Hambei 18d

Fugita Kinsuke 19b
Fujihei Jihei 18c
Fujihei Shirōbei 18c
Fujii Issō 18d–19a
Fujiye Bunsuke 18c
Fujiye Kubei 19a
Fujimura Kiyemon 18b
Fujimura Sōsuke 19a
Fujimura Zenyemon 18bc
Fujiwara Zenyemon 18b

Genkosai 19b. This man was also
 a master designer of *inrō* and
 engraved a book of designs for
 these. He may have engraved
 other work.
Giokkiosha Sensei 19ab
Giokkwosha Chōsei 19b

Hamako ? 18d
Hangiya Gembei 18c
Hata Kuhei 18d
Higuchi Gembei 18d
Higuchi Yōhei 19ab
Hōgendō 19d
Horikane 19bc
Horikuma 19bc
Horimasu Ota 19c
Hōritatsu 19c

Ichida Jirōbei 19a–c

Inouye Jihei 19a
Inouye Shinshichi 18c–d: sealed
 Shunshō:
Ise Shin 19a
Ishihara Ambei 18b
Ishikawa Sukejirō 19a
Itakura Seijirō 19c–20a
Iwasaki Isaburō 19bc

Kamimura Yasugorō 19c
Kasuke ? 19b
Kawawata Tōzaburo 19a
Kikuji Mohei 19a
Kimura Tokutarō 19d
Kinoshita Jimbei 19a
Koizumi Shimpachi 18d–19a
Komindō 196
Kumazō ? 19abc
Kurehara Jirōbei 18b
Kurehashi Tokubei 19b

Machida Chōchu 18cd
Machida Sukeyemon 18d
Mataichi ? 18d
Matsui Chuzō 19a
Matsushima Fusajirō 19b
Miyata Kitsusai 19ab
Mori Kichigorō 18d
Morishita Richō 18c
Murakami Genyemon 18b
Murakami Kuhei 18d–19a

Nakade Toen 18c
Nakamura Bunsuke 19d
Nakamura Nichō 19bc
Nakamura Onozō 19bc
Niwa Ezayemon 18b
Niwa Shōbei 18b
Noshirō Ryuko 18d
 (SHUMPŌDŌ)

Ogita Tōbei 19c: also a printer
Okada Mohei 19b
Okamoto Shōa 18d
Okamoto Shōgyō 18cd
Ōkubo Kazutomi 18b
Omori Jihei 18d
Omori Kumasichirō 19b
Ōnō of Ōsaka 19bc
Ōtsuka Yuji 20a

RANKŌDŌ Gokuhi 19a
ROKKŌDŌ Tōhei 18c

Sakaki Jimbei 18c
Sakamoto Jimbei 18c–19a
Sakata Chugorō 19b
Sakata Yasubei 19b
Sakaye Yonesuke 19a
Sasaki Shōbei 18bc
Sawagi Shōbei 18c
SEIKŌDŌ Tani Takuboku 19ab
Seki Jiyemon 18d
Sekiguchi Jinshirō 18d
Sekine Kaei 18c
Sekine Kihei 18c
Sekine Shimbei 18c
SEKŌDŌ alternative reading of
    SEIKŌDŌ
Shimizu Riuzō 19c
Shimonura Tukifusa 16d–17a
SHINODŌ Enshi 19a
Shioyama Yoshibei 19bc
Shirai Tōsuke 18d
SHŌKAIDŌ Sadakichi 19b
SHOMODŌ Giokkiosha 19a
SHOMODŌ Kokotei 19ab
SHUMPODŌ Noshirō Riuko 18d

SHUMPODŌ Riukotsu 18d
Sofue Samon 19b
Sugita Kinsuke 19ab
Suzuki Ejirō 19a?

Tadashobe 18d–19a
Takahashi Matsubito 19a
Takahashi Rōsen 18c
Tampa Yezayemon 18b
Tanaka Heibei 18c
Tanaka Jirōkichi 19d
Tanaka Shuchichi 18c
Tanaka Tadashichi 18c
Tanaka Yebei 18c
Tanaka Yoju 19d
Takahashi Rosen 18c (engraved
    some of Harunobu's prints)
Takenouchi Heishirō 18cd
Tani Takuboku 19ab =
    SEIKŌDŌ
Tani Tōri signs 'Tōri' 19b
Tokubei 19bc
Tsuji Kazumune 18cd
Tsusen 18bc
Tsusen 20a
Tzumiya 18a

Uemura Yezō 19a
Umesawa Minokichi 19d

Yamaguchi Bokuyō 18c
Yamaguchi Hanshirō 18c–19a
Yamaguchi Seiga 18d
Yamaguchi Seizō 19a
Yamaguchi Shichibei 18d–19a
Yamaguchi Tatsunosuke 19a
Yamaguchi Yashichirō 18d
Yamamoto ? 19d

Yamamoto Chōzayemon 18d
Yamamoto Kihei 18b: seals
  'Takeho'
Yamamoto Wayemon 18bc
Yamamoto ? 19bc

Yamazaki Shōkurō 19a
Yasudō Yanagi 19cd
Yokogawa Takejirō 19bc
Yoshida Kyōsen 18bc
Yoshimi Niyemon 18c

LIST OF PRINTERS

Daikyu ? 19c

Fujihei Shirōbei 18c seals 'Ike'

Hōri Kisaburō 19a

Iida 19abc
Isumiya Gorōbei 18d–19a
Itakura Seijirō*

KAKUSHŌDŌ Toyemon 19a
Kakuso Nanori seals Kanamori
  Shōsai 18cd
Kasaharu Sahei 19c
Kataōka ? 19bc
Kikuya Sahen 19a
Kikuya Yohen 19a
Kwakuseidō 19abc

Matsumura Senkichi 19c
Motohashi Teijirō 20a

Nukatomi ? 19b

Ogawa Hachigorō 18cd
Ogawa Hatchō 18c
Ogita Tōbei 19c also engraver
Oriki Saburō 19ab

Sadagorō ? 19c
Sekiguchi Jinshirō 18cd also en-
  graver
Sekiguchi Tōkichi 18cd
Senritei 19b
Shinoda Yashitarō 19b
Shirai Tōsuke 18cd
Suritoyo 19bc
Suzuki Kichitarō 19d

Takekawa Minosuke 17c
Tomekichi? 19ab

Uemura Yōhei 19a

Yamamoto Genshichirō 18cd
Yumoto Koshi 18c

*An interesting account in Japanese of this man, will be found in
  Yamada, K: Itakura Seijirō; 'Woodblock Printer' *Ukiyo-e* Art:
  No. 2 (1963)

CALLIGRAPHERS

Chikwa Tōryu 18d–19a

Fuji Karamaru 18d–19a

GANSHŌDŌ Shujin 18cd

Hanada Kiukwa 19b
Hokuoshi Shagiō 19a

Ishihara KOMACHIDŌ 19a

Kawata Hirōyoshi 19b
Kensai 19a
Kihō 19a
Kinsai Seyu 19b
Kitao Shigemasa 18c–19a. This
is the *ukiyō-e* artist

Mikifusai 19b
Minagawa Gen seals 'Kihen' 18d

Niwa 19a

Ōka Sanchō 19a
Ōson seals Bunsen the name of
the painter Hōitsu 19ab

Rokuroku Kanjin 18cd
Rokuzotei 18d–19a: used also the
name Kwakei Rōgyō

Sangakushi seals 'Kiushi' 19ab
Sankio Tokoki seals 'Tokoki'
and 'Shisan' 18d
Sayama? 18cd
Sendōjin seals 'Kosendōjin' 19a
Shikura Tōryu 18d–19a
Sōhin seals Nakajima 19ab

Tanaka Shōzō 19ab
Tōgetsu Nanshu 17d
Tsune Isome 17d–18a

Watanabe Ōko 19b

Yamazaki Ryu 18a

LIST OF EDO PUBLISHERS

Adzumaya Daisuke 19bc = TŌKINDŌ or KINSHUDŌ
AIKINDŌ = Hiranoya Kichibei 18ab
Akamatsuya Shōtarō 19b
Amamatsuya Hōsuke 19a
Aridaya Kiyoyemon 19bc = YUYEIDŌ
Aridaya Seiyemon 19abc = YUSUIDŌ
Asakura Hachiyemon 19a
Asakusa-an = Kurōkawa Harunobu, 1799–1866, a scholar of the
Japanese classics and a noted Kyōka poet.
Azumaya Daisuke 19a

BAISHUKUDŌ 18a = Nishimuraya Ichirōyemon
BAITARŌDŌ 19a
BANKAKUDŌ 18ab = Nishimuraya Genroku
BANKIŌDŌ 19b
BANKIUKAKUDŌ 19b = Hirabayashi
BANSHUNDŌ 19a
BUNEIDŌ 19a = Maokawa Zembei
BUNEIDŌ 19d = Takeda Denyemon
BUNGIOKUDŌ 19b
BUNJUDŌ = Maruya Bunyemon 18d–19a
BUNKEIDŌ 19ab = Chōjiya Heibei
BUNKEIDŌ 19c = Shiuwaya Bunshichi
BUNKIDŌ 18ab = Igaya Kanyemon
BUNKINDŌ 18cd–19a = Toyojimaya Bunjiemon
BUNGWADŌ 19c = Minoya Seishichi
BUNKWADŌ 19b = Shioya Shōsaburō
BUNRINDŌ 19a
BUNSENDŌ 19a = Yoshidaya Shimbei
BUNSHŌDŌ 19a–c = Kobayashiya Matsugōrō
BUNSHŌKADUDŌ 18c = Suharaya Saburōbei

Chichibuya Shōzayemon 18d
Chōjiya Heibei 19ab = BUNKEIDŌ
Chōjiya Kiyemon 19a
Chusuke ? 18d

Daikokuya Heikichi 19a–20a = SHŌJUDŌ
Daikokuya Kinjirō 19bc
Daikokuya Kyubei 19bc = SHŌJUDŌ
DAIKWANDŌ = Fushimiya Zenroku 18c–20a
DAIYEIDŌ 18d–20a = Iseya Sōyemon
DANSENDŌ 19bc = Ibaya Sensaburō

Note. For other names sometimes commencing with 'E' see under
   'YE', an older and more common transliteration.
Ebijuya Shōshichi 19b
Ebineya? 19bc
Ebiya Rinnosuke 19bc = KAIJUDŌ
Echigoya Chōhashi 18d–19c

Echizenya Hachiyemon 19ab
Echizenya Heisaburō 19bc
Eirakuya Jōsuke 19b
EISENDŌ *see* YEISENDŌ, etc.
Ejimaya Kiseki 18a
ENKAKUDŌ 19bc
Enomoto Heikichi 18d–19a
Enomoto Sōyemon 18d–19a
ENSEKIRŌDŌ 19b
Enshuya Hikobei 19bc
Enshuya Matabei 19bc
Enshuya Yaskuka Yashichi 18bc
ERINDŌ (probably this is the name used by the engraver Suzaki
    Ejirō as a publisher in 1813)
Ezakiya 18c (*see* Yezakiya)

Fuchizenya ?
Fujihiko 19b
Fujikei Keijirō ?
Fujiokaya Hikojirō 19c
Fujiokaya Hikotarō 18d–19b = SHŌGENDŌ
Fujiokaya Keijirō 19bc = SHŌRINDŌ
Fujiwaraya Bunjirō 19bc
Fujiya Munesuke 19ab
Fukitaya Takichi 19b
FUKOKWANDŌ 19a
FUKUSENDŌ 18d–19b = Kawaguchi Uhei
Funaki Kasuki 18c
Fushimiya Zenroku 18c–20a = DAIKWANDŌ
Fushimiya Zenzō 18d
Futaya Takekichi 19b
FUYŌDŌ = Takasu Sōshichi 18d–19a

GIOKUNANDŌ 19bc = Fujiwaraya Bunjirō (also with a branch in
    Ōsaka)
GIOKUYODŌ 19a
Gojishachu 19a
GUNKIOKUDŌ 19a = Kawayachiya Mohei (also of Ōsaka)

Gusokuya Kahei 19c
GWANGETSUDŌ 18d–19a = Nishimiya Shinroku
GWASENDŌ 19a = Mizunoto Hitsuji

HAKUAIDŌ 19c
HAKUBUNDŌ 19d
HAKUBUNKWANDŌ 19d
Hamadaya Tokubei 19abc
Hanabusaya Bunyō 19ab = SEIUNDŌ
Hanabusaya Daisuke 19b
Hanabusaya Heikichi 19a
Hangiya Shichirōbei 17d–18a
Harataneya Suimoto 19d = SHŌDŌ
Hashimoto Jubei 17d
Hayashiya Shōgorō 19a
HEIRINDŌ 19b
Hirabayashiya Shōgorō 19b = SHUBUNDŌ or HEIRINDŌ
Hiranoya 19bc
Hiranoya Kichibei 18ab = AIKINDŌ
Hirayama Takeshirō 19d
Hiroaki 19bc
Hiro-okaya Keisuke 19c
Hishiya Jihei 19a
Hishiya Tomoshichi 19b
HOEIDŌ 19ab = Takenouchi Magohachi
HOEIDŌ 19ab
Honchō Mohei 19b
Honchō Naosaburō 19b
Honchō Rensuke? 19ab
Honya alternative reading of Motoya
Honya Kiubei 19b
Honya Shōsuke 19b
HŌRAIDŌ 19a = Sumiyoshiya Masagōrō 19ab
Horikoshi ? 19ab
Hori Masaji 20a = KWŌKWADŌ
Hori Takichi 19bc
HŌSENDŌ 18abc = Maruya Yamamoto Kohei
HŌSHUDŌ 19abc

HŌYEIDŌ 19b = Take-no-Uchi Magohachi (some prints sealed 'Take')

Hyakumambo Machu 19b

Ibaya Kyubei 19bc = KINSEIDŌ

Ibaya Sensaburō 19bc = DANSENDŌ

Idzusan ? 19c = ? Idzutsuya Zembei 19b

Igaya Kanyemon 18ab = BUNKIDŌ

Igetamura

Igetani Ebibaya ?

IKWANDŌ 19b

Imafukuya Yusuke 19a

Imaiyu Gōbei 19b (associated with Kyōto firm)

Inokuchiya Matsunosuke 19d = KWAISHINRŌDŌ

Inomoto Heikichi 19a

Inomoto Sōyemon 19a

Irihan

Iriya Maka

Isekane Kawaguchi 19bc

Iseya Chubei 19c

Iseya Heibei 19bc

Iseya Isaburō 19ab

Iseya Jisuke 18d–19a

Iseya Jiyemon 19a = KOSAIDŌ

Iseya Kanekichi 19be

Iseya Kimbei 18a–19a

Iseya Komatarō 19c

Iseya Magashirō 18d–19a

Iseya Rihei 19ab = KINJUDŌ

Iseya Sanjirō 18d–19b

Iseya Sōyemon 18d–20a = DAIYEIDŌ

Iseya Tōkichi 19bc

Iseya Tokubei 19ab

Iseya Uyemon 19ab

Ishimiya Soshirō 18c

Ishiwatari Heihachi

Ishiwatari Risuke

Iwaiya ? 18b

Iwamoto Chuzō 19c

Iwamoto Kyubei 19bc
Iwamoto Shun 19d
Iwatoya Gempachi 18cd
Iwatoya Kisaburō 18d–19b
Iwatoya Yamagata 17d and 19bc
Izumiya Chōbei 18a
Izumiya Gonshirō 18ab. Said by Morishima Churyō, a poet, to have
    invented the *benizuri-e*
Izumiya Hambei 19ab
Izumiya Ichibei 18d–19c = KANSENDŌ = 'Senichi'
Izumiya Kiyoshichi 19b
Izumiya Kōjirō 18d
Izumiya Mohei 18a
Izumiya Shōjirō 19ab
Izumodera Izuminōjō 18d
Izumoji Izumono ?
Izutsuya Chuzayemon 17d–18c = SEISUIDŌ
Izutsuya Ihiko 18d
Izutsuya Kanyemon 18d
Izutsuya Kanyemon II 19abc
Izutsuya Sanyemon 18abc
Izutsuya Zembei 19b (evidently a branch of the Kyōto firm)
Izuya Gankichi 19ab

JAKURINDŌ 18d–19c = Wakasaya Yoichi
JŌKINDŌ 19bcd = Jōshuya Kinzō
Jōshuya Juzō 19b = KINJUDŌ
Jōshuya Kinzō 19bcd
JUKWAKUDŌ 19abc = Maruya Seijirō or Kiyojirō

Kadomaruya Jinsuke 19a = SHINSEIKAKUDŌ
Kadomaruya Tokusaburō 19a
Kadzusaya Iwakichi 19bc
Kagaya Kichibei 19abc
Kagaya Kichiyemon 19b
Kagaya Yasubei 19b
Kagiya Shōjirō
KAIJUDŌ 19bc = Ebiya Rinnosuke

Kamaya Kihei 19b
Kameya Iwakichi 19b
Kameya Taihei 18c
Kamimura (an alternative reading of Uyemura 18b–19a)
Kamiya Gembei 18c
Kamiya Gorōbei 18d–19a
Kamiya Tokuhachi 19bc = TŌSHŌKENDŌ
Kanaya Eiyemon 18a
Kanesa
KANSENDŌ 18d–19b = Izumiya Ichibei
Kariganeya Ihei 18c
Kariganeya Jisuke 18cd
Kariganeya Seikichi 18cd
Kasentei Tōjin 19a
Katashima Gonshirō 19b
Katoya 19bc
Kawachiya Kihei 19a
Kawachō ? 19bc
Kawagendō 18d
Kawaguchiya Chōzō 19bc
Kawaguchiya Shōbei 19bc
Kawaguchiya Yuhei 18d–19b = FUKUSENDŌ
Kawaju ?
'Kawashō' ? 19ab
Kawamuraya Genzayemon 18a
Kawamuraya Giyemon 18c
Kawashō ? 19b
Kazusaya Iwazō 19b
Kazusaya Rihei 18c
Kazusaya Shiosuke 18d–19a
KEIUNDŌ 18d = Uyemuraya Zenroku
Kenya Shōgorō 19b
Kichimonjiya Ichibei 18c
Kichimonjiya Jirōbei 18d
Kikuchiya Takemura 19c
Kikuya ? 18ab
Kikuya Ichibei 19bc
Kikuya Kōzaburō 18d–19c = KINKŌDŌ
KIKWAKUDŌ 18d–19c = Sanoya Kihei

KINCHŌDŌ 19b = Jōshuya Juzō
KINJUDŌ 19ab = Iseya Rihei
KINKŌDŌ 19c = Kikuya Kōzaburō
KINKŌDŌ 18c–19c = Yamguchiya Tōbei
Kinoshita Jinyemon 17d–18c
KINSEIDŌ 19bc = Ibaya Kyubei
KINSHINDŌ 19abc = Moriya Jihei
KINSHŌDŌ 19bc = Yebisuya Shōshichi
KINSHŌDŌ 19bc = Nakano Nihei
KINSHŌDŌ 19ab = Shōjiya Shōshichi
KINSHŌDŌ 19bc = Tsujiokaya Bunsuke
KINSHUDŌ 19ab = Asumaya Daisuke
Kintsusha 19c
KINZUIDŌ 19c
Kiriya 18bc
Kitajima Chōshirō 19a
Kiya Sōjirō 19c
Kiyomidzuua 19bc (an alternative reading of Shimidzuya)
Kobayashiya Bunshichi 19d–20a
Kobayashiya Kimbei 19b
Kobayashiya Matsugorō 19abc = BUNSHŌDŌ
Kobayashiya Shimbei 19ab = SUZAMBŌDŌ
KŌEIDŌ 19abc = Tsutaya Kichizō
Kogaya Katsugorō 19bc
KOGOKATSUDŌ 18d–19a
Kōjimaya 19c
KOGOKATSUDŌ 18d–19a
Koizumi Chugorō 18c
KŌKWADŌ 19b
Komatsuya Dembei 18ab
KŌRINDŌ 19bc
KŌSAIDŌ 19a = Iseya Jiyemon
Koshimuraya Heisuke 19bc
KŌSHODŌ 18c–19b = Tsutaya Juzaburō
Koshōdō Karamarō 19a
KŌZANDŌ 19c
Kureganeya Gisuke 18cd
Kuwagataya 19a
KWAISHINRŌDŌ 19d = Inokuchiya Matsunosuke

KWAKUJUDŌ 18abc = Okumuraya Genroku (this is Okamura
    Masanobu)
KWANGETSUDŌ
KWŌKWADŌ 20a = Hori Masaji
Kyōkaya Utahiza 19ab

Maekawa Rokuzayemon 18d–19a
Maekawa Zembei 19a = BUNEIDŌ
Manjuya ? 19c
MANYŌDŌ 18d
Muraichiya ? 19ab
Marubun ? 18d
Marujin
MARUKŌDŌ 18a–19a = Yamamuraya ?
MARUKYUDO 18cd = ? Takeya
Marumatsuya
Marumuraya
Maruya Bunyemon 18d–19a = BUNJUDŌ
Maruya Gorōyemon 18a
Maruya Jimpachi 18c–19c = YENJUDŌ
Maruya Kiyōjirō 19bc = JUKWAKUDŌ
Maruya Kōhei 18abcd = HŌSENDŌ (see the family name
    Yamamoto)
Maruya Kuzayemon 18b
Maruya Kyushirō 19bc
Maruya Seijirō 19abc
Maruya Tetsujirō 19c
MASUGINDŌ 19bc
Masuya 18bcd
Masuya Jimpachi 19ab
Masuya Kichigorō 19b
Matsuazakaya Kikujirō 19b
MATSUBARADŌ (a mistaken reading for SHŌGENDŌ sometimes
    found in catalogues)
Matsumoto Sahei 19abc
Matsumura Tatsuemon 19a
Matsumuraya Yahei 18b–19a
Matsuyasu ? 19a
Matsuya Shiōzō 19b

Matsuya Tetsujirō 19bc = YENJUDŌ
Matsuye Sanshirō 17d
Matsuzakaya Kinnosuke 19c
Matsuzaki Nakaba 19d
Mikawaya Rihei I 18bc
Mikawaya Rihei II 18d–19a
Mikawaya Sahei 19ab
Mikawaya Tetsugorō 19b
Mikuraya Sōkichi 19b
Minatoya Kohei 19b
Minoya Heishichi 18c
Minoya Seishichi 19c = BUNKWADŌ
Mitaya Kihachi 19ab = YEISENDŌ
Moriji Jihei (not Jirobei) possibly this is the same publisher that seals
   'Mori' on prints on Shigemasa
Moritaya Hanjirō 19bc
Moritaya Hanzō
Moriya Jihei 19ab = KINSHINDŌ
Motoya (alternative reading of Honya)
Muraichiya ? 19abc
Murataya Ichibei 19bc
Murataya Ichigorō 19b
Murataya Jimpachi 18d–19a
Murataya Jirōbei 18b–19b = YEIYUDŌ
Musashiya Isaburō 19b

Nagagawa Shinshichi 19a
Nakabayoshi ? 18cd = SEIYEIDŌ
Nakajimaya Risuke 18abc
Nakajimaya Sakai 18ab
Nakajimaya Sōsuke 19ab
Nakamuraya Katsugorō 19ab
Nakamuraya Shinshichi 18a
Nakamuraya Shōsuke 18d
Nakano Kimei 19d
Nakano Nihei 19bc = KINSHŌDŌ
Ningyōya Takichi 19bc
Nishikiya Takemura 19bc
Nishimiya Shinroku 18d–19a = GWANGETSUDŌ

Nishimiya Shunsoken 18d possibly this man did not do more than
   reprint old and valued plates which were in his possession
Nishimuraya Dembei 18d
Nishimuraya Genroku 18bcd = BANKAKUDŌ
Nishimuraya Hambei 17d
Nishimuraya Ichirōyemon 18a = BAISHUKUDŌ
Nishimuraya Magosaburō ?
Nishimuraya Shoshichi 19a
Nishimuraya Soshichi 18c = SHINRŌKODŌ
Nishimuraya Yohachi 18b–19b = YEIJUDŌ
Nishinomiya Shinroku 18d
Nōshuya Yasubei 19b

Odamakitei 19b
Odawaraya Yashichi 19c
Ōdaya Takichi ?
Ōgawa Hikokura
Ōgawa Shichirōbei 18bc
Oguraya Magobei 19d
Ōhara Jokichi 19d
Ōhashiya Yashichi 19bc
Okadaya Kahei 19c
Okadaya Kashichi 18cd
Okamuraya Shosuke 19b = SHUMBIDŌ
Okanoya Manjirō 19ab
Okanoya Taheiji 18d–19a
Okazakiya Mohei 19b
Okazaya Jubei 19ab
Okazaya Kihei 19bc
Okumuraya Genrokurō 18abc = KWAKUJUDŌ
Okumuraya Kihei 18c
Ōkuraya Magobei 19d
Ōkuraya Yasugorō 19d–20a
OKURINDŌ = Nishimiya Yahei 19b
Ōmiya Heihachi 19bc
Ōmiya Kuhei 18b
Ōmiya Yohei 18d–19a
Ōmiya Yojibei 18a
Onogiya Yasubei 18c

Ōoka Shunboku 18ab (a branch only of the Ōsaka house)
Ōsakaya Gembei 19b
Ōsakaya Mokichi 19b
Ōsakaya Shōsuke 19ab
Ōshimaya Denyemon 18d
Ōshimaya Sayemon 19a
Owadaya Yashichi 19a
Owadaya Yasubei 18c = ZEIGIOKUDŌ
Owariya Dembei 19ab
Owariya Kiyoshichi 19bc

RANKŌDŌ 18a–19a = Yemiya Kichiyemon
RENPŌDŌ 19a
RIKWAKUDŌ 18abcd = Urokogataya Magobei
RINSHŌDŌ 19bc
Ruiya Zembei 19bc

Sagamiya ? 18ab
Sakaiya ? 18bcd
Sakaiya Kurōbei 18c
SANJINDŌ 19d
SANKINDŌ 18c–19a = Yamazakiya Kimbei
SANKODŌ 18cd = Sanukiya Tōbei
SANMAIDŌ 19b
Sanoki 18d–19c
Sanoya Kihei 19bc = KIKWAKUDŌ
Sanoya Sadashichi 19ab
Sanoya Tomigorō 19c
SANRINDŌ 17d–19a = Yamadaya Sanshiro
SANSEIDŌ 19a = Yamazaki Heihachi
Sanukiya Tōbei 18cd = SANKŌDŌ
SANYUDŌ 19b (this appears to be the *dō-go* of the Inoue family of
    Edo when publishing privately)
Sasaya Matabei 19ab
Sawamuraya Rihei 19bc
Sawaya Jisuke 18cd
Sawaya Kōkichi 19bc
SEIKYUDŌ 18d–19a

SEISUIDŌ 17d–18c = Izutsuya Chuzayemon
SEIUNDŌ = Hanaya Kinjirō (Hanabusa Bunzō)
SEIYEIDŌ 18cd = Nakabayoshi ?
Sekiguchiya Masajiro 19d
Sengaku-ji temple 18a
Senichi 19a–c = Izumiya Ichibei
SENKIŌDŌ 18d = Takegi
SENKWAKUDŌ 17d–19c = Tsuruya Kiyemon
SENYA 18ab
Sessuiken Chajō 19b author, artist and publisher of several private
    publications
SHIKWADŌ 19a
Shimaya Tetsuya 19b
Shimidzuya ? 19bc (an alternative reading of Kiyomidzu)
Shimidzuya Naōjirō 19b
Shinagawaya Kiusuke 19c
Shin Iseya Kōhei 19bc
Shinoya Tokubei 19a
SHINROKUDŌ = Shunsoken Nishimiya
SHINSHODŌ 18cd = Suwaraya Ichibei
SHINSENYENDŌ 19a
SHINEIKAKUDŌ 19a = Kadamaruya Jinsuke
Shinyutei 19b
Shioya Shōsaburō 19b = BUNKWADŌ
SHIZENKWANDŌ 19a
SHŌGENDŌ 19bc = Fujiokaya Hikotaro
Shōjiya Shoshichi 19bc = KINSHŌDŌ
SHOJUDŌ 19a–20a = Daikokuya Heikichi
SHŌKWAKUDŌ 18b–19b = Yamashirōya
SHŌRINDŌ 19bc = Fujiokaya Keijirō
SHŌYEIDŌ 19ab = Kawaguchiya Shōzō (also said to be the *dō-go*
    of Yamaguchiya Shōjō, another reading)
SHUBUNDŌ 19c = Hirabayashi Shoguro *see* HEIRINDŌ
SHUGIOKUDŌ 19b (produced some very fine but rare *surimono*)
SHUMBIDŌ 19b = Okamuraya Shōsuke
SHUNRŌDŌ 19ab = Yamazakiya Seishichi
SHUNSHŌDŌ
Shunsoken Nishimiya = SHINROKUDŌ
SHUNYŌDŌ 18d

Shunyutei 19bc
SHUSEIKAKUDŌ 19b = Suwaraya Mohei
SHUYEDŌ
SOKWAKUDŌ 18d–19b = Tsuruya Kinsuke
Sonoharuya Shōsuke 19b
Sōshuya Yōhei 18d–19c
SŌYODŌ 18d
Sudareya Matayemon 18a
SUDŌ 17d–18a = Yamaguchiya Gombei
Sugiwaraya Kiyojirō 19bc
Suirenya Matayemon 17d
Sumimaruya Jinsuke 19ab
Sumimasa ?
Sumiyoshiya Masagōro 19ab = HŌRAIDŌ
Surugaya 18bc
Surugaya Sabujirō 18d–19a
Suwaraya Eisuke 19a
Suwaraya Ichibei 18d–19a
Suwaraya Ihachi 19a
Suwaraya Mohei 17d–19d = SHUSEIKAKUDŌ
Suwaraya Saburobei 18c = BUNSHŌKAKUDŌ
Suwaraya Sasuke 19c = KINKWADŌ
Suwaraya Shimbei 19b = SUZAMBODŌ
Suwaraya Shirobei 18c
Suwaraya Shiroyemon 18c
Suwaraya Sōbei 18c
Suwaraya Zengōro 18d–19a
Suyehiro-an 19a
SUZAMBODŌ 19b = Suwaraya Shimbei
Suzuki Kichitarō 19d

TAIKWANDŌ 18d = Takatsu Isuke
TAIYEDŌ 18d = Iseya Sōyemon
Tajimaya Yahei 19bc
Takadaya Takemasa 19b
Takahashiya 19bc = BUNEIDŌ
Takasaya (a firm established at Shiba in the suburbs of Yedo)
Takasu Sōshichi 18d–19a = FUYŌDŌ
Takatsuya Isuke 18d–19a = TAIKWANDŌ

Takedaya Denyemon 18d (seems only to be known as the publisher of Mori Genkwosai's 'Inro Fu' designs for inro)

Takegawa Tōbei 19a

Takegawa Tosuke 18d

'Take' this is the seal of HOYEIDŌ = Takenouchi Magohachi 19b

Takegi 18d = SENKIŌDŌ

Takemago ?

Takemuraya Tahei 18d

Takenouchi Magohachi 19b = HŌYEIDŌ

Takeya ? 18cd = MARUKYUDŌ

Tamaya Sōkichi 19ab

Tamaya Sansaburō 19b

Tambaya Hanshichi 19bc

Tambaya Rihei 18c

Tanaka Jubei 17d

Tanaka Yubi 19d

TENJUDŌ 18d–19b = Yegakiya Kichibei

TŌENDŌ 19a

Tōhonya Tahei 17c (this was the Edo branch of a Kyōto firm and seems to have published only Chinese works)

Tojimaya Hikobei 19bc

Tomitaya ? 18a–d

Tomitaya Yoshijirō 19d = BUNYŌDŌ

Tomiya 19c

TŌSHŌKENDŌ 19bc = Kamiya Tokuhachi

Toyojimaya Bunjiemon 18cd–19a = BUNKINDŌ

Tsujiokaya Bunsuke 19bc = KINSHŌDŌ

Tsujiya Yasubei 19bc

Tsuruki ? 18d–19a

TSURUSHINDŌ (this seems to have been the *dō-go* of Moriji Jihei which he used between the years 1751 and 1768)

Tsuruya Kihei 19bc = SENKWAKUDŌ

Tsuruya Kinsuke 18d–19b = SOKWAKUDŌ

Tsuruya Kiyemon 17c–18a (the same firm published from Nagoya, Kyoto and Osaka. Uncertain which were merely branches)

Tsusen 18c

TSUTAJUDŌ 18d

Tsutakuchi ? 19b

Tsutaya Juzaburo 18c–19b = KOSHŌDŌ

Tsutaya Kichizō 19abc = KŌEIDŌ

UEMURA *see* Uyemura
UMEMURA Yaichirō 18b
Uoei ? 19c
Uoya Eikuchi 19c
Urokogataya Magobei 18abcd = RIKWAKUDŌ
Urokogataya Sanzayemon 17d
Urokoya 17d
Uweda ? = Ueda
Uyedaya Kiyujirō 19b
Uyemura Kichibei 18b   } There may be some confusion
Uyemura Kichiyemon 18bc }   between these two
Uyemura Tōzaburō 18b (also at Osaka)
Uyemura Zenroku 18d = KEIUNDŌ

Wakabayashi Seibei 19a
Wakamatsuya Gensuke 18c
Wakamatsuya Yoshirō 19bc
Wakamidori Tei 19a
WAKARINDŌ 18d–19c = Wakasaya Yoichi
Wakasaya 18d–19a
Wakasaya Yoichi 18d–19c = JAKURINDŌ
Wanya Hisaburo
Wasenya Ichibei 18d–19a

Yamaboshi
Yamadaya Dembei 18d–19a
Yamadaya Juhei 19bc
Yamadaya Sanshirō 17d–19a = SANRINDŌ
Yamadaya Sasuke 18d–19a
Yamadaya Shōbei 19c = KINKYŌDŌ
Yamadaya Shunshio 19a
Yamadaya Shunshirō 19a
(Yamaguchi in 17d seems to have been the family name of Yama-
    gataya Iwatoya, seemingly a very curious combination which I
    do not understand)
Yamaguchiya Chusuke 18d–19a
Yamaguchiya Gombei 17d–18a = SUDŌ

Yamaguchiya Shōzō 19ab = SHŌYEIDŌ
Yamaguchiya Tōbei 18d–19c = KINKŌDŌ
'Yamahan' 18d
Yamakichiya ? 18d
YAMAKINDŌ 18d
'Yamakiya Kimbei' 18c = Yamazakiya Kimbei 18c ?
Yamamaru ?
Yamamatsu ?
Yamamotoya Heikichi 19abc = YEIKYUDŌ
Yamamotoya Kichibei 18d–19a
Yamamotoya Kohei 18ab = Maruya Kohei
Yamamori ?
Yamamuraya ? 18abcd = MARUKŌDŌ
Yamanakaya Yōsuke 19a
Yamashirōya Heisuke 19b
Yamashirōya Kambei 19a
Yamashirōya Niiroku 19b
Yamashirōya Sahei 18d–19c
Yamashirōya Sōhei 18d–19b
Yamashirōya Tokei 18b–19b = SHŌKWAKUDŌ
YAMASHŌDŌ 19ab
Yamatoya Kihei 18a–19b
Yamatoya Shōbei 18d–19a
Yamatoya Yasubei 19c = ZUIGYOKUDŌ
Yamazaki Heihachi 19a = SANSEIDŌ
Yamazaki Kimbei 18c–19a = SANKINDŌ
Yamazaki Seishichi 19ab = SHUNRŌDŌ
Yebisuya Shōshichi 19bc = KINSHŌDŌ
Yedoya Matsugōrō 18b–19c
YEIJUDŌ 18a–19b = Murataya Jirōbei
YEIJUDŌ 18b–19b = Nishimuraya Yohachi
YEIKYUDŌ 19abc = Yamamoto Heikichi
YEIRINDŌ 18d–19b = Iwatoya Kisaburō
YEISENDŌ 19ab = Mitaya Kihachi
Yemiya Kichiyemon 18a–19a = RANKŌDŌ (family name
    Uyemura)
'Yenami' 18c–19a
YENJUDO 18c–19c = Maruya Jimpachi = Matsuya Tetsujirō 19bc
Yenomoto Kichibei 18d–19a

Yenshuya Matabei 19bc
Yenshuya Yashichi 18c
Yezakiya Kichibei 18d–19b = TENJUDŌ
Yezakiya Tatsukura 19abc
Yezakiya Tatsuzō 19bc
Yorozuya Kichibei 19bc
Yorozuya Seibei 18a
Yorozuya Tajiyemon 18a–19a
Yoshidaya Gempachi 19bc
Yoshidaya Kimbei 19d
Yoshidaya Shimbei 19a = BUNSENDŌ
Yoshikawa Hanshichi 19d
Yoshikawa Kōbunkwan 20a
Yoshimaya Sonokichi 19bc
YUISUIDŌ 19abc = Aridaya Seiyemon
Yurien Toshu 18c (may have been only an owner of printing blocks, *zōhan*)

ZEKUNTEIDŌ 19c probably a private publisher
Zugwa Kankokwai 20a when publishing an important series of reprints of famous old Japanese books in the series *Nihon fuzuokudzuye* before 1914, he signed *Nihon fuzuoka dzuye* 'Kamkokwai' but does not appear to have used this form after 1914
ZUIGYOKUDŌ 18c = Yamatoda Yasubei

LIST OF KYŌTO PUBLISHERS

Aiba Chōbei 20a
Akatiya Tōbei 18d
ANSEIDŌ 19a = Tennojiya Rinzō

BUNCHŌDŌ 19ab = Yoshida Shimbei
Bundaiya Jirōbei 17cd
BUNKWADŌ 19a
BUNSHODŌ 19ab = Yoshida Shimbei

Chōjiya Genjirō 19a
Chojiya Nihei 17b

Daimonjiya Tokugōrō 19b

Fugetsu Shōzayemon 17c–18d
Fugetsu Sōchi 17b
Fujii Magobei 19abcd
Fukui Genjirō 19b
Fukui Kōsuke 19a
Fukuroya Sōshichi 19a
Fushimiya Sakubei 19a
Fushimiya Tōyemon 19a

Gakuryōken 19bc
GASENDŌ 19a = Higashiyama
Gataya Magobei 18b = UROKŌDŌ
GŌSHUDŌ
GYOKUSHŌYENDŌ 19a

Hachimonjiya Hachizayemon 18a
Hachimonjiya Hatsuyemon 17cd
Hachimonjiya Senjirō 18bc
Haifukiya Yōhei 18ab
Hangiya Genzayemon 17c
Hasegawaya Ichirōbei 17c
Hashiya Zensuke 19a
Hattoriya Kuyei 17d
Hattoriya Yōyemon 18d
Hayashi Ihei 18d
Hayashi Izumi-no-jō 17cd
Hayashi Kyujirō 17d
Higashiyamiya 19a = GASENDŌ
Hinoya Hambei 18b
Hiranoya Mōhei 18c
Hishiya Jihei 18b
Hishiya Kichibei 19b
Hishiya Magobei 18d–19a
Hishizawa Jubei 19d
Honjō Kōhei 19b
Honya Sōshichi 19a

Ibaraki Tazayemon 17d = HŌDŌ

Ichigoya Jihei 19bc
Ichigoya Rihei 19bc
Ikushima Kōhei 19a
Imai Kihei 18c–19a
Imai Shichirōbei 18b–19a
Imai Zembei 18b
Inouye Chubei 18b
Inouye Jihei 19b
Ishiya Jihei 19ab
Ishiya Magobei 18cd = SHŌAKUDŌ
Isoda Tarōbei 18a
Izumoji Bunjirō 19b
Izumoji Izumi 18c
Izutsuya Chubei 19b

Jakushō-ji: 18d; a temple in Kyōto which published Geisen's '*Reisen Zusan*' ('Portraits of Sennin')
JISHINDŌ 17b
Jōkyō 17d

Kajikawa Shichirōbei 18b
Kameya Gisuke 19a
Kameya Hambei 19c
Kamisaki Sōhachi 18cd
Kanaya Heiyemon 18a
KASETSUDŌ 19b
Kasusai Ichirōbei 19b
Kato Shinjirō 19b
Katō Shōkirō 17c
Katsumura Jiyemon 19a
Kawakatsu Gorōyemon 18a
Kawaminami Kihei 19ab
Kawaminami Shirōyemon 18b
Kawamiya Kihei 19a
Kawano Dōsei 17c
Kikuya Jimbei 19a
Kikuya Kihei 17c–18c
Kikuya Kimbei 19a
Kikuya Shichirōbei 18b–19a

Kikuya Tahei 19a
Kikuya Yasubei 18c
KINKWADŌ 19d = Nakamura Satarō
Kinoshita Jinyemon ?
Kiorenken 18d
Kitamura Shirōbei 18d
Kobayashi Shōbei 19b
Kōjima Yazayemon 17b
KŌKANDŌ 18c = Sumaya Kembei
KŌUNDŌ 19b = Ōmiya Risuke
Kōyasan Kozan-in 16d. A temple which published certain works
Kumuraya Ichirōbei 18d
Kurimoto Kihei 18d
Kurokawaya Shirōbei 18b

Maekawa Moyemon 17d
Marakami Kambei 19d
Maruya Zembei 19bc
Masuya Kambei 18c
Matsuya Kihei 18b
Medogiya Jisuke 18d
Medogiya Kambei 18ab
Medogiya Kihei 19a
Michizawa Tayei 17d
Mikiya Subei 19b
Minoda Shinzayemon 17c
Mizutaya Jinzayemon 19d
Momoya Sōbei 19c
Morikawa Yasuyuki 19b
Morimoto Tasuke 18d
Murakami Heirakuji 17c
Murakami Kambei 19c

Nagamura Gōhei 17cd
Nagamura Kasuke 18d–19a
Nagamura Tasuke 18d
Nagano Ichiyemon 17c
Nagano Kimei 19d (this man had in his possession many plates of
    Korin's designs from earlier work)

Nagano Shōzayemon 17b–18b
Nagano Sōyemon 19d
Nagano Zesai 17c
Nagaro Ichiyemon 17b
Nagasawa Heiyemon 18a
Nagata Chōbei 18a and 19c
Nakagawa Tōshirō 19a
Namariya Yasubei 19b
NIKIUDŌ 18b
Nishimuraya Ichirōyemon 17d–18d = BAISHUKUDŌ
Nishimuraya Kuzayemon 17d
Nishimuraya Matazayemon 17b
Nishimura Sozayemon 19d
Nōdō Dembai 19a
Nōdō Jihei 18d
Nōdō Kasuke 19a
Nōdō Kiyobei 19c
Nōdō Tohachi 19b
Nōdō Yahei 18d
Nukadaya Shōbei 19a
Nukadaya Shōzaburo 18b

ŌBUNDŌ 18cd = Onogiya Ichibei
Ogawa Bunyemon 18ab
Ogawa Gembei 18a
Ogawa Gohei 19a
Ogawa Kyubei 18b
Ogawa Tazayemon 18d
Okiya Gihei 18a
Ōmiya Heizayemon 17d
Ōmiya Jirōkichi 18d
Ōmiya Risuke 19b = KOUNDŌ
Ōmiya Shimbei 18d
Ōnaya Nihei-no-jō 17c
Ondoya ? 17d
Ōnisha Shimbei 18d

Sakaiya Katsubei 17c
Sakaiya Nihei 19a

Sasada Yahei 19d
Sasaki Kōtarō 20a
Sasaki Soshirō 18d–19a
SHŌAKUDŌ 19a = Ishiya Magobei
Shōhonya Kichibei 18d
SHŌKWAIDŌ Sakutan 17d
SHŌSHIDŌ 17cd
SHUNSHUDŌ 18c
Suminokura Sōan Yoichi 17a published various *Saga-bon*
Sumiya Gembei 18cd = KOKANDŌ
Suwaraya Hihachi 19a

Tachibanaya Jihei 18d
Takeuchi ?
Tanaka Heibei 18d
Tanaka Jihei 19d–20a
Taniguchi Kōkyō 19d
Tanioka Schichizayemon 17c
Tatsumi Sayemon 18d
Tawaraya Kambei 18d
Tawaraya Seibei 19c
Tennōjiya Ichirōbei 19a
Tennōjiya Rinzō 18d–19a
Teradaya Yoeji 17d
TŌBUNYENDŌ 19b
Tōgai Tōbei 18c
Tohon-ya Kichizayemon 17c publisher of Chinese illustrated
    books
Tohon-ya Seibei 17c publisher of Chinese books
Tomikura Tahei 17d
Tsuruya Kiyemon 19a

Umemura Ihei 19ab
Umemura Saburōbei 18cd
Umemura Sōgorō 18c
Umemura Toyemon 18b and 19abc
UNKINDŌ 20a
UNSŌDŌ 20a = Yamadaya Naosaburo
UROKODŌ 17d = Gataya Sanzayemon

5 A & B. *Left:* Kiyomasu I; Watanabe no Tsuna and the demon of the Rashomon. *Benizuri-e. Hashira-kake: c.* 1760: unsigned. *Above:* a *Takarabune* print. The Seven Gods of Good Fortune coming into port on New Year's Day in the Takarabune. *Kakemono-e* in three colours and black. Signed: Yoshiyuki; this artist was a pupil of Sadayoshi of the Ōsaka School and was active for a short time about 1860.

These *takarabune* prints are rare; some modern ones show decided *avant garde* characteristics in their design: it was believed that pictures such as these, bought on New Year's Day and put under one's pillow, ensured lucky dreams.

6. Two *Hashira-e. Left:* Shunchō (*fl. circa* 1780–95). Girl at the Entrance to a Temple: signed; Shunchō gwa. Sealed: 'Kiwame'. Publisher's seal: 'Yamakichiya'. *Right:* Kiyonaga (1752–1815). A Gust of Wind. A girl under a wistaria tree draws her skirts about her in a gust of wind. Signed: *Kiyonaga gwa*. The theme of young women in the winds of spring, summer and autumn seems to have been introduced to Ukiyo-e by Toyonobu (1711–85).

Urokogataya Magobei 18b
Uyeda Hanzaburō 19a
Uyezaka Kambei 19a

Wada Koreshirō 20a

Yamadaya Ichirōbei 17c
Yamadaya Naosaburō 20a = UNSŌDŌ
Yamagataya Kichibei 17c–18a
Yamaguchi Mōhei 18ab
Yamamaka Zembei 19a
Yamamori Rokubei 17c
Yamamoto Chōbei 18d
Yamamoto Ezayemon 18d
Yamamoto Gōhei 17c
Yamamoto Kuhei 17c
Yamashiroya Fujii Sahei 18b
Yamashiroya Sahei 19bc
Yamatoya Hihei 18c
Yamatoya Kinshichi 18d–19a
Yamazakiya Seishichi 19a
Yasuda Jubei ?
Yorozuya Shōbei 17d
Yoshida Jihei 19ab
Yoshida Saburōbei 17d
Yoshida Shimbei 17d–19b = BUNCHŌDŌ
Yoshimura Kichizayemon 18c
Yoshinaga Shichirōbei 17d
Yoshinoya Nihei 19bc
Yoshinoya Rihei 19b
Yoshinoya Tameachi 18d
Yoshinoya Tōbei 18a

Zenya Shōbei 18c

LIST OF ŌSAKA PUBLISHERS

Akashiya Ihachi 18d
Akitaya Tayemon 18c–19c

Asano Hisuke 18bc
Asano Settsuyo 18c
Asano Yahei 18c
Awaya Bunzō = JUBAIDŌ 18b

BUNEIDŌ = Maekawa Zembei 19a
BUNKAIDŌ = Tsurugaya Kubei 19b

Choya Chubei 19a

Fujiya Kuhei (perhaps this is the same as the following publisher, but
    two works in which the publisher is thus cited, although undated,
    appear to belong to the period 18d)
Fujiya Tamura Kuhei 19ab
Fujiya Tokubei 19a
Fujiya Yahei 18c–19a

GASENDŌ 19a = Higashiyamiya (a branch of the Kyōto firm)
GIOKUNANDŌ 19b
Giokusentei 19b (probably a *dō-go*)
GIOKUTOENDŌ 19b
Goshintei Sanhen 19b
GOSHUDŌ 18d
GUNGIOKUDŌ 19b = Kawachiya Mohei
GUNGIOKUDŌ 19c = Kawachiya Tōbei (This and the previous
    entry represent one of the rare instances of two persons of different
    given name having the same *dō-go*)
Gwaikotsu Miyatake 20a

Hachimonjiya Hachizayemon 18d–19a
Harimaya Inosuke 19b
Harimaya Shimbei 18d
Higashiyamiya 19a = GASENDŌ
Hiranoya Shōzayemon 17d
Hirosawa Kahei 18ab
HONSEIDŌ 19abc
Honya Kichibei 19b
Honya Seibei 19ab
Horiuchi Shōbei 18d

Iida Kihei 19c (published some striking *surimono* of Sadanobu II)
Imazuya Tatsusaburō 19a
Inose ? 18d (probably a *dō-go*)
Ishihara Mohei 18c
Itamiya Mohei 17d
Itamiya Shimbei 18a
Itamiya Shinshichi 18a
Itamiya Zembei 17c and 19ab
Itōya Heihachi 17d
Itōya Ichibei 18d
Izumimotoya Hachibei 18d
Izumiya Tatsusaburō 19a

JUBAIDŌ = Awaya Bunzō 18b

Kamisakaya Kinshirō 19c
Kariganeya Shōbei 17d
Kariganeya Shōzayemon 18a
Kashimaya Chubei 18d–19a
Kashimaya Kyubei 19a
Kashiwabaraya Seiyemon 19a
Kashiwaraya Gihei 19bc
Kashiwaraya Kahei 18d
Kashiwaraya Kuzayemon 19c
Kashiwaraya Seiyemon 18bc = SHŌKODŌ
Kashiwaraya Seiyemon 18d–19a = SHIBUKAWADŌ (Shibukawa
    was the original family name)
Kashiwaraya Seizayemon 19b
Kashiwaraya Yoichi 17d–18c
Kashiwaraya Yōzayemon 18c–19c
Katsuoya Rokubei 18d–19a
Kawabeya Otōjirō 19b
Kawachiya Chōbei 19ab
Kawachiya Genshichirō 19c
Kawachiya Heishichirō 19a
Kawachiya Kasuke 19a
Kawachiya Kichibei 19b
Kawachiya Kihei 19abc
Kawachiya Mohei 19b = GUNGIOKUDŌ

Kawachiya Sōbei 19a

Kawashiya Tasuke 17d and 18d–19ab

Kawachiya Tōbei 19c = GUNGIOKUDŌ

Kawachiya Tokubei 19a

Kawachiya Yuhei 18c–19a (this publisher sometimes signs with his
family name, Ueda Yuhei)

Kawachiya Wasuke 18c

Kichimonjiya Ichibei 18bcd

Kichimonjiya Ichizayemon 18d

Kimuraya Kasubei 18ab

Kimuraya Kasuke 18cd

KINKODŌ 18c = Yamaguchiya Tōbei (this firm seems to have
started in Ōsaka but moved to Edo about 1778)

KINKWADŌ Konishi 19abc

Kitamura ?

Kobayashi Kimbei 19b

Kobayashi Rihei 19ab

Kobayashi Rokubei 18c

Kobayashi Shimbei 18d–19b

Kyōya Kōsuke 18a

Maekawa Zembei 19a = BUNEIDŌ

Matsubaya ? 19ab

Matsumoto Zembei 18c

Matsumura Kyubei 18b

Matsuya Kihei 19b

MENTEIDŌ 19a

Mineta Fukō 19bc (an author and publisher who seems only to have
published his own books)

Moritaya Shōtarō 18ab

Mukai Hachisaburō 18a

Murakami Genyemon 18a

Murakami Sakichi 19a

Nakabayashi Matabei 17d

Nakagawa Kōtei = SHIBUNDŌ 19a

Naniwaya Chugorō 18c

Nishizawa Ippu 17d–18b

Nishizawa Kuzayemon 19 ?

Nodaya Riyemon 18b
Nunoya Chuzaburō 18c

Ōbundō 18cd = Onigiya Ichibei
Ōgiya Kamesaburō 19b
Ōgiya Risuke 19ab
Ondaya Manyemon 19a
Onogiya Ichibei 18cd = Ōbundō
Onogiya Rihei 18b
Ōoka Shunboku 17d–18c
Oriuchiya Shōbei 18d
Ōsakaya Shingoro 19b = Shokodō
Ōtsukaya Sobei 18cd
Ozakiya Masayoshi 19ab

Ritsukwaen Shōchō 19bc

Sakamotoya Kiichirō 19a
Sakaya Kimbei 19b
Sanshōbodō ?
Sekigiokudan ?
Senkwakudō 19a = Tsuruya Kiyemon
Senritei 19b
Setomonoya Dembei 18a
Shibukawa the family name of the Kashiwaraya and used in books
  published by the first Seiyemon, Seizayemon, Kiyoyemon and
  Yōichi
Shibundō 19a = Nakagawa Kotei
Shikwadō 19ab this firm and a branch in Edo
Shimada Bunsa ?
Shiōya Chōbei 18d
Shiōya Heisuke 17c and 18d–19a
Shiōya Yashichi 19b
Shobakudō Shōbo 19a
Shokodō 18c–19a
Shoseikakudō 19b
Shunkosai 19a
Shuōchōdō 19ab
Sueido 19bc

Takahashi Heisuke 18d
Takekawa Zenyemon 18a
Tanaka Tanyemon 18c–19c
TATSUSHINDŌ 19a
Temmanya Kihei 19ab
Tenriya ? 19bc
Teradaya Yōyemon 18ab
Tomaya Kihei 19b
Tsujiya Kimbei 18c
Tsurugaya Hikoshichi 18c–19c
Tsurugaya Jisuke 18c
Tsurugaya Kihei 19a
Tsurugaya Kuhei 18c
Tsuruya Kiyemon 19a = SENKWAKUDŌ

Ueda Yuhei 18c–19a
Uemura Tozaburō 18b (seems to have moved to Edo in 1738 or
   1739)
Umibeya Kambei 18d

Washiya Tatsuburō 19a
Wataki ? 19bc

Yamaguchiya Mataichirō 18d
Yamakaya 19ab
Yamamatsuya 19ab
Yamatoya Kahei 19b
Yamatoya Shirōbei 19a
Yanagiwara Kihei 18c–19a
Yōkōe Iwanosuke 18d
Yorazoya Hikotarō 17d
Yorozuya Nihei 17d
Yorazuya Seishirō 18d
YUSENDŌ 19c

LISTS OF PROVINCIAL PUBLISHERS

ARIMA (near Kōbe)
Ōyamaya Gempachi 18bc described himself as a publisher of prints
   of bathing girls

FUSHIMI
Ariwara Baizan 19a
Kaneharu Ichinojō 19b
Kinoshita Jimbei 19a (also an engraver)
Tambaya Shinzayemon 19b

HAGI (in Nagato province)
HAKUKŌDŌ 19bc

KII
KWANDŌ Nanrei 19a

KURASHIKI (in Bitchu province)
Kozanrō 19a (a society which seems to have published the work of
   its own members)

NAGASAKI
BANPŌRŌDŌ 19cd
BUNKINDŌ 18d–19a
BUNSAIDŌ 19a–c = Yamatoya
Hariya 18bc
Imamiya 19abc
Nakamura Sanzō 18b ?
Ogiya 19c
Toshimaya Bunjiyemon 18cd
Toshimaya Denkichi 18d
TŌSHUNDŌ Rōjin 19c (author and publisher, doubtfully of this
   place)
Wataya 19bc
Yamatoya 17d–19c = BUNSAIDŌ

NAGOYA (capital of Owari province. Some of these publishers
give their address simply as Owari; presumably they lived in
the capital)
BANONDŌ 19b
EIRAKUDŌ 18d–19c = Eirakuya Tōshirō
Eirakuya Toshirō 18d–19c = EIRAKUDŌ
Fugetsu Magosuke 18d
Hishiya Kyubei 18c–19a

Hishiya Tōbei 19bc
Kadomaruya Jinsuke 19a
Katanoya Tōshirō 19a
KEIUNDŌ Tōhei 19a
Kobayen 19b
KOGETSUDŌ Bunsuke 19b
Matsuya Kihei 19b
Matsuya Zembei 19a = SHŌKWADŌ
Minoya Ichibei 19a
Minoya Iroku 19abc
Minoya Seishichi 18d
Mitsuboriya Mosuke 18d
Niwa Komakichi 19d
Ōhashiya Yeizaburō 19d
Sakaiya ? 19b
SENZAIYENDŌ 19b
SHŌKWADŌ 19a = Matsuya Zembei
Sumiyoshiya Yasaburō 19b
Terazawa Matsunosuke 19d
TOEKIDŌ 19a
Tsuruya Kiyemon 19a
Uemura Tozaburō 18b
Yorōzuya Tōbei 19a

NARA
Nakanishi Tōshichirō 18bc
Okamoto Seiyemon 18b

SENDAI
Nishimura Jiyemon 19a

SUNPU (in Suruga; now Shizuoka)
Yamada Sadazane 19b

TAWARA (in Mikawa)
Watanabe Kai 19d

TOYAMA (in Etchu)
BUNKWAIDŌ 19c

Kami-ichi-ya Shijō 19ab
KWANDŌDŌ 19ab
Mifukuya Bunjirō 19bc
Sanada Zenjirō 19b
TOZENDŌ 19b
Ugawa Shichibei 19ab
Ushijima Keikwadō 19bc

YAMADA (in Ise)
Jakushōji 18d

YOKOHAMA
SHOKWAIDŌ 19d = Ōbuya ?

Part II

The Subjects of the Prints

CHAPTER IV

Shunga ('Spring Pictures'): The Erotic Print in Japan

E. B. DE FONBLANQUE, a not very typical Englishman of the Victorian age, writing just over a century ago[1] has this rather remarkable passage in his now long-forgotten book on Japan: 'The Japanese are depraved, sensual and obscene in every sense. The men of all classes—from the first Daimyō in the land to the meanest of his retainers—delight in contemplating human nature in its most animal form. Respectable mothers of families and young girls of otherwise irreproachable conduct, will take an undisguised pleasure in sights and scenes which would shock an English street-walker; and little innocent-eyed children, toddling by their fond father's side, or nestling in their mother's bosom, may be seen playing with toys so indecent, that one longs to dash them from their tiny hands and trample them underfoot.' To this there is a footnote which reveals more personally the difficulties which mid-nineteenth century westerners found in Japan: 'In shopping in Japan, the greatest care must be exercised to guard against the acquisition of indecencies which are found not only in books and pictures, but are painted on their porcelain, embossed on their lacquer, carved in their ivory, and surreptitiously conveyed into their fans. Mr Alcock made a purchase of some illustrated books destined for some children in England, and it was only by a fortunate accident that he discovered among them, before they were despatched, pictures which would have disgraced Holywell Street.' Such report is neither isolated nor, probably, much out of focus; a decade before this Dr (later Professor) Wells Williams writes[2] in his diary made during the famous expedition of Commodore Perry, under the entry of Tuesday 13th June 1854, '. . . and made a complaint in addition against the obscene books which the Japanese had given the sailors and thrown into the boats . . .' Without doubt it was but one more instance of *autres temps* (*et autres pays*) *autres moeurs*.

A strong current of erotic play is present in Japanese literature from the earliest times; for example, in many of the quite obscene passages of the *Kojiki*, the first Japanese chronicle, it is prominent and it is sometimes not far below the surface in the great *Genji Monogatari*. Yet it is not really until Momoyama times that it quite throws off the romantic trappings and becomes more frankly sensual. By Tokugawa times a literature of more or less overt eroticism was well established and the *ukiyo-zōshi* were much concerned with sexual situations; as a literature contemporary with that life which made sensual pleasure, the cult of the courtesan and a resolute disregard for money and the morrow its most socially acceptable criteria, it was natural that it should be so. It was inevitable that the pictures which illustrated these works should choose such situations for their subjects.

It is difficult, unless one has made a closer and more extensive study of this *genre* than the present author, to determine how much of the total output of the *ukiyo-e* is made up of these sex pictures. James Michener[3] who, judging by his own account of them seems to have seen more of this kind of print than most other western authors, has two somewhat contradictory statements on this matter; firstly he writes: 'Certainly compared with western art, *ukiyo-e* is singularly free from erotic content . . .' but in the very next paragraph he says: 'But if one were to conclude from this that *ukiyo-e* ignored the erotic element of life, one would be guilty of maximum error. No art of which we have record produced more sex pictures than *ukiyo-e*.' Nor can I find any Japanese statement that is much more to the point although it is true that the '*Nippon empon dai-shusei*' (Bibliography of Japanese erotic books)[4] gives a very impressive list of these, covering the whole period from the Heian to the present day. A moderately experienced student of these matters might conclude that the percentage of the whole output of prints made by the works of sexual import was markedly increased in the nineteenth century and there is some little evidence to support this but nevertheless, it will probably prove to be due to a sampling error consequent upon more of these ephemeral productions having survived from the later times than from the earlier. However, it may well be that, at least as far as the courtesan books are concerned, the output was smaller in the first three quarters of the seventeenth century when the larger part of the clientele of the brothel quarters were samurai. As the fortunes of these dwindled in relation to the accumulating riches of the townsmen the latter, becoming a much more significant factor in the total economy of brothel keeping and the associated trades, demanded the production of more and more new and up-to-date guides to the courtesan quarter with its rich store of accumulating customs, lore and tradition as well as to the expert assessment and description of the finer points of its inmates.

This was almost certainly the position when the *Shin* (New) *Yoshiwara* was founded in Edo in 1657; the old *Moto Yoshiwara* had been opened in 1618 and previous to this all prostitutes had been scattered over the whole city. Earlier the *Shimabara* district of Kyōto and the *Shimmachi* district of Ōsaka had evolved their own customs, usages and technical vocabularies and, almost at the commencement of the seventeenth century, we find these places shown in *ukiyo-e* style paintings which could only have been afforded by the samurai class. However, before the century had closed, all these places had their guides, e.g. the *Yoshiwara Kasen* (Song of a Yoshiwara Recluse), and these showed erotic representations of the leading ladies, each in one of the traditional forty-eight copulatory positions and a great number of other incidental customs. By 1660 there had appeared the '*Yoshiwara makura-e*' (Pillow Pictures of the Yoshiwara) and the '*Yoshiwara Kagami*' (Mirror of the Yoshiwara), prototypes of works that were to appear for nearly the next two centuries. In these, and in the books of the next decade, almost all the male figures that appear are either samurai, brothel servants or, very occasionally, priests. However, by 1678 works like the *Komurasaki* depict the richer kind of young merchant—or the pampered sons of such—with prostitutes and there is no doubt but that this class became more and more important as potential customers of this type of publication.

For many years before then, Kyōto had been producing black and white erotic prints including guides to its own brothel quarter, the Shimabara, and about 1640 these were coloured with *tan* red, green and yellow. The earliest Kyōto ones were, for the most part, poorly designed and often show sex in a joking context: a few show what, in the West, would be considered abnormal sexual practices. Very few indeed are those that show any tenderness of pose or expression and fewer still have tenderness of composition such as we find in some of the erotic works of Utamaro. Michener (l.c.) has called attention to the fact that Kōetsu (see page 37) produced an erotic work from his press, soon after 1600 and tells us that the first half, which is founded on a Chinese work, has some aesthetic quality, whereas the second half is 'an atrociously poor Japanese original'.

The impact on a western mind of these startling early erotic prints and paintings is extraordinary indeed, yet it is by no means impossible for a cultivated occidental to appreciate the exceptional beauty of some of them. For example there is in existence a fan print of the last quarter of the sixteenth century reproduced as a frontispiece to the *Nippon empon dai-shusei* (l.c.) which shows three girls engaged in the frankest of lesbian activities yet the total effect is one of a strangely beautiful design—not lacking in a certain tenderness too —carried out in the usual orange, green, yellow and black colours which perfectly accentuate the frieze of these three nude figures with their lovely tracery of interwoven arms and the powerful, sweeping, black masses of the coiffures which give an effect of quite extraordinarily April-like charm and innocence.

Not all Japanese erotic works have this quality; indeed it is probably true to say that artistic merit is rarer in this *oeuvre* than it is, at any level, in all the rest of the *ukiyo-e* output. Much of it is the sorriest, crudest pornography and even as works of fun, the humour is so immature that it rises little above that of the *graffiti* of the young rustic boor on the walls of a country station convenience. However, some of these erotic albums do rise to great levels as works of art. Much of Sukenobu's sex pictures must rate not only among the finest of his own output but among the loveliest erotic art in the world. Michener says that most of them are masterpieces. One notices especially the extreme tenderness of many of them especially those involving a pair of young lovers or an older man and a younger woman. Yet other designs of this artist show a curiously touching and wondering seriousness in the celebration of the sex rites depicted and equally moving are the representations of women which show them with drawn brows expressive of that pain which lies at the heart of so many moments of sexual ecstasy. However, even in the erotic prints of this great artist it is often true, as Lane says[5] that 'the faces and figures . . . are less delicate than the childish, dreamlike visages of his finest work; indeed this is a phenomenon seen in many of the *ukiyo-e* artists, who could not but be insensibly influenced by the voluptuous and worldly nature of their subject matter when they executed erotica.'

7. Two *Surimono*.
Above: Gurenkei (art
name of an amateur,
'the humble Renkei').
Butterflies and a
poem: the name is not
otherwise known.
Below: Shuman Kubota
(1757–1820). A
surimono of a fan, an
eboshi and a spray of
cherry, pine and
camellia. Part of an *Ise
Monogatari* series.
Printed in tones of
red, pink, green,
brown, yellow and
blue with gauffrage
printing embellished
with copper and silver

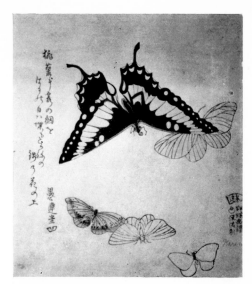

8A. Yokohama-e. Yoshitora: an English couple holding an umbrella *ai-gusa* fashion. Title: *Gaikoku Jimbutsu zue*; sub-title: *Igirisu*. Publisher's seal: Yamadaya Shōhei. Censor seal: *Aratame Tiger* (year) tenth month, i.e. 1866. Signed: Yoshitora.

8B. Yokohama-e. Yoshitora. A Russian couple; the woman shakes a cornet, the man, seated, plays an accordian. From the series *Gaikoku Jimbutsu zue*; sub-title: *Raroshiya*. Publisher's seal: Yamadoya Shōhei. Censor seal: *Aratame Tiger* (year) tenth month, i.e. 1866. Signed: Yoshitora.

Albums of erotic prints were very frequently in twelve sheets of which the first and the last are quite innocuous and very often one finds that these have been pulled from the book in earlier times and sold to collectors as separate sheets. Such twelve-sheet albums were produced by most of the *ukiyo-e* artists and Michener (l.c.) gives pride of place to an unnamed album of Masunobu's. Certain of the erotica of this artist are undoubtedly very fine—among the very best of the whole of the output of this school. Other great early masters of this genre are Moronobu and Tsukioka Settei. Michener (l.c.) describes some of the work of the former as 'poetic compositions with lyrical figures and the most gracious harmony of design and execution.' This may well be so but the few sheets of this kind that I have seen would not lead me to think of them in terms of such high praise: perhaps I have been less fortunate. Tsukioka Settei's work has been rightly praised by Mr Hillier[6] and he especially draws attention to the excellence of the warrior pictures of this Ōsaka artist. Yet his erotica seem to me to be among the very finest of those produced by *ukiyo-e* artists; they are extremely characteristic and the white flesh of the figures is emphasized by great flowing, juxtaposed, black masses. Among other of the 'primitive' print artists, those of Kyōto and Ōsaka were both active in this genre. Of the former, possibly those prints of the greatest impact were the work of Yoshida Hambei; Lane (l.c.) reproduces a page from a dictionary of sex terms which shows a man attacking a young girl and at the same time kicking out at an older woman who attempts to interfere. At the top of the print are two characters which read '*inran*' meaning 'debauched' or 'licentious'. Of the latter city perhaps the foremost artist of erotica was Shimomura Shichirōbei who worked in a black and white of the utmost contrast and whose work has a kind of nineteenth century French cartoon air about it.

In later times, when the colour print technique was fully developed, almost all the Edo *ukiyo-e* artists tried their hands at erotica: outstanding are the works of Harunobu and, of even greater achievement in this kind of art, Kōriusai, his follower. Utamaro, Hokusai, Kunisada, Kuniyoshi and, one whose best designs for sex pictures are, I think, the greatest of the later masters, Eisen, all designed notable sheets in this genre. It gives some idea of the output of erotic prints by these artists when we recollect that Utamaro produced some thirty-five albums of this kind between 1784 and 1804 and these

8

certainly contain some of his loveliest work and most ingenious designs.

Several other kinds of sex picture besides those dealing with the Yoshiwara were in existence. Small books, the successors to earlier and similar scroll paintings, were designed to serve as manuals of sex technique and were intended for the use of young ladies entering upon marriage. It is interesting to note that these are very much better informed and for the most part more scientific than the more famed works on sex instruction of India and the Near East. But there seems to be some evidence that this kind of work developed a sophistication much more suited to the tastes and needs of the young man about town than its original clientele. China may not have been a negligible influence in this respect since very similar works, of superior artistic attainments, were being produced and designed by artists and *literati* in the vicinity of Nanking during the Ming dynasty and Dr R. H. van Gulik has treated one of these with very scholarly analysis;[7] this is the *Hua-ying-chin-chen* ('Variegated Battle Arrays of the Flowery Camp'). In the later Japanese work in this *oeuvre* we find that the artist moves a very long way indeed from the simple instruction manual for brides and provides his public with illustrated ideas for types of copulation in such unlikely situations as on horseback; hardly likely, one would have thought, to have fallen to the necessary experience of the young Japanese newly-wed!

Probably from this last type of sex book there arose the humorous sex picture which has always had a great vogue. Indeed, scroll paintings as early as the Heian period show situations of this kind and the ancestry is therefore an old and honourable one. These pictures, generally known as *warai-e*, are the ones which the collector most commonly comes upon and then they are those of the latter half of the nineteenth century. These are crude in the extreme and one will not usually find a good design in the whole book, yet here and there, as in some of the work of Yoshitoshi, there eventuates a print of quality but for the most part these sheets are exemplified by the repulsive crudities of artists like Yoshitora. Related to the *warai-e* are the novelettes or short tales of gross sexual import called *makura-zōshi*. These draw on the themes of those universal sex myths which are to be found in civilized communities in all times and places. The young man who is cast away on an island of young women and who eventually dies of exhaustion; the unseen artist peeps through the *shōji* and sees some scandalous happenings which involve ladies of the court and actors or teahouse waitresses and wrestlers; Komachi, the beautiful poetess of ancient times, comes back into the modern tougher society and, instead of being responsible for the death of her true lover, we are made to see a very different fate overtake her; the artist becomes very small and is led to see many old things from new and surprising angles; all these are part of a universal sexual mythology. What is new in the Japanese version is that the artist may show himself as a protagonist or else provide us with recognizable likenesses to living contemporaries, especially actors, who are favourites of the day. For nearly all of this class of illustrated pornography and for the *warai-e*, it is probably true to say that fine design, careful drawing and good colouring are more rarely to be met with here than elsewhere.

A few books and single sheets deal with various abnormal sexual practices with what is, to western eyes, startling frankness. Such are likely to occur as single page compositions in almost any of the erotica of this school and among the events recorded from a visit to the Yoshiwara may be a scene showing *cunnilingus* in progress or indeed, as in at least one later album, in all its stages. Masturbation is not infrequently the subject of a design as are certain sado-masochistic occurrences and in all of these one may find the occasional sheet which has aesthetic quality of a fairly high order. At least one extremely fine album series was devoted to such kinds of perversion: this is Masanobu's *Danshoku Hiyochidori* ('Double Birds') which is, in fact, a detailed treatise on sodomy. Published in 1707 in six volumes, it comprises forty black and white plates of great beauty and is indeed what could well be described as a practitioner's guide to the whole art of the subject! It is interesting to note that a copy that was in the Haviland collection bore the seal of a former owner, the famous novelist Fukuda Shikitei.

Shunga exist as albums, incidental illustrations to *makura-zōshi* and as single sheet prints, a few being in the rare format of the horizontal 'pillar-print' (*hashira-e*); the last appear to have originated with Harunobu and most of the leading artists produced a few of these throughout the latter half of the eighteenth and the whole of the nineteenth centuries. Among these single sheets perhaps none are more powerful and original as works of art than a few of those of Hokusai. Most of the erotic sheets of this artist are mere 'publishers' feed' done, no doubt, to meet a demand which could be relied upon to raise sufficient for the bare minimum of subsistence. But a few sheets seem to me to be terrible in the manner in which some of Goya's etchings are. Although I would disagree with Michener that these are in any sense typical of *ukiyo-e* itself, yet Michener does indeed describe them in most apposite terms. He says, 'The old man set down scores of agonizing human beings caught up in the *reductio ad absurdum* of sex. Here, in these demonic sheets, each with a dozen frenzied couples, one sees the ultimate in human experience: the longing, the savagery, the bitterness, the joy, the ridiculousness and the unsatiated hunger of sex. These sheets are greater, I believe, than the mad visions of Hieronymous Bosch . . . this was the final irony he permitted himself, this savage comment on sex . . .'

NOTES ON CHAPTER IV

[1] Fonblanque, Edward Farrington de: *Niphon and Pe-che-li or Two Years in Japan and Northern China*, London, 1862.

[2] Williams, S. Wells: 'A Journal of the Perry Expedition to Japan'; *Transactions of the Asiatic Society of Japan*, vol. xxxv, part 2п, Tokyo, 1910.

[3] Michener, J.: *The Floating World*, London, New York and Toronto, 1954. Michener gives a racy account of these erotic books in chapter 10 of this work under the somewhat coy title of 'The Other Books'. It contains some interesting facts and some very amusing comment which is obviously founded on a wide experience of this kind of work.

[4] *Nippon empon dai-shusei* (Bibliography of Japanese Erotic Books from the Heian Period to the Present day), edited by the Research Society of Erotic Books. Uozumi Shōten, Tōkyō, 1960. In Japanese.

[5] Lane, R.: *Masters of the Japanese Print*, London, 1962. An excellent and scholarly work which gives much prominence to the paintings as apart from the prints of *ukiyo-e*. References to erotica are scattered but in general the index is fairly adequate for finding them.

[6] Hillier, J. R.: *The Japanese Colour Print; a new Approach*, London, 1960.

[7] Gulik, R. H. van: *Sexual Life in Ancient China*, Leiden, 1961.

CHAPTER V

The Prints of Beautiful Women
(Bijin-Ga) and of Children

MICHENER says that during the period 1660–1860 pictures of beautiful women made up about 40 per cent of the total output of *ukiyo-e* and this estimate may well be approximately correct. Even allowing for the fact that it may be somewhat on the high side for certain periods it is still obvious that a very large part of the subject matter of all the prints of this school can be put under this heading. From the occidental point of view, the intricate nature of the themes, the wealth of allusion, the alien nature of the actions which the subjects perform and even the manner in which the face of this or that particular beauty is represented, may well be barriers of no inconsiderable magnitude to an enthusiastic enjoyment of these prints.

The curiously stiff attitudes in which many of the artists show courtesans, their exaggerated mannerisms and almost theatrical gestures, the flat white, often almost featureless faces and the distracting gorgeousness of the patterns of their amply folded dresses, are all matters to which the student and connoisseur of such subjects must accustom himself. Louis Aubert[1]—perhaps rather exaggeratedly but certainly revealingly—well says: '... un geste, un mouvement de la tête ou du bras, suffisent à révéler toute la force d'un sentiment: se détachant sur du vide, la moindre inflexion du corps une éloquence singulière. Et encore dans la lenteur de la démarche des belles, dans le très léger balancement de leur busts, dans le port de leur tête, dans la fixité de leur regard, dans leur art de soutenir avec leur bras et leurs coudes l'ampleur de leurs vastes manches et de développer les plis de leurs *kimono*, dans leur mouvements sans brusquerie, dans les glissements à plat de leurs pieds sur le sol, on retrouve l'harmonie classique des anciens drames lyriques.' These prints, in fact, are not stylized abstractions from the living woman of the day but do indeed give us a more or less accurate representation of her as she was and as she no doubt appeared to her admirers and, if the technical means employed by the artist are always those of the school or sub-school to which he belonged yet they do no less, define an ideal type of the day to which some women, by both nature, the accessories of fashion and artifice, came to approximate and exemplify.

Pictures of beautiful women are among the very first subjects to be portrayed by the *ukiyo-e* school and lasted as favourite themes of both designer and public until late days—until, in fact, the commencement of the present century. Women are quite frequently shown in Tosa-style paintings and occur in some of the illustrations of the Nara-bon (see page 36), e.g. 'Kohada Kitsune'. The courtesan is in evidence even as early as the end of the sixteenth century, and by the second quarter of the seventeenth century she is firmly established. The *shunga* apart, the nude is always rare in this art and the whole interest of the design centres upon the face, the hair and more particularly, the *kimono*. Not only did the ever-changing patterns and colours of this last provide endless interest (and one has only to think of the frequency with which passages concerned with the appraisal and evaluation of *kimono* hues and motifs occur in the *ukiyo-zōshi*) but many of the gestures—the withdrawal of the arms inside the kimono for example—have a vaguely erotic suggestiveness —a suggestiveness frequently heightened by stray, disordered strands of hair at the side of the temples.

There are certain characteristics of the dress of women which it is useful to have in mind when looking at these prints. Courtesans are seldom shown with any footwear since they traditionally went about with bare feet although in winter they usually wore the high clogs called *geta*. *Geisha*, out of doors in summer, wore a single thonged sandal, the *zōri* and, in winter, the *geta* whilst the apprentice *geisha* of Kyōto wore characteristic clogs, very high and lacquered black, called *koppori*; these are sometimes seen in book illustrations of views of that city. Ordinary women wear simple divided socks, *tabi*, and clogs which at different times went through various fashion changes and show variously shaped cross pieces which are lacquered, usually black but sometimes red; the latter colour is especially prominent in prints of the mid-eighteenth century but is most commonly to be found on the clogs worn by men. In summer, the wear for ordinary women was a simple sandal with a single thong going straight across the foot. Sometimes clogs were also worn at this season but these were usually made of a whole block of wood lightened by a central, broad U-shaped cavity. Peasants are shown wearing woven sandals made of bamboo sheaths on a curious straw 'bootee' (*waraji*) often worn by pilgrims.

It is a curious fact that, although authorities on the print frequently describe a work as representing one or more 'girls', there is often very little to indicate, even approximately, the age of the women shown. In the prints of Sukenobu, Kiyomitsu and a few others, as well as some of the earlier Kyōto prints, the older women are represented by omitting the eyebrows and putting two V-shaped marks over the nose to denote wrinkles. From the eighteenth century almost to the present day, *kimono* with very long sleeves (*furisode*) were worn only by young girls and this is a definite indication of the age of the subject and, equally definitely, shows that she is not married. Marriage itself is seldom shown but an important set by Harunobu is devoted to this subject.

The *kimono* itself underwent many changes of fashion, not only of design and colour but of style and cut. In the seventeenth century until about the middle of the eighteenth the garment was long in front but when moving about a woman held up this front part and this very characteristic gesture is the one so frequently seen in the courtesans of the Kaigetsudō school of print artists.

Apart from the *kimono* the artists very frequently made the most important part of their design the sash or *obi*, especially the intricate and variously shaped bow (*obijime*) in which it was tied. The style of these *obi* is sometimes an auxiliary help in dating prints and book illustrations; if used with some care and a knowledge of their styles, it helps in identifying types of women shown and in the general understanding of the illustrations. All *obi* were originally tied in front and in illustrations dating from the Genroku and Kyōho periods (1688-1736) it is not possible to use this feature alone for distinguishing the courtesan from other women. During the period Genbun (1736-1741) with the very swift changes of fashion that followed one another in those years, this custom became much less stable, and after 1741 only the courtesan—always with a *penchant* for the archaic— wore the bow in front; all other women now tied it behind and so from the mid-eighteenth century this can be used to distinguish the prints of courtesans. There were, of course, over the centuries many styles of tying the *obi* and the following are to be found in various illustrations:

Kichiya musubi which was originated by the Kabuki actor Uemura Kichiya in Empō (1673–1681)

Mizuki musubi originated by the actor Mizuki Tatsunosuke at the beginning of the eighteenth century

Gōsho musubi the 'five part' knot worn in Kyōto in the seventeenth century

Otaiko musubi the 'drum tie knot'

Tateya no ji a knot in the shape of the character '*ya*'.

The width of the *obi* too is important. Before the period Kyōho (1716–1736) the *obi* was only about three or four inches wide but during that period the wide *maru-obi* came into vogue; this was about two feet broad and folded double. Later, for more informal wear, there was introduced the *chuya-obi* which is about ten inches wide or a little less.

The underwear (*shitagi*) of women is comparatively seldom seen in prints but does occur in some book illustrations. Over this was worn a long under-dress, the *naga-juban*, which frequently had a different coloured lining and it is the differently coloured upper and under surface of this garment which is often made to show in colour prints when the hem (*suso*) of the *kimono* is turned back. The most easily perceived differences in the cut of the *kimono*, as it is represented through the centuries in prints, are in the collar (*eri*) and the cuff (*sodeguchi*). The styles favoured by artists for their fashion plates are indicative, sometimes of the public taste of the period, sometimes of the individual taste of the artist. Certain of the illustrated books give details of women's garments that are useful in a study of the prints themselves; thus those of the seventeenth century are to be found in the *Onna shorei shu* published by Yamada Ichirōbei of Kyōto in 1660, the illustrations of which have been credited to Moronobu although there seems to be rather little evidence to support this. Again in 1773 publishers at Kyōto and Nagoya published the *Onna imagawa oshie-bumi* with illustrations by Kitao Sekkōsai which shows twelve different costumes of that date.

It is perhaps not too much to assert that, for nearly half a century, from the commencement of the last twenty years of the eighteenth century, no artist who was concerned to achieve success with large single sheet prints of women could afford to neglect current fashions. Such an artist might even be expected to give his ideas of new *kimono* fashions and to show those worn by the inmates of the

Yoshiwara and by favourite tea-house waitresses. In this field no fame exceeded that of Kiyonaga who, season by season, met the public demand with the assurance of an inexhaustible supply of new ideas of such felicity that today, as in his own time, he seems to us pre-eminent. Of an earlier decade, perhaps Koryusai with his immense series *Hinagata wakana no hatsumōyō* (New patterns for young Leaves) has most claim to fame as a designer of this type of print. It argues how well this met the taste of the *edoko* that Kiyonaga himself later produced a series with exactly the same title: both show *oiran* as models for the new season's styles. The words '*waka-na*', i.e. 'tender young leaves' are often used as a metaphor for young girls in the titles of such prints. A later artist whose works, if without the supreme distinction of the best of Kiyonaga's, are yet of a certain powerful although obviously derivative beauty, is Eizan. Such series of his as *Tōsei imayo bijin hana awase* (A set of Beauties in the Fashions of the Hour), *Furiu bijin soroi* (A Harmony of fashionable beauties) and *Furiu bijin Matsu-no-uchi* ('Fashionable Beauties within the Pine', i.e. during the fifteen days of the New Year festival) serve to show the unwearied public demand for such prints during the first quarter of the nineteenth century. They also give an indication of the titles which these prints commonly bore—titles in which certain evocative words that caught the public mood were used over and over again.

It is a matter very frequently commented upon by writers on *ukiyo-e* that, just as artists played a part in creating a public taste in certain fashions, so did certain of them create a taste in a style of woman. It would indeed be an interesting piece of research to trace the delineation of women of various physical types by the artists of different periods. Something of this kind has, of course, long been accomplished but it remains to be discovered how far these types predominated in the literature of the time as indeed how much influence this may have had in creating a demand for this type of woman in the gay quarters of the great cities. More than one author has commented upon some of these characteristics but not always with justice. For example, attention is sometimes called to the tiny hands of the girls in the prints of Harunobu as if they were unique to that artist but they are to be found, although not exclusively, in many of the figures drawn by artists such as Kiyomitsu and Toyonobu.

Individual physical features like this are nearly always the result of

an artist's personal choice but sometimes they result—or seem to do—
from a weakness in the drawing. There are, for example, some prints
in the great *Musume hidokei* (Series of Women) set by Utamaro—
recently designated a 'Registered Important Cultural Property'—in
which one notices the contrast between the beautiful drawing of the
lovely arms and the stubby fingered hands and badly drawn wrists.
Certainly, only a minority of the prints have this defect yet, if we
compare this with prints of equal eminence by Kiyonaga, we shall
hardly find one in which the hands are not joined to the forearms by
wrists beautifully shaped and contoured.

The style of woman delineated by any artist is best seen in the
representation of the facial features, somatic type, hands, arms and
the nude breast. This last is sometimes very characteristic: Shigemasa,
as in his drawing of the nude generally, keeps very close to nature
with all its variants; Toyonobu and Kiyomitsu almost always show
the nude breast erect, its axis making an approximate right-angle
with the thorax and with its upper surface a convex curve; most
frequently Harunobu shows it with the axis at a slightly obtuse angle
to the thoracic wall whilst Kiyoshige and Toshinobu favour a representation which depicts it as somewhat pendulous.

As an accompaniment to the prints of women are often to be found
the figures of children and sometimes these latter are the sole subject
matter of the print or series of prints. Certain artists, on occasion,
excelled in their prints of children; one might instance, Toyomasa,
Muranobu, Harunobu, Kōriusai, Utamaro, Kiyohiro and Kiyomitsu
as producing the rare and especially charming print of child life.
Children were shown as the twelve months—often engaged in the
game appropriate to the month, e.g. Utamaro's *Osana asobi juni
tsuki* ('Amusements of Children in the Twelve Months'). This was a
series catering for the same public demand as Shunchō's *Fuzoku
juniko* (Customs of the Twelve Seasons *a la mode*') or Kōriusai's
Furiu juni tsuki (Twelve Months *à la mode*'). Among the occupations
of children shown in such prints are ones of boys making a snowball
(December), children writing large calligraphic characters and hanging them up (a common practice on New Year's Day), children
spinning tops or blowing 'soap' bubbles and, as in some especially
lovely prints of Kiyomitsu, young girls playing battledore and
shuttlecock, usually with the players in a ring.

Much more rarely, children are shown in some of the playful

representations of personages and activities commonly found in prints of women but they seem never to have been in great demand. Most frequently met with is probably the odd print from such series as Kōriusai's *Furiu Kodomo Rokkasen* ('The Children's Rokkasen or Six Poets'). Boys dressed as wrestlers are not perhaps quite so un-common as the last but they are still a rare subject; Utamaro gave at least one print to this theme as did some later artists. Children play-ing with dogs and, more rarely, cats may be found but apparently more popular were prints showing young mothers or servants with small children; the latter, most frequently held in the mother's arms, reach out for a butterfly or some other insect and nearly all of them have an immediately perceptible charm which no doubt endeared them to a section of the Edo public.

The sale catalogue of the Ikeda collection (Paris 1910) shows that this collection had some important and charming prints that por-trayed children. For example there is a rare print by Kitao Shige-masa which shows a young girl demonstrating a magic lantern to some children. There are also several prints of children by Shunzan; one shows six Chinese children playing, some making music and the others doing acrobatics. Another shows a young mother who has a baby in her arms looking at two older children chasing fireflies about a hedge of chrysanthemums. Most interesting of all is a beauti-ful diptych by Toyokuni I, the subject of which is a group of two mothers with their young sons who are grimacing and gesturing in front of a lacquer wainscot in which may be seen their reflections: not only is this a beautiful design but the printing is superb, the wains-cot being touched with the so-called 'lacquer' of the earlier *urushi-e* which gives the whole, even in reproduction, a most brilliant and delightful effect.

Other activities in which children are sometimes shown in prints are kite fighting and top spinning, both games for the New Year (*shōgatsu*). Tops of different shapes are spun on a mat placed on top of a box and if the top went outside this small arena it was forfeited. Other prints—especially later ones—show children wearing fox masks and playing. This seems to have been customary on the first 'horse' day in February when various rituals were carried out at the Inari shrines throughout the country, the servants of this deity being foxes. Some prints show girls arranging their dolls at the doll festival; in this some fifteen special dolls are arranged on a stand of either five or seven tiers and white *sake* is poured for them. The Boys Festival (*Tango no Sekku*) celebrated on 5th May, is of fairly frequent occurrence on prints of children. This may be shown by the paper or cloth carp or *koi* fish, attached to poles outside a house and flying free in the air. Some *surimono* will be found to show these together with other emblems of this festival such as iris leaves and a small wooden sword. Another ceremony occasionally shown in the prints is that of the *obi-toki* or 'changing the sash'. This took place when a girl was seven years old, on which day the little girl took to an *obi* for the first time, previously her *kimono* having been fastened by tying together two pairs of narrow strips of cloth on the front of it.

Reverting to prints of young women and girls, it remains to list briefly some of the activities and relationships in which they are commonly shown, a knowledge of which will help in identifying many of the themes common to these *bijin-ga* in the eighteenth and nineteenth centuries. Perhaps one of the most famous of such themes is that of young women representing the *Nana Komachi* (Life of Komachi in Seven Scenes). The individual scenes are: *Amagoi Komachi;* Komachi invoking rain; *Sōshi Arai Komachi*; Komachi washing a rival poet's manuscript; *Kayoi Komachi*, 'Frequented by the World', usually depicting the young nobleman, Fukakusa no Shōshō outside Komachi's house where he waited for 100 nights to earn admission only to die of the cold. *Kiyomidzu Komachi*, Komachi talking to a priest in the garden of the Kiyomidzu temple; *Sekidera Komachi*, the old Komachi, poor and wretched, talks to priests at the gate of the Sekidera temple; *Onai Komachi*, Komachi returns the Emperor Yosei's poem with only one character altered; *Sotoba Komachi*, Komachi among the tombs; this was also the title of a famous *Nō* play.

When they are shown reading, girls sometimes represent famous poets, especially on autumn evenings, the autumn sky being a symbol of the changing heart. A single print of two girls reading may however be intended to recall the two worthies Kanzan and Jitoku (Chinese *Han-shan* and *Shih-te*) and in this instance one of the girls will hold a *samisen* or some other article which distinguishes this one as Jitoku who is normally depicted holding a broom. In this class of print, girls may also represent the Six Accomplishments which were considered to be *rei*, etiquette; *gaku*, music; *sha*, archery; *gio*, horsemanship; *sho*, calligraphy and *su*, arithmetic. Continuing with the numerical categories so favoured in the Far East, girls are depicted in prints as the five virtues, viz. *jin*, charity; *gi*, dutifulness; *rei*, courtesy; *chi*, judgment; *shin*, fidelity. Perhaps rather more common are prints of girls as the four classes, i.e. samurai, farmer, artisan and merchant and typical of this class is the series *Furiu shinō kōshō* ('Popular Four Classes') by Kōryusai. In this connection girls are often shown as fan sellers or print sellers (merchant), planting rice (farmer), making prints (artisan) and as lady samurai. Women shown engaged in silkworm culture are not usually part of such a series but rather of some set designed to show the stages in the raising of the silk moth caterpillars; those of Utamaro as well as those of Shunsho and Shigemasa (in their joint work '*Kaiko Yashinai Kusa*') are particularly famous in this connection. Women may be found masquerading as the Six Famous Poets (*Rokkasen*) and in this instance, not uncommonly, the syllable '*ka*' of the title is changed to another character of the same sound meaning 'odour' and suggesting 'flowers' so that this may give rise to such titles as the *Seirō bijin Rokkasen* (by Yeishi) or 'The Six Flower Goddesses of the Beauties of the Greenhouse' (i.e. Yoshiwara). As in a series by Shunchō, women may be represented as the Seven Sages of the Bamboo Grove, a club of literati and musicians formed in China during the third century A.D. Plates from such series can be told by the attributes held by the women: these correspond to the Chinese originals thus: attended by a boy (Yüan Chi = Genshiki), with fan and staff (Yüan Hsien = Genkan), carrying a book (Liu Ling = Keiko), with an unrolled *makimono* (Hsiang Hsiu = Kyōshin), with plums (Wang Jung = Ōju), with a staff (Shan T'ao = Santo), with a 'guitar' (Chi K'ang = Ryurei).

Other prints of women whose titles fall into the numerical category are those representing the *Omi Hakkei* ('Eight Views of Omi' or Lake Biwa—in imitation of the *Shōaho no Hakkei*, the eight classical views of Lake Tung Ting in China. For a list of these see under landscape page 185). The corresponding views are sometimes shown in a reserve panel in the corner of the print but quite often they are to be deduced only by analogy from some such title as *Furiu Zashiki Hakkei* ('The Eight Elegant Interiors'). Another kind of series in the same category is that represented by such titles as *Edo Hakkei* ('Eight Views of Edo'—sometimes mimicked by girls and youths—and often with landscapes in the background) and *Edo Jisho*

Zekkei ('Ten Famous Views of Edo'). Women may also be depicted as the *Shichi Fuku Jin* ('Seven Gods of Felicity') in the Takarabune or Treasure Boat, a feature which helps to identify the intention of the design at once.

Women are often shown in scenes that are intended as a parody on various more or less classical themes. In this connection are to be noticed girls representing the Korean envoys (to be identified by the Korean style dress). A famous seven-sheet composition of this subject by Utamaro exists. Girls parody scenes from the *Chiushingura* (see page 162) of which that most commonly the subject of sheet prints is the incident in which the spy Kudaiyu reads Yuranosuke's letter. Finally, there are parodied versions of the romances of the *Genji Monogatari* and the *Ise Monogatari*. The incidents so depicted in these novels were part of the literary heritage of the Japanese people and would have been, for the most part, easily identified by the public which made the market for the colour print. Usually, but not always, the first of these works can be determined by the presence on the print of one of the peculiar devices known as the *Genjimon*, each of which refers to one or other of the chapters of the book: for a list of these see Koop and Inada's *Japanese Names and How to Read Them*. Perhaps best known are the so-called *mitate* pictures in connection with the Genji tale—as they are indeed in so many of the themes now under discussion. The word *mitate* can be translated 'analogue', 'travesty', 'parody' or simply 'a modern version' of which perhaps the first and the last are the best (see Plate 22). A common *mitate* of *Genji* is that which shows a courtesan in a cage and a young man kicking a ball. This is to be identified with the football scene of the novel, the girl representing the character Nyosan and the youth Kashiwagi. Yeishi designed a famous series of triptychs, *Furyu yatsushi Genji* ('Popular Stories of Prince Genji').

The *Ise Monogatari* is a tenth-century novel in 125 chapters, each of which tells the circumstances surrounding the composition of one of the poems of the great poet and lover Ariwara no Narihira (A.D. 825–880). It is impossible to detail all one hundred and twenty-five of these but those most frequently met with in prints are basically identical with those chosen by the artist Shunshō in his series of twenty-four prints on this theme. These are:

1. Narihira composing a poem whilst watching two court ladies behind a fence.

2. A servant on the veranda of a house delivers a love-letter from N. to Takako; the lady being seen inside the house.

3. N. finds a doorkeeper asleep when making a night call on a lady love.

4. N. carries Takako on his back whilst abducting her from the harem of the mikado Kōkō-tennō.

5. N. with a companion visits the iris pond of Yatsuhashi and composes an acrostic poem on the Kakitsubata (*Iris laevigata*).

6. N. looking at the snow-capped Mount Fuji.

7. N. by the Sumida river sees the *miyakodori* (oyster catchers) fly up reminding him of home and causing him to wonder if his first love is dead or still alive.

8. N. and his current sweetheart hide in the long grass of a moorland whilst men with torches come to set it afire.

9. N. and a lady at a well.

10. A lady on the veranda of a house speaks, in a poem, of her yearning for her lover, N., who is hiding behind a fence.

11. A cockerel on the roof of a house crows to mark the dawn whilst N. stands beside a seated lady who composes a poem marking her vexation that the night closes so soon.

12. A lady whom N. has deserted, sits beside a river contemplating suicide.

13. A lady standing with her sleeve to her face, in a great palace, is being persuaded by N. not to marry.

14. A girl stands mournfully under a tree repining for N. who does not reciprocate her love.

15. Three of N.'s companions sit by a pool of water listening to N. read his poems.

16. N. seated beside his servant renounces his intrigues, addressing a lady, also seated.

17. N. says his farewells to a court lady seated on a mat in the next room.

18. The lady mounts the fence and, standing by the *torii*, views N.'s departure.

19. N. under an umbrella, makes his way through the snow to visit Prince Koretaka.

20. N. is smitten by love for a fisherman's daughter who carries pails of sea water for evaporation at a salt kiln, seen in the distance.

21. N. stands by a waterfall composing a poem which expresses the wish that a rival in a love affair could be thrown in.

22. One of N.'s deserted mistresses leans against the *shōji* with her child whilst N. himself kneels by a pillow.

23. A lady picks up maple leaves and bemoans the fact that N. has not come at this season as he had promised to do.

24. N. kneels before Prince Koretaka holding a poem which assures the prince of his fidelity. A pheasant perches on a flowering plum branch.

Two circumstances in which women are inevitably frequently depicted and which are to be found even amongst the earliest subjects of the colour print are the *Kyodai mae bijin* (Beauty in front of a Mirror) (see Plate 21) and *Yuagari bijin* (Beauty after the Bath). In later prints women are shown even more commonly in other situations. For example, girls are to be seen at the *Kangetsu no yen* ('Banquet for the Contemplation of the Moon') admiring the moon and quite frequently beside the shore or on a river bank. The reference here is probably to the belief that the hare (*usagi*) conceives by running on the waves on the eighteenth day of the eighth moon, if the sky is clear. Ladies are also often shown on an outing for viewing the cherry blossom at Asukayama or Gotenyama or some other place famous for this flower. Sometimes a mixed party of girls and youths are shown on a pleasure outing to the beach at Enoshima and indeed parties of young people on a picnic are amongst the earliest themes of *ukiyo-e* paintings as they are of the prints of all periods. In a similar way girls are often shown at the gate of a temple or standing by a sacred pine-tree in the precincts of a temple.

A few of the situations in which women are depicted are not so easily recognized by the uninitiate whilst others are straightforward enough. Of the latter, one that is repeated over and over again by *ukiyo-e* artists is that of a young girl dreaming of her own seduction; it is exceedingly common throughout almost the whole of the eighteenth century and, in its elements, goes back to the work of Kiyonobu. Nearly as common, at least in the earlier part of that century is the design which shows a girl being carried on the back of the youth who is eloping with her. Such a print usually represents the two lovers, Ohan and Choyemon, but sometimes the intention is to present an analogue to the Japanese Romeo and Juliet, Hinadori and Kuganosuke.

9A. Ōsaka School. Hirosada
Nishikawa; portrait of an actor
of the Ichimura School
(Uzayemon XII?). *Chuban circa*
1840.

9B. Koriusai Isoda (*fl.*
1765–84). A small boy
playing with a puppy:
from a series of twelve
sheets depicting children
with the twelve zodiacal
animals. *Chuban.*
(See page 123.)

意太里亞
タ
リ
ヤ

10. *Nagasaki-e*. An illustration from one of the *bankoku* (works devoted to foreign peoples). 'Italians', from the *Shijuni-koku Jimbutsu zusetzu* by Nishikawa Jōken, published at Nagasaki in two volumes and dated the fifth year of Kyōho, i.e. 1720. The dress appears to be that of the early seventeenth century. (See page 213.)

Young women are to be found on prints which depict them standing inside or outside a house in the early morning; they often hold an instrument of some sort and the allusion here is to the training of musicians who traditionally practised before daybreak. A common theme of all periods is that of women at their toilet and sometimes a young mother will have one or more children with her who play with her combs as she does her hair. Girls with pet animals are a not uncommon subject and the latter may be either a cat or a dog or, more rarely, a monkey or even a frog. Also involving animals is that favourite subject of the middle part of the eighteenth century, a young girl having a lucky dream which takes the shape of two falcons.

Quite frequently young women are shown smoking long stemmed pipes; much more rarely they smoke short ones. Usually near at hand is a box of smoking utensils (*tabako bon*) and this is sometimes carried by an attendant. Very rarely women are depicted with blow-pipes and Harunobu has a most charming print of young girls in a blow-pipe gallery (*fukiya-mise*).

Ladies are not infrequently shown in prints with their maids (*koshimoto*) and these may be of any number from one to three or even four. Young couples were a favourite subject of most of the eighteenth-century masters other than the Torii school. When the young man and woman are shown sharing the same umbrella (*aigasa*) this suggested to the Edo public that they had been living together without telling their parents and when green plums are either shown in the design or mentioned in the accompanying text it is an indication that the young lady is already pregnant.

The theme of women threading needles has reference to the Tanabata festival (the seventh day of the seventh month) on the eve of which women threaded seven needles in honour of the Heavenly Weaver, Shokujo. Young girls carrying New Year offerings are a fairly common subject both of the sheet prints and of *surimono*. These offerings take the shape of rice cakes (*mochi*), dried persimmons (*kushi gaki*), dried chestnuts (*kachiguri*), pine seeds (*kaya no tane*), crayfish, *tai* fish, cuttle fish (*surume*), radish (*daikon*), strings of cash and edible seaweeds. Sometimes too, girls are shown carrying branches of willow: they are returning from the temple of Temmangu which was customarily visited on the first 'hare' day of the first month of the year.

9

Finally there is the almost inevitable comparison of women with flowers, a subject found in many forms and among all the artists whose reputations rested mainly on their delineation of feminine beauty. Harunobu produced the series *Ukiyo bijin hana ni yosuru musume fu* (Contemporary Beauties: Young girls typified by flowers); Chōki has a series of designs entitled, *Furiu ikebana kwai* (Refined meetings for flower arrangements) which shows young women making various types of these arrangements and, nearly always, actually putting a flower into a vase. This pose is not adopted solely for aesthetic reasons since the phrase '*te-ike no hana*' which means literally 'to put a flower in a vase with one's own hand' also carries the figurative meaning 'to have one's will of a beautiful woman'. Utamaro produced several series which incorporate women and flowers such as the *Gosetsu hana awase* or 'Flower competitions for the five festivals'. His pupil, Utamaro II also made similar designs and the series *Tengachi bijin ikebana awase* (Beauty's rivalry with living flowers) is attributed to him.

It is, of course, obvious that women will very commonly be shown in all prints that could be generally classified under the loosely generic title of 'figure studies' but the foregoing paragraphs have considered only that type of print, the chief purpose of which was to show the beauty of young girls and women other than *geisha* and the inmates of the Yoshiwara. As will be seen, more than half of all these prints are devoted either to depicting women in the course of their common occupations or else to the role they are made to play in the parodied representations of historical or literary incidents or as analogues to such abstractions as virtues and even vices. (An exceptionally rare series of Hokusai's is recorded under the title *Furiu nakute nana kuse*, 'An elegant representation of the seven bad habits'). They may even be likened to such unlikely things—at least to the occidental mind—as famous beauty spots, hours of the day, seasons of the year or the chief annual festivals.

To illustrate this last category it will perhaps serve to mention, as typical of its class, the series by Utamaro, 'Mutual love as the five festivals' which shows pairs of young lovers in the various festival occupations. These are:

1. *Shogatsu.* A girl tries to recover a shuttle-cock which a young man has hit into the pine and bamboo branches of a New Year decoration (*kadomatsu*).

2. *Hina matsuri.* A doll playing a little drum, lying in its box, is presented to a delighted girl by a boy.

3. *Tango.* A girl watches a boy paint a huge figure of Shōki on a kite.

4. *Tanabata.* The girl's lover watches her write poems on pieces of coloured paper preparatory to hanging them on bamboos.

5. *Chōyō.* A girl rolls up rice cakes which she packs into a box beside her. Her lover holds a vase of chrysanthemums, this being the festival of that flower.

In this series, as in so many others, it is the attributes and accessories that identify the scene for what it is. Thus Shunchō has a series based on the five festivals but uses the courtesans of the Yoshiwara as figures and often in a completely different setting to those of Utamaro but with much the same attributes.

Women of the noble classes are very rarely shown in prints unless they are representing literary or historical personages or scenes or, as may be supposed, they are being mimicked by some of the young beauties of the day. Very occasionally their purpose seems to be that of evoking the charm and luxury of the life of the upper classes as in a famous triptych of Yeishi's which shows noblewomen floating cherry blossoms on paper boats which they set adrift on a stream.

Apart from the young girls of the town, the inmates of the brothels were undoubtedly the commonest theme of all the *ukiyo-e* designs that featured women as the main motif. Yet an appreciable number of prints, in all periods, were concerned to show two other classes, the waitresses at tea houses and *geisha*. In the days of the old Yoshiwara and in the early years of the new, the tea houses were situated outside the main gate of the quarter and part of their income was obtained by selling tickets which enabled the purchaser to enter the Yoshiwara itself. In later times they were all moved inside the quarter and in various ways came to have a controlling interest in its activities. So powerful was their influence that, in effect, one could not have access to the courtesan chosen without having recourse to the intermediary services of the tea house. In the course of time it became customary for the visitor to be entertained whilst waiting and the scale of this entertainment was an indication of the status of the patron.

In a few years the tea house came to act as the agent for the free-lance entertainers who, in Edo, were called *geisha* and in Ōsaka and

Kyōto were known as *geiko*—the *ko* being a diminutive ending of female names. There was also a kind of male *geisha* known as the *otoko geisha* who played something of the same role as that of the jester in the court society of medieval Europe. *Geisha* do not appear in prints until about 1760 but more than forty years were to elapse before they become at all common in the single sheet prints and their occurrence becomes more frequent as the nineteenth century progresses. In 1799, by government decree, all qualified Yoshiwara *geisha* had to obtain a licence from the central official registry office (*kemban*) and this did something to give them a professional status which they seem never to have lost. The *geisha* tie the *obi* behind and usually have less elaborate hair ornaments than the courtesans whilst the face has a curious flatness due to the heavy white make-up which is prepared on a basis of white-lead powder. When going to entertain at a party outside the Yoshiwara they had to be attended by a manservant, the *hakoya*, who carried the box which held the samisen and, on occasion, a lantern as well: sometimes a maidservant is holding the lantern and in many prints the *geisha* may be identified by the presence of either or both of these two attendants. There is a very beautiful print of a female attendant with a lantern, looking into the face of a *geisha* setting out to give an evening's entertainment, in Toyokuni's series, *Furyu shichi komachi ryaku sugata-e* ('Sketches of the Seven Elegant Paragons of Beauty').

Another distinguishing characteristic of the *geisha* is the fact that, unlike the courtesan, they only very rarely wear their *mon* or badge; indeed it was only worn by this class of entertainer at the New Year festivities and when a *geisha* can be identified in a print and is wearing such a *mon* it is virtually certain that the print in question will have some reference to the New Year itself. In later times the *geisha* and *geiko* have adopted the custom of giving a yearly exhibition of dancing, the *odori*. The *miyako odori* of Kyōto was started in 1872 and that of Ōsaka in 1882: a large print of the somewhat unusual *bai-ōban* size shows the former, rather prettily, and bears the inscription 'by Okamura after a drawing by Hideteru'. Tōkyō has its own *Azuma Odori* which is performed by the *geisha* of that city but this did not start until 1925.

For the most part prints of *geisha*, unlike most actor and courtesan prints of the period 1790 to the opening of the twentieth century, do not come into the category of the *nigao-e* or 'pictured likenesses';

instead they seem to show the 'style' of a *type*. What this style is in fact, is difficult to define. The aim of the *geisha* is to be '*ikki*' and this adjective is really quite untranslatable. It applies to the dress and its accessories, to the behaviour, to the way in which the clothes are worn and even to gesture and stance: certainly it involves a spontaneity and vivacity which moves easily and naturally from joy to sorrow and back again and which involves all the endless nuances of emotional tone between the two. It is vivacity, it is repose; in short, it is the 'stylishness' of the *geisha*.

Their 'style', their amiability, their wit and their quickness of repartee are most often the reasons for their appearance in prints— these and the mood of gaiety and conviviality which is naturally associated with them. By no means were they necessarily noted beauties. Yet noted beauties of the town, neither courtesan—at least officially—nor *geisha*, do appear in the work of several artists who were especially devoted to *bijin-e*. Quite frequently these were shop assistants and such was their ephemeral renown that their names and anecdotes about them occur in the *yomiuri* or news sheets that sold weekly about the streets of Edo; a few achieved the further fame of having plays written around their personalities. Such were two of Harunobu's favourites, Ō-Sen who, about 1768, was a waitress at the Kasamori tea house in the precincts of the Kanōji temple of Yanaka, and Ō-Fuji an assistant at the Yanagiya shop, a stationers. Another, at the end of the eighteenth century was Ō-Hisa of the Takashima-ya, a shop selling rice-crackers: she was the subject of a famous print by Toyokuni. Utamaro's portraits of Ō-Kita of the Naniwa-ya tea house are perhaps the most noted of all and the business she made famous, as well as some of the other waitresses there, can be seen in a rare triptych by Chōki.

Reference has been made to some of the most notable themes in which women appear but the list of such themes is by no means exhausted. Often the beauties are nameless; sometimes neither courtesan nor *geisha* but merely delineations of lovely women used merely to create a mood or to capture a moment of enraptured loveliness (see Plate 14). How various the situations shown and how anonymous the personages, may be seen from a few titles taken at random:

Tonda chagama (A beauty with attendant) by Harunobu.

Fune ni noru bijin (A beauty stepping into a boat) by Harunobu.

Kiku miru bijin (A beauty looking at chrysanthemums) by Tanaka Masunobu.

Natsu sugata (A beauty in summer) by Shunshō.

Okawabata sambashi ni bijin (Two beauties by the riverside) by Kiyonaga.

Koshi saki bijin (A beauty looking out of a door) by Shunchō.

Sechu bijo (A beauty admiring the snow) by Shunsen.

NOTES ON CHAPTER V

The literature on the subject of this chapter is excessively scattered and very fragmentary. Restriction of space precludes anything like a detailed listing and, indeed, much that bears on these matters is most easily approached from a study of the prints themselves. The few works that follow have interesting sidelights on some aspects of the general subject.

Hashimoto Sumiko: *Japanese Accessories*. Japan Tourist Library 2nd series, No. 26. Tōkyō, 1962.

Iwadō Tamotsu: *Children's Days in Japan*. Japan Tourist Library 1st series, No. 12. Tōkyō, 1936.

Kawakatsu Kenichi: *Kimono—Japanese Dress*. Japan Tourist Library 1st series, No. 13. Tōkyō, 1936.

Saitō, R.: *Japanese Coiffure*. Japan Tourist Library 1st series, No. 28. Tōkyō, 1939.

Scott, A. C.: *The Flower and Willow World*. London, 1959.

Stratz, C. H.: *Die Korperformen in Kunst und Leben der Japaner*. 4th edition, Stuttgart, 1925.

The most informative of all books on dress and accessories known to me is the Japanese work *Kinsei Onna fuzoku Ko* (Modern costumes of Japanese Women), Tōkyō, 1896.

CHAPTER VI

Libertine and Courtesan: Prints of the Yoshiwara and its Inmates

THROUGHOUT the history of the *ukiyo-e* prints the courtesan is depicted as entering into almost all the themes which have been discussed in the last two chapters yet so important is the life of the Yoshiwara, so frequently is some aspect of it the subject of a print or book illustration, that it is necessary to devote a separate chapter to this subject. Indeed, so many aspects of the strange, exclusive life of the brothel quarter of Edo and its inmates are reflected in literally hundreds of prints of the eighteenth and nineteenth centuries that some knowledge of it is necessary for the identification of their subject matter.

The Shin (New) Yoshiwara, as mentioned on page 111, was founded in 1657. Sole access to it was along an embankment, the *Umamichi* ('Horses' Way'), which ran across the rice fields and swamps and by the eighteenth century it had become what was almost a separate town. By the time of the shōgun Tsunayoshi (died 1709) its fortunes were assured and for the most part, it had taken on the form which was to be maintained throughout the whole period of the colour prints. The idle samurai, the newly rich merchants, actors, artists, some of the dangerous rōnin (i.e. samurai without an overlord) and members of the *otokodate*, all frequented its brothels, tea houses and streets: in no part of the period 1700 to 1870 could there have been less than two thousand prostitutes permanently living there and this figure might perhaps easily be trebled if one were to add all the host of attendants, servants, pimps, debt collectors, cooks, merchants, singers, musicians, jesters, *geisha*, adventurers and intermediaries of every kind and description. It became, in truth, the gay quarter and was called, not without reason, *fuya-jō* 'the nightless city'.

The name Yoshiwara (the usual derivation is from *yoshi* 'a reed' and *hara* 'a moor' but it is sometimes written with another character for *yoshi* meaning 'lucky') is the name given to the prostitute quarter of Edo; it is not the name of similar quarters in other towns which are usually designated by such words as *yujoya* and *kuruwa*. Such prostitute districts in cities like Ōsaka, Kyōto, Nagoya, Nagasaki and others are sometimes shown in illustrated books but are only of very rare occurrence in the sheet prints and in these they are almost confined to the latter half of the nineteenth century. Due no doubt to its isolation and to the devotion of its inmates to a single over-riding calling, in course of time, special customs, special arts and even special words were used and observed by those who frequented the place and allusions to these are not uncommon in the prints. Those students who are interested in such details will find much information in the scholarly work of J. E. de Becker.[1]

In so far as these historical details affect the understanding of prints and of printed books dealing with the life in the Yoshiwara there are only a few matters to which attention need be called. On some prints of courtesans we find short epigrammatic comic poems, the so-called *Yoshiwara no Kyōka*, which were always of unending delight to the public. As an example one of those composed by the novelist Bakin may be cited: 'Without questioning one knows that the *miyako-dori* ("oyster-catcher") lives by the Sumida river; she for whom I long lives in the Yoshiwara,' i.e. the bird calls out the river's name continuously and the poet talks equally continuously of the Yoshiwara.

A general plan of the Yoshiwara is shown in the figure on page 137. Important features are the division of the whole 'town' into wards (*chō*) and districts (*machi*) as well as the great gate (Ō-Mon) which last appears in several prints especially some notable ones by Hiroshige. Formerly there were four shrines inside the Yoshiwara all dedicated to Inari the so-called Fox God—originally a god of daily food—and the protector of prostitutes. One of these is sometimes depicted in prints as is also the *Mi-kaeri Yanagi* or 'looking back willow tree' because, passing it, the visitor looks back reluctantly to the scene of his late pleasures.

Peculiar to the Yoshiwara are certain dances and festivals, some of the former now long extinct but still to be seen in various old books that were designed as guides for the visitor or to serve maybe as souvenirs. Among these dances were the *Daijin-mai no koto* (Dance of the Millionaires) popular in the period 1711–1715 and performed

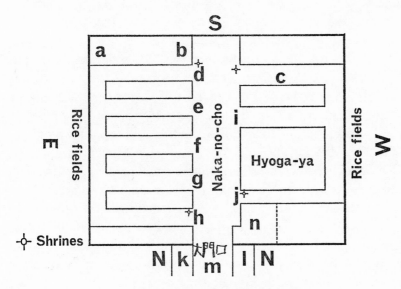

Plan of the Shin Yoshiwara

a. Shrine of Kurosuke Inari
b. Water supply
c. Kyomachi Itchōme
d. Shin-chō
e. Sumi-chō
f. Sumi-chō
g. Yedo-cho 2 Chome

h. Fushime-chō
i. Akeya-chō
j. Yedo-chō Itchōme
k. Tea house
l. Streets of tea houses
m. Great gate leading to the Emonsaka Highway
n. The Tomoe-ya

The Yoshiwara is in the Asakusa quarter of Edo. To the west of the *Emonsaka* was the temple of the *Yoshiwara-jinja* devoted to the spiritual needs of the inmates. NOTE: E.W.S.N. are not true points of the compass but merely denote the sides. Adapted from Kurth and Becker.

to certain songs said to have been composed by the actor Nakamura Kichibei and later sung and danced by *hōkam* or jesters. Another dance was the *Daikoku-mai* performed by special *daikoku-mai* dancers who seem originally to have been beggars. It was danced from the beginning of the eighteenth century until about the end of the first half of the nineteenth century. Formerly the dancers gave their performance in the houses of the Yoshiwara from the second day of the first month to the first 'horse' day of the second month but later they seem to have entered the quarter on all the major festival days especially that of the last day of the year. It was customary for the courtesans to give the dancers various articles of cast-off clothing. The dance has its name from the fact that one of the dancers wore the mask of the god Daikoku-ten, god of riches.

More famous than either of the above and more frequently seen in prints is the *Niwaka* dancing. This is a semi-dramatic presentation performed by the *hōkan* and *geisha* and took place about the end of August or beginning of September. The performance was given for a whole month, the first half of the month being taken up by *geisha* who did 'lion' dancing and '*kiyari*' singing. Such dancers drag a great wooden lion's head behind them and are often dressed as men. The performance was given from a wheeled car about eighteen feet square and nearly as high (see Plate 15). This was followed by a *soko-nuke ya-tai* or 'bottomless car' which housed the orchestra, both cars being pulled by coolies. In the seventeenth century the Niwaka seems to have been only a series of impromptu burlesques but later the cars were introduced in imitation of the Gion festival at Kyōto. Burlesque processions remained throughout the eighteenth and earlier part of the nineteenth century as a regular feature of the Niwaka and many prints show the *geisha* dressed as nobles, pilgrims, musicians, foreign envoys, etc. Originally, this festival was of some religious import, a conclusion which is supported by the fact that during the eighteenth and earlier nineteenth centuries a bamboo plant in leaf was set up on either side of the great gateway whilst the Niwaka was in progress and a straw rope was slung across in order to purify the place within. Formerly the various grades of prostitutes as well as the *geisha* took part in this ceremony.

Another Yoshiwara ceremony shown in several prints is that of the feast of lanterns, *Tōrō no koto*, which takes place in August. It is said to commemorate a famous courtesan, Tamagiku, who died in 1715 but hanging out lanterns for the souls of the dead at this time of year, is a very ancient custom all over Japan. Every tea house hangs out a pair of lanterns which are long and narrow in shape and are easily recognized in prints.

The cherry blossom festival is yet another of the great annual occasions of the Yoshiwara that can be seen in prints and book illustrations. This began some time between 1741 and 1743 and at this season of the year, when the cherry trees are in full bloom—varying from late March to early April—all the houses are hung with brilliantly coloured curtains and at night, lanterns are placed to illuminate the blossom-covered trees. In older times this always commenced on the third day of the third month. Formerly the *kamuro* and *shinzō* were allowed to visit various localities famous for their cherry flowers—Ueno, Asukayama, Mukōjima—at this time of year and on another day all the inmates of the brothels attended *sake* parties for viewing the cherry in the *Naka-no-chō*.

On the 'Cock' days of November occurs the *Tori-no-matsuri* or 'Cock festival'. It was customary for great crowds to visit the Yoshiwara on these days, many of them having attended the fair of Asakusa which was held then and which is situated quite close to the Yoshiwara.

Most gorgeous of all occasions in this quarter and the one most frequently seen in prints of the nineteenth century was the promenade of the *yujo*. This seems to have grown out of the custom in earlier times of the courtesan going to her guest when ordered through the tea houses but, from about the middle of the eighteenth century until the middle of the nineteenth century or a little later, this ceremonial promenade was especially associated with the more or less ceremonial viewing of the newly-planted flowers in the brothel quarter; in spring was the cherry, in summer the iris and—perhaps even more important—in autumn the chrysanthemum. Then, the *yujo*, dressed in the most magnificent style with silks and brocades of incredible richness, her *obi* tied in front in an enormous bow, her hair dressed in a high pyramidal coiffure with combs up to three feet long stuck through it from side to side, walking on clogs (*geta*) nearly a foot in height and accompanied by her *shinzō*, *kamuro* (pages), *yarite* (chaperone), and *wakaimono* (porter) would parade very slowly through the quarter watched by an enormous and admiring crowd. Many prints of these times show these parades and indeed they were one of the notable sights of Edo. At night each of these great courtesans would be preceded by an enormous lantern on which her crest was emblazoned. A specially intricate step was used by *yujo* in these parades and this added to the dignity and impressiveness of the whole. Many special customs grew up and flourished for a time in connection with this display and in some periods even the colours of the outer and under garments became a set fashion. All these detailed changes may be studied in the prints which illustrate this subject.

In the Yoshiwara the highest ranking prostitutes were, in many ways, the leaders of their society and indeed, in the matter of fashion, they were, to some extent, the leaders of society as a whole. For this reason they were never spoken of as *jōro* but by the more euphonious name of *Ōiran*. These great *ōiran* were never numerous and records show that at no period did they exceed twenty in number and on occasion the class might be represented by but a single one. The *Ōiran* naturally belonged to the highest class of prostitute and members of this class in Edo were called *Tayu* whilst the inferior ones made up a group which originally were designated *hashi-jōro*. During the early years of the period of the Shin-Yoshiwara this last category was done away with and in the Genroku period (1688–1703)—the golden age of *ukiyo* ideals and customs—four categories of the inferior class were recognized: *kōshi-jōro, kirimise-jōro, sancha-jōro* and *umecha-jōro*. The three last categories originally seem to have lived outside the licensed quarter but eventually all were brought into its confines. This multiple origin of these women of the Yoshiwara—and some, called *yakko*, even came from the samurai class—entailed not only a complex and detailed classification but the changes of fortune and fashion ensured that some classes ceased to be recognized whilst others, formerly obscure and minor, rose to favour. For this reason many names are found in the native texts which are difficult to interpret but the reader who is interested in this will find much information in the work of Becker (l.c.) and there is a useful table of periods and classifications on page 74 of his volume.

Often to be seen in prints of courtesans are the little girls called *kamuro* or pages. These usually entered the profession between the ages of five and seven and acted as attendants on an older courtesan. Originally their clothes were of white linen dyed with a pine-tree pattern and they may sometimes be seen in the *ukiyo-e* paintings of the Tosa school and in the prints of the early Hishikawa school. *Tayu* and *Kōshijōro* were entitled to three and two of these *kamuro* respectively whilst a *Sancha-jōro* had one. After the period Hōyei (1704–1710) the last class were often attended by two *kamuro* when out walking, on the pretext that one was not a personal servant. In later times the *kamuro* wore the same fine dress as their mistress and the pine-tree pattern was only worn during the first week of January. The higher courtesan to whom they were attached was called their *ane-jōro* and she was expected to play a considerable part in furthering their fortunes. Names given to *kamuro* were poetical fancies that would be naturally associated together; thus one might be called 'Namiji' (Waves) and the other 'Chidori' (Plover).

When the *kamuro* were about sixteen they might, at the discretion of their *ane-jōro* be made into *shinzō*. This usually entailed expensive ceremonies, which were paid for by the *ane-jōro* (or her wealthy patrons!) and were accompanied by many gifts and special customs. One may sometimes see in a book illustration a brothel with a row of vessels containing hot food set on a white wood table, outside the entrance: scenes of the interior of the brothel sometimes show a similar table laden with dress materials, fans, etc.; both of these are part of the ceremonies carried out on the day that the *kamuro* became a *shinzō*. For a week following this the *shinzō* would not appear in the *mise* (shop where the courtesans were on view to prospective customers) but would parade the *Naka-no-chō* under the guidance of her *ane-jōro*. Such parades—and a different dress was used each day— are sometimes to be seen in the contemporary colour prints since, for their public, this was something of an occasion.

The *kamuro* were mostly the children of peasants from whom they were bought by the pimps (*zegan*) who scoured the surrounding countryside. Since this was illegal they had to be smuggled into the Yoshiwara but once there they were entered on the official papers as the adopted daughters of the brothel proprietor (*rōshu*). It was in his private quarters (*naishō*) that the young girl was taught the techniques of harlotry. However, a part of the supply came from the numerous children of the Minowa district where the Yoshiwara's secret maternity hospitals offered their facilities to pregnant courtesans. As a *shinzō* the girl acted as a kind of personal secretary to the *ōiran*, these duties being called *myōdai* and, by the custom of the place, it was accepted that one's attentions should not be given to the *shinzō*: no doubt this was a rule proven by the numerous exceptions.

In general the colour prints show only courtesans of the *tayu* class with their attendants and this is certainly true of all those prints which are, in their own particular way, portraits of the person concerned. For this reason it is important to know the names of these leading prostitutes and of the houses to which they belonged and it is often possible to see the different treatment accorded by different artists to the same woman. But these names can be deceptive: firstly, because the name may be handed down for several generations or it might skip a generation; secondly, because the *mon* or badge of the first of the name may or may not be changed. Thus, for example, with Shizuka of the Tama-ya brothel, the name remained the same but the *mon* was changed. Another complicating factor comes from the fact that the brothels each had their own 'house' *mon* and this was sometimes used by the inmates on certain occasions only whereas, in other instances, one of the *tayu* class might take the 'house' *mon* as her own at least on such accessories as lanterns, etc. Help in the identification of some of the most famous of these personages may be obtained from the list at the end of this chapter. Once one of these individuals has been identified in a print, facial resemblance will be a fairly certain means of identifying them in other illustrations.

In colour prints the names of the houses to which the courtesans depicted belonged are often shown in the form of various articles which are pictured in a reserved field at the top of the print. The names of these articles are to be read as a rebus and several of the leading brothels may be identified in this way. The following is a short list of some of the ones most frequently in use. Tobacco pipe = *kise-ru* (shortened to *kise*); a stream or river = *gawa*; pine needles or pine-tree = *matsu*; arrow = *ya*; cherry blossom = *sakura*; coiffure in the form of a butterfly = *chōji*; house = *ya*; cup or bowl = *wan*; hills or mountain = *yama*; clove = *chōji*; fan = *ōgi*; lobster = *ebi*; ivy leaf = *tsuta*; a trident-headed spear = *hishi* (but more often this house was designated by a rhombus = *hishigata*).

Very commonly in prints dating from the middle of the eighteenth century onward courtesans are shown displaying themselves by walking about on their very high clogs called *hachimonji geta* or 'sign of eight clogs'. From the Hōreki period (1751–1763) only the two classes of prostitute called *yobi-dashi* and *chusan* were permitted to wear these clogs and the possession of them shows the rank of the woman depicted. The *yobi-dashi* were themselves divided into two grades and only the first of these corresponded to the older first grade *tayu*.

Since the printed books sometimes deal with the brothel quarters of Ōsaka and Kyōto a word may perhaps be said about these. The courtesan district of Kyōto was called the Shimabara and that of Ōsaka the Shimmachi. The top rank courtesans in these cities were called *Tenjin* although in earlier times, i.e. late seventeenth and very early eighteenth century Kyōto seems to have had a *Tayu* class that ranked above these. In Ōsaka the *Tenjin*, on ceremonial occasions had more attendants and were in fact accompanied by *shinzō*, *taiko-joro* and *kaburo*. It is a curious fact that the so-called Ōsaka school of *ukiyo-e* does not depict the courtesan life at all and it is only in the earlier publications emanating from this city that they are at all common.

The Yoshiwara courtesans appear in the colour prints not only as being part of the everyday life of that quarter but in almost all the themes that formed the subject matter of the *bijin-ga*. They are shown, very fancifully, as taking part in the different occupations carried on by artisans and peasants; forming processions dressed as nobles and samurai (often these were part of the *Niwaka* festival); as warriors and poets; as gods and Chinese heroes (e.g. by Gakutei); compared to beautiful scenery; as fashion plates, or in more straight-forward roles such as Utamaro's series *Gonin bijin aikyo kisoi* ('A competition of five lovely women'.) Titles of some others of Utamaro's series suggest variations on themes that in one form or another were perpetuated by many artists, viz. *Komei bijin rok'kasen* ('Celebrated beauties as the six famous poetesses'); *Fujin ninsō jippin* ('Ten Physiognomies of Women') and *Fujin so gaku ju-tei* (Ten types of learning in women'). Both these last series are signed 'The phrenologist, Utamaro'. In many single sheet prints the courtesan is shown holding one end of a cloth (*tenugui*) in her mouth—a sign of stifled tears—or else writing a love letter. More rarely the calligraphy of famous courtesans is shown with their portrait and in this connec-tion autographs are not very uncommon. An example of this last is Masanobu's *Yoshiwara keisei shin bijin awase jihitsu kagami* ('Mirror of the autographs of the latest Yoshiwara rival beauties.')

It remains to list the main houses of the Yoshiwara, the inmates of which are represented in colour prints or some of the more im-portant books. The latter often listed and portrayed those not of the first rank but almost all those that are delineated in the single sheet colour prints belong to the two top classes and usually only to the *tayu* class and they are moreover those to whom the name *ōiran* would be given.

In listing these brothels and courtesans any worker must necessarily lean heavily on the work of Professor Julius Kurth;[2] inevitably I have done so here but I have also added substantially to the list given by him especially for the later periods in which his work is markedly deficient. This is the period however for which the novice collector will most often require information. Generally the name of a brothel was taken from an object which appeared on the house flag but this was not always so as, for example, the Echizen-ya which was named after the province of that name. Certain prefixes must be noted too: '*kado*' (side) and '*naka*' (inner) denote associated houses whilst '*dai*' (large), which can also be read '*Ō*', denotes the main house. '*Ko*' (small) designates the branches of the main business, usually to classify a dependency of the main house and quite often these would seem to have been a separate concern financed from individual sources. Then the name would become extinct and a completely new name takes its place.

Besides the Yoshiwara there were other unlicensed quarters of prostitution called *okabasho*. For the most part these were illegal and government action was taken against them from time to time but seemingly it was never very successful; perhaps it was not seriously intended to be. The most important of these quarters was the Yagura-shita of Fukugawa which some connoisseurs of these pleasures prized the more highly because of its simplicity. Single sheet prints show these unlicensed quarters only rather rarely but one can see them in certain of the *meisho-ki* and other such works.

Some novelettes refer to still more pleasure quarters about the city. That of Nakasu was situated on a sandbank in the river and comprised inns, tea-houses and firms who hired out boats. It existed only from 1775 to 1788. Yet another on the island of Kusaki had at least two notable houses, the Masu-ya and the Daimon-ya but they disappeared with the destruction of the whole quarter by the great tidal wave of 1791. The suburbs of Shinjuka and Shinagawa were noted prostitute quarters but were low class and often dangerous. Kunisada depicted most of these other Pleasure Quarters in three series referred to in an article by Mr Shigeo Miyao in *Ukiyo-e Art*, No 8 (1964), pp 23–30.

But female prostitution is not the only kind dealt with in the prints. Male prostitutes, mostly effeminate and vicious young men, are not uncommon in eighteenth-century colour prints and there is more than a hint of this relationship in many of the actor sheets. Indeed, some actors specialized in the so-called *wakashu* parts, i.e. those of effeminate boys (see Plate 13), one such being Onoe Kikugorō I (1717–83). The poems inscribed on such actor prints sometimes have erotic overtones although these are generally

11. The Classical School. Gesshō: two doves. A sheet from the *Gesshō Sogwa* of 1828, printed from seven colour blocks and black. The birds are reserved in a grey background: all colours are shaded on the block with, here and there, an extremely light over-printing of white: if this print is compared with that by Sugakudo on Plate 12, the differences between the treatment of *Kwa-cho* themes by the classical school and *ukiyo-e* will at once be apparent.

12. *Kwa-Cho* print by Sugakudō Shujin (*fl.* 1858–61). A plate from the series *Shō Utsushi shiju hachi Taka* (Exact Representations of Forty-eight Hawks, i.e. Birds) published by Koyeidō in 1858. This shows the Narcissus Flycatcher (*Kibitaki:* Zanthopygia narcissina) with a clump of narcissus.

equivocal. Mr D. B. Waterhouse in his book *Harunobu and his age* (London 1964) has an excellent example of this. A print by Kiyomitsu of the 1760s shows the actor Nakamura Tomijurō as a young girl. The short poem is thus translated by Mr Waterhouse:

Kite wa hore	At his coming—infatuation
Kaerite wa home	At his going—applause . . .
Koku-botan	The black peony!

But the phrase '*koku-botan*' in eighteenth-century Edo slang meant an artificial model of either the male or female genital organs. The inference in the poem is not far to seek and brings near to us the bawdy, salty atmosphere of the society for which these delicate and seemingly wistful prints were made.

Fashionable young men are sometimes shown in attitudes which are intended to suggest analogies with the Bodhisattva Monju Bosatsu who sought supreme wisdom and, as a child, was so wise that he confounded his teachers. He became the patron deity, not only of wisdom but of homosexuality and in Edo society of the seventeenth and eighteenth centuries the words '*Monju jiri*' (Monju's arse) were a slang expression for homosexual love. Just as courtesans are sometimes playfully depicted as Fugen Bosatsu (Sanskrit, Samantabhadra), the dispenser of knowledge, seated on an elephant —and it possibly adds to the point that this divinity was the patron of a markedly ecstatic sect—so youths in the role of Monju Bosatsu were shown with a lion and often with peonies. This flower in China, and later in Japan, was not only an emblem of wealth but the Chinese phrase, 'the dew in the peony' denoted the climax of a sexual orgasm. In the light of these references the overtones of such prints will be readily apparent.

Finally, what will not perhaps be so obvious to the student col-lector of courtesan prints as to the more experienced, these courtesans may very frequently be identified by mere facial likeness to one whose name is known. In a certain sense many *bijin-e* are portraits— just as are the actor prints—and the features, especially the propor-tions of the face and the shape of the chin and eyes, are mostly enough to make the identification of the subject fairly certain. Although we can see resemblances, often amounting to identity, between many of the young men shown in prints, they are generally anonymous and most often nothing whatever is known of them.

10

NOTES ON CHAPTER VI

[1] Anonymous (Becker, J. E. de): *The Nightless City or the History of the Yoshiwara Yukwaku*. Yokohama, 1899. Two other useful works, full of much erudite information but both in Japanese, are Doke, Sai-ichiro: *Baishun-fu ronko*. Tōkyō, 1927 and Yamaji, Kanko: *Kuruwa no hitobito: Kamuro, shinzō, yarite sono ta*. Kaishaku to Kansho, Vol. 28, No. 3, 1963; pp. 88–93. The latter work, however, was not available to me at the time of writing this book.

[2] Kurth, J., *Die Geschichte des Japanischen Holzschnitts*; Vol. 1; Introduction. Leipzig, 1925.

List of the Brothels of the Yoshiwara, Edo, which appear on Colour Prints and some of the Inmates portrayed by the ukiyo-e Artists

Abura-ya. Some; (Utamaro).

Akatsu-ya (Red Ivy House). Rinzan (Eishō), Ukishima (Hidemaro).

Asahi-maru-ya. Hayama (Kōriusai).

Chi-ya. Haruhino (Eishō).

Chōji-ya (House of the Clove). Hinatsuru (Harunobu); her *kamuro* were Kochō and Tsurui Hinatsuru III (Utamaro), her *mon* a crane in a circle. Hinatsuru II (Eishi). Chōzan *mon* a crane; Meizan same *mon*; Senzan I *mon* orange in a circle; Kara-uta I same *mon*, her *kamuro* were Matsuno and Takeno (all these by Kōriusai); Senzan II (Kiyonaga); Chōzan II (Utamaro); *Kamuro* Shiori and Tsumaki, Hinamachi, Kaoyo, Nishikigi, Toyosumi, Senzan (I?), Tamazuru, Miyamagi, Hinaji, Nishikido, Futamura, Meizan (I?), Hinatsuru (I?) (all given by Harunobu), *Kamuro* of one Senzan seem to have been Yasōji and Isōji Misayama; her *kamuro* were Isōji and Hachiuji and are shown by Eishi. Another Misayama given by Eishō. Toyotsumi and Michiyama (Eishō) Utamaro in different prints gives four *kamuro* for Hinatsuru III, namely Sarano, Korano, Yahashi and Kotoguki as well as the *shinzō* Takeba-e, Karakoto her *mon* a Glycinia leaf, her *kamuro* Akeba and Yayoi; Morokoshi Nishiki-ko (Utamaro); Tokiwa, (Eishi); Yoshito, Gōkyō, Karakoto II, (Eisui); Hinatsuru, (Kiyonaga); Ko-Tokiwatsu, (Eishi).

Chumanji-ya. Utamaro shows an unnamed courtesan of this house which was seemingly a subsidiary of the Daimanji-ya.

DaiEbi-ya see *Ebi-ya*; *DaiHishi-ye* see *Hishi-ya*; *KaiKane-ya* see *Kane-ya*; *DaiManji-ya* see *Manji-ya*; *DaiMonji-ya* see *Monji-ya*.

Ebi-ya (House of the Lobster). Chief house was DaiEbi-ya with dependencies of KadoEbi-ya and MaruEbi-ya. Utanosuke Ebira of

DaiEbi-ya (Harunobu), the *ōiran* Tsushima inaugurated a game to mark the festival of the first day of the eighth month; it was seemingly played with a large feather ball and a bat. Enomachi of Kado, Ebi-ya Aisome of Maru Ebi-ya; Hatsura, her *mon* a *Glycinia*.

Echizen-ya. Konosato, Wakoku, Morokoshi, Kotoura, Senzan (all Harunobu); a Morokoshi is given by Kōriusai and may be different. Kayoiji (Torii IV); Kokonoe (Eishi); Ō-Karashi (Utamaro); Morokoshi II (Utamaro II).

Ezashi-ya. Shown in a single sheet print of Moronobu of 1707.

Gankaizenya. Dōkai and Shigenoi (Utamaro II).

Hirano-ya. Ō-Saya (Utamaro).

Hishi-ya. Contracted form of *Hishigata-ya* (House of the Rhombus); *DaiHishi-ya* Kisagata, her *mon* a wreath of cherry blossom, her *kamuro* Sawano and Sayono. Hitoe, Hinakoto, Mitsunotsu. (all given by Harunobu). Isawa had same *mon* as Kisagata, Mitsunoha, her *mon* a fallen cherry blossom, Mitsubana her *mon* a single cherry blossom. Mitsukona fl. *circa* 1778. The subsidiary house *KiriHishi-ya* had Himegiku, Katsuragi, Agemaki, Senzan, (compare she of Chōji-ya), Ariake, Hananobe (all given by Harunobu).

Hyōgo-ya (name of a State). It was situated in the Central Street. Ōshu, Umegae (both by Harunobu); Mitsuhama (Eishi); Hanatsuma (Utamaro); The chief *ōiran* was Tsukioka (Utamaro); a Tsukioka, perhaps the same, is also given by Toyokuni, Mitsuma (Utamaro).

IchiMonji-ya; see Monji-ya.

Ieda-ya. Konoharu (Utamaro).

Ise-ya. Hanachō, Mitsuyama, Shigezuru (all Harunobu). A subsidiary house of this establishment appears to have been the *Gaku-Ise-ya* which seems to have persisted until the third decade of the nineteenth century since it is figured in a print of Kunisada's. However, only the following of its inmates have been recorded by name; Shiranami, Harukaze, Hatsune, Haruzono and Kureha, all by Harunobu; also Tōra (Kiyohiro). A 'Shiranami' of an unspecified house in a print of Kunisada's may have belonged to this house. It seems possible that later in the nineteenth century the management was taken over by the great house of Matsu-ya since in some few late nineteenth-century prints an *Ise-Matsu* is met with very rarely.

Kado-Dai-Sato-ya; see *Sato-ya*, *KadoEbi-ya*; see *Ebi-ya*, *Kado-Kairō*; see *Kairō-ya*, *KadoKane-ya*; see *Kane-ya*, *Kado Tama-ya*; see *Tama-ya*, *Kado Yamaguchi-ya*; see *Yamaguchi-ya*.

KadoManji-ya. Shizuhata, Shizukaze (Harunobu).

KageManji-ya. Kiyohana (Kōriusai).

KageManji-ya; see *Manji-ya*.

Kairō-ya (Old Pond House). The sub-house *KadoKairō-ya* was only found in Utamaro's time and in more than one print he gives unnamed courtesans who belonged to this house. Meinare, her *mon* a *Glycinia*, Rikiserō, Kasumino, Daii (All Utamaro and his school), Ainare, (Kikumaro).

Kana-ya. (The name is taken from the *kana* syllabary and probably for this reason the names of Ōiran of this house appear always to be written in *hirigana* script.) There are two houses, the main one *DaiKana-ya* and *ShinKana-ya*. Of the first the following are recorded on prints, Nishikigi, Fujinoto, Sumaginu, Itsuhata, Kasane, Ichinoe (all Harunobu), and Nishikiku by Bunchō. Of the *ShinKana-ya* are Utena, Konoura, Tokiwagi, Nana-aya, Nana-uta, Shigaraki, Nanaginu, Kasugano, Ayasato (all by Harunobu). Some of these names occur in the work of Kiyonaga and other later artists without any indication of their house but it is reasonably certain that most, if not all belong to the *Kana-ya*.

Kane-ya (The Yellow House). The main house had Namo-e and two others unnamed all with the same *mon* of a fan (*ōgi*) and two crossed leaves. The *KadoKane-ya* had Shichijō, Imaoka and Nana-aya (Torii IV).

Kashiwa-ya. Hana-no-i, Hanakazure, Tamashiba, Koiyama, Toyosumi, Kaneyama (all in time of Harunobu).

Katsumoto-ya. Kurth (2) reads this uncertainly as 'Kwatsumae-ya' which seems to be erroneous. Monekoshi, Hanaoe, Wakoku (Eishi); also two other unnamed ones all with *mon* of two flying large-billed cranes which was probably the house *mon*. Eishi has Karashi with a *mon* of five ivy leaves.

Kazusa-ya. The main house *DaiKazusaya* had Makiro-o, Shigenosuke, Agemake, Ne-mo-hi, Makishino (Harunobu and mid years of eighteenth century). The subsidiary house (?) *NakaKazusa-ya* had Sumaginu, Hanakoto, Katsuyama.

Kikumoto-ya. O-Han (Utamaro).

Kimura-ya. Iosasa (Harunobu).

Kiri-ya (Pawlownia House). House *mon Glycinia*; Mizubana *mon Glycinia*; Hanakiri *mon* five stars; Aakinoha (all mid-eighteenth century).

Kirimo-ya. Shiragiku *mon Glycinia*; Hogiku *mon* a whole cherry blossom; Kamegiku same *mon*; Tamagiku (another Tamagiku in Manji-ya).

Kuragira-ya. Tsukimasa (Utamaro).

Kurata-ya. Sata *mon* three oak leaves in a circle.

Mame-ya (Bean House). The five leaves probably were the house *mon*. Kōriusai has a painting of an *ōiran* of this house.

Manji-ya (House of the Swastika). This was a large house with several dependencies. It persisted down to the twentieth century but in the last part of the nineteenth century its fortunes failed and it fell to a *ko-mise* or third class house. In the era Shōtōku (1711–1715) lived the famous and beautiful Tamagiku. *DaiManji-ya*, Hinasato, Waka-usa, Kurenai, Asagiri (all Harunobu), Manshu, Mitsuharu, Chiyo-hana (Kōriusai), Tokoshie (Torii IV), Hitochi (Utamaro), Fuji-e (Utamaro II). Four unnamed courtesans are depicted by Kunisada all of this house. Hana-murasaki, Rinzan (Harunobu).

Maru-ya (The Round House). Sonomume, Toyoyama, Naniwase, Chiyozuru, Muraōgi, Tanshu (Harunobu), Konomachi with *mon* of two feathers in a circle. Kazusano with *mon* of two crossed pine branches.

Matsuba-ya (Pine Needle House). One of the most famous of all the houses of the eighteenth century and of the first third of the nineteenth century. It seems to have declined very rapidly and was extinct in the last half of the nineteenth century. The house *mon* was a circle of pine needles broken in three places. Somenosuke is a famous name in several decades. Somenosuke had for a *mon* the *maru chigai taka no ha*, i.e., two crossed hawk's feathers in a circle. This *mon* is sometimes found in other houses and seems to have functioned in later times as a *mon* of *ōiran* in general. Women with the name of Somenosuke are shown by Harunobu, Kōriusai, Bunchō, Eishi, Utamaro and Kunisada. Utamaro gives as her *kamuro* Wakagi and Wakaba, Wakana, Ukifune, Matsushima, Sonoume, Hatsukaze, Someha. Segawa I, *mon* three oak leaves in a cartouche of Gingko leaves; she was famous as a poet. Segawa II, same *mon*; her *kamuro* were Takeno and Sarinō. She was a calligraphist of note and is famous for a letter sent to her intimate friend Hinatsuru of *Chōji-ya*. She was eventually ransomed by the owner of a large business called the *Eichi-ya*. She was also known as a poet and is shown by Utamaro, Toyokuni and others. Segawa III, same *mon* shown by Kunisada and some of his followers. She too was eventually ransomed by a blind musician named Toriyama. Agemaki, Utahime I (Kōriusai), Uta-hime II (Kiyonaga). Tamagoto, *mon Glycinia* with spiny leaves. Hatsuito, *mon* orange in a circle, Matsuyama, *mon* a star of six arrows in an octagon. In the time of Utamaro there were Matsunoi, Nak-agawa. Ichikawa a noted beauty; *mon*, feathers in a circle, *kamuro* Mitsumo and Tamamo. Utagawa (same *mon*), Yoso-oi with *kamuro* Nioi and Daidaitoshi. Utamaro also has Kisegawa with *kamuro* Takeno and Sakuno, and this might be the same as Segawa II. Yoyotose (Utamaro). In later times were Somegawa and Harukaze, Matsumura (Eisen); a Kisegawa is given by Eisui and a Wakana by Gōkyō. Utamaro also shows a Yoyojiku and Yogozuro in one print and Yoyomachi and Yoyohama in another print. Toyotosei (Utamaro).

Matsu-ya (Pine House). Branches of the main house were *Sa-no-Matsu-ya*, (situated on the left of the main house) *Matsugane-ya* and *Ko-Matsu-ya*. There is some evidence that the last was indeed the original house or perhaps the original name of the house. For the main house, Eishi has Ukimatsu, Kawasumi, Kawanoto, Matsukaze, Kisegawa (cf. Matsuba-ya).

Of the *KoMatsu-ya* are Takamura, Nanamachi, Tokiwa, Kayoiji, Shigarami, Hideoke, Kozakura, Tomioka (all Harunobu). Koriusai gives *ōiran* with the *mon* of an orange in a circle with a *noshi* bundle flanking it (cf. actor school of Segawa) all in a circle. Takamaki with *mon* of three water-lily blossoms.

Of *Matsugane-ya* is Azumaya (Kiyonaga).

Of *SanoMatsu-ya* are Utamachi and Myoharu (Torii V).

Miura-ya (House of the Three Coasts). A very old house going back to Genroku times. It was one of the small houses in the first block of Kyo-machi. In the 'lacquer' print (*urushi-e*) times was Takao with *mon* maple leaf in a circle; a later version of her is given by Kikumaro.

Monji-ya (The House of the Written Character). There were two houses, the *Daimonji-ya* and the *IchiMonji-ya*. Kurth says the last was a dependency but this seems doubtful since it was an old house and may have been named after the famous one at Kyōto. The other house may have become the main house in later times. The *Ichi-Monji-ya* had Suma-ura, Matsuyama, *mon* a leaf of the paper mul-berry in a circle, Shikitae, Hanamino (all Harunobu), Ichimoto, Hanakota, *mon*, leaf in the form of a lobster (Utamaro), Daijutsun.

DaiMonji-ya had Tagasode (Kitao Masunobu), Minazumi (Shunman), and Tsukimaro has two unnamed courtesans of the *Daimonji-ya*. Motosue (Ryukoku). Itsumoto, Motowasa (Utamaro).

NakaManji-ya. Ōtowaji (Chōki).

NakaManji-ya; see *Manji-ya*.

NakaŌmi-ya; see *Ōmi-ya*.

Nishita-ya (The Western Rice Field House) in Edo-machi. The house *mon* was the great sign 'Nishi-ta' in a circle. Kokonoe, *mon* a black and white chrysanthemum bloom. (Kurth says this is only known in a single sheet print by Hanegawa Chinchō).

Obishi-ya. Kurth says that it is only known from a print of Kōriusai's of the *ōiran* Mitsuhana.

Oe-ya. The house is depicted by Kōriusai; it was noted for having a hot spring.

Ōgi-ya (The House of the Fan). This was probably the most famous house of the whole Yoshiwara. The house *mon* was three fans in a circle (*mitsu-ōgy-maru*). There was another house of this name equally famous in Kyōto. It was the property of a fan-maker Ōgiya Uemon who had the literary name of Bokuka and was a prolific poet. The most famous name amongst its *ōiran* was Hanaōgi (Flower Fan). Hanaogi I had house *mon*; her *kamuro* were Yayoi and Yoshino. Surprisingly enough Hanaōgi II does not seem to be figured in prints. Hanaōgi III was the most famous *ōiran* in the whole of the Yoshiwara. She was a great beauty, famous as a poet and calligraphist and noted for her filial devotion to an old mother. Among her known *kamuro* were Hanamazu, Hanakazu, Hanayama, Daisaburō, Yoshino, Tatsuta and several others. She used two *mon* of which the first has two forms, being either two blossoms near a fan or three blossoms and a fan, or secondly she sometimes used the house *mon* coloured yellow and blue.

Tokiwado, Takigawa I, Matsukaze, Ninoaya, Yoyohana, Ureshino, Takamura and Kōnōito (all Harunobu), Yuba-e, Nahakoshi (Kōriusai), Hanando, (Eisui), her *kamuro* were Onami and Menami, (Shizuka of the Tama-ya had *kamuro* of the same name); Kukigawa, Kisagawa, Hanamichi and others. The last seems to have been a favourite of Utamaro and Toyokuni. Takigawa III is shown by Eishō and Tsukimaro. All seem to have had the same *mon*.

Tsukaki was the third most famous *ōiran* of the first years of the nineteenth century; Ainame, Ayame, Karakoto with *kamuro* Keriba and Wakaba; Shichikoshi, Nioteru with *kamuro* Ōmi and Miji; Yoshinobu (all Kōriusai), Matsukaze II, Chōyan, Nioteru II or III, Nanakoshi II with *kamuro* Takane and Imane, and later Miwano, Katachino with *mon* two crossed feathers in a circle and *kamuro* Shikeno and Makino, Tomioka, Takehime, Ogino with house *mon* and *kamuro* Isami and Susami (all Torii IV, i.e. Eishi). Of the time of Utamaro are Tsukasu, Hanabito, Haruhino, (Kasugano 'Spring Day Field' of Tama-ya), Sekiyu, Yōkoto, Takino-ō, Tsushima, Yoshibito. Shuman depicts a Takigawa (?) II and Eizan shows a Takigawa III or (?) IV; Miyabitō (Utamaro).

Okamoto-ya (House of the Hilly Ground). Chief *ōiran* Hanatsuru, *mon* two carnation flowers. There were several of this name, possibly four in all spanning the time from mid-eighteenth to mid-nineteenth centuries. Yoshidaka, Ihateru, Oribata. Utamaro shows Onodaki and Shushō. Both Eisen and Eizan show unnamed courtesans of this house. Ino-oka, Shirasuru, (Kiyomine).

Okana-ya. Suminoto, (Kōriusai); but see *Kana-ya*.

Okatomo-ya. Hōzan (Tominobu).

Ōmi-ya. (This was the name of a province. Also Lake Ōmi with the eight famous views.) Had a dependency the *Naka Ōmi-ya*, Utamaro depicted the main house. Ninomachi, Makiginu, Handayu, Azuma-ya, Orikoto, Azumano, Azumado (Harunobu), Handayu, Miyakaji (Kōriusai). The *Naka Ōmi-ya* in the time of Utamaro had Handayu II, *mon* clump of bamboos in a circle. Mizuura, Konomachi, and four others unnamed.

Otawazo-ya. This name occurs on an early black and grey print of Toyohiro's. It is painted on a lantern that hangs above the head of a courtesan and is probably the name of a small brothel.

SanoMatsu-ya; see *Matsu-ya*.

Sato-ya (The Village House). Kurth says he knows this house only from the work of Shunshō and Shigemasa who show a *Kado-Daisato-ya* with Hateyoe and Tamakaira, *mon* a butterfly.

Sekichō-ya. Imose (Shunkyo).

Tachibana-ya. Ō-tatsu (Utamaro).

Take-ya. Utamaki (Eishi), Eizan (Eishō).

Tama-ya (The Jewel House). House *mon* three Jewels. One of the greatest and best known houses of the Yoshiwara. It had two dependencies, the *Kado Tama-ya* and the *Yahachi Tama-ya*. The *ōiran* of the first two houses are often the same. Of the third house Kurth says 'Of this I know only Wakaume by Eishō.' Hanamurasaki, Sode-ura, Miyato, Tamagawa, Shizuka, Shinomaki, Shizutaki, Namigiku (all by Harunobu). Shizuka, *mon* kiri-*Glycinia*, *kamuro* Matsuno and Matsuyo (Kōriusai); a later Shizuka (?) II in the time of Eishi and Utamaro, with *mon omodaka* (water plantain) and *kamuro* Onami and Menami (cf. Takigawa of Ōgi-ya). Also Kōriusai gives in both houses Kasugano, (Haruhino 'Spring day Field' of Ōgi-ya), *mon* a crane in a circle, Matsuyama (Bunchō). There is a later Kasugano with *mon* three fans in a circle and *kamuro* Kochō ('Little Butterfly'), and Wakana ('Young Leaf'), and *shinzō* Uraba. Also later in both houses Tsukioka (Utamaro and pupils), Shiratama (Kōriusai), *mon Glycinia*, and in the time of Utamarō, Komurasaki, Shiraito, Sugatano, Akashi, Tagasode and Shizuhata.

Of the *Kado Tama-ya*, Komurasaki (Kōriusai), and a Komurasaki II, (Eishi), *mon* crane in a circle, *kamuro* Kikuno and Haruii. Hatsune, Shirabe, Komurasaki III by Utamaro, *mon Glycinia*, *kamuro* Kochō and Haruki. The second Komurasaki is extremely famous; a fine poet and calligraphist she committed suicide on the grave of her lover Gompachi who had been executed for robbery and murder and was later buried with him. She is looked upon as the ideal of the faithful courtesan. Hanamurasaki III, *mon* an open fan, *kamuro* Kochō and Teriba; Sekiya (Utamaro), Miyato, Haruka, Haruji, Kiyohana (Kōriusai), Tamagiku, (cf. *Manji-ya*) by Eishi. Kasugano (Utamaro), *shinzō* Uraba.

(*Shizutamaya*: a house with this name existed in the eighteenth century and may have been connected with the *Tama-ya*. The prefix is an obsolete Japanese word meaning 'poor' or 'humble' and it was obviously a cheaper and probably third-class house engaged in a more plebeian type of business. Only known in a print of Eishi's showing Shizuka, *mon* a starfish. The name of the courtesan strengthens the possibility of a connection with the Tama-ya itself.)

Tawara-ya. This house disappeared at the end of the first half of the eighteenth century and had one or more dependencies the names of which do not seem to have been recorded on prints. Of the main house are known, Yoshide, Inanome, Wakamatsu, Tamanoi (Harunobu).

Tomimoto-ya. Toyohina (Utamaro).

Tomoe-ya (House of the Tomoe figure). This was an old house which closed down before 1730. The house was situated in the Naka- and Edo-machi on the right of the great door of the Yoshiwara.

From 1688 to 1703 it was famous for the great *ōiran* Takaboshi, there was also a Hana-Ōgi. This house is often shown in the early *shunga* and in the sketches of Sukenobu.

Tsuru-ya (The House of the Crane). The house *mon* was a white crane flying on a blue ground. This was, of course, also the name of a famous publishing house. Sugawara I (Harunobu), *mon* prunus blossom, Michihana, Sugatami, Tsuru-no-o (Kōriusai); both the last named had *mons* of an ivy leaf. In Utamaro's time Shinowara was famous with *kamuro* Shinobu and Utano and *shinzō* Shinojike. Shinowara was a pupil of the artist Eishi. Later times had Shinobito, *mon* four prominent double braces making a cross with *kamuro* Niragi and Hatsuse, Sugawara (?) III, *mon* prunus blossom; Shino-shike. Utamaro gives also Ariwara. Mutsu (Eisui), Fujiwara (Eizan).

Tsuta-ya (House of the Ivy). A similar name was that of a famous printing house. The name does not appear very frequently and considering that this was a house of the first class its rarity in prints is rather surprising. It is much more frequent in the early prints and books and possibly by the mid-eighteenth century its great days were over. Shioginu, Michisato, Michiharu, Michitose, Sanshu I, Misao, Miyoshino, Senshu (all Harunobu), Hachishio with *kamuro* Futagon and Meshiki. Kurth cites another unnamed with *mon* mulberry blossom *kuwa* and *kamuro* Midori and Tokiwa; Sanshu (?) III (Gōkyō).

Utamina-ya. Shirataie (Kōriusai).

Wakamatsu-ya (House of the Young Pine). Probably a house associated with *Matsu-ya.* Kikunoe (Torii V), Midorigi, Fuchimoto (Kiyonaga).

Wakana-ya (House of the Young Greenery). Karasaki, Wakaura, Michiura, Hanagishi, Hatsukaze, Shiratama, Hanazono (all Harunobu), Shirashino, Shirayu with *kamuro* Kochō and Tomegi (all Kōriusai), Shirayu II, (Torii IV). In Utamaro's time were Shiratama with *kamuro* Kaoru and Tomaki; Wakaba, Harugiku, Shiratsuji, Shiratsuyu, Nishikie.

Yahachi-Tama-ya; see Tama-ya.

Yamaguchi-ya (Mountain gulley House), with the branch *Kado-Yamaguchi-ya* of which Kōriusai gives Ōshu. The *ōiran* Kakuyama also of this house who lived in Hōei (1704-1710) inaugurated the custom of holding a supper on the Festival of the Moon Viewing, when cups of rice wine were handed round.

Yamamoto-ya (The House at the Base of the Mountain). Found only in very early prints. The *ōiran* Katsuyama had a sister with the same name in the *Hyōgo-ya*.

Yamashiro-ya (Mountain Stronghold House). Rather rare. Matsukaze, Hatsuito, Hanazuru, Naniwazu, Miyakono, Onomatsu (all Harunobu), Karahata, *mon* a crane in a circle (Torii IV), also two other unnamed *ōirans*.

Yogo-ya. Mitsuhama (Eishi).

Yoshimura-ya. Tagasode (Harunobu).

Yotsume-ya. (The '*yotsume*' is a figure of four concentric squares inside one another with another smaller one inside these). Tomiyama, Kinzan, Sayoginu, Utagawa, Sugatano (all Harunobu), Kasugano, Tomiyama (?) II, *mon* three Water Caltrop blossoms, Tamanoi, *mon* triple '*tomoe*' in a circle; Katsuyama, *mon* three oranges with a leaf above them; Suzuyoginu, *mon* fully opened cherry blossom; Atsumaji, same *mon*, (all Kōriusai); Matsuyama I (Kōriusai), Matsuyama II (Torii IV); Nanasoto and Utagawa (Masanobu).

KYŌTŌ

The courtesan quarter here was called Shimabara: *Ichimonji-ya* in the Naka-no-chō and a similarly named house in Edo. Hantayu in *urushi-e* times.

Kokyo-ya: Hanamurasaki (cf. *Tama-ya* in Edo).

Ogi-ya: house of similar name in Edo. Yugiri died in 1678: see actor Sakata Tojurō.

ŌSAKA

The courtesan quarter here was called Shimmachi. One of its streets was the Echigo-chō.

Ibaraki-ya: Echigo-chō. Tamahagi, Yugiri in *urushi-e* times: cf. Kyotō's Ogi-ya.

Tsuchi-ya. Diagaku (Nagayoshi).

NOTE: Early in the eighteenth century it seems that the brothels of the Yoshiwara were divided into some six classes, all variously named at different times. In the era Kwansei (1789–1800), five classes were recognized: these were distinguished by the height of the bars of the cages, the bars of the lowest class running horizontally while the rest were vertical. Since 1872 the brothels have been classified into three classes. The charges are, of course, proportional to the grade of the house which does not necessarily follow the classification of a main or a branch house.

CHAPTER VII

The Stage and the Actors:
Prints of the Kabuki

OF THE three main forms of Japanese drama, the Nō, the Ayatsuri (i.e. the manipulation of puppets to an accompanying recitation, the Jōruri) and the Kabuki, only the last is an important source of subject matter for the colour prints and printed books. The Nō was always something more than mere entertainment and its appeal was almost restricted to the learned and noble classes. Very occasionally accessories of the Nō may appear on *surimono*—some prints by Shunman come to mind—and incidental wood-block illustrations may be seen in books on the Nō but in general it is not subject matter for the colour prints until the Meiji era. In those later days some rather fine designs illustrating this dramatic *genre* were produced by several artists, an especially fine set of thirty-five sheets being the work of Kōgyō who died as late as 1919.

That the Nō should not have been a subject for *ukiyo-e* is not surprising; its insistence on more profound and spiritual values precluded its acceptance by an art dedicated to the salty joys of the passing world, but that the puppet drama should also be virtually absent from the colour prints is not so easily understood since, in the seventeenth century it had had a strong appeal to the populace of Edo and continued to hold this popularity in Ōsaka and Kyōto during the first part of the eighteenth century. Koheita Yuya (Jirōyemon Toraya) had taken the doll dramas to Edo about 1635 and after he retired a new style, the Kimpira Jōruri, had immense popularity in the Shōgun's capital. However, in 1657 the fire of Meireki (see page 44) caused the doll manipulators to seek refuge in Ōsaka and whilst in that city further developments in this drama were still to be unfolded, it never regained its former favour with the Edo public. Illustrations of the Ayatsuri are to be found here and there in books: for example, the puppets are shown in one of the illustrations in the second volume of Sukenobu's *Ehon Nishikawa Azuma-warabe* (1767) and Hokusai did a number of illustrations of scenes from *jōruri* for Bokusen's *Jōruri Zekku* (1815?). The first of these was published in Kyōto and the second in Edo or, more likely, Nagoya.[1]

Kabuki, the theatre of live actors, blazing colour and superhuman tensions, from the last quarter of the seventeenth century, was a major part of the subject matter of the wood-block prints. Its popularity with all social classes in Edo was phenomenal and the demand for prints of the favourite actors and scenes remained unabated for almost two hundred years. Moreover, in several ways it stimulated new techniques and styles in *ukiyo-e* designs, without which the whole *oeuvre* would have been very much poorer.

As an example of this one may cite the fact that we seem to owe the *okubi-e* or bust portrait to its having first been used, according to recent researches,[2] to delineate actors. From such portraits on fan prints of Kabuki actors, it would appear that this kind of design was in use at least as early as the 1740s, whereas hitherto, dates between 1780 and the later 1790s had been suggested. Besides these designs, the cult of the actor and the publicity needs of the theatre brought other prints into being. As part of the publicity, painted sign boards (*kamban*) were exhibited outside the early theatres and it seems that this work was originally undertaken by some of the actors themselves. The print artist, Kiyonobu I was the son of one such and in 1696 produced the first single sheet (*ichimai-e*), black and white designs of actors which achieved an immediate popularity; in the same period too, Kiyonobu designed his first play-bills (*banzuke*) for reproduction by wood-blocks. This, of course, was the origin of the *oeuvre* typical of the Torii school and for which it was to be famous for nearly a century. At the end of the eighteenth century and for the first half of the nineteenth—especially after 1820—there grew up a demand for memorial portraits of deceased actors. These prints, *shi-ni-e*, literally 'death pictures', showed the actor in Buddhist robes and usually with a rosary and, since they seem to have been popular, it is somewhat difficult to understand why they should have become comparatively scarce. Rare too, are the prints showing the interiors or exteriors of theatres. Although the outside may be reproduced, by such artists as Hiroshige, merely as one of the 'sights' of the capital, the inside of a theatre seems usually to appear on the prints when the purpose is to show some notable performance or occasion such as the 'benefit' performance in favour of some leading actor, this being announced by the three characters '*hi-i-ki*' (i.e. 'favour') on the drapes above the centre of the stage.

But the so-called 'actor' prints comprise, for the most part, portraits of the actor in character—sometimes really no more than a mere delineation of a role and not a portrait, even as such are understood in *ukiyo-e*—and of scenes from the many and various dramas which have had ephemeral or lasting popularity on the Kabuki stage. A detailed study of them must obviously be heavily interwoven with a close study of the history of the Kabuki itself and to list and shortly to comment upon the larger part of the plays, scenes from which are delineated on the prints, would obviously be far beyond the scope of a book such as this. What can be done to enlarge the understanding of these prints and therefore to heighten the appreciation of them by connoisseurs, is to explain briefly some of the salient and unique features of Kabuki and the traditions of its actors.

The identification of actors and plays is by no means easy even when one has some knowledge of the Japanese written language; without this knowledge it is often impossible although, here and there, in certain instances, one may expect to find a helpful clue. The name of each actor is frequently inscribed on a print and where not, or where this cannot be read, it is often possible to identify the actor by his *mon* or badge, an additional aid being found to hand when the date of the print and the name of the artist are known. However, even this may sometimes be misleading since some roles in certain plays also carried their characteristic *mon*. But this is rare and possibly in ninety-nine instances in a hundred one may rely on the *mon*, if present, to identify its wearer. Occasionally a print of one actor would be re-furbished and re-issued as a portrait of another; thus, Kiyotada's *urushi-e* print of Monnosuke I (died 1729) published by Izumaya had a new name inserted in the block and a new *mon* put in place of the old one, the whole being re-issued as a portrait of Arashi Wakano in 1730, the latter having commenced his acting career in that year.

The play depicted upon a print may often be put into one or other of the categories into which the Kabuki repertoire is divided. First are the *jidaimono* or classical plays which treat, for the most part, of historical subjects although most of the actual events of the play may be pure inventions. The wigs and costumes are generally extremely elaborate and often gorgeous since they deal with princes and great nobles. Acting here is often a matter only of gesture and movement was frequently much reduced or absent. Secondly come the *sewamono*, plays of common folk, which took their themes from the everyday life of the times. The first of these plays was the *Kuruwa Bunsho* written by Chikamatsu Monzaemon in 1679 for the actor Sakata Tōjurō and, for more than two centuries such plays were favourites of the Edo play-goer. The plot of the play centres around the love of a courtesan, Yugiri, for the rich young man, Izaemon and such a plot proved to be one of the most popular in the long history of these dramas but, unlike most of the later ones, this one ends happily. The highlights of such plays were often the *nureba*, i.e. 'wet scene' or less literally, 'tear jerker'. These are generally played with great reticence, tenderness and delicacy, shades of expressive meaning being conveyed by movements of the fan (*ōgi*) or towel (*tenugui* see page 120). Sometimes, in the later prints, especially those of the later Utagawa school, one may find plays which make a special sub-division of the *sewamono*, namely the *kizewamono* or later plays of every-day life. These plays deal with the borderlands of the Edo underworld; prostitutes, gamblers and crooks of all kinds; poverty, bullying and the sordid shifts to maintain social status are the stock situations. Scenes represent peasant hovels or slum dwellings or else well-known public places such as Asakusa or the gate of the Yoshi-wara. For the most part the surroundings are squalid and the dress and general style of the characters impoverished. Such plays are by no means commonly shown in prints and a study of the few that survive, although often lacking aesthetic appeal of any kind, would yet be extremely interesting.

A few plays may be identified by the dress of the actors. Thus the *Chushingura* or more fully the *Kanadehon Chushingura* can always be named with certainty when many of the characters are seen to be wearing the curiously bold designs of black and white wedges which signified night and day and were symbolical of the fact that the loyal league of *rōnin* were ever watchful. Similarly in plays of the Sōga cycle the two brothers wear characteristic patterns on their dress; the *kimono* of Jurō is ornamented with plovers (*chidori*) whilst that of Gōro has a pattern of butterflies. Again the play *Shibaraku* is often depicted in prints by one or other of the long line of actors named Ichikawa Danjurō in the role of Gongōro, the chivalrous man. The pattern of five red lines on each side of the face, the excessively long,

13. Bunchō Ippitsusai (1725?–94). Portrait of a young actor in a female role. From the *Ehon Butai-no-Ogi* (Portraits of Edo Actors on Fans) by Shunshō and Bunchō jointly. Published by Karigane-ya in 1770. (See page 144.)

14. Utamaro. Three notable beauties of the Kanei period, Takashimaya Ō-Hisa, Tomimoto Toyohina and Naniwaya Ō Kita. Signed: Utamaro hitsu. Published by Tsutaya Jusaburō. Sealed: *Kiwame*. (See page 133.)

angular garments with their trailing trouser legs and equally long
sleeves, ornamented with the huge *mon* of 'the three rice-measures',
i.e. the three concentric squares of the Ichikawa, all proclaim the
character at that moment when, standing at the end of the *hanamichi*
(the long gangway leading at a right-angle from the stage) he
thunders, 'Shibaraku' ('Tarry a moment!').

Most actor prints show the actor in a special pose (*mie*) and very
frequently this is of the kind which involves a peculiar glaring with
crossed eyes called a *nirami*. *Hippari no mie* or 'casting a *mie*' was a
special part of the actors' art and was reserved for moments of great
emotional tension. It should by no means happen at once but very
slowly, all movement being gradually congealed into a kind of
tableau which will be held for some little time without motion of
any kind. The audience are warned that this will soon take place by
the beating of a small clapper, the *tsuke*, on a flat board. These poses
are of several kinds and in plays of the *aragoto* style (see below) are
especially exaggerated. Westerners sometimes find the delineations
of these *mie* in prints peculiarly repellent, but once the significance
of them is understood and appreciated, such an attitude quickly
passes and is no longer found to be a bar to the appreciation of the
aesthetic qualities of the work. However, it is of course true that the
tasteless exaggerations of the later Utagawa artists destroyed by over-
statement the very qualities which they sought to make impressive.

Mention was made in the last paragraph of the style of acting
known as *aragoto*. This name, which might be translated 'rough-
house stuff', is given to a form of the actor's art characterized by the
intensely bombastic nature of the performance which uses exaggerated gestures and expressions and clothes of vast proportions
decorated with enormous patterns. It was invented by the great
Ichikawa Danjurō I at the commencement of the eighteenth century
and was perfected by him and some of his successors. In general it is a
vehicle for the display of an intensely aggressive temperament and is
used to portray a kind of super-man. The make-up used with this
style is called *kumadori* and consists of broad lines drawn on the face
in such a way as to emphasize the structure of the nose, cheekbones
and chin, the colour of these lines varying with the temperament of
the character but being most often of red which symbolizes the brave,
impetuous and choleric nature. There are many types of this 'striped'
kind of make-up and they are used in roles other than those occurring

in *aragoto*. Small dark patches over the eyes signify that the character is of noble birth whilst a predominantly purple colour on the face shows haughtiness. Red faces are a sign of the loyal man and red and white of the chivalrous one; indigo and black both suggest evil whilst green is used for ghosts and light blue for calmness of spirit: examples of all of these can be found in the prints and will help to elucidate the role.

Of all the prints which showed actors in character none were more popular than the ones portraying an *otokodate* or 'chivalrous commoner': this somewhat 'Robin Hood' spirit, often a poet and musician and so very frequently shown with a flute, was dedicated to upholding the rights of commoners against the over-bearing, arrogant samurai. Their popularity with the ordinary theatre-goer was obviously assured and not least because the *otokodate* themselves were invariably the younger sons of samurai who had renounced rank and privilege to right the wrongs of the poor and revenge them on their oppressors. Skilled in judo and swordsmanship they were unmatched for strength and valour. Besides the fact that they carry but one sword and often a flute they may be identified in a print by the showy, dashing and even ostentatious pattern of their *kimono*.

Colour prints were used as programmes for theatrical performances; such have the portraits of the chief actors in the particular play and above them the title of the play and other written matter all in a very heavy type of script which is exceedingly decorative. The titles of Kabuki plays were indeed often chosen simply for the decorative possibilities of the characters used in writing them and have no very obvious meaning in many instances.

It would be impossible, except in a fairly lengthy volume, even to outline the plots of the many *kabuki* plays shown on the prints that have come down to us over two centuries. The late Mr Basil Stewart gives an explanation of some theatrical prints in two of his books[3],[4] and a very detailed account of the *Chushingura*, mentioning many of the famous prints that illustrate this play. Mr and Mrs Halford in their handbook[5] give the plots of many more, besides other details that need to be mastered by any student who would undertake a detailed survey of these theatrical prints. Of the *Chushingura* there have been many versions since the first to appear on the Edo stage in 1706 and the present version dates from 1749: scenes from this play are probably those of most common occurrence in all the colour prints that have reference to Kabuki. Almost as popular with the public who bought the prints were the plays of the Soga cycle which began when the first of such plays was performed by Ichikawa Danjurō I in 1655. This was founded on an historical incident which occurred in 1193 and which involves a fairly simple tale of revenge against great odds and of that filial piety which was so much prized in mediaeval Japan; in some instances, having the same romantic appeal to the later Edo public. In the course of time other plays were written on this theme, many of them very far-fetched and having little relation to the original facts whilst others elaborated parts of the story in a manner for which there was but little warrant. All of these make up the plays of the Soga 'world' and two of them, *Sukeroku* and *Yanone* are numbered among the eighteen plays of the Ichikawa collection.

The *Juhachiban* or eighteen most popular plays of the Ichikawa family were collected together by Danjurō VII in the first half of the nineteenth century and all of them, because so successful in their day, have appeared on prints at one time or another. Almost all contain roles that can be played in the *aragoto* style and all are spectacular in a most extreme degree. The titles are, *Kanjincho, Shibaraku, Sukeroku, Gedatsu, Yanone, Kagekiyo, Narukami, Kamahige, Kenuki, Fudō, Fuwa, Kanu, Nanatsumen, Zobiki, Ōshimo Doshi, Wuranari, Wirouri* and *Jayanagi*. The synopses of the first seven of these are given in Mr and Mrs Halford's book (l.c.).

At least one of the colour print artists left an illustrated book on the history of the *kabuki*; this is Shuntei's *Kabuki Nendai-ki* (not dated but probably about 1808). It seems, unfortunately, to be a rare work but is useful in identifying plays previous to that date. Of great importance for the identification of the plays shown in prints is the recent work of Kawatake Shigetoshi[6] which has many extremely useful plates.

If the identification of the plays represented on prints presents some considerable difficulty, the identification of the actors represented is perhaps somewhat easier. Yet even here the matter is not so simple as it might at first appear. Usually the name is written near to the actor (in a reserve in later prints) or somewhere at the head of the print; with the help of one of the works for reading Japanese names mentioned in the general bibliography and a little knowledge of the language, such as most serious students gradually acquire, it is not an impossible task to read many of these. But the names themselves can be very puzzling. The name usually given to the actor on a print is his *geimei* or professional name—the name by which his public knew him. This includes his family name, i.e. the name of the family of actors to which he belongs but not necessarily the name of his own family by birth since many actors were, and are, adopted into an acting family. Along with this is his 'given' name of which every acting family has several of varying degrees of prestige. As he progressed in professional excellence therefore, he might take on another 'given' name and so his *geimei* could be different at different times of his career. Added to this name is a number which shows his order in the succession of the name; thus, the last Ichikawa Sumizō was the sixth to hold the name and was therefore known as Ichikawa Sumizō VI or Ichikawa Sumizō *rokudaime* (the sixth). These names did not follow one another continuously but were often left in abeyance in the absence of a candidate of suitable merit.

Besides the *geimei* the actors had a literary name, *haimyō*, which however is very seldom used on prints except memorial portraits, unless it is added to the *geimei*. This was not all; each actor possessed a *ya-gō*, similar to those of tradesmen, and these all end in the syllable '*ya*'. These '*ya*' are, in effect, titles and are often founded on family associations and so have a variable origin. By strict application of the law, the '*ya–gō*' was the only one an actor was allowed to use in Tokugawa times when only nobles and samurai were allowed to have more than a 'given' name.

Apart from names however, actors may often be identified by their '*mon*' or badge: even so, some *mon* are the badge of the role being played and these can only be identified with experience; thus the *mon* of the role Ō Shichi in the play *Arashi Soga* was originally that of Arashi Kiyosaburō who first made the part famous when it was introduced into the play in the spring of 1708. Another similar role-*mon* is that of Ōboshi Yuranosuke in the Chushingura—a double *tomo-e*. *Mon* were of two kinds, the *jō-mon* which is generally that of the '*ke*' or line to which the actor belongs and the *kae-mon* which is more personal. The former is the one most often shown on prints since it is the one worn by the actor on his stage costume. Only very rarely does the *kae-mon* appear on prints showing actors in character: it was usually reserved for the private clothes although sometimes it may appear on stage clothes along with the *mon* of a role.

In any list of actors it is inevitable that one should draw heavily on that given by Kurth (l.c., see bibliography, chapter 6). In the list given here a certain amount of simplification has been introduced and several other names have been added; particularly to be noted are those of actors that appear very frequently in the prints of the Ōsaka school, and some more modern ones of the Edo stage. The subject is a very large one and only a selection can be made with special reference to the prints which however, would obviously have covered all the important actors and not a few of the others that showed some promise or who had, for a time, an obvious following among the theatre-goers.

Finally, perhaps a word should be said about two kinds of *mitate* pictures that may occur in prints of actors. One usually likens courtesans to actors or, more commonly, to dramatic roles: this is not so extraordinary as it may at first seem to be since actors specializing in female parts (*onnagata*) often set the fashion for courtesans. Such actors wore a purple square of cloth (*murasaki boshi*) on the front of the head, a custom that originally was made compulsory, by order of the shogunal government, when young men played such roles and homosexuality became rife (see Plate 13). The other *mitate* picture is not easily characterized beyond the fact that it shows a most intricate ingenuity. A good example is a print, *oban beni-e*, by Kiyohiro which shows two courtesans, Shōshō of Okamoto-ya and Tōra of Ise-ya, manipulating marionettes representing Yoshitsune and Jōrurihime in a play from the Soga cycle which is being played by the actors Sanogawa Ichimatsu and Nakamura Tomijuro. An accompanying poem compares the flower of the prunus to that of the cherry: this has reference not only to the beauty of the two girls but to the comparative excellence of the two actors, the two stage characters and the virtues of the Ayatsuri and Kabuki theatres. Such prints are rare. The art of the actors taking female parts was both difficult and delicate and great achievement in these was somewhat unusual. Schools like the Segawa specialized in these *onnagata* roles exclusively and others, like the Sanokawa, changed later in their history to portraying women. Toyokuni produced a famous series entitled *Edo Waka Onnagata* ('Actors of Edo in Female Roles') and from the undoubted success of such prints we may see how much this kind of acting was appreciated by the Edo public.

NOTES ON CHAPTER VII

[1] A few very rare single sheet prints showing one or other of the forms of *ayatsuri* have been recorded. There is a rare print by Teigetsudō (or Jōgetsudō, as read by Gookin) dating from about 1745 which shows a puppet performance being held in the Great Hall of a noble house. Also of about the same date is a print by Kiyomasa II of the puppet master Tatsumatsu Hachirōbei giving a performance with the *Tezuma-ningyō* puppets. Both Kiyomasa I and Masanobu produced prints having reference to *jōruri* plays. As an example one may cite No. 5 of Masanobu's series *Yamato Irotake* which is entitled *Teika no Michiyuki*, the name of a *jōruri* drama.

[2] Shigeo Miyao and Sutezo Kimura: *Edo Kabuki Uchiwa-e. Genroku-Enkyo Hen*, Tōkyō, 1962. Also an important review of this work by Toyohisa Adachi, 'Primitive Fan Prints': *Ukiyo-e Art*, No. 5, pp. 3–9 (Tōkyō, 1964) who shows that they were published by Iba-ya for a fan wholesaler in Horie-chō, Nihonbashi, Edo.

[3] Stewart: Basil, *Japanese Colour Prints and the Subjects They Illustrate*, London, 1920.

[4] Stewart: Basil, *Subjects Portrayed in Japanese Colour Prints*, London, 1922.

[5] Halford, Aubrey S. and Giovanna, M.: *The Kabuki Handbook*, Rutland, U.S.A. and Tokyo, 1956.

[6] Kawatake, Shigetoshi *Nihon Engaki Zenshu*, Tōkyō, 1959. The standard work on the history of Kabuki plays and their presentation is Tatekawa Emba *Kabuki Nendai Ki*. (The Chronological Record of Kabuki Plays.) 10 vols. Tōkyō, 1905. This has several hundred illustrations and is essential for research into the subject of this chapter; unfortunately no copy was available to me when writing this chapter. Also of use to those students of the prints who wish to become more exactly informed about the plays is the rather little known bibliography, Sakanishi, S.: *A List of the Translations of Japanese Dramas into English, French and German*, Tōkyō, 1935. A most useful work for the identification of actors and details of plays, especially those of the nineteenth century, is Ihara, T. *Kinsei Nippon Engekishi*, Tōkyō, 1913. This deals with the theatres of Ōsaka and Kyōto as well as those of Edo.

ADDENDUM

Actors of the Edo and Ōsaka Kabuki who appear in the ukiyo-e Prints

Here only the *geimei* of the actors are given. The *ya-gō* and *haimyō* of an actor seldom appear alone and it was the fairly consistent practice of the Katsukawa school not to use these other names by themselves. Thus we find on prints of this school, Iwai Hanshirō (Yamatoya Tojaku), Ishikawa Yaozō (Sakatakaya Takasuke) or Sakata Hangorō (Sangyō). (f. = female roles). (Ōsaka = Ōsaka school print artists).

Agemaki Rinya. Name taken between 1756 and 1760 by Azuma Tōzō I.

Ageno Hisaburō (Kiyomasa).

Anekawa Chiyozō (Torii II), Shinshirō, Magosaburō.

Arashi (This school had a much longer history than Kurth suggests.) Kiyosaburō (Torii I), Sangorō I, Sangorō II (Torii IV), Shirōgorō, Wakano (f.), Sankatsu (Torii III), Hinaji, Hikokichi, Shichigorō, Koshirō, Sanshirō Ichizō, Sampachi, Ryuzō, Tokusaburō, Sankatsu II (all early Katsukawa), Shichigorō II, Ryuzō II, (Sharaku); from this time onwards mostly male roles. Shichigorō III, Sampachi II, Jonosuke, Kanjurō, Otohachi, Shimpei. Others are, Kōkorō (f.), (Kiyomasa II), Kichisaburō I (Ashimaru) Kichisaburō II (Ōsaka), Hinaji (Bunchō), Rikan I (c. 1820 Ōsaka), Rikan II (c. 1835 Ōsaka), Tokusaburō III (Ōsaka), Otohachi I (Bunchō), Tomisaburō (Ōsaka), Koroku (Masanobu).

Asahina Saburō (Yoshikatsu).

Asao A late and rare school; first in Edo, later in Ōsaka. Yuzaemon (Toyokuni), Kozaemon, Tomijurō (Ōsaka), Gyokuroku (Yoshitaki).

Azuma Tōzō (f.) see under Agemaki. (He is shown by both Shigemasa and Bunchō.)

Bando Hikosaburō I (*urushi-e* times), Hikosaburō II (1749–1768),

Hikosaburō III (1759–1811), Aiso (Torii III), Matatarō, Mitsugorō I, Shumagorō, Kichizō, Shōzō, Umeji, Hyakushō, Hyakujirō, Sampachi, Kichizō, Nanzō, Koijurō, Kinsaburō, Hikoji (all Shunshō or Shigemasa), Mitsugorō II, Hikosaburō III, Yasutsuke (all Sharaku), Hikosaburō IV, Zenji, Mitsugorō, Minosuke, Hachijurō, Hikozaemon, Kukujurō (all Toyokuni). Hikosaburō (?) V (Kunichika), Mitsugorō IV (Sadafusa), Jutarō (1830 Ōsaka), Sucho (Kunisada), Shuka (Kunisada), Kamesaburō (late), Kunigōrō (Yoshikuni).

Eruja Tomoemon (Kunisada).

Fujikawa Murajirō (f. Sharaku), Bunzaemon (Toyokuni), Tomokichi (had considerable fame, Ōsaka).

Fujimura Hantayu (f. c. 1693–1716), Hanjurō (Torii I).

Fukawa Dairō (f. Torii II).

Fukishima Masunori (Yoshikata).

Hajino Denzaburō (Sharaku).

Hayakawa Shinkatsu (f.), Denjurō (Torii II), Hasse (f. 1703–1713, 27–28).

Ichikawa The most famous school of actors, specialists in male roles and in *aragoto*. The *mon* is of three concentric squares (rice measures) now used by junior branches of the family. There are several other *mon* of which the 'prawn and wave' and 'paeony' are now used by the senior branch when more than one *mon* is to be worn. Most famous, and the senior branch, is the Danjurō. Danjurō I, founder and leader of the school and the most famous actor of Japan. Born of samurai stock in 1650 in Narita (hence *ya-gō* of the Narita-ya). Was assassinated by Sugiyama Hanroku on the stage, 1704. He was often shown by Kiyonobu in prints.

Danjurō II (1697–1756 acting), famous as Gorō in 'Soga Yano-ne'.

Danjurō III (Kiyonobu II, *urushi-e* but not well known).

Danjurō IV at Nakamura theatre in 1758 (Torii III).

Danjurō V. Was formerly Matsumoto Kōshirō III. He was given the name Ebizō and was also known as Hakuen V. 1754–1802 (Shunshō, etc.).

Danjurō VI. Still a youth in 1790 and several prints show him as a mere boy. Born 1778, died 1799. Excelled in mime.

Danjurō VII. Born 1791. Shown by Toyokuni and Hokusai.

Danjurō VIII. Kunisada and followers.

Danjurō IX. Died 1903. After Danjurō I was most famous. He was known for his female roles. Was the first to perform before the Mikado and, with the producer Morita Kanya, was the founder of the modern stage. The title has been in abeyance since his death.

Danzō I (1684–1740) shown by Torii I and II. Danzō II (Kiyotomo), Danzō III (Shunshō), Danzō IV (Shigemasa), Danzō ?V (Toyokuni) a Danzō V is certainly shown by Kuniyoshi. Monnosuke I (acting 1700–1727, early Torii), Monnosuke II (acting 1756–1794), said by Kurth to have admitted female roles to the school. I cannot find confirmation of this. Monnosuke III (Sharaku), Monnosuke IV (Toyokuni); Yaozō I (acting 1747–1759) (Torii school); Yaozō II (acting 1751–1757) (Shunshō, Bunchō, etc.) Yaozō III very famous actor and noted for *sewamono* roles. Had the soubriquet of Tachimiya which occurs on several prints (Sharaku, Toyokuni I etc. There is also a good print by Enkyō (1796) of him which necessitates a modification of the estimate of this artist given by Binyon and Sexton). Yaozō IV or V ? (Baichōrō Kunisada); Kōmazō I (Shunshō), Kōmazō II (acting 1770–1801) after which he became Matsumoto Kōshirō V (Toyokuni, Bunchō); Tosaburō (acting 1731–1753), Masugorō (acting 1727–1741) (m. and f.) became Danjurō III in December 1735; Raizō I (m. and f.) (acting 1743–1766), later the Raizō were established at Ōsaka and appear very probably in later prints of that school; Somegorō (Kurth says middle Torii times); Tomozō; Benzō; Kōdanji; Daisaburō, Ichizō; Oyazō; Shunzō; Yuzō; Fukagorō; Reiemon; Kuzō; Dangorō; Aragorō (earlier Nakamura Kumejirō); Sankizō; Kamekichi; Chozō; Tsuruji (all Shunshō, Shigemasa, etc.). Tomozō; Omezō I (acting 1776–1800 and 1804–1824); Danzaburō; Ichizō II; Monzaburo (all Toyokuni); Ebijirō I (Hokushu)—an Ebijirō, perhaps II is shown in a print by Shunshi who also shows a Goemon; Sanen (Kunisada); Sansho ? II (Kunisada); Ganjurō (Ōsaka, 1824); Kuzō (Ōsaka, 1841); Udanji (Ōsaka, Hironobu and Yoshitaki); Kodanji (Kuniyoshi). Late prints (Meiji era) show, Somegorō, Chusha and Sumizō. There is also the long line of the Ebizō, the number and order of which are not, in my experience, to be determined from the prints. There have, according to the Halfords (l.c.) been nine up to and including the present one. The first seems to have been Danjurō II who took this name in December 1735 but the line of succession is not clear to me. Yonejirō (Kunisada), Hakuen (Yoshikuni), Yonezō (Yoshitaki).

Ichimura One of the oldest established of all schools that are still in existence. Takenojō IV is shown by Torii I and II; Kamezō (Torii I and II) and Komezō? II (Torii III); Mitsuzō (Shigenobu); Uzaemon VIII (1709–1759), Uzaemon IX (acting 1731–1785). The VIIIth was evidently a favourite since he is shown by many artists, e.g. Shigemasa, Masanobu, etc. The Xth and possibly the XIth appear to be shown by Kunisada, the XIIth by Kunisada II. The present holder is the XVIIth; Kichigorō; Hanyemon (Shunshō); Sōemon (Shigemasa); Kichigorō II; Hikosaburō III (Sharaku)—I can find no records on prints of earlier holders of this name. The Halfords (l.c.) give the name of a present member of this family as Kakitsu XVI but I can find no former ones on prints. Somewhat mysteriously the Ichimura as a whole have been much neglected by the print artists, only the VIIIth was really an exception to this. Tamakashiwa (Kyōto actor but performed in Edo in 1715) (Kiyoharu; Shichijirō (became Uzaemon X) (Kiyomitsu).

Ichiwara Yakidōgon. (This actor is recorded for a print by Kunisada. I know nothing of him or the school.)

Ichiyama Kurth knew only of Shimagorō, mentioned in a list of *mon*. I know of no others in prints.

Ishikawa Goyemon (Hirosada).

Itō Kōtayu (f.) late seventeenth century. Kurth says that he went mad and died during the Shōkyō era (1684–1687).

Iwafuji ? Applied to an actor in a male role in a print by Kuniyoshi. It may not indeed be part of the *geimei*.

Iwai This school specialized almost exclusively in female roles. Several of the great *onnagata* belong to this line.
Sagenda (acting 1700–1715); Hanshirō II (acting 1700–1710); Hanshirō III (m. and f.) (acting 1722–1756); Hanshirō IV f. (Shunshō); Hanshirō V m. (Toyokuni Kiyonaga); Hanshirō VI f. (Kunisada, Kuniyoshi); Shijaku III (Kunisada); Tamanoko (Chinchō); Kumesaburō (Shunshō)—he later became Hanshirō V (Sharaku, etc.), the drama 'Ōsome and Hisamatsu' was

written for him by Tsuruya Namboku (1755–1829); in this he took seven roles himself. Kiyotarō Koyeda (m. and f. Toyokuni, etc.); Kidaitarō; Shigaku II (Ōsaka school).

Jitsukawa Yaozō; Enzaburō; Enjaku (all in prints of the Ōsaka school and more particularly those of Yoshitaki). Enzō (Kunisada).

Kametani Jujirō (Shigemasa); Kikusan.

Kamimura Early school specializing in female roles. Kichisaburō I (Torii I); Kichisaburō ? II (Torii II).

Kanazawa Goheiji (Torii I) said to have specialized in warrior roles.

Kanzaki Miwano f. (Torii II).

Kasaya Matagurō (Shigemasa); Matagō.

Kataoka Nizaemon (Toyokuni, Kunisada), Gatō (Hironobu).

Katsuyama Matagorō (acting *c.* 1716).

Kikuchi Kojumarō (Kunisada records this name on a print).

Kirinami Onoe f. (Torii II) famous for *ōiran* roles. Mitsujirō (early Torii).

Kirinodami Kurth says that he knew only of a Monzō in Toyokuni times. I have never met with this name.

Kishita Tōtarō (Shigemasa).

Kogawa Kichigorō. In 1693 he acted with Danjurō I in Tsuwamono Soga.

Kumaju Hangorō ? I (Shunshō); Hangorō II (Hokusai).

Manazura Masakichi (Kunisada).

Matsumoto Members of this school played both male and female roles. Kōshirō I (Torii I); Kōshirō II (Shigemasa); Kōshirō III later became Danjuro V, only male roles, Kichizō (Torii I); Shujirō; Daishichi; Kojirō (all Shigemasa); Yonesaburō f.; Hachizō male roles only (both Sharaku); Kokugorō, Yonesan (Toyokuni); Kumesaburō (Kunimasa). The second Kōshirō exemplifies some of the difficulties inherent in these actors' names; he became Danjurō IV in 1754 reverting to Kōshirō II in 1770 and in 1772 he became Ichikawa Ebizō II. Koshirō IV (Sharaku) see Plate 16, also Kiyonaga.

Matsushima Hyōtarō f. (Shigenobu); Kichisaburō (Kiyomasu II produced a *hoso-e beni-zuri* print, dated 1744 showing Danjurō II as a samurai watching Segawa Kikunōjō as Ō Chiyo from whose mouth emerges her own image impersonated by Matsushima Kichisaburō from the play *Imagawa Chushingura* produced at the Nakamura-ya in that year).

Mimasuyu Sukebana (Shigemasa); Gennosuke; Inemaru (both Ōsaka school).

Miyagi Asojirō (Kunisada).

Momomura Hyakutarō (Ōsaka school, *c.* 1840).

Morita This school played male and female roles. Kanya f. (Torii II) probably was fifth of the name and certainly different from that referred to by L. Binyon and J. J. O'Brien Sexton in their authoritative book on prints (see bibliography) as Kanya VI. However, Shunyei and Sharaku depicted one identified as Kanya IX by H. G. Henderson and L. V. Ledoux in *The Surviving Works of Sharaku*, New York, 1939. If this last is truly definitive then the two former will surely have to be renumbered. The present holder of the title is Kanya XIV.

Murayama Shirōji acted *c.* 1680.

Musashugata Innosuke (Kunisada).

Nakajima All male roles. Kanzaemon I (acting 1700–1710, Torii I *tan-e*); Kanzaemon II (Shigemasa); Mioemon I (acting 1714–1762); Mioemon II (1755–1782); Sambōzō; Miōzō (Shunshō); Kanzō; Wadaemon (both Sharaku).

Nakamura A very large school with a long history and flourishing right down to the present day. Played both male and female roles. Kurth divides these actors into several groups—a practice which is also followed here.

Time of the two first Torii

Rennosuke (warrior roles Torii I); Kichisaburō (acting 1700–1708); Senya (acting 1716–1718); Takesaburō II (acting 1700–1720); Shichisaburō I (acting 1700–1707); Denkurō I (acting 1700–1713); Kansaburō I (acted 1693); Shimahachi (acted a demon king, 1693); Kojirō. (Senya acted some female roles.) Gennosuke (1715).

Time of the middle Torii

Kichibei (acting 1716–1739); Shichisaburō II (acting 1711–1773); Sukegorō I (acting 1725–1763); Utaemon I (1757–1770); Denkurō II (acting 1733–1775); Tomijurō (acting 1731–1778); Kiyosaburō II (acting f. roles, 1749–1758); Kumetaro I (acting f. roles 1748–1755); Noshio I f. (1772); Nakazō (acting 1745–1789). Shoko I f.

Time of Shunshō and Katsukawa

Matsue f. (acting 1761–1785); Sukegorō II (acting 1761–1798);

Nakazō II (acting 1778–1796); Banzō f.; Chōemon; Dengorō; Denkurō III; Gokyohachi; Gorōsan; Hanji; Juzo II, male roles only; Kaemon; Kanematsu; Katsugorō; Kinji; Kiyosaburō III; Kumejirō (was earlier Ichikawa Aragorō); Matsusai f.; Ōtarō m.; Riko f.; Senzō f.; Shichisaburō III f.; Shichizō; Shimagorō; Shingorō m.; Sukeji, Tokusaburō f.

Time of Sharaku

Mansei f.; Noshiō II f.; Tomisaburō II.

Time of Toyokuni

Daikichi; Denkurō; Komatsu; Matsue II f.; Shichisaburō III and ? IV; Kanzaburō III.

Time of Kunisada and Kuniyoshi

Utaemon III and IV; Shibajaku I and II; Denkurō III; Shikan; Sekisanjurō III. Keishi; Matsue III; Shibajurō; Enzō (Kunisada).

Time of Ōsaka print school

Baigyoku; Utaemon ? IV? Sojurō; Koraku; Matsuya; Shikan II = later Utaemon IV; Utaemon III; Sennosuke; Kumanosuke.

Nakayama A more recent school originating around 1770. Kurth suggested that it might have originated in the *onnagata* line of the Nakamura. This seems indeed to have been the case and certainly Nakayama Tomisaburō and Nakamura Tomisaburō as depicted in the prints of Sharaku are one and the same person. Raisuke (Shunkō); Tomisaburō (Sharaku and Shunshō); Kumejirō (Shunshō); Kumetarō (Sharaku). All of these acted only in female roles. Its *mon* was very close to the Yoshizawa and may denote kinship.

Ogawa Zengorō (acting 1711–1732).

Ōgino An old established school which seems to have been active at all times but is not often recorded in prints. Isaburō m. and f. (acting 1724–1747); Tatsunojō f. (Torii I); Isaburō II (Toyokuni); Senjō (Shunshō); Daikichi f. (Kiyohirō). Makinōjo (Toshinobu).

Okuna Kurth knew only Kokugorō (Shigemasa).

Onoe Played both male and female roles. Kikugorō I (acting 1769–1773); Matsusuke (acting 1756–1814); Kikugorō II (three-colour print times); Kikugorō III, noted for horror roles (Toyokuni); Tamizō (*c.* 1769); Minzō; Seizō; Kyusuke (all Shigemasa); Monzaburō; Baikō; Denzaburō; Raisuke; Eisaburō (all Toyokuni); Sanchō (Shunshō); Matsusuke II (Kunisada) (this certainly appears to be a different actor to Matsusuke I who, however, had a long stage career, Toyokuni having a print of him in character at the age of 71). Kikujirō; Baikō ? II (Kunisada); Takanōjo; Tamizo ? II (both by Yoshitaki of the Ōsaka school). Shoroku (Yoshitaki).

Osagawa Tsuneo I f. (acting 1750–1766); Tsuneo II (acting f. roles, 1763–1808).

Ōtani An old established school but its members played only male roles. Hiroji I (Torii I) was the founder of the school. Hiroemon I (acted *c.* 1693); Hiroemon II (acting 1725–1747); Hiroji II (he changed his name to Bandō Matatarō in 1736 and to Ōtani Oniji I in 1748, acted 1735–1756); Hiroji III, known as Oniji II in 1758 (acted 1755–1798); Hirozō; Uemon; Ōhachi; Senji; Tokuji (all Shunshō); (Tokuji; Oniji II, the first a noted comedian, were depicted by Sharaku); Tomoemon; Tomosaemon (Toyokuni); Tomomatsu (Sadahiko, Ōsaka school). There were others with the name Tomoemon in later prints.

Ōtomo Kuronushi (Ōsaka school).

Sagawa A small and late school. Kurth suggests that it may have been an offshoot of the Kosagawa. Shinkurō (*c.* 1770).

Sakakiyama An early school which later died out and was forgotten. Matagorō acted about 1693; Sangorō (Torii III).

Sakata An older school. After about 1770 its members became affiliated with other schools. The great Tojurō (1645–1709) acted only in Kyōto and Ōsaka. Hangorō I (early Torii times); Hangorō II (acting 1742–1782); Hangorō III (acting 1756–1795) in 1783 he changed his name to Hanjurō; Oginojō (early Torii). (Dr Florenz says that the first *kabuki sewamono* was written and acted by Tojurō in 1678; this was 'Yugiri Nagori no Shōgatsu' (The memory of Yugiri's parting in January) and Izaemon acted in this from 1678–1709). Sajurō; Dempachi; Tomigorō; Daizō; Kunihachi (all Shigemasa).

Sanjō An early school of short life. Female roles prevailed. Kantarō (acted both male and female roles, 1714–1749. He was quite famous and is shown by Torii I and II, Sadanobu, Kiyotomo and Toshinobu) = Kurth says that a Sanjō with a name ending in '. . . zo' occurs in later times.

Sankoku Kurth knew only Tomitarō.

Sanokawa In its early days its members appeared in male roles but in the middle Torii times it went over to female roles which it afterwards devoted itself to exclusively. Mangiku (acting m. and f. roles 1714–1743); Ichimatsu I (older Torii times); Ichimatsu II (acting m. and f. roles 1741–1762. He acted f. roles under the name Aizō). Ichimatsu III (Sharaku); Kokichi (about 1770); Senzō (Kiyomasa).

Sawamura A very famous school, active down to the present day and with very numerous members pictured on the prints of the Katsukawa school. The school has only acted male roles and the chief name is Sojurō, the present holder of which is the eighth. Kōdenji (acting 1700–1702); Sōjurō I (acting 1718–1755) he changed his name to Chōjurō in 1747. Sōjurō II (acting 1750s and 1760s, Torii III); Sōjurō III (acting 1759–1800, Sharaku); Sōjurō IV (Toyokuni); Sōjurō V (Kunisada); Harugorō (Torii I); Kakuzō (played a boy's role in 1778), Engorō, Tanosuke, Morijurō, Saijurō, Sawazō, Watazō, Fukumatsu (all in prints of early and middle Katsukawa school); Tatsunosuke, Tanosuke ? II; Gennisuke (all Toyokuni); Tosshō (Kuniyoshi); Tomosuke (Kunichika); Shōzan, Kunitarō (both Ōsaka school).

Segawa One of the most famous schools, active at all periods and giving only female roles. Some of the most famous *onnagata* belonged to this school. Kikunojō I (acting 1730–1748); Kikunojō II (acting 1750–1772); Kikunojō III (also took the names Tomisaburō, Rokō and Senjō, acting 1774–1810); Kikunojō IV (possibly him on a sheet by Baichorō Kunisada); Kikunojō V died 1830 but Kunisada has a posthumous portrait of him. He is shown by many of the lesser artists of the Utagawa school. Kikusaburō I (Torii I); Kikusaburō III (Shunshō); Kikusaburō IV (Sharaku); Kikujirō I (Torii I); Kikujirō II (acting 1731–1735); Yujirō (was Sawamura Shimbei, in 1767 became Shirogorō and in 1769 Segawa Yujirō reverting to Shirogorō in 1777, was Ichikawa Yaozō III in 1779, acting in all roles 1764–1808); Shichizō, Kichimatsu, Yuji, Tomisaburō (all main Katsukawa times); Kikunosuke, Osaburō, Ronosuke, Rosaburō, Michinosuke, Rokkō (all Toyokuni); Ginjirō (Kunisada). There is also a print by Toyokuni of a Segawa Senjō as a *sarumawashi* but I find no other mention of this actor anywhere. Rōkō (Toyokuni).

Seki Only known are Sanjurō I (time of Toyokuni) and Sanjurō II (Kuniyoshi and later the Ōsaka school).

Shibazaki Kōdenji (Kiyoharu).

Shimagawa A small school of first half of eighteenth century known to Kurth only by Sanemon and Ōjurō.

Shinotsuka Wakiemon.

Shubiyo Evidently a small ephemeral late school. Kanshagiko (Kunisada).

Sodeoka Shōtarō f. (acting 1716–1733).

Sodezaki Specialized in female roles. Nuinosuke (acting 1702–1711); Miwano (acting 1725–1735); Iseno (acting 1726–1745, Torii I and II); Sambuha (Torii II and Toshinobu).

Sugiyama Hanroku. (He assassinated the famous Danjuro I on the stage in 1704.)

Suketakaya Shirōgorō (Kurth gives this but it seems more likely to be a *ya-gō*.)

Takenaka or *Takinaka* All female roles and, in earlier times probably courtesans. Kasen (He called himself first Takenaka and then Takinaka; in 1743 he changed to Utagawa Shirōgorō and under this name is shown in a print by Kiyomasa. In 1749 he changed to Sawamura Sōjurō II acting 1734–1769.)

Tamazawa Saijirō f. (acting 1733–1751).

Tanimura Several actors in the last part of the eighteenth century seem to have had this name and all of them called Torazō. Sharaku depicts one such in 1794. According to Kurth there is evidence to suppose that all of them were connected with the Nakamura school. Most seem to have been identical with the Utaemon and Chōemon of that school.

Tatsuoka Hisakiku (Masanobu).

Tomijima Hachizō (first half eighteenth century).

Tomizawa Hansaburō (acting 1710–1718) he was probably the second of the name since Kurth refers to another who acted the role of Asahina in 1693. Tamijurō; Tanuji; Montarō (all first half of eighteenth century).

Tsugawa Old, ephemeral school, female roles. Hantayu; Fujimura (Torii I); Kamon (with similar *mon* to that of Fujimura Hantayu the courtesan) depicted by Torii I and II.

Tsuruya Namboku (acting 1732–1752).

Tsutsui Kichijurō f. (acting 1704–1715).

15. Tōrin Tsutsumi (1780–1820). The Niwaka Matsuri car (see page 138) caught in a rainstorm: this was the car used in the Niwaka festival of the Yoshiwara.

16. Sharaku Toshusai: Matsumoto Kōshirō IV as the fishmonger Gorōbei, from the play *Katakiuchi Noriai Banashi* performed at the Kiri-za Theatre in May 1794. Koshirō IV was noted for his good looks and his success in romantic roles. (See page 171.)

Tsu-uchi Monsaburō. Before 1730 was Ōtani Rokuzō; changed to Tsuyama Tomozō in 1751 (acting 1734–1751).

Yamakami Gennaizaemon also shown in a later print by Kiyomine.

Yamamoto Kansuke (Kunisada).

Yamanaka Heikurō (acting 1700–1722). Kiyomine in 1744 designed as a print a copy of a portrait of Heikurō acting in 1701.

Yamashina A school rarely depicted, the members of which played only male roles. Tomijurō (Sharaku); Shirōjurō (Toyokuni).

Yamashita Members of this school always acted female roles. Kinsaku I (acting 1711–1742); Karumo (early Torii); Kinsaku II (formerly Nakamura Hantayu, acting 1749–1794); Kintaro; Shōjirō; Kamekichi; Monshirō; (all early and middle Katsukawa school period); Mansaku; Taminosuke (Toyokuni); Mangiku (Kiyonaga).

Yoshizawa All acted female roles. Ayame I (acting 1713–1714); Ayame is said to have been the greatest of all the *onnagata* and wrote a book on the art entitled *Ayame-gusa*. Gokōichi; Kiyotsune; Naminosuke; Iroha.

CHAPTER VIII

Sumō: Prints of Wrestlers

JAPANESE wrestling (*sumō*) is an ancient sport; a racial dispute is mentioned in the Kojiki as having been settled by the wrestling of champions. Definite rules are known to have been introduced to govern the sport in the eighth century and at the same time the great festival of wrestling, held in July, was started. Such accounts as there are, however, make this early form of the sport seem more like *judō* but true *sumō* matches, taking place in a special ring, began in 1570 and became very popular in Tokugawa times. During this era, too, it became customary to hold the *Kanjin-zumō* (Benefit Exhibition of Wrestling) in order to raise money for the repair of temples or roads and other such charitable causes. At least as early as the middle of the eighteenth century woodcuts were used for the printed programmes of wrestling tournaments and these are usually in the same heavy script as that used for the kabuki posters.

The finer points of this sport, in which mountainous men with bulging bellies make titanic efforts to push each other out of the ring or to lift the opponent in a throw, have never aroused much enthusiasm among Europeans. The throw is made mostly by grasping the special loin-cloth made of very heavy silk and called *mawasi*. No part of the body except the soles of the feet may touch the ground nor may any part of the body slip outside the ring; either event means defeat for him to whom this has happened and therefore, apart from the throw, there is an extraordinary amount of pushing— a situation in which weight obviously counts for much. In all there are some thirty-three kinds of technical throw, push or trip.

The grades of wrestler may be told by their hair style; the highest grade wears the *ō-ichō-mage*, a *coiffure* with loose coils, like vertical wings, at the side and a queue knotted low down and fastened so that the whole stands out from the head in a loose loop in profile, looking a little like a 'bun'. Lesser grades, who are in training, wear the *kuri-mage* in which the knot is higher on the head, the hair being pulled rather more tightly from the nape and the side wings much reduced.

Beginners have the hair in a simple queue pulled up tightly from the nape of the neck, bunched together and tied on top. This is the *chon-mage*. Wrestlers of the top grade wear a long apron with a heavy and intricate fringe together with a silk sash when in ceremonial dress. The highest rank of this top grade are *Yokozuna* wrestlers and as such are entitled to wear the heavy *yokozuna* rope for a girdle together with the pendant *gōhei*. This is but one more sign of the many ways in which *sumō* is connected with the native Shintō religion.

The umpires carry a special type of fan similar to that which generals used in mediaeval times to direct battle operations and sometimes to ward off arrows. This is called the *kumbai uchiwa* and, by the colour of the cords which are attached to it, one may know the rank of the umpire. With the first, or lowest rank, the cords are black, with the second green, with the third pink and white and with the fourth, or highest, scarlet. The first rank go bare-footed into the ring, those of the second and third rank wear white socks, whilst the highest rank are entitled to white socks and straw sandals.

In prints, wrestlers are usually shown either in their ceremonial clothes or in ordinary outdoor costume. Often they are pictured with a courtesan and it was not unknown for their supporters to raise funds among themselves in order to hire such a girl for the solace of their own particular champion. A few prints show a pair of competitors and others the great *sumō* festival itself. As an example of this Kunisada designed a print entitled *Kanjin Ōsumo Kōgyō no zu* (Pictures of the exploits at the great *sumō* festival). There are also triptychs by Kunisada, Yoshitora and Yoshichika which show wrestling festivals whilst another triptych by the first named artist shows *sumō* wrestlers at a meal after a contest. Shunei made the most prints of wrestlers and interesting among these as an important document for the identification of such personages, is a print which is divided into thirty-five compartments of which thirty-two show various named wrestlers of the day and the others, umpires.

Boys certainly engaged in *sumō* and it seems at one time to have figured among the list of acceptable 'school sports', to use a term forever associated in the minds of the British with such occasions as 'Sports' Day' and 'Speech Day'. Kyōsai has left an amusing print of a Japanese equivalent (see Plate 19).

SOME WRESTLERS APPEARING IN PRINTS

Shunei Hakusai-no-suke; Raiden; Onogawa; Shachihoko; Nishi-kigi; Kurokomo; Kagami Iwahana-no-suke; Kashiwata Sogorō; Gorōmaru; Soga no Gorō Tokimuni; Suketsune; Ho-Shoei; Kin Honkei-no-tsuke; Kurokomo Otōzo; Kashiwadō Sogorō; Kusanoki.

Shunchō Onogawa; Tamikaze Kaginosuke.

Shunshō Onogawa Kichisaburō; Arakuma; Hamiwatari; Edogasaki; Washigahama; Kimenzan; Kajigahama; Sekinoto; Nishigodake; Fude no Umi; Onogawa Kisoburō; Kurate Sanko Taifu; Shusuisen Rinsaemon.

Sharaku Kumonryu Seikichi and Wadagahara Kanshirō. (These were issued as prints by Shotarō Sato of Kyōto about 1920, based on unpublished drawings by Sharaku.) Daidozan Bungorō.

Shunrō, i.e. early name of *Hokusai*. Dewanoumi and Kimenzan.

Kunisada Ibuki Shimasaemon; Arauma Kichigorō; Kimenzan Tanigorō; Haraishi Shichidaiya; Jimmaku Hisagorō; Unryu Hisakichi; Nijigadake Senyemon; Hibikinada Tatekichi; Washi-gahama Otoyemon; Shirazubi Mitsuemon.

Toyomaru Wada Hara; Ashiwatori.

Kōriusai Shaka-sa-daka. (This giant is shown in Kōriusai's print with a young girl hanging from his finger.)

Note: An important and interesting article in Japanese on prints of *sumō* is: Hoichi Naka; *Sumō as depicted in Ukiyo-e*; *Ukiyo-e Art*, Vol. I, No. 2, pp 19–27.

CHAPTER IX

The Landscape Prints

In some ways, landscape prints have seemed like an alien plant among the lush growth of *ukiyo-e* genre subjects: in some ways they were, for there is little doubt but that the interest shown by artists such as Shiba Kōkan and Toyoharu in European copperplate engravings of western views which were imported by the Dutch at their Deshima factory, contributed quite substantially to the rise in importance of the landscape theme in *ukiyo-e* prints. But the appearance of landscape, like most other aspects of these productions, did not have one single, more or less simple origin. As far back as 1690 Moronobu had published his *Tōkaidō Bunken Yezu* ('An Accurately Measured Pictorial Map of the Tōkaidō Road') in five volumes *gwajō* form, i.e. as a folding album, published by Hangiya Ichirōbei at Edo. Undoubtedly such a publication was put on the market with a view to its sale to those who had to travel in the trains of the great *daimyō* between Edo and Kyōto and the provinces served by this great highway.

Books on the art of garden making also contained illustrations which constituted, in certain instances, something akin to landscape and indeed Moronobu had produced a work on hill gardens, *Tsukiyama-zu niwa-e dzukushi*, in the year following his Tōkaidō work. There is not much doubt but that such books as these, designed as they were for practical use, were making tentative exploration of the means by which landscape could be represented in terms very far removed from the classical landscapes of the Kanō or Chinese schools of painting.

Yet another kind of book which called for illustrations of landscapes, began to appear around the year 1640: this was the *meishō-ki* or guide book. It usually contained many illustrations and was popular with pilgrims and other travellers and sightseers. Except for the purpose of pilgrimage it was difficult for the ordinary people to travel about their country in pre-Tokugawa Japan but after the time of Ieyasu the restrictions imposed on travel became progressively lighter and, for purposes of pilgrimage, the common folk organized themselves into pilgrims' clubs under a *sendatsu* or club president and set out annually on their travels some time between the end of the first half of July to the end of the first fortnight of September. For these, the *meishō-ki* served not only for a guide but as a souvenir of travel and places seen.

Representations of famous views were also used in the so-called 'magic lantern' or 'peep show' (*megane-e*). In this, the picture was put in at the bottom of a box and its reflection, in a mirror let into the top, could be viewed from a hole in the side. Many eighteenth-century prints show young girls and children with this toy and there can be no doubt of its popularity: if we rate it no higher, it seems likely that such things were playing a part in building up a demand for the pure landscape print; a demand which was to be met in the works of Hokusai, Hiroshige and a few others.

Yet the work of these artists is very different to that of the earlier illustrators of landscape. If we compare some of the well-drawn pages of more or less pure landscape in Sukenobu's great *Ehon Yamato Hiji* with a little known print by Shiba Kokan illustrated in the Hayashi sale catalogue, we can see an important stage in the transition from one type of landscape to another. The former work was produced from 1738 to 1742 and the style is not far removed from the straightforward representations of the *meishō-ki*. Shiba Kōkan was born five years after the final volume of Sukenobu's work was published yet this large print of his, dating perhaps from around 1780, imports into the art of these landscape prints new atmospheric effects, obviously drawn from western sources. These are achieved by means utterly alien to the traditional school of Japanese picture making. The scene represents Waka-no-Ura in Kishu and has been engraved on stone, printed in black and coloured by hand, the inscriptions being superimposed by wood-block engraving after printing from the stone. No doubt, for its time, this was *avant-garde* stuff and by no means popular but it was surely playing a part in slowly conditioning the Japanese *bourgeoisie* to accept an 'atmospheric' type of landscape—one showing a mood of nature or an impression of the overall aspect of a locality—and as such helped to create the market which was to absorb the enormous output of the great landscape artists of *ukiyo-e* who still lay a decade or so away in the future. Mr J. A. Michener[1] explains the sudden demand for landscape prints as the outcome of the growing mania for travel among the Japanese populace of Hiroshige's time: it is true that this was an important factor but it is not the whole explanation. We have to account not only for the demand and the sudden growth of that demand but must seek an explanation of the fact that a fully formed style, in keeping with *ukiyo-e* taste, was already in existence and that this, making use as it did of techniques utterly different from those of traditional Japanese and Chinese landscape painting, should have been immediately acceptable to the Edo public.

Mr Michener (l.c.) says that landscape probably made up some 15 per cent of the total *ukiyo-e* output. This is no doubt an accurate figure if applied to the surviving works but is probably overestimated if one includes all the prints from early times which must have perished without a trace. Even so the number of landscape prints is enormous; Uchida Minoru[2] estimated that the total number of Hiroshige's prints was 5,460 of which by far the greatest proportion were landscapes. One must add to this not only the very large proportion of Hokusai's output which was devoted to this genre but the rarer landscapes of Eisen, Kunisada, Kuniyoshi, Kunitora, Sadanobu, Sadahide and many lesser artists, as well as the fairly numerous but largely unpopular designs, in the European manner, by such artists as Shuntei whose essay in this style is not wholly unsuccessful. On looking over such a list of designers of landscape prints it is at once obvious that many of them were working in the late 1840s or after, and there is, of course, no doubt at all but that the government edict of 1842 which forbade the production of actor and courtesan prints and exhorted the artists to choose as subjects the more heroic events of history and legend, did in fact provide, as a side effect, a stimulus to draw the famous views in which so many of the travelling public were interested. Yet, although it did much to increase the number of landscape prints, it was manifestly not a proximal cause of their existence since even Hiroshige had produced some of his greatest work of this kind a whole decade earlier.

In general terms one may roughly classify the landscape prints of the late eighteenth and early nineteenth centuries into the following categories: 1. Prints in which the scenic background is of equal or greater importance than the figures. 2. The various kinds of *uki-e* ('bird's eye') print. This is the name given to those showing the influence of European perspective and of these two varieties may be discerned; *a.* those mostly figuring interior views of theatres, stores or brothels and; *b.* those devoted wholly to outdoor themes such as the ones for which Toyoharu is famous: these were evidently considered to be a new advance since many of that artist's prints of this kind have the word '*shim-pan*', i.e. 'new style' before the description *uki-e.* 3. The purely topographical print such as appears in most of the *meishō-ki.* 4. Poetic, dramatic or atmospheric interpretations of nature in which the individualistic portrayal of the moods of the weather or the season play a much larger part (see Plate 23a). In this last category, so far as the *ukiyo-e* artist is concerned, there are, apart from the very rare masterpieces of landscape by Eisen, Kunisada and a few others, only the names of Hokusai and Hiroshige. It is true that there were other artists who attempted the delineation of the dramatic quality of some natural scene or aspect of the weather but almost all of these fell into the banality of the merely melodramatic.

Of all the themes to which the landscape prints are devoted probably none proved to be so popular as the posting stations of the Tōkaidō road, that great highway between Edo and Kyōto, much of its length skirting the shore, along the 323 miles of which were fifty-three stations. Since all manner of folk, including the multitudinous retinue of the great *daimyō* had perforce to use this road it could very fittingly be considered as a theme to which the art of *ukiyo-e* might be devoted. Although many of the numerous series of prints given to this subject are entitled 'The fifty-three stations of the Tōkaidō Road' there are usually fifty-five plates: this is because a view is given of both the termini. The titles of the prints in Hiroshige's great set, the *Tōkaidō Go-ju-san eki zu-e tsuzuki yoko-e* (this full version appearing only on the cover of the original volume) serve to give in order all the stations which, with only minor variations, appear in countless other similarly named series. These are: 1. The Nihonbashi, Edo. 2. Shinagawa. 3. Kawasaki. 4. Kanagawa. 5. Hodogaya. 6. Totsuka. 7. Fujisawa. 8. Hiratsuka. 9. Oiso. 10. Odawara. 11. Hakone. 12. Mishima. 13. Numazu. 14. Hara. 15. Yoshiwara. 16. Hambara. 17. Yui. 18. Okitsu. 19. Ejiri. 20. Fuchu. 21. Mariko. 22. Okabe. 23. Fujiyeda. 24. Shimada. 25. Kanaya. 26. Nissaka. 27. Kakegawa. 28. Fukuroi. 29. Mitsuke. 30. Hamamatsu. 31. Maisaka. 32. Arai. 33. Shirasuka. 34. Futagawa. 35. Yoshida. 36. Goyu. 37. Akasaka. 38. Fujikawa. 39. Okazaki. 40. Chiryu. 41. Narumi. 42. Miya. 43. Kuwana. 44. Yokkaichi. 45. Ishiyakushi. 46.

Shono. 47. Kameyama. 48. Seki. 49. Sakanoshita. 50. Tsuchiyama. 51. Minakuchi. 52. Ishibe. 53. Kusatsu. 54. Ōtsu. 55. Kyōto (the long bridge).

Less famous and indeed less used, since more remote and mountainous, was the Kisokaidō road which constituted the inland route to Edo. This had seventy stations along its length, although Ōtsu was common to both routes. For this reason too the famous set of prints, the *Kisōkaidō Roku-ju-ku Tsugi*, i.e. 'The sixty-nine stations of the Kiso road', by Hiroshige and Eisen jointly, leaves out Kyōto (see Plate 23b). The stations, in order, are: 1. The Nihonbashi, Edo. 2. Itabashi. 3. Warabi. 4. Urawa. 5. Ōmi-ya. 6. Ageo. 7. Okegawa. 8. Konosu. 9. Kumagae. 10. Fukaya. 11. Hondō. 12. Shimmachi. 13. Kuragano. 14. Takasaki. 15. Itahana. 16. Annaka. 17. Matsuida. 18. Sakamoto. 19. Karuizawa. 20. Katsukake. 21. Ōiwake. 22. Odaii. 23. Iwamurata. 24. Shionada. 25. Yawata. 26. Mochizuki. 27. Ashida. 28. Nagakubo. 29. Wada. 30. Shino no Suwa. 31. Shiojiri. 32. Sema. 33. Motoyama. 34. Niegawa. 35. Narai. 36. Yabuhara. 37. Miya-no-koshi. 38. Fukishima. 39. Uematsu. 40. Suwara. 41. Nōjiri. 42. Mitono. 43. Tsumagome. 44. Magome. 45. Ochiai. 46. Nakatsu-gawa. 47. Oi. 48. Okue. 49. Hosokute. 50. Mitake. 51. Fushimi. 52. Ōta. 53. Unuma. 54. Kano. 55. Kodo. 56. Meiji. 57. Akasaka. 58. Tarui. 59. Sekigahara. 60. Imazu. 61. Kashiwara. 62. Samegai. 63. Bamba. 64. Torii-moto. 65. Takami-ya. 66. Echigawa. 67. Musa. 68. Moriyama. 69. Kusatsu. 70. Ōtsu.

If much of Hiroshige's fame rests on his delineation of the scenery of the Tōkaidō and Kisokaidō so, in similar manner, does Hokusai's rest on the set of views entitled *Fugaku sanju rokkei* ('The Thirty-six Views of Fuji'). It is to be noted in passing that these numerical titles do not always mean quite what they say: for example, in this instance a supplementary group of ten views brings the full number of plates to forty-six. The beauty of the peerless mountain had long been celebrated by Japanese artists and poets and Hokusai, as Hiroshige too in his late series of upright views, was but paying his tribute as one of a long succession of painters. Unlike so many other landscape subjects these views were not fixed either by locality or season.

A fundamental classification common to several series of landscape prints is the 'Eight Views'. This idea was borrowed from Chinese poetry, the term *Pa Chieh* being applied to 'The Eight Verses' or

'The Eight Periods of the Year'. The idea of the Eight Views (*Hakkei*) could be adapted to various scenes in Japan but the actual subject for each scene is the same whatever the locality. These subjects are: 1. Snow; 2. Evening Rain; 3. Autumn Moon; 4. The Evening Bell; 5. Boats returning at evening; 6. Geese Flying to Rest; 7. Sunset; 8. Clearing weather after rain. Most famous and favoured of all such series is probably the *Ōmi Hakkei* or 'Eight Views of Lake Biwa' (which is in the province of Ōmi). By custom the localities here were fixed by long usage and these were: 1. The evening snow on Hiriyama; 2. Evening rain at Karasaki (usually showing the famous Karasaki pine in a torrential downpour); 3. The autumn moon seen from Ishiyama; 4. The evening bell at Miidera; 5. Boats sailing into Yabase; 6. The wild geese alighting at Katada; 7. The sunset in Seta; 8. Clearing weather with strong breezes in Awazu. Toyohiro, Hokusai, both Hiroshige I and Hiroshige II as well as Sadahide—to name only a few—all produced one or more Ōmi Hakkei series. The last named produced all his eight on a single triptych. About 1830 Kunitora also made some extraordinary designs for an *Ōmi Hakkei* showing western influence.

In Japanese prints the category of the 'Eight Views' is to be found applied to several other localities besides Lake Biwa. To mention only a few there are the *Edo Kinkō Hakkei* ('Eight Views of the Environs of Edo') by Hiroshige; *Meishō Edo Hakkei* ('Eight Famous Views of Edo') by Hiroshige; *Kanazawa Hakkei* ('Eight Views near Yokohama') by Hiroshige and also some by other artists, this being another classical subject: *Edo Hakkei* ('Eight Views of Edo'), the most noted perhaps being Eisen's; *Meishō Hakkei* ('Eight Famous Views') by Gosotei Toyokuni; *Tōto Hakkei* ('Eight Views of Edo'—Tōto being an old poetical name for this city) by Hiroshige; *Tōto Shiba Hakkei* ('Eight Views of Shiba', a district of Tōkyō) by Hiroshige; and, closely related to these by a simple extension of the number, one could perhaps add Hiroshige's *Tsuki Niju Hakkei* ('Twenty-eight Moonlit Views'). Lastly, mention might be made of what is probably the best work of that unfortunate artist, Hiroshige II, published in 1861 by Hiranoya, the *Sumidagawa Hakkei* ('Eight Views of the Sumida River').

Prints showing beautiful women of the day as 'The Eight Views' are not so strange as at first they appear to be. The term '*Hakkei*' may be punningly written with different characters which give to it the meaning either of 'The Eight Rivalries' or of 'The Eight Assignations'.

Rather rare but typically *edoko*-like in spirit is a series of prints issued by the publisher Izumiya in the period 1830–1844; these are entitled *Irozato Sanju-san kashō musoko junrei* ('Pilgrimages to the Thirty Three Places of the Gay Quarters'). This is an intentionally irreligious travesty on the usual thirty-three places of religious pilgrimage and the set is mentioned in the article by Mr Shigeo Miyao referred to on page 144.

Yet another favourite theme for landscape prints is the *Mutsu Tamagawa* ('Six Jewelled Rivers'). Here the themes for each river were fixed by reference to an ancient poem and all were linked together by the fact that each river shared the name *Tama*. The rivers and the associated poems are:

1. Kinuta River, Settsu Province: 'The soughing of the wind in the pine trees deepens the autumnal loneliness, where the fullers beat by the Tama River.' Toshiyori.

2. Noji River, Yamato Province. 'Perhaps, coming again across the fields of *Lespedeza* to the Tama River, we may find once more the reflected moon awash in the ripples.' Toshiyori.

3. The Ide River, Yamashiro Province. 'Reining my horse by the Tama River of Ide, he drinks his fill where the yellow roses are blossoming.' Toshinari.

4. The Chōfu River, Musashi Province. 'In the vale of the jewelled river, the cloth hung high on the hedges shakes off the morning dew.' Sada-iye.

5. The Kōya River, Kii Province. 'Taking the waters of the Tama River of Kōya in a spell of forgetfulness, the traveller may enter oblivion.' (These waters were thought to be poisoned. The poem has overtones of Buddhistic significance.) Kobo-Daishi. (Prints usually show the Kōya waterfall with pilgrims.)

6. The Noda River, Mutsu Province. 'Salt blows the evening wind in Mutsu, carrying the cry of the plovers over the far expanse of fields.' Nō-in.

Other subjects which are of fairly frequent occurrence in landscape prints are those depicting waterfalls and bridges. Of the former the most famous set is probably the *Shokoku Takimeguri* (lit. 'Going the round of the country's waterfalls.') of Hokusai. The plates in this series show waterfalls in the different provinces, all of them noted beauty spots. Perhaps most famous of these, and the one most frequently found in prints is the *Roben* Fall in Sōshu—Kuniyoshi has a triptych devoted to it—a sacred locality of Shintō: men are often shown standing under the fall in the ice-cold waters. Famous bridges were also a favoured subject of the landscape artists and especially noteworthy in this category is Hokusai's *Shokoku Meikio Kinran* ('Views of Famous Bridges in the Various Provinces'). Hiroshige's *kakemono-e* ('Monkey Bridge') is perhaps, with Hokusai's 'Great Wave', the most famous of all Japanese landscape prints.

Views of Edo were always in great demand and especially, one would suppose, among its multitudes of visitors. Hiroshige produced many series of such views with titles such as *Tōto Meishō*, *Edo Meishō* and *Kōto Meishō*, the so-called 'Hundred Views of Edo' (*Meishō Edo Hyakkei*) (actually 118 plus the title page) being composed of some of the most frequently met with of all landscape prints: by the same token the series contains some of the weakest of his designs.

Fairly frequently met with also are plates from various series of views in the different provinces of Japan. Hiroshige II produced a set—the *Shokoku Meishō Hyakkei* ('A Hundred Views in Various Provinces') in imitation of the famous series by the first Hiroshige, *Rokujuyo Shio Meishō Dzu-e* ('Views in more than Sixty Provinces'), actually a set of sixty-nine plates plus the index. This set contained several plates that rank amongst the finest prints that that artist ever designed. Hokkei also published a series of thirteen designs with the title *Shokoku Meishō* (Famous Views in Various Provinces) but they are rarely met with.

Hiroshige particularly, produced several series of landscape designs which depict scenes other than those mentioned above. These are, for the most part, rare and one would suppose that the demand for them was never so great as for the traditional themes and places which have been previously listed. Possibly the most esteemed of such series is the *Kyōto Meishō* ('Famous Views in Kyōto') which comprises ten sheets of *oban yoko-e* format. The finest of this series is generally considered to be the snow-covered Gion temple. Another rare series is the *Honchō Meishō* ('Famous Views of the Main Island'). Ōsaka also had at least one set devoted to it—the *Naniwa Meishō* ('Celebrated Views of Ōsaka') but it would not appear to contain any very noteworthy prints and does not seem ever to have been reprinted. One or two of the Ōsaka school of *ukiyo-e* artists, particularly Sadanobu, seem to have been inspired to make an attempt to emulate these and other prints by Hiroshige but, with very few exceptions, their designs are entirely mediocre.

In 1858 there appeared a curious series of views by Hiroshige, the *Sankai mitate sumō* ('Mountains and Seas compared to Wrestlers'). Each of the plates has the title printed on a fan-shaped panel similar in outline to that of the fan used by umpires at wrestling bouts. Earlier than this had appeared the same artist's *Nihon Minato Tsukushi* ('The Harbours of Japan'): such a theme seems to have had a fairly widespread appeal since ships entering a harbour appear not uncommonly on more than one sheet in such series as Gakutei's *Tempōzan Shokei Ichiran* ('Views of Tempōzan, Ōsaka') of 1838 and Hokkei's *Shokoku Meishō* ('Some Celebrated Views in Various Provinces').[3]

Whilst almost all landscape prints were issued in a series with a single title a few were in fact issued as separate sheets. Such were Hiroshige's famous *kakemono-e* prints and the remarkable designs of Hokujiu, who worked in a curiously strong idiom of European derivation and in a personal style, the products of which were works of great impressiveness.

NOTES ON CHAPTER IX

[1] Michener, J. A.: *The Floating World*, London, 1954.

[2] Uchida Minoru: *Hiroshige*, Tōkyō, 1930 (in Japanese).

[3] For those students of the print who wish for more detailed information on landscape prints as well as descriptions of many of the series, sheet by sheet, reference may be made to Stewart, S.: *Subjects Portrayed in Japanese Colour Prints*, London, 1922. The larger part of this very large work is devoted to the landscape prints and is invaluable as a work of reference. It is lavishly illustrated, by modern standards, and one can hardly agree with Michener's unnecessarily harsh stricture that 'the majority of prints illustrated are boring'. Mr Michener however is one of the few modern writers who have made acknowledgement to this work although it is obviously consulted by many.

CHAPTER X

The Prints of Birds, Flowers and Fish

A RECENT important article by Dr R. T. Paine[1] has thrown much light on the origins of this kind of print and should be consulted by all who are likely to be interested in this subject. Originally bird and flower themes—the exact association of which seems to have depended on their mention in old poems—were derived from Chinese sources and as such would obviously have made their appeal to a more cultured and erudite audience than that to which the ordinary *ukiyo-e* print was directed. However, in the Kyōhō era (1716–1735) there appears to have been a developing taste for this kind of subject among the *chōnin* class and the theme had the added attraction, as far as the publisher was concerned, of being one that had the approval of the government.

The earliest single sheet prints of this subject seem to have been those of eagles and hawks drawn by Torii Kiyomasa I and published in 1716. They were all of large *kakemono-e* size and for the most part show these powerful predators about to attack their prey. This large format for bird and flower prints seems to have lasted until 1735 after which such subjects appeared on *hoso-e* sheets. Dr Paine has shown that Masanobu produced several notable works in this genre but that for the most part his designs seem to have been copied from the well-known book, *Wakan Meihitsu Ehon Tekagami* by Ōoka Shumboku published in Edo in 1720. Indeed, both Masanobu and his follower Toshinobu seem to have copied quite slavishly from various book sheets—a custom common enough at that time. The same article also illustrates and discusses a most interesting calendar print of 1727 by the little known artist Hanegawa Wagen (active 1716–1735) which shows small birds with the leafy culms of bamboos, the characters of the long and short months being hidden between the leaves of the bamboo. No doubt a careful search would show other such prints of birds and flowers (*Kwa-chō*) put to such a use in the eighteenth century. Shigenaga is another artist who produced several sheets in large *kakemono-e* form and some of these seem indeed to have been copied from the work of Masanobu. The bird which figures very commonly in these illustrations, and other later ones, is variously called by authors an eagle or a hawk; it is in fact the *kumataka* or hawk-eagle (*Spizaetus nipalensis orientalis*). In several prints however the golden eagle is depicted. This bird, called by the Japanese *Inu-washi*, is most frequently shown attacking a monkey and Kiyomasu was responsible for a magnificently vigorous print of this subject.

Many later artists set themselves to the production of *Kwa-chō* and the greater number are probably in the form of complete albums rather than single sheet prints. Of this kind, most noteworthy are Masayoshi's *Raikin Dzu-e* or 'Depictions of Foreign Birds' of 1789.[2] The first volume has ten double-page illustrations of birds and flowers and two pages showing Chinamen who are said to be the importers of the birds figured. In 1793 the same volume was again published with Utamaro's signature, and later another edition appeared, once more with Masayoshi's signature but without the plates of the Chinamen. Utamaro also published an extremely fine album of bird studies in 1796; this was the *Momochidori kyōka awase* ('Contest of Humorous Poems on Innumerable Birds'). It seems that the publisher, Tsutaya Juzaburō, ran a competition among the buyers of his books in which they were invited to send in *kyōka* verses to match the subjects of the plates announced by him. These were selected by Yadoya no Meshimori and printed, with illustrations by Utamaro. The work really forms part of a three-volume publication of which the first was the famous *Ehon Mushi Erabi* ('Book of Insects') and the third the *Shiohi no Tsuto* ('Book of Fishes').

Hokusai designed two famous sets of *kwa-chō* which, because of their size, are known as the small and large flower sets respectively. The earlier, smaller sheets—each of which has a poem as well—derive fairly markedly from Chinese painting although they show a charming adaptation to the *ukiyo-e* colour print style. The larger, and incomparably the finer, dating from about 1830, have no poem but show a freedom of approach and a rhythmic sensibility that make them masterpieces of their kind. Hiroshige was responsible for several bird and flower sets and especially notable are those in *ō-tanzaku* and *chu-tanzaku* form (see Plate 3). Nearly all of these sheets are among the greatest works he ever produced and are much sought after. Since these sizes are those used for the slips of paper on which poems are written it is fitting that each should have on it a short verse. Besides these artists, some fine sets of prints of birds and flowers were produced by Sekkyo, Sugakudō (active 1850–1860) and Bairei (active 1880–1895). The best of Sugakudō's designs are of high quality, the finest being perhaps the red parrot and the white heron (see Plates 12 and 17). His fame rests on two sets of prints, the *Shiki-no-kwachō* ('Birds and Flowers of the Four Seasons') of 1861 and the *Shō utsushi shiju hachi taka* of 1848 distinguished by the canary-coloured borders of the prints and the finely *gauffraged* printing; a supplement was published in 1860.

Fishing was a pastime indulged in by court nobles during the Heian era but other classes gradually became interested in it and in at least one locality, namely the Izu peninsula, the samurai practised it in Kamakura times. In Tokugawa times more and more of the towns-folk of the *chōnin* classes took up angling as a pastime and several books on it were published. Of the greatest importance in populariz-ing the sport however, was the publication in 1820 of the *Chōkyaku-den*: it stimulated the manufacture of various new patterns of rods, reels, floats and such and increased research into the habits and kinds of fish generally.

The sudden and widespread interest in angling must have been a very powerful inducement to publishers to commission prints of fish. It is true that for a long time before this fish of one sort or another are to be found in illustrated books (e.g. the third volume of the *Kenshi Ga-en* by Kanyōsai of 1775) and in *surimono* (e.g. Mr Hillier[3] reproduces a *surimono* of horizontal *ō-tanzaku* format show-ing *ayu* fish (*Plecoglossus altivelis*) with carnation, iris and other plants. This is by Kubo Shunman and would probably date from about 1805). But the fish print did not become a significant part of *ukiyo-e* output until the later *surimono* of Hokusai, Gakutei and Hokkei together with the notable single sheet productions of Hiroshige. Of the latter's work in this genre there are two sets, generally known as the large and the small. The large sheets have each a poem and the small are without; both represent some of the artist's best work apart from that of the finest of his landscapes. Much later in the nineteenth century, several albums of designs figure some charming studies of fish, perhaps the most notable among them being those of Kyōsai. Unlike the associations of birds with plants there

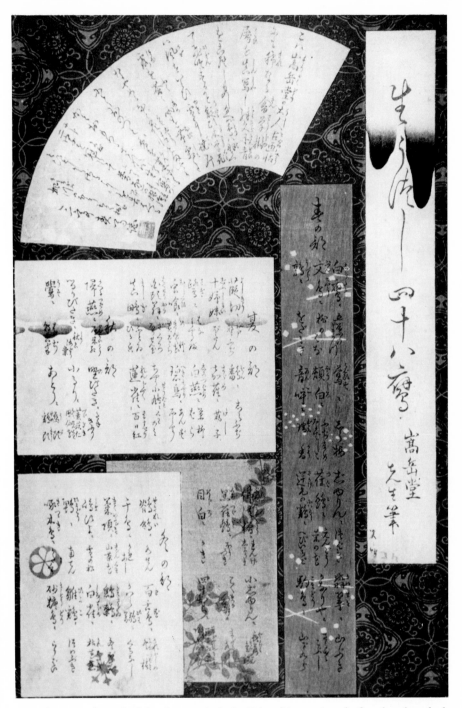

17. Title page of Sugakudo's *Sho Utsushi hachi Taka*: this was issued after the plates had been published and is dated one year later, i.e. 1859. The publisher, Koeidō, first issued these as *ichimai-e* and later in book form. The titles of the plates are represented as being written on poetry papers (*shikishi*). (See page 244.)

18. Kunisada II (1823–80). Scene from the *Genji Monogatari* with the Genjimon in the top left-hand corner denoting Chapter VI: 'The Saffron Flower'. This is really a *mitate* picture since the young couple carrying the umbrella *aigasa* fashion are in the dress of Tokugawa times and the incidents are scarcely related to those of the sixth chapter of *Genji* in which Genji, in a time of thick snow, visits the ugly, red-nosed daughter of Prince Hitachi. Signed: Baichōrō Kunisada. Sealed: *Aratame* with date seal, Snake Year First Month (1857). (See page 197.)

appear to be no fixed relationships between fish and plants or anything else.

In the cataloguing of bird and flower prints there is a good deal of inaccuracy: a useful work for this purpose will be found to be that of the Marquis Hachisuka.[4]

NOTES ON CHAPTER X

[1] Paine, R. T.: 'Japanese Prints of Birds and Flowers by Masanobu and Shigenaga'. *Oriental Art* (new series) vol. IX, No. 1, pp. 22–34. Spring, 1963.

[2] An interest by Japanese society in birds is very ancient. Even in the tenth century aristocrats held contests (*Kotori-awase*) between singing birds and in these contests, colour, song, plumage and rarity were all taken into account in judging the entries.

[3] Hillier, J.: *The Japanese Print; a new approach*, London, 1960. Plate 38. There is also an extremely interesting print of fish on plate 39. One of the fine flower studies of this same artist, always to be considered as rare, is shown on plate 37.

[4] Hachisuka, M. U.: *The Birds of Japan and the British Isles*, C.U.P., London, 1925. This gives, besides the scientific names of all the species of birds, the Japanese and the English names and all of them so correlated that identification of the various kinds of birds shown in prints, is greatly facilitated.

CHAPTER XI

Prints of Heroic, Historical, Legendary and Mythological Subjects

SUBJECTS from this vast field were not well represented in the *ukiyo-e* colour prints until the last few decades of their existence. During the eighteenth century a few sheets, it is true, are given up to historical and legendary events and personages, but they are decidedly uncommon: this is somewhat strange since there are several books of the seventeenth century with many illustrations of this kind, e.g. *Shōgun Ki* (Records of the Shōgun) 1664; *Honchō Kokon Retsujo Den* (The Lives of Ancient and Modern Heroines) 1668 and several illustrated versions of the historical work, the *Heike Monogatari* (Tales of the *Heike*). No doubt the urban *chōnin* of Edo, like those of our larger cities in Elizabethan times, responded more readily to the lurid versions of the stage than to the more sober, if highly selective, heroic and semi-historical accounts of the older writers. Yet, during the second decade of the nineteenth century, stimulated no doubt by the various prohibitory edicts of the government, by its general policies and by the internal situation of the country after more than two centuries of semi-isolation, there arose an ever-growing public demand for this type of print. Artists such as Hiroshige, Kunisada, Kuniyoshi and, in a later generation their followers, combined in the production of an ever-increasing flood of such subjects, the numbers of which seemed only to stimulate the demand for more. The part that these played in the re-vivification of the strong nationalistic sentiments of the people has yet to be studied in detail.

So great is the range of the material from which artists drew for illustrations of this kind that the student must necessarily consult both the work of Stewart mentioned in the notes to chapter 10 (or his earlier and shorter book of similar title[1]) and the famous work of Joly[2] or perhaps preferably, the more usable and accurate volume by Edmunds,[3] which last however is completely unillustrated. In this present chapter only a few of the main themes can be mentioned, besides which, a few series, the titles of which are likely to puzzle the student and collector, are singled out for explanation.

The earlier members of the Torii school seem to have been especially drawn to illustrate the story of Watanabe no Tsuna and the demon who haunted the Rashōmon in Kyōto (see Plate 5a). The hero, told of the demon which infested this gate of the city, decided to wait all night for its appearance. At two in the morning, when dozing, he felt a tug at his helmet whereupon he drew his sword and cut off the arm of the demon who was hovering above him. Several pillar prints, the form of which was eminently suited to the vertical composition required by this subject, are to be found among the productions of the first half of the eighteenth century.

During this period Masanobu produced several prints devoted to the illustration of incidents in the life of Benkei. This giant, who lived in the twelfth century, was said to be eight feet tall and as strong as a hundred men. He posted himself at the end of the Gōjō bridge in Kyōto and challenged all comers. Finally he met and was overcome by the young Yoshitsune who, little more than a boy, had yet been trained in swordsmanship by the *tengu* king, Sōjōbō. In a few prints Benkei is sometimes referred to by his alternative name of Sen-ninkiri.

Yoshitsune and his half brother Yoritomo are often depicted in incidents which occurred during the Gempei wars. These two belonged to the Minamoto clan who fought the Taira or Heike family which was finally annihilated at the battle of *Dan no Ura*—in part a naval battle—the crowded incidents of which have become legends, each being the subject of more than one print especially in the nineteenth century. The other famous battle of these wars was that of *Ichi-no-tani*, the castle of which name belonged to Tomomori the son of Kiyomori. This castle faced the sea and at the back of it was the steep mountain pass of *Hiyodori Goye* which traditionally was said to be too steep even for monkeys. Yoshitsune descended the pass at the head of his troops and at full gallop, so surprising the enemy at the back gate of the castle. This battle is shown in many prints and Kuniyoshi has a fine triptych showing Yoshitsune looking down from a great height at the castle and troops below. It was after this battle that the young Taira noble, Atsumori, who had betrayed his presence by playing on the flute, was killed by the old warrior Kumagai who later, filled with remorse, became a monk. Kuniyoshi has several prints of all these and other incidents from the Gempei wars: so has Hiroshige in a rare and unnamed series published by Fujihiko about 1840.

Scenes from the lives of the poets Narihira and Komachi (described on pages 124 and 126) are shown as illustrations of historical events and not as *mitate* pictures only. In the same manner we find sheets illustrating the story of Ōta Dōkwan the *daimyō* who, caught in a rainstorm, went to a poor cottage to borrow a raincoat (*mino*) but the young girl there brought him instead a yellow rose (*yamabuki*) thus signifying that she had no raincoat since the *yamabuki* has no seed (= *mino*).

Scenes involving swordplay, murder and assassination were also seemingly much in demand in later times and typical of these is the rare series by Hiroshige 'Chiuko-adauchi dzu-e' (Illustrations of instances of fidelity in revenge).

In the fourth and fifth decades of the nineteenth century prints of warriors seem to have become almost as popular as those of beauties in the same decades of the eighteenth century. The following are a few titles of this kind of subject as given by Mr B. W. Robinson[4] in his invaluable monograph on Kuniyoshi and his work:

Tsuzoku Suikoden gōketsu hyaku-hachi-nin no hitori (The one hundred and eight popular heroes of the Suikoden). A popular Chinese historical novel.

Tsuzoku Sangokushi yeiyu no ichi-nin (Popular heroes of the history of the Three Kingdoms).

Seisuki jimpin sen (Characters in the Gempei (=Seisuki) wars. Taira and Minamoto heroes).

Buyu hyaku den (One hundred stories of warriors).

Buyu nazoraye Genji (Warriors compared with the chapters of Genji): a very novel form of the *mitate* picture!

Honchō kendō ryaku den (Abridged stories of our country's swordsmanship).

Oguri ju yushi no ichi-nin (The ten brave retainers of Oguri Hangwan).

This very short selection will serve to show the almost endless subjects that could be obtained from the biographies and legendary history of warriors, noted swordsmen and loyal retainers.

The hundred poets and the six famous poets also provided subject matter for many series but none were perhaps so famous as Hokusai's *Hiakunin-isshiu Ubaga yetoki* (The Hundred poems recited by the nurse). Similar series by Kuniyoshi and other Utagawa school artists followed in later years.

The Six Famous Poets (*Rokkasen*) were: Kizen Hoshi in a priest's robes with a fan; Ariwara-no-Narihira with a quiver of arrows on his back; Sōjō Henjō in a priest's robes; Ōtomo-no-Kuronushi in full ceremonial court costume; Bunya-no-Yasuhide, also in court dress and the poetess Ono-no-Komachi.

Central to the understanding of hundreds of prints of diverse kinds is the *Genji Monogatari*, the work of the tenth-century novelist, the Lady Murasaki Shikibu. Every one of its fifty-four chapters has been the subject of illustration by woodblock prints and many form the essential point of one or other of the numerous *mitate* themes based on it. Western readers know it through the fine and moving translation by Arthur Waley and those familiar with this work will not be greatly troubled to place the subject matter of the prints that were designed to illustrate it. This is simplified by the *Genjimon*, a device found in one or other of the upper corners of the print, each of the fifty-four forms referring to a separate chapter of the work. A list of these with their respective *mon* will be found in the work of Koop and Inada (see page 247). Only the first thirty-one chapters deal with the life and loves of Genji himself and several series were devoted to the illustration of these, particularly so in the nineteenth century when the novel became more popular through Bakin's *Ehon Genjio meizo* (1804). One such series, not entirely negligible, is that by Kunisada II, a sheet from which is illustrated on Plate 18.

Myths, legends and bits of folklore were sometimes used to make a kind of Tōkaidō road *mitate* series. Several of these exist by such artists as Hiroshige, Kunisada, etc. and there is a series in which Hiroshige, Kunisada and Kuniyoshi all collaborated, the *Tōkaidō go-ju-san tsui* (Pairs for the fifty-three stations of the Tōkaidō). There are series too in which famous ghosts are paired with the stations of the Tōkaidō and such subjects are chosen as the Goblin cat; Ubume, the old woman of the underworld who gives the lone passer-by a child to hold which becomes heavier and heavier (see Plate 20) and Umi Bōzu, a kind of apparition of the western ocean—a sort of tortoise with a human head. Ghosts and apparitions are indeed the subjects of several prints (see Plate 5a) and the citizens of Edo evidently had a considerable taste for the supernatural which was seemingly shared by those of Ōsaka since some of the prints of the

Ōsaka school also show them (see Plate 20). In a similar way historical, heroic and ghostly scenes were associated with the Kisokaidō, e.g. Kuniyoshi's *Kisokaidō rokuju-kutsugi no uchi* (The sixty-nine stations of the Kisokaidō), one sheet of which shows Abe no Yasuna with his wife who is changing into a fox—her true form.

Chinese themes for this class of subject are not uncommon. Of such is the curious series by Kuniyoshi, *Ni-ju Shi ko Dōji Kagami* (The Twenty-four Examples of Filial piety). Illustrations of scenes from classical Japanese stories are fairly common and there are several series devoted to both the Genji Monogatari and the Ise Monogatari, the former having the chapter denoted by the presence of the *genjimon* on the print. The five festivals (*Go-sekku*) are also a not uncommon theme for a series and may consist either of straightforward representations of the subject or else be some kind of *mitate* or analogue of it. The five are as follows: first day of the first month (*Shogatsu*), i.e. New Year's Day. Congratulatory poems were written on this day. Third day of the third month (*Yayoi*). The doll's festival for girls. Fifth day of the fifth month (*Tango*). The boys' festival. Often shown with emblems of iris sword or paper carp. Seventh day of the seventh month (*Tanabata*). The Weaver's festival. On this day strips of coloured paper with poems written on them were hung over the doors of houses. Ninth day of the ninth month (*Chōyō*). The chrysanthemum festival.

Somewhat related to these are prints of the *Takarabune*, the treasure ship that sails with the gods of good fortune. This boat sails into port on New Year's Day and to sleep with a picture of it under one's pillow ensures lucky dreams. Such prints are rather uncommon in the West but they were produced by many artists including Hiroshige, Hanabusa Itchō, Taiga and many later artists (see Plate 5b). A very fine series from the collection of Mr C. H. Mitchell of Chicago were auctioned by Sotheby in October 1962. The Seven Gods of Good Fortune are:

Daikoku. Attributes are the mallet and a rat. With the former he produces riches.

Ebisu. Son of the above. Bearded, smiling and wearing a cap with two points. He is the patron of fishermen and god of daily food: he often carries a rod and a carp or basket of carp.

Fukurokujiu. Tall, bearded and with a tall head: attributes are the crane and the tortoise. He is god of longevity.

Benten. The goddess of learning and speech and also the goddess of love.

Hotei. With an enormous belly and wreathed in smiles. He carries a great bag full of precious things and is the god of contentment.

Jurōjin. A solemn old man with a tall head and a hat with the circle of the sun on it. He carries a staff and a scroll. He is a god of longevity.

Bishamonten. Clad in full armour and carrying a pagoda shaped shrine and a lance. He is a god of riches of Hindu origin and not often shown with the others.

The first, second, third and sixth of the above are sometimes shown alone on prints and with a frequency of about that order. They appear more especially on *surimono* where they are also sometimes represented only by their attributes.

Somewhat related to the above but derived from Chinese sources is the rare series by Hiroshige, *Fukutoku Kane no Naru ki* (Money Bringing Trees). This, in a sense, is a *mitate* on a theme that is to be found in the folk prints of China. The sheets show women as emblematic of such things as 'The Tree of Good Behaviour' and 'The Tree of Good Looks'.

The illustration of pure Japanese myths is rather rare in *ukiyo-e* art: the reasons for this are obscure. Certain single sheets by later artists were, however, given up to well-known themes of this kind and Stewart (l.c.) mentions a rare series by Hiroshige (*Honchō nen reki dzu-e*—'An Illustrated Calendar of Japanese Events') which depicts some of the most popular myths. Three are listed and these are, in fact, of subjects which have been treated also by other artists; they are:

1. Izanagi and Izanami, the husband and wife sent by the gods to consolidate the land and to people it with their progeny.

2. The dance of the immortal Ame-no-Uzume to lure the sun goddess, Amaterasu from the cave into which she had retreated from her brother.

3. Urashima and the Daughter of the Dragon King. He had caught her when she was in the form of a turtle. He married her and lived three years with her under the waves but, returning for a brief visit to earth, he found three centuries had passed and shortly after he dropped dead.

Related to such myths is that of the wild women of the mountains who have the generic name of Yama Uba. Many prints from as far back as the first half of the eighteenth century show the famous strong boy, Kintarō or Kintoki, with one of these women or, as one version has it with his real mother Yaegiri, or as another version records, the woman who found him when lost, Sakata no Tokiyuki. This infant Hercules is often shown suckling his mother. He may, however, be seen with an axe or wrestling with a bear. This was a favourite subject of Utamaro. Kuniyoshi illustrates this theme under the title Sarashina-hime and her son Shika-no-suke.

Two dances are frequently shown in prints in one form or another. One is the *Shakkiyō* or lion dance, in which the performers wear long reddish hair reaching to the ground and carry peonies in their hands. The other is the *Sambasō*; in this the dancer wears a mask and a peculiar shaped hat which in profile looks somewhat like a mitre but from the front is conical and painted black with a red disc on it. Usually he carries a fan. The mask is that of an old man with tufts of hair on the forehead and at the corners of the mouth.

In this chapter no more has been attempted than the briefest survey of some of the more frequently occurring themes associated with this type of subject matter. It should, however, be sufficient to illustrate the great diversity of the sources from which *ukiyo-e* artists drew, in later times, for material on which to base their illustrations. Moreover it may help to direct the student as to where to search in order to identify the subject of any print that may fall into this category and for this the references here given are essential.

NOTES ON CHAPTER XI

[1] Stewart, B.: *Japanese Colour Prints and the Subjects they illustrate*, London, 1920.

[2] Joly, H. L.: *Legend in Japanese Art*, London and New York, 1908.

[3] Edmunds, W. H.: *Pointers and Clues to the Subjects of Chinese and Japanese Art*, London, 1935.

[4] Robinson, B. W.: *Kuniyoshi*, London, 1961. The student will find this is a particularly useful book for reading the titles of such series as illustrate the subjects covered by this chapter as well as being a model of what a monograph on a single print artist should be. Since Kuniyoshi lived late on in the history of *ukiyo-e* this book will be found to be extremely helpful to the student in many ways quite remote from the restricted field of the study of this artist's prints.

Part III

The Print Productions of Cities other than Edo

CHAPTER XII

'The Classical School': Print Albums of the Kamigata

THE TITLE, 'The Classical School', is the name given by Mr O. E. Holloway to albums of prints produced in Ōsaka and Kyōto during the eighteenth and nineteenth centuries. Mr Holloway's book[1] is indeed the basic reference for the student who wishes to extend his studies into this field which may be considered relatively unworked and uncollected when compared with the Edo *ukiyo-e*. There is evidence in the very considerable rise in the prices commanded by these albums in recent years that Mr Holloway's study is doing for the Kamigata prints what Professor Kuroda's essay did for the Nagasaki-e in 1924: no doubt it will prove to be germinal for a whole range of future research.

The social life and outlook of the townsfolk of Kyōto, Ōsaka, Kamakura and other cities of the Kansai was completely different from that of Edo which lay in the Kantō region to the east of the dividing control point in the Hakone pass. Kyōto, besides being a centre for the older 'court' culture of Japan was also the centre of a rich manufacturing district and some great industries, like the textile industry, were almost entirely in the hands of its townsfolk. Wealthy, with aristocratic tastes and a certain amount of feeling for the distant past—a not too serious antiquarianism—the Edo *ukiyo* culture appeared to them somewhat vulgar and shallow. Nor was the judgment of the populace of Ōsaka very different: rich city of millionaires, centre of the great granaries and of the rice Exchange, proud possessor of ancient rights which even the shōguns had been unable either to take or filch from it, the population was one which, for the most part, depended upon and modelled its tastes upon those of the great merchant bankers. The Swedish scientist Thunberg, who visited it in the last half of the eighteenth century, likened it to Paris and there must indeed have been several similarities. The two cities were the chief centres of the Kamigata.

During the first two decades of the eighteenth century this vast non-samurai population of cultivated clerks and artisans was in the midst of a crisis of uncertainty and disorientation. Buddhism was distrusted, Shintō neglected and Christianity forbidden. The art of the Tosa school was palling; that of the Kanō tiring, whilst the ideals of *ukiyo-e* had little to offer these careful, meticulous, somewhat tradition-orientated folk. After the fall of the Ming dynasty in China in 1644 more and more refugees from the Manchus reached Japan through the Chinese trading post at Nagasaki. With them came the ultra-Confucianism of the Chinese literati and the associated ideals of the gentleman-scholar and the amateur painter and calligrapher.

This culture of the *bunjin* or literary man was typified by the seemingly careless and unstudied paintings called *bunjinga*. Because during the Yuan and Ming dynasties the Chinese *bunjin* lived south of the Yangtse river, their school of painting was called *Nanga* (Southern Paintings) to differentiate it from those of the northern school (*Hokuga*)—the art of the academies. The soft, sensuous poetical brushstroke of the *Nanga* was more easily mastered than the nervous, modulated, sinewy stroke of the *Hokuga* with its emphasis on the value of ink tone. Many were the would-be teachers of the *Nanga* style; still more were the would-be pupils. From this situation two things arose very quickly: firstly there came into being a number of 'professional', in the sense of career, artists of this style and secondly, there arose a great demand for albums of their work, partly for the intrinsic aesthetic enjoyment to be obtained from them and partly because they could serve as manuals of instruction. Prints of the work of these masters, designed by them and beautifully printed, making use of most of the techniques which had evolved to that date and deriving a style from the *Chieh-tzu Yuan hua chuan* (Handbook of the Paintings of the Mustard Seed Garden) (see page 24) were in ever greater demand in the cities of the Kamigata. These are the albums of 'The Classical School', a title selected by Mr Holloway because the *Nanga* school returned to the roots of the humanism of the continent: in this sense it is indeed apt.

In 1731 the notable Chinese artist Shen Nan-pin arrived in Japan and the two Japanese artists, Kusumoto Shiseki (1712–1786) and Ryōtai (Kanyōsai) (1719–1774), the latter a poet-priest, went to Nagasaki to study with him. Taiga Ike (Taigadō) (1723–1776), a distinguished literary figure, calligrapher and Zenist, learned the

Nanga style of painting from a Chinese work, the Pa Chung Hua P'u.
By 1780 the whole of the 'Mustard Seed Garden' had been translated
into Japanese and had been published by Hishiya Magobei of Kyōto.
Before long native manuals were appearing in apparently fairly large
editions. Studies of the work of Shen Nan-pin by Ganku (1749–
1838) were published in eight volumes under the title Ransai Gafu in
1772 and influenced a generation of Nanga painters, the leader of
whom, Chikuden (1777–1835) a Confucian of the Oka clan, published his influential Sanchujin-jōzetsu (Talks on Painting). By this
time the Chinese influence had been given a purely Japanese
character and it is the illustrations of these albums and many other
such, that constitute the prints of this school, 'The Classical School'.

It is to be noted that these prints are album prints: the single sheet
was never utilized by this school for any of its work although, in the
west, one may often come across single pages that have been torn
from their albums and are consequently very difficult to place
(especially in the absence of a signature) without a knowledge of the
albums in their original state. Pornographic works (shunga) are likewise never met with in the work of this school: in view of the
overall adherence to the Confucian code it would have been strange
if these artists had turned to such productions.

Most of the work which fills these albums was designed for the
printed form; their pages are not transcripts of paintings. One has
only to compare such paintings as that by Taiga Ike, the Shunju
Sansui Byōbu ('Spring and Autumn Landscapes on Folding Screens')
in the collection of Mr I. Dan of Tōkyō or the Shuchu Baishōgyō Zu
('Picture of Fishermen Selling Octopuses from their Boat') by
Chikuden[2] with prints by these artists in Mr Holloway's book, to see
how true this is. Yet the printing of these albums differs in some ways
from that of many ukiyo-e sheets: prints of the classical school make
much greater use of colours shaded on the surface of the printing
block; many passages are printed, in the manner of the Chinese
albums, without outlines (see Plate 11) and in some instances the 'outline' is actually printed over the graded wash which has been first
applied by blocks to the same area. There is also another rather
curious matter concerning the printing of these works, it is this: the
Chinese editions of the 'Mustard Seed Garden' and the 'Ten Bamboo
Studio'—at least the earlier ones—used stencils in part, both for their
effect and also because, according to the original introduction to the

first volume of the former, great difficulty was experienced in finding capable block-cutters and printers. Later Japanese editions of these two works seem to have made use of stencils for their reproduction and this was done with very great success—so much so, that it is not always easy to tell whether a plate has been printed by stencils or by wood-block. The art of stencilling had reached an extraordinary degree of perfection in Japan where it was almost exclusively used for the printing of textiles. This being so it is almost unbelievable that stencils were so seldom used for Japanese prints.

As might be expected in view of the position of Kyōto as a textile centre, the few artists who did design stencil prints were inhabitants of that city and almost all of them seem to have been actively at work there only in the last decade of the eighteenth and the first of the nineteenth centuries. Some like Chōshu (Nagahide?) worked in the *ukiyo-e* idiom—a rare occurrence in Kyōto—others published albums of prints representing several schools. The best known of the artists who designed for stencil prints are Hotta Renzan (Shimbei Yukinaga), Yanagawa Shunsui, Chōshiu and Harukawa; all appear to have been residents of Kyōto. In addition, certain very cheap prints were produced by the method of stencilling and, since they were often given away with patent medicines, they are known as 'medicine prints'.

Many of the prints of this classical school give the impression of being in the nature of sketches and certainly one feels that the artists eschewed anything that might seem to be academic. The titles of many of these albums support this view since it is characteristic of the school to use for this only the artist's name followed by the word *Sōga*, i.e. 'rough sketches', a word intended to be in opposition to *mitsuga* (detailed drawings). Even more commonly the titles of these books of the classical school end in the word *Gafu*, i.e. 'a picture book'. The artist's name may precede the word, e.g. *Chikuto Gafu* (An album of pictures by Chikuto) or, more rarely, a descriptive title may be followed by '*gafu*', e.g. *Yamato Jimbutsu Gafu* (A Picture book of Japanese Figures). Never, in the works of this school, do we find the title preceded by the word '*Ehon*' (An illustrated book) as in so many works of the *ukiyo-e* school; indeed, the word itself never seems to appear in the titles at all. Sometimes, where the work of various artists has been collected together, the word *Bunko* (a library or collection of books) is used in the title. Such a work is the *Ariwara*

Bunko (Ariwara Library), an extremely important collection of drawings by artists of the *Nanga* and Chinese schools, collected and published by Ariwara Baizan of Fushimi.

A perusal of the Ariwara album, as of many another such work of this group of artists, shows that the subject matter of their art could be almost anything and everything. Many of these sheets are conceived as *haiga*, i.e. as illustrations to *haiku* poems. Illustration is not perhaps a very good word for this since the picture is almost a visual extension of the verbal experience of the poem itself. These tiny poems—only seventeen syllables in length—aim at a kind of transcendent *significance* rather than a *meaning* in the ordinary sense of that word. Mr Holloway, quoting Professor Blyth, well says, 'In *haiga* as in *haiku* the most delicate feelings are to be portrayed as though they were everyday occurrences. The subjects are usually small things, or large things seen in a small way.' It was in keeping with the concepts, techniques and ideals of this school that much of the best work should be associated with the *haiku* poem and probably this is an orientation fundamental to the Japanese outlook on life and art as many of the *ukiyo-e* prints are accompanied with the joking or satyrical *kyōka* poems. The difference between the *haiku* and the *kyōka* is also to a certain extent the quintessence of the difference between *ukiyo-e* and *nanga* as between the ways of the Kamigata and of Edo.

Human figures—poets or peasants for preference but any class or calling except heroic or mythological beings—were subject matter for the drawings of this school. Mostly they are a kind of recollection of the figures seen in classical Chinese landscapes and nearly always they are treated with humour and humanity. Not only is this kindly humour in keeping with Zen, an influence near to the surface in many of these sheets, but it is also redolent of the true Confucian virtue of 'jen' or 'human heartedness'. Flowers also are a very common theme, indeed the orchid, bamboo, prunus and chrysanthemum were the four basic models set for the practice of the beginner who desired to command the fundamental brush-strokes of the school. Birds, fish, insects, frogs, shells, puppies and bats appear almost in that order of diminishing frequency. Landscapes too, are of frequent occurrence in these albums: in general, they are in the nature of *interpretations* of Chinese landscape paintings rather than anything like direct copies.

Mr Holloway gives the titles and short particulars of some fifty-nine of these albums and this list is an essential reference for the would-be collector. Not very uncommonly however one meets with single sheets torn from some book of this sort and, in the absence of any data concerning their provenance, only a search through the original volumes in one of the larger libraries, will give the necessary details.

NOTES ON CHAPTER XII

[1] Holloway, O. E.: *The Graphic Art of Japan; the Classical School*, London, 1957.

[2] Convenient reproductions of these paintings and of others of the Classical School will be found in Professor Tokuzo Sagara's *Japanese Fine Arts*, Japan Travel Bureau, Tōkyō, 1949.

19. Chikamaro (=Kyōsai). From the series Tōkaidō Nanwa Tempōzan (The Tōkaidō at Tempōzan, Ōsaka), a noted beauty spot: it has the sub-title *Kodomo sumo shōran* (viewing children wrestling). Seals: 1 of the Carl Meinzi Collection; 2 of the publisher "Daikin" = Daikakuya Kinjirō; of the censor: *Aratame Tiger 6* (sixth month = 1866). (See page 179.)

20. Ōsaka School. Kunimasu (*fl.* 1830–50). The ghost Ubume, an old woman of the underworld who asks passers-by to hold the child she carries. Gauffrage printing and colours with delicate silver-powdered lines in the hair. *Chuban Tate-e.* Kunimasu Goshotei used the name Sadamasu on actor prints published about 1830–44. In the absence of other identification it might seem possible to identify the subject of this striking print with the ghost of O-Iwa from the *sewamono* play *Yotsuya Kaidan* by Mamboku Tsuruya. Since most Ōsaka School prints are illustrations of Kabuki actors in roles, this would have the advantage of being in keeping with the usual subjects of these prints but the child is certainly not a recently-born one and the face of the ghost is not hideously deformed.

CHAPTER XIII

The Nagasaki-e

ONLY during the last forty years have these prints been invested with any importance. The scholarly essay of Professor G. Kuroda[1] first brought them to the notice of collectors in Japan and of western scholars. Two years later, in 1926, appeared Mr Nagami's[2] two contributions to their study but as all these works were in Japanese, these prints were still not greatly valued by the comparatively few western collectors who had acquired them. In 1939 N. H. Mody[3] published his collection of Nagasaki prints and paintings in two rather sumptuous volumes and, marking a decided rise in the interest of scholars and connoisseurs, prices began to increase. After the last war this trend continued but by this time three great collections had come into being; Professor C. R. Boxer's, General Pabst's (later bequeathed to Professor Boxer) and the late Mr Ikenaga's, now in the Kobe museum. Professor Boxer himself has added much to our knowledge of these prints by the publication of two very scholarly essays on the subject.[4]

The *Nagasaki-e* are colour prints made by printing from woodblocks and published in the port of Nagasaki during the eighteenth and first half of the nineteenth centuries. A few of them have colour added by hand but this is usually confined to the brighter hues, the browns, blacks and deeper reds all being printed from blocks. These prints have nothing whatsoever to do with the *ukiyo-e* prints of Edo and their subject matter is very much more restricted: apart from maps it is confined entirely to the ships of China and Holland, to illustrations of the Chinese and Dutchmen who had reached the trading posts at Nagasaki and to as many aspects of the life and learning of the Dutch as the artists could become acquainted with. Neither have they anything to do with the woodcuts produced in the Nagasaki district by the Jesuit missionaries and Japanese Christians (*c.* 1595–1610), very rare specimens of which have survived to this day: nor must they be confused with the *Yokohama-e* (see chapter 14). For the most part the prints are unsigned and of those that do bear a signature almost all belong to the nineteenth century; moreover, the names of these artists signify little since nothing is known of them and it has been supposed that most of them were interpreters and servants of the Dutch in their tiny island trading post of Deshima in the bay of Nagasaki.

The designs of most of these prints show foreign influences. Many of those depicting China and the inmates and incidents of the Chinese trading station were derived seemingly from native Chinese illustrations of the Ming dynasty whilst those showing the Dutch and other foreigners were often free transcriptions of European copper-plate engravings, some of which can still be identified as the source material, but mostly the originals remain unknown.

The sizes of these *Nagasaki-e* were larger, as a rule, than the *ukiyo-e* sheets of Edo and this is especially noticeable in the earlier prints: indeed it may be taken as a character useful for dating (although with a good many exceptions), that the oldest are the largest. The earliest known print produced in Nagasaki, according to Professor Boxer, measures 80 × 60 cm. but this size is exceeded by other eighteenth-century prints, e.g. one of a Dutch ship of 1790 measures 53 × 99 cm. whilst the oldest *dated* map of Nagasaki—one published by the firm of Toshima-ya in 1764—exceeds this since it measures 100 × 65 cm. In the nineteenth century the tendency was for the sizes to be reduced and by the 1860s they are not noticeably different from the prints of Edo.

The colours used in the last half of the eighteenth century were a light brown (called *cha-iro* or 'tea colour'), indigo blue, a bright *tan* red and black but after about 1795 the colours of the *ukiyo-e* prints were used. The marked degradation of colour caused by the importation of German aniline colours which so affected the Edo prints was not so marked in the latest *Nagasaki-e*. This blue used in many of the *Nagasaki-e* prints is usually of a more vivid and intense hue than that to be found in the *ukiyo-e* prints and in those prints that date from about half way through the second decade of the nineteenth century it would seem to play an increasingly dominant part in the colour scheme. The range of the greens in these productions is also rather more than one will usually find in *ukiyo-e* sheets of the same date.

The subjects depicted in these prints are more restricted in their range than those found in the popular plebeian art of Edo although the variety within that range was probably originally fairly extensive. In keeping with the sources of their inspiration they may be divided into two main groups; the first comprising subjects derived from the inhabitants of the Chinese factory and the second, subjects—often parallel ones to those of the former—derived from the Dutch factory. In Europe at least, the Chinese subjects seem to be decidedly the rarer of the two and are seldom to be met with in salerooms, a position which, to judge by the evidence of old sale catalogues, was not very different half a century ago. No doubt to the Japanese the nationals of China would never have seemed so strange and exotic as the *Oranda* (Hollanders), and the very strangeness of the latter would no doubt have ensured better sales for any prints that dealt with them.

The Chinese subjects which are represented in these prints are: views of the harbour of Nagasaki with Chinese ships in the offing, views of the Chinese factory, portraits of Chinese either singly or in twos or threes, Chinese with Japanese prostitutes at a party (but these are never obscene either in the design itself or in the inscription and always the interest lies, most clearly, not with the lady but with her foreign patrons). More rarely one finds prints of the things imported from China and more especially exotic mammals and birds, and finally there are the *Nagasaki-e* prints which are copies—usually somewhat free—of original Chinese wood-block prints of the late Ming or early Ch'ing dynasty: since, in fact, many of the Chinese who came to Nagasaki seem to have been in effect refugee sympathizers of the deposed Mings and so strictly traditionalist, the obviously Ming inspired pictures vastly predominate. As in prints of Hollanders, children are fairly frequently represented and one of the commonest of this kind of print shows a beautiful young Chinese mother and child on a balcony whilst another depicts two young Chinese boys, one teaching the other to read. The first is obviously 'from the life'; the second, equally obviously, from a late Ming print.

If we substitute Dutch for Chinese in the descriptions contained in the last paragraph we shall have a very generalized account of the main subjects of the *Nagasaki-e* so far as they were concerned with the Hollanders. But there are some other matters, based upon the people and trade of the Dutch factory at Deshima, that greatly extend the range of these prints. It must be remembered that the ordinary Japanese citizen had far less opportunity of seeing the 'red-haired barbarians' than he had of encountering the visitors and refugees from China since the latter were allowed much greater freedom to move about than the former who, confined to their little island only some three acres in area, were scarcely ever allowed to leave except once a year when some of them made the journey to Edo to pay homage and to give presents to the *shōgun*. Even on these occasions, as Kaempfer tells us, they were surrounded by such a host of guards and inspectors and so hurried upstairs or into the back rooms of the inns at which they stayed on the journey, that the populace would scarcely ever catch a glimpse of them. In addition, once or twice a year, a few, and those mostly the physicians under the pretext of gathering medicinal herbs, were allowed to walk in the adjacent country but this proved to be so expensive that it was a privilege which was probably seldom utilized. Under such conditions and with their added strangeness, prints of the Dutch would be likely to have a greater appeal.

It is characteristic of the 'Dutch type' of *Nagasaki-e* that these yearly journeys to Edo form the subject matter of quite a number of prints. These show the *Opperhoofd* or factory director accompanied by several of his compatriots, most of them playing various instruments, Indian and Javanese servants as well as, in earlier prints, negro slaves. The Dutch flag is usually carried ahead. In later prints there are, in addition, such adjuncts as elephants, chariots and camels and the designs for many of these were no doubt taken from European engravings. The influence of these engravings was very considerable for, since the Dutch introduced books and prints originating in other European countries than Holland, the *Nagasaki-e* drew for inspiration on a rather wider range of illustration in the 'Dutch type' than in the 'Chinese type'. Since several of these transcriptions of European engravings have no wording in European character upon them whereas others have the words 'Hollandsche' or 'Hollander' it might well be that the former, in some instances, originated in other countries of Europe.

Other countries, and especially their peoples, were, as we know, a very considerable source of interest to the Japanese of the eighteenth and early nineteenth centuries. This interest was fed by a series of illustrated books, all of them published by firms in Nagasaki. These *bankoku* (i.e. works on foreign peoples) are all very rare today and, since their sources were mostly from European works, many of which, if used in similar manner now, we should consider 'out of date', the illustrations therefore show some of the peoples of Europe in dress that may well be a century or more earlier than the date of their printing in Nagasaki (see Plate 10). The most important of these books are:

Kwaitsu Shōko and the *Zōho Kwaitsu Shōko*, published in five volumes by Nishikawa Kurinsai, probably in the last decade of the seventeenth century. There is a largely imaginative map of China with representations of Chinese men and women and Chinese armed junks. There are maps of North and South America, Europe, Africa and Asia and there are woodcuts of various foreigners and of foreign sailing vessels.

Bankoku Jimbutsu Dzue. Printed at Nagasaki in two large sized volumes on very good paper in 1720. Natives of many foreign countries are shown in the woodcuts and their names are taken from both Dutch and Latin. It is exceptionally rare (see Plate 10). The work is by Nishikawa Jōken.

Bankoku Ichiran Dzusetsu by Furuyama Genrin, illustrated by Ōoka Naokatsu of Ōsaka. It was published in two volumes in 1810 and deals with the customs of foreigners, their houses, furniture and appurtenances.

The contents of such books show clearly some of the major subjects illustrated in the *Nagasaki-e*; thus there are pictures of Hollanders and their women-folk (although only two of the latter are known to have been at Deshima because European women were forbidden), views of the Dutch settlement, views of interiors of Dutch houses (although these were confined to book illustrations), representations of ships and quite often other foreigners, in the form of Indian or African servants. In the earliest years of the nineteenth century the interest of the designers and their public widened to include some aspects of European scientific techniques and instruments and we find such things shown as a Dutch doctor performing a surgical amputation. In addition to subjects like this, several maps of Nagasaki itself were published and these are among the oldest productions of the Nagasaki printers; indeed, it has been claimed that a map of the world, showing forty-two different types of foreigners, produced during the Shōhō era in the year of the Cock and hence in 1645, is the oldest known of the surviving Nagasaki prints. The late Mr Ikenaga and Professor Boxer considered it more likely to have been a production of Ōsaka or Kyōto and this certainly seems more in keeping with what we know of the development of printing at that time.

The publishers of *Nagasaki-e* are given in the list of publishers (page 103) but of these, four firms are by far the most important. That of Hariya is the one that produced the earliest dated prints but very few designs by this firm are known. They probably started production around 1720 but their oldest known print cannot be earlier than perhaps a little before 1750. The prints of Toshimaya are very rare—nearly as rare, at least the early ones, as those of Hariya —whilst those of Bunkindō and Yamatoya are later and very much more common. Most of the publishers marked the prints that they produced in later times, either with their seal or with the full name of the firm but, as a rule, the earlier prints can only be attributed to a particular firm on grounds of style.

NOTES ON CHAPTER XIII

[1] Kuroda, G.: Professor, *Seiyo no Eikyo wo uketaru Nihongwa*, Kyōto, 1924.

[2] Nagami Tokutaro: *Nagasaki Hangwa shu* and *Zoku Nagasaki Hangwa shu*, Tōkyō, 1926.

[3] Mody, N. H.: *A Collection of Nagasaki Colour Prints and Paintings showing the influence of Chinese and European art on that of Japan*; 2 vols., London and Kōbe, 1939. According to Professor Boxer, Mr Mody died during the last war and the fate of his collection is unknown: this is a very serious loss but the two volumes of what is really a catalogue of his collection, although now become very rare, have salvaged much for us.

[4] Boxer, C. R., Professor, *Jan Compagnie in Japan, 1600–1850*: The Hague, 1950. The first part of chapter 5 of this extraordinarily interesting work deals with the *Nagasaki-e*. It provides a very detailed discussion of some of the early prints and is the most accessible of all these sources of reference. Professor Boxer has also provided for scholars a painstaking account of a single type of these Nagasaki-e in his essay, 'Rin Shihei and his picture of a Dutch East-India ship, 1782.' *Trans. Asiatic Soc.*, Japan. Tōkyō, 1932.

A more recent and very important article is that by Mr Kurasuke Watanabe: 'Nagasaki kyu no han hajime Yamatoya'. *Ukiyo-e Art*, No. 2, Tōkyō, 1963. This deals with the origins of the Yamatoya firm and lists and dates some of their important nineteenth-century prints. The author argues that there was not the same decline in the Nagasaki print as in the contemporary *ukiyo-e* ones.

CHAPTER XIV

The Yokohama-e

THE HISTORY of the *Nagasaki-e* was to be repeated in quite extra-ordinary detail in the prints which depicted foreigners in Yokohama (and later elsewhere) after the advent of the Americans and other western nations into Japan following on the arrival of Commodore Perry and his 'black ships' in 1854. Yokohama had been a mere fishing village before it was opened as a trading port for Europeans and Americans in 1859 and native interest in the foreigners—now much easier of access than the Dutch had been at Nagasaki—was even more intense than it was in the eighteenth century. It was in-evitable that the *ukiyo-e* print artists, at this late date left with little more than a few now thread-bare themes, should have turned their attention to this exciting new subject. Moreover, it would seem probable that the now hard-pressed government commissioned at least one of these artists, Sadahide, to make drawings of the American officers and warships some years before Yokohama was declared an open port.[1] Thus the stage was set, an interesting new theme for the prints had been provided and government approval had been gained; it is little wonder that, for a few years, these prints were to enjoy a popularity almost greater than any others of the time.

Yet, unlike the other kinds of print dealt with in this section, they were not products of Yokohama itself: all of them were, in fact, printed in Edo by the same publishers who produced the *ukiyo-e* prints and indeed, by the same artists. Some eight or ten publishers in all seem to have been responsible for them but by far the most prolific were the firms of Kawaguchiya and Yamaguchiya. For the most part the artists who designed these prints were late members of the Utagawa school and were of that generation that had been pupils of Kunisada and Kuniyoshi. As Dr H. P. Stern[2] has shown, these artists probably played the very important role of public relations officers to the foreigners that were now coming to Japan in increasing numbers. The most important of these artists was undoubtedly

Gountei Sadahide (1808–1874), a man who certainly had the makings of a great artist (as I have argued elsewhere!) but whose misfortune it was to have worked in the latter part of the period of the decline of the prints. By the time of his death the days of the true *Yokohama-e* were over and even prints of foreigners and their buildings and inventions—at least prints of any pretensions to qualities of design and excellence of engraving—were not to last beyond the end of that decade and by this time most of these kinds of picture had Edo and not Yokohama as their locale.

The subjects chosen by these artists are extremely similar to those of the *Nagasaki-e*. The earliest, as in the case of the latter, were maps both of Europe and America and, a little later, others of the port of Yokohama and of places which were under guard in these times of national emergency: all of these map prints are now very rare indeed and are seldom to be seen in the salerooms of Europe and America although probably rather more common in Japan. Also, as with the *Nagasaki-e*, a theme almost as early in its development in the Yokohama-e is that of the foreigners' ships and Sadahide especially seems to have had an interest in these. Mostly they are depicted on three, five or six sheet prints which show the roadstead at Yokohama with a group of foreign ships at anchor or coming to anchor, all of them of the old paddle-wheel kind and of a size which is greatly exaggerated. The foreigners are rowed out to them, stores are taken aboard and sailors climb about the rigging—the latter a matter which seems to have had perpetual fascination for Sadahide.

Later come pictures of the foreign merchants and their ladies (see Plate 8); first of all, in twos and threes, but later in larger groups; at parties in foreign houses and also in prints of coteries of the foreign gentlemen, in the gay quarters, with Japanese courtesans. As with the *Nagasaki-e* too, there are portraits of Chinese merchants and servants, for the nationals of this country extended their trade with Japan at the same time as the Europeans and Americans. Yet some of these prints, particularly perhaps those of interiors, in certain instances, are copied from American and European engravings as Stern (l.c.) has shown. This practice became increasingly common in the next few years as trade with the west opened up and communications became speedier and so we find prints of balloons in America as well as views of London, Nanking and Paris; most of such prints are the work of Yoshitora. It is perhaps of some interest to note in passing that these copies of European engravings were not completely new to the Utagawa school for, nearly thirty years ago, G. A. Wainwright[3] showed that Kuninaga was responsible for a *ukiyo-e* style print of the Meroe pyramid of Egypt which was based on several lithographs of F. Cailliaud whose work was published from 1823 to 1827. Since Kuninaga's print is dated 1829 it is obvious that, even in those days, European work could become available in Japan with quite surprising rapidity.

As with the *Nagasaki-e* there are, too, prints of exotic animals—a tiger in a cage, an elephant—imported by the foreigners, whilst their sports and entertainments become the subjects of these prints with increasing frequency. Indeed, some of these latter left their mark on the *Yokohama-e* for several years: a notable example of this is the visit of the French Circus—Mons. Soulier's Cirque Imperiale—in August 1871. Portraits of the *equestrienne*, Madame Soulier, did duty for prints of the women of several European nationalities during the immediately succeeding years.

The following artists are known to have designed one or more of these *Yokohama-e*: Gōuntei Sadahide (1808–1874), Issen Yoshikazu (working 1850–1870), Ikkeisai Yoshiiku (working 1850–1870), Shozan (?), Sensai Eiko (?), Ichimosai Yoshitora (working 1850–1880), Ichigeisai Yoshitomi (?), Ichiryusai Yoshitoyo (1830–1866), Yoshifusa (?), Ikkeisai Yoshinobu (1838–1890), Yoshimori (1831–1885), Ippōsai Yoshifuji (working 1850–1880), Ichieisai Yoshitsuya (1822–1866), Ikkaisai Yoshitoshi (1839–1892), Yoshikata (?), Hiroshige II (working 1839–1864. He went to Yokohama in 1865 and called himself both Risshō and Hirochika II. He was also known as 'Tea Box Hiroshige' because he was reduced to painting scenes of the port on boxes of exported tea), Hiroshige III (1843–1894), Utatora (?), Ippōsai Kuniaki (working 1850–1865), Kunimaro (?), Baichōrō Kunimasa (?), Ikumaru (?), Sadashige Kuniteru II (1830–1874), Ikkosai Keirin (1828–1910), Ikkei (?), Baiju Kunitoshi (?), Kunimatsu (?), Yoshiyuki (?), Kunizuru (?), Toyoshige II (?), Kunitsuru (?), Ogata Gekkō (1859–1920), Toshinobu (?), Naomasa (?), Sensai Eitaku (?). Many of these artists were very obscure but, taking them all in all, the very best work of themselves and their period is to be found in their Yokohama-e and an extremely extensive collection of their work is to be seen beautifully reproduced, in the volume by Mr Tamba.[4]

NOTES ON CHAPTER XIV

¹ *Turk, F. A.*: 'Sadahide and the Yokohama-e Prints: a study and a re-appraisal'. *The Connoisseurs Yearbook*, pp. 126–129. London, 1962, gives the fullest study yet available in English of Sadahide and his work together with some notes on the *Yokohama-e*.

² *Stern, H. P.*: 'America: a View from the East'. *Antiques*, vol. 79, No. 2, pp. 166–169. Feb. 1961, New York. Has some interesting notes and re-productions of rare prints of American interest.

³ *Wainright, G. A.*: 'The Pyramids of Meröe in a Japanese Colour-print'. *Antiquity*, vol. 11, No. 4z, pp. 229–233. London, June 1937. Traces the inspiration of this important print to F. Cailliaud's 'Voyage à Méroé, au fleuve blanc, an-delà de Fâzoql . . . 1819–1822'. Paris, 1823–1827.

⁴ *Tsuneo Tamba: Yokohama Ukiyo-e*, Tokyo, 1962. In Japanese but with 418 very good illustrations and indispensable to the collector or student of these prints.

CHAPTER XV

The Ōsaka Ukiyo-e

IT IS a curious comment on European taste that only one book, that of Dr Lubor Hajek,[1] has been devoted to the Ōsaka woodcuts; in this relative neglect an aesthetic snobbism has no doubt played no small part although it is true that, on the continent at least, these prints are rather rare. In Britain, however, they are not at all uncommon and fine designs may still be bought for a pound or so.

As Mr Holloway (l.c.) makes clear in his book on the classical school, the cultures of Edo, Kyōto and Ōsaka were very different one from another. In fact, in the seventeenth and eighteenth centuries they probably differed more from one another than any of the major cities of Europe. Edo by reason of its history (see pages 35–36) was the centre of government, the focal point of the country's administration and, because of its immense population, it was, apart from the few bankers (*fudasashi*) the home of the small shopkeeper, the artisan and the craftsman. For the most part its culture was that of the middle class which found its expression in *kabuki*, *kyōka* poems, the *ukiyo-e* woodcuts with their emphasis on courtesans and actors and the literature of the *ukiyo-zōshi*. Ōsaka, on the other hand, was the home of the great wholesale merchants, centre of the immensely wealthy banking, shipping and marketing concerns. Still more important, it was the place of the country's great granaries, of the rice exchange, of all the mercantile activity which grew up from the handling of the products of the estates of the *daimyō* and, above all, it had the power that comes from being able to grant credit.

The great merchant bankers and their families pursued, as far as they could, the old culture of the court nobles and the great Buddhist ecclesiastics; for them the prints of the 'Classical School' existed as did the many albums devoted to the reproduction of paintings of the Kano, and to a much less extent, the Tosa school. If this was the culture of the employers it was certainly beyond the reach of the employees—the main class of Ōsakan society. Moreover, their status, their means of livelihood and the strongly paternalistic relationships on which they lived with their employers, all combined to prevent them from taking over the pursuit of luxury, the splendid disregard of economic prudence and thrift, the life of enjoyment and entertainment which were the characteristics of the small shop-keepers of Edo. For this city of clerks, Ōsaka, the *kabuki* was still the major source of entertainment but their interest is not in the personality of the actor but the power of the role or the tension in the *tableaux* with which the play was punctuated.

It is just this absence of personality which characterizes every aspect of the Ōsaka woodcuts. Although it is certainly overstating the matter to say, as some have done, that they might all be the work of one man, there is nevertheless an absence of individual style about the whole of the production of this school. Dr Hajek (l.c.) has pointed out that instead of the many publishers that issued the wood-block prints of Edo, only some ten produced those of Ōsaka and of these only four are at all common; these four are Honseidō, Wataki, Temmanya Kihei and Kinkwadō Konishi. Moreover, the range of engravers and printers was almost equally restricted; among the former the commonest are Ōnō, Kumazō, Horikuma and Horikane, whilst the printers most frequently found are Suritoyo, Kwakuseidō and Iida.

The restriction of these prints to a comparatively small group of artists, a very much smaller group of publishers and an even more restricted group of engravers and printers is obviously an important factor in the bringing about of the clearly characteristic, isolated but eminently coherent style which demarcates so clearly the Ōsaka woodcut. But not only was the circle of men engaged in their production limited but there was also a fairly marked degree of co-operation and interchange between them, for it is not uncommon to find that different prints in the same series bear the seals of more than one firm of publishers. Here, evidently, was no desire to be different, to show that originality of style or design or that capacity to titillate the public palate which was so important for the Edo artist. Nor were there here, individual connoisseurs for whom prints were designed 'to special order' (*motome ni ōjite*): if anybody in Ōsaka did order these prints it was the owners of the theatres who desired only a vibrant, even febrile, dramatic rendering of some role or situation in a new play.

Dr Hajek (l.c.) has argued very cogently the effect of some of the characteristics of the old *yamato-e* style of painting on that of the Ōsaka colour print and any student interested in this matter could not do better than read the whole of his account of this. Unlike the unlovely innovations of much of Kunisada's output, shown still more markedly in that of his followers—the earthquakes of draperies and the breaking up of the print surface with tiny fragments of unrelated coloured patterns—in the Ōsaka print, at least in its developed form, all is controlled. The colour harmonies are in low, even very low keys; the colours are continued over large areas which only rarely and sporadically are broken by smaller areas in a different colour. The pigments themselves are often mixed with black which has the tendency to make them opaque and to keep all in a low and sonorous key. Possibly this is not so true of the earlier prints that began to appear in the second decade of the nineteenth century nor yet of some later prints—those, as it seems, the work of followers of Hokusai—which keep to bright, light colouring but these are in no sense typical. Apart from these factors of the highly characteristic style of the school there are others that may be cited: the designs are contoured by hard clean outlines, beautifully cut on the blocks and the more obvious in that only very, very seldom does one see a print which has been taken from a worn block—the editions of each print being, one supposes, smaller than those customary for the Edo *ukiyo-e*. Moreover the printing itself is among the most technically perfect that can be found in the whole range of colour prints. The register is exact, the colours beautifully and carefully graded or overprinted on the block and the whole often enriched with *gauffrage* printing, with mica and particularly with metal dusts. The clear, hard style, the uncluttered design, the masterly engraving and the perfect printing are, in short, the unmistakable *cachet* of the Ōsaka print.

In a sense it is probably true to say too that the quality of the materials used is much better than that in most of the contemporary prints of Edo. The colours are far purer: the blue is a true ultramarine, reminiscent of the *Nagasaki-e*—and it may not be without significance that the red is very like the brilliant orange-red also to be found in the *Nagasaki-e*—whilst the greys show a very wide range indeed and are of exceptional purity, both they and the blacks exhibiting an altogether impressive vibrancy. The paper too is of very good quality for the time at which these prints were produced;

it seems to be both thicker and smoother than that used for the Edo prints and it is absorbent but only so far as to take up the requisite amount of pigment, not allowing the colours to smudge.

The earlier examples of these prints, like those of Edo, were of *oban* size but later (i.e. beginning in the latter part of the 1830s) the smaller *chuban* size came into use, firstly for bust length portraits of the actors but later for the full length figures as well. The number of sheets that make up a series is, with the Ōsaka prints, always an even number whereas, as we have seen already in the section on the subject matter of the prints, those issued by the Edo publishers were almost always in an uneven number. Dr Hajek has suggested that this is probably because the people of Ōsaka did not paste these prints on the walls of their rooms but kept them between covers or mounted as folding albums (*orihon*).

The origins of this school are obscure; its end hardly less so. The Edo *ukiyo-e* went into a fairly rapid decline from the 1860s onwards but even so it took quite an appreciable time to die. Some of the reasons for this decline are discussed in detail in Dr Koshima Umidzu's much neglected book,[2] the last chapter of which is given up to a critical study of the life and work of Toyoharu Kunichika. As a sample of the processes of decline in operation, nothing could have been more happily chosen and western students will find it nearly incredible that the same artist who designed the terrifyingly powerful portrait head (reproduced there in colour), which is surely one of the supreme masterpieces of the Utagawa school if not of all *ukiyo-e*, should have been responsible for the tawdry, garish crudities which the European collector associates with this name. A careful comparison of the meticulously chosen and rare prints reproduced in this book with the later prints of the Ōsaka school will show that the falling off in the quality of the design of the latter was similar in both instances. Yet in the Ōsaka prints it does not proceed as far as it does in the work of the Edo artist. There is the same loosening of the design, the tendency to clutter the print surface with detailed but purely decorative accessories—baskets of flowers, cherry trees and such—and then, print production in Ōsaka ends. No doubt the troubles of the 1860s and finally the damage to the city when the Shōgun's forces fled after the battle of Fushimi in 1868, all helped to reduce the market for the prints and perhaps to disperse the artists themselves.

As was pointed out above, if the end is obscure the beginning of the school is no less so. Prints of the Ōsaka school first appear about 1820: printed books had previously been produced in this city but one finds in them no outstanding excellence of technique and certainly nothing to suggest the beginning of a tradition of printing which in many respects was to be reminiscent of that of the best *surimono*. At the most there cannot have been more than two generations of artists engaged on the design of these prints and perhaps, for the most part, there was only one. E. F. Strange[3] was, I think, the first to suggest that the major influence in the formation of the Ōsaka style came from Shunshō by way of his pupils, Shunkō and Shunyei. A study of the prints themselves does much to support this view yet nothing seems to have come to light to connect the Katsukawa school with Ōsaka. Shunyei's pupil Shunyō worked in this city but his prints are rare and he can hardly have had a formative role in this style.

Hokusai visited Ōsaka in 1818 and had several pupils there and one can believe that his influence is occasionally to be seen but in these figures of actors it is usually his earlier style that seems to find an echo and, sometimes, one is reminded of a few of the figures and especially faces in some of his *shunga*—a kind of production entirely absent in the work of the Ōsaka artists. Among his pupils here were Shunkosai or Sekkwatei Hokushu, who worked until the 1830s producing these actor prints, Hokuei (signing Shunkōsai, Shumbaisai, Shumbaitei and Sekkwarō), Hokuju (Shunshōsai), Hokusen, Hokuchō, Hokumiō, Hokusei, Hokutsui, Kokui and Shigeharu. Several of these artists illustrated books as well as designing prints and Hokushu was also responsible for some *surimono*. He was also a publisher doing business under the name of Shunkōsai about 1815 to 1818. One of the books published by him has the name of the printer given as Kwakuseidō and this name also appears on at least two of his Ōsaka style prints. If one is to look anywhere for the sudden origin of this school of print artists Hokushu would seem to have some claim on our attention.

Some of the followers of Kunisada who worked in Ōsaka were: Sadakage, Sadafusa, Sadanobu, Sadamasu, Sadatsugu, Sadahiro, Sadayoshi and Yoshitsugu as well as some much rarer ones. Perhaps also to be classified here is Hirosada who had, rather more than most Ōsakan artists, a somewhat individual style and a fairly prolific output.

A curiously isolated group of uncertain affinity is the small circle of artists whose names begin with the syllables 'Ashi' and include: Ashiyuki (by far the most common), Ashimaro, Ashihiro, Ashikiyo and Ashikuni. They were mostly employed by the publisher Shuōchōdō but a few prints by these men were published by the firm of Honseidō. Possibly the most interesting of this school is the artist Enjaku whose prints are of most outstanding quality, mostly very low in key with much use of black and a very striking, dramatic shade of dull brown which often covers large areas of the design, the background of which is often more detailed than is commonly found in the work of this school. Nothing is known of him but the name appears among the actors of the Sawamura school and he himself may have been an actor.

NOTES ON CHAPTER XV

[1] Hajek, L.: *The Ōsaka Woodcuts*, London n.d. (1960). The best illustrations of the work of the school are to be found in this book.

[2] Koshima Umidzu: *Edo matsugo no Ukiyo-e*, Tōkyō, 1932. An important study, scholarly and beautifully produced. It has been somewhat unjustly neglected by students of the Japanese print. It deals entirely with the decline and decease of the Edo genre pictures.

[3] Strange, E. F.: *Japanese Illustration*, London, 1897, and *Japanese Colour Prints*, London. Victoria and Albert Museum. Six editions, 1904–1931. These two books contain the most complete factual information about the artists of this school yet available in English.

CHAPTER XVI

A Note on Toyama Prints

OF ALL the regional centres of print production in Japan this is one of the most interesting. It is also the one most recently discovered by Japanese scholars and collectors and for this reason, the published literature on these prints is small indeed, all in Japanese and none of it very easily accessible to European students. Most easily available is Mr Seizō Murakami's excellent summary, *Toyama hanga*, based on several years collecting and study, which was published, in Japanese, in Ukiyo-e Art, No. 5, pp. 13 to 17, with an English *résumé* by Mr C. H. Mitchell. In Britain, at least, the prints are but rarely met with and the later ones have hitherto been largely disregarded.

Toyama lies on the west coast of Japan some one hundred and fifty miles from Tōkyō but shut in by great mountain ranges dominated by the peak of Hakusan. This situation has always ensured for it and for the province of Etchu in which it lies, a certain remoteness. Even today the only rail approach to the city is along the very narrow coastal strip and before the coming of western ways to Japan, Toyama was isolated indeed. Yet, notwithstanding this isolation, it had in earlier years a reputation for having the least number of illiterates of any of the provinces of the country. This may well have been due, in the first instance, to the influence of the enlightened *daimyō*, Masatoshi Maeda, Lord of Toyama who, during the Tenna Era (1681–1683) founded the patent medicine industry which, until the last war, was the main industry of the prefecture. Maeda was much interested in manufacturing medicines from Chinese plants and assembled scholars and physicians from all over the country in order to consult them on the matter. In the second year of Genroku (1689) he was asked by the *daimyō* of other provinces to send travelling salesmen to them with prepared medicines and thus were laid the fortunes not only of the clan but of the city.

This history has influenced the prints as well. It was the custom of these salesmen to distribute various kinds of advertising matter and, in the preparation of such, many artists and several publishing houses did good business. During the middle years of the nineteenth century many of these circulars were designed by some of the lesser artists of the Utagawa school and Mr Murakami especially cites pupils and relatives of Kunikazu. It would seem that the firms that published these *ichimai-e* were, in the main, different from those which produced the illustrated books; nor were these single sheets restricted to serving the sales of patent medicine, for many other kinds of print were issued in this form including tickets for lotteries and mutual aid associations together with advertisements for the various spas in this district which abounds in hot-springs, the water of which has for long been thought to have a curative effect. The centre of the region of spas and noted beauty spots is Kanazawa which, in feudal days, was the seat of the Maeda family and, since it is only some fifteen miles or so from Toyama, it is natural that the publishers of that city should have undertaken its publicity.

Mr Murakami also mentions certain religious prints, printed solely in black (*sumizuri-e*) and mostly unsigned. Seemingly most commonly met with are those bought by pilgrims to the famous temple on the peak of Go-honsha, highest of those that make up the group known as Tateyama. He says that these prints and other Buddhist inspired designs issued at temples and shrines in the district, are among the finest surviving specimens of religious prints, the earliest ones so far recorded dating from the Shotoku era (1711–1716).

At least one famous book came from the Toyama publishers, the *Honzō Tsukan Shōzu*, published in 1853. The author is said to have been the Lord Maeda, a noted botanist, and the work deals with information on all kinds of herbal medicines. The two illustrations from this book given in Mr Murakami's article would certainly seem to justify his claim that it is the finest example of wood-block printing to come from Toyama. Its illustrations would also appear to rank among the very best flower prints that came from Japan. To judge from the two reproductions given by Mr Murakami the illustrations of this work may owe something to the *Honzō Dzufu* of Tsunemasa Iwasaki published in 1828. If one compares the treatment afforded to the representation of the backs of leaves in these Toyama woodcuts with that of plates in Mattioli's *Commentarii in sex Libros Pedacii Dioscoridis* (Venice 1544), one may be assured how very much finer the Japanese woodcut is than anything produced for the great Venetian herbalists by the European wood-engravers.

Toyama publishers were also noted for their production of *Haiga* (drawings in various styles with associated poems). According to Mr Murakami these works were first published in Etchu province in the early 1800s, a matter to be explained—as Kyōto was already the recognized centre for this kind of print—by the fact that Etchu had become a popular centre for the making of *haiku* since it was visited by many poets following the example of the famous Bashō in the seventeenth century. Chief of these productions was the *Haikai Tamahiroi* with illustrations by the local artist Ōshinsai Moriyoshi (1824–1886) but including others by such different hands as Seishō, Shōho, Kunzan and Bunkei. The true *ukiyo-e* style prints from this centre seem negligible and of the same inferior quality as those of the late Utagawa in Edo.

Part IV

A Miscellany of Notes on Prints and Printed Books

CHAPTER XVII

Surimono and Fan Prints

THE WORD *surimono* has the literal meaning of a 'printed thing' and it is applied to a special class of printed sheet which, although distinctive, is somewhat difficult to define. Its purpose was always to commemorate an event or to congratulate a person yet, by itself, the purpose is hardly sufficient to define it since many single sheet prints were designed to commemorate an event such as, for instance, the death of an actor. Nor is its origin anything but obscure and this probably for two reasons; firstly, this kind of print only gradually developed a separate entity in the public consciousness and secondly, having thus developed, the name *surimono* was applied in retrospect, as it were, to things not so considered when they originated.

The origin of some kinds of *surimono* is known to us. According to Dr C. Ouwehand,[1] the *kyōka* poet, Ōta Shokusanjin (1749–1823) says that, about the year 1780, the poet Ōne Futoki introduced the custom of sending New Year *surimono* (*saitan-surimono*) whilst in 1781 the actor Bandō Katitsu of the Ichimura family designed the first of the theatre *surimono* (*shibaikyōka-surimono*). Shokusanjin was an eminent student of both Chinese and Japanese literature and the author of a long series of books on these subjects and it is unlikely that such a statement was made at random. Yet more than a decade before this, some of the *egoyomi* (picture calendars, see page 54) were called *Daishō-surimono* (long-short *surimono*) because they enabled one to tell the long and short months. Indeed, the first exhibit listed in the catalogue of the exhibition for which Dr Ouwehand was writing was one such *surimono*, depicting a bowl with goldfish in it with a smaller bowl and hand-net by the side; it was attributed to Harunobu and was dated 1765. Jan Tschichold[2] has suggested that *surimono* may have originated in the Chinese letter papers such as those published in 1644 under the title of the 'Collection of the Ten Bamboo Hall'. This may well be so since, by the middle of the eighteenth century, as we have seen (page 211), many such Chinese books, ideas and works of art were being brought into

Nagasaki by the supporters of the Mings, refugees from the new power of the Manchus.

Surimono represent the acme of the printer's and engraver's art. Always they are on the best *hōsho* paper (i.e. 'edict paper', so called because in Kamakura times it was used for writing the official pronouncements) and the full range of the printer's colours are used together with metal powders, gold, brass, silver and bronze, mica and even, in a few rare prints which seem to reach the ultimate in luxurious refinement, mother-of-pearl.

Yet these adjuncts to the printer's palette are by no means always employed although, even where they are not, the printing is careful in the extreme and with many, perhaps not quite so obvious, refinements. Sometimes an area of colour will be applied to the print by the means called *atenashi-bokashi* (i.e. 'random shading') in which a certain unevenness is achieved by floating the colour on to a wet block; often the shading will be produced by carefully wiping the block over the area which it is desired to shade—a technique called *fuki-bokashi* or 'wiped shading'—and, very frequently indeed, special effects are obtained by embossing parts of the design in the manner called *gauffrage* printing which is considered by the Japanese printer to be divisible into two kinds; a. *kimekomi* when the figures or whole objects are outlined or b. *karazuri* when the patterns or designs upon a figure or object are embossed. There is indeed a third kind, *tsuyazuri*, used when it is desired to burnish the embossed surface of the pattern. It will be seen that almost every resource of the printer's craft is called into play in producing *surimono*.

It is said that originally this kind of refined and special production of the *daishō-surimono* originated—although not of course in *nishiki-e* colours—in the Kyōhō era (1716–1736). In the course of time, these became a kind of New Year print and had short, seventeen-syllable *haikai* poems on them. For this reason, no doubt, they came to assume a form and shape not very unlike the square poetry papers (*shikishi*) on which were spread faint colours and specklings of gold and silver. Many of such prints were the products of certain rather Bohemian clubs (*ren*) composed of artists, poets, actors, courtesans and scholars and it became customary for members of such clubs to exchange these prints one with another: thus there came into being the so-called *zōtōsurimono*. Poets who specialized in the witty or satyrical *kyōka* poems wrote them especially for these and other purposes and artists illustrated them although in some instances the one man might do both things; such a one was the artist Kubota Shunman. In this manner the *surimono* gradually became a separate kind of print and indeed, with the frequent emphasis on texture that they showed—differing in this, in format and in other ways from the *ichimai-e*—they formed what was thought of almost as a separate art. A very much larger proportion of the population of Edo had become literate in some degree by the end of the eighteenth century and many of them wrote poems (*kyōka, haikai, tanka*) which, with a suitable design, would be turned into a *surimono* and circulated to friends. These might mark anniversaries, the occasion of a change of name, the assumption of a new art name, the opening of a theatre, the announcement of a dance performance or they might be simply invitations to, or records of, a gathering of poetry club members. Later, as it seems, possibly towards the end of the first decade of the nineteenth century, *surimono* became increasingly used for more private and personal matters—to notify a marriage or the birth of a son, to congratulate a friend or relative on attaining their seventieth birthday, to thank them for the pleasure of a musical performance or simply to invite them to a private party for flower arrangement or some other aesthetic pursuit.

As the *surimono* came to serve more private purposes without its use diminishing in any way among the small societies of aesthetes and connoisseurs, it became *à la mode* for people with some amateur artistic talent to design their own and it is for this reason that we find so many of these small sheets with signatures that are not met with elsewhere. But in all of these sheets there is this rather intimate welding together of poem and design, the *haikai*, as it might be and the *haiga*, i.e. the picture which goes with such a poem. Almost always the poem is present, its allusions, its overtones, its secondary meanings (which often lie in the almost endless puns of serious intention of which the language is capable), are all enhanced by the *haiga*; poems and *haiga* being complementary. In the course of time however there is to be seen a falling off in this characteristic and in the last half of the nineteenth century, designs copied particularly from pictures of the Shijō school, were produced as *surimono*, leaving the purchaser to add a poem of his own. So, in this and other ways, the decadence which overtook the *ukiyo-e* print also fell, in time, upon the *surimono*. Probably the last great master of the *surimono* was the lacquerer Shibata Zeshin (1807–1891) and few of his designs are likely to be later than the seventies of the century. In all, the *surimono* proper may be said to have been in production a little over a century, i.e. from about 1750 to 1870 but these dates may be extended backwards a little if the meaning of the word *surimono* is not so precisely drawn. In this connection Strange[3] draws attention to a statement by the minor artist, Hokui, on a print in the Victoria and Albert Museum which purports to outline the history of wood-engraving: this says, 'in the period of Genna (1615–1623), Katsukatsubō Hōkiushi, a comic poet who lived in Musashi, ordered Chikamatsu Riusai to engrave on cherry wood a picture of a pine branch and this was the beginning of *surimono*.' This would appear to have been a poetry paper and was probably designed to receive a hand-written congratulatory poem to be sent to someone on the attainment of their seventieth birthday.

In size, *surimono* vary much: perhaps the commonest is the *kakuban* (about 18 × 21 cm.). This nearly square form, derived from the standard poetry papers, is customary for these prints. Rather rare are the long *surimono*, horizontal compositions, often with the design occupying only a part of the surface of the print, the other part being used to convey a message or wish. The sizes of these are somewhat variable but the largest known to me is that of one designed by Hokusai for a professor of music, Niyo Dayu of the Tokiwazu school, notifying the fact that he is willing to receive pupils and give instruction; the design shows the sea-shore and the tea house Echizenya, in front of which some travellers have stopped to take refreshment. This print is about 19·5 × 52·5 cm. and a black and white sheet of text is attached to it; the whole is probably in imitation of the *makimono* scrolls. Other 'long *surimono*' of several sizes exist; a common size for this kind of print is said to be about 20·25 × 56 cm. It is true that Hokusai and a few other artists produced some even larger sheets of which the greater part of each is taken up with a collection of poems; these are always records of poetry which was written at a meeting of a *ren* (poetry club) and, in so far as their length merely depends on the number of poems recorded and but little on the design, a consideration of them is not likely to be helpful to any general statements about the size of these prints. Of the smaller and commoner sizes, most fall between 12·5 × 18 cm. and 16 ×

23 cm.; more commonly the composition is vertical on such sheets but several horizontal ones are known.

The subjects of the designs of *surimono* are altogether endless but since the majority were used to send felicitations to friends at the New Year, it is natural that we should find the objects associated with the New Year festivities occurring most frequently. Thus designs may be found incorporating the *Takarabune* ('Ship of Good Fortune') with the Seven Gods of Good Luck aboard; *Manzai* dancers or only the special hat which is worn by them, the *manzai-eboshi* (see Plate 7); the *Shimenawa*, a left-handed straw rope with tufted pendants in the sequence three, five, seven, alternating with paper *gohei*. Attached to the rope or, in many *surimono* shown alone or in a group, may be fern leaves (*urajirō*), charcoal (*sumi*), leaves of the *Yuzuri*, Bitter Oranges (*Daidai*) or a crayfish. Special arrangements of pine and bamboo called *kadomatsu* are sometimes found and the *shimenawa* is occasionally shown attached to these. The special kinds of food offered to the household gods are also commonly the subject of such designs and the presence of one or more of them is often sufficient to identify the print as a *saitan-surimono* or New Year *surimono*. These objects are: rice cakes (*mochi*), dried persimmons (*kushi gaki*), dried chestnuts (*kachiguri*), pine seeds (*kaya no tane*), black beans (*kuro mame*), the sardine (*iwashi*), herring roe (*kazunoko*), crayfish, *Tai* fish, dried cuttle (*surume*), flowers made of rice and straw (*mochibana*), a large radish (*daikon*), a string of cash and edible seaweeds such as the *kobu* (a pun this on *yorokobu* meaning 'peace').

All the zodiacal animals are commonly met with on New Year *surimono*, the particular year being in fact designated by the appropriate animal. Sometimes however they represent the days on which various festivals are held in January. Branches of willow loaded with lucky symbols are sold in the gardens of the temple of Temmangu and these too are occasionally to be seen in *surimono*, as are emblems of prosperity like Daikoku's mallet, *Okame* masks, toys and *maidama* —a kind of sticky cake representing a coconut. Indeed, many of the objects to be found worked into the designs of *surimono* are not easily identified by the uninitiated and some are of an archaic significance which perhaps would not have been recognized by the ordinary citizen since they were chosen for some *recherché* meaning or message such as would delight and flatter the mind of a connoisseur or antiquarian, many of whom belonged to the poetry clubs. For this class of more scholarly person these prints often incorporated personages of Chinese history or Chinese lore and not a few of the *surimono* of Gakutei make use of this kind of *motif*. Many of these could no doubt have been recognized by the man-in-the-street, as indeed would have been the various popular Japanese heroes but in almost all such *surimono* there is some subtle allusion which suggests the senders' good wishes.

Thus, although figures and even landscapes do occur in such compositions nevertheless, more than any other type of print, they include in their designs what we should call 'still life' and so give unrivalled opportunity to the artists to render textures to a degree which, had such prints not been known, one might have thought impossible for the technique of wood-engraving. These 'textures' are by no means always those natural to the object shown but are a kind of transposition, the probity of which will be apparent in almost all instances when the design is well considered. Occasionally the object depicted is such that it can convincingly carry another picture of its own; as an example of this one might cite that of fans which are themselves emblematic of good fortune or even of forthcoming ennoblement.

Allied to these still-life compositions are the several *surimono* that utilize flower arrangements and some early *surimono* by Utamaro are known which make use of this. Of other natural objects shells are possibly those most commonly found and a fine series of *surimono* by Hokkei are known which record the poems written by members of one of the literary clubs of the capital; each sheet of this series being decorated with various species of shells beautifully printed and with an embellishment of silver powder.

Perhaps the greatest masters of the *surimono* among the noted *ukiyo-e* artists were Shunman (see Plate 7), Gakutei, Hokkei, Shinsai, Chōsho and Hokusai; there were also some masters of the 'Classical School' who were noted for their *surimono* and the most famous of these were probably Kawamura Nihō and Kikukan Geppō but, as would be expected, the style of these *surimono* is quite different from that of the other masters, being less highly wrought and far more impressionistic in the treatment it affords the subject.

FAN PRINTS

It seems that the production of this kind of print was very much greater than would appear likely from those that have actually survived. As these prints exist in Europe today they are distinctly uncommon and it is very seldom indeed that one finds any dating from the eighteenth century and almost never one from the seventeenth. Undoubtedly they were fragile and subjected to a certain amount of rough usage; easily torn, stained or creased, it is probably only those leaves that were never actually put to the use for which they were intended that have survived.

Fans are roughly of two types; *a.* the folding kind (*ōgi* or *sensu*) and *b.* the non-folding type (*uchiwa*). As might be expected, the first of these is excessively rare and a search through many old catalogues reveals only two unmounted leaves of this sort—the so-called *ōgi-e* prints—and both were signed 'Hiroshige'. The first was a landscape *Takanawa Aki-no-Tsuki* or 'Autumn Moon at Takanawa', one of a series of *Tōto Hakkei* ('Eight Views of Edo') and the other a *Kwachō* print of Sparrows and Passion flower published by Shōgendō. Of course a few mounted leaves—usually on plain wood sticks with the bases lacquered—are to be found but almost always they are of the late type brought home by the Victorian and Edwardian traveller and not infrequently they depict one of the European hotels of Kyōto or Tōkyō.

Uchiwa-e are more common and often of very high quality, quite high prices being given for the work of comparatively late artists like Sadahide who indeed produced some of his finest work for fans. One of his fan prints of a fishergirl in a boat beneath a willow tree, published by Iseya Sōyemon, was sold in 1963 and fetched the surprisingly high price of £20.

Kuniyoshi was responsible for several *uchiwa-e* but seemingly by far his favourite subject for this type of print was one in which cats played the main roles. So we find prints by him of cats playing various scenes from the *Genji-Monogatari*, a fanciful and witty print of the *Neko no Sakari* or Festival of Cats which shows an assembly of cats on a terrace by moonlight and a third depicting a cat, a *kappa*, a badger, a toad, a fox and a bat dancing to the music of a samisen played by another cat.

Most of those designed by Hiroshige were landscapes, possibly the best of them being from the series *Hakone Shichito no dzu* ('The Seven Hotsprings of Mount Hakone') published by Ibaya and another series *Edo Jiman mitate Gōgyo* ('The Five Elements compared with the Glories of Edo'). However, Hiroshige—indeed, neither the first, second or third of the name (for they all seem to have worked in this form)—does not appear to have produced any landscape of much merit for fan-leaves.

Unsigned fan sheets by members of the Utagawa school are those most commonly seen and usually these are of scenes from well-known dramas such as the *Chushingura*, on the theme of which Kunisada made several *uchiwa-e* including a *mitate* series of unknown number, none of them being very pleasing. Toyokuni was responsible for some very rare and very charming *uchiwa-e*, one or two of which give us a glimpse of his work in the realm of landscape subjects. Utamaro is known for a few fan prints of courtesans although none have much merit, the best of them known to me being that of the courtesan Ariwara of Tsuru-ya. All the fan prints of Shunko's of which I have any record are of portraits of actors and there are a few unsigned prints to be found in *uchiwa-e* form which are, in fact, theatre programmes. One wonders whether this idea could have been copied in England since the British Museum have a theatre programme in the form of a fan, issued by the old Gaiety Theatre for Robertson's drama *Dreams* and Gilbert's *Robert the Devil*, these designs being lithographed in colour. Possibly some of the finest fan leaves of the *ukiyo-e* school are those by Zeshin but they are not often seen. Some, like those of Kyōsai, have reference to the Nō drama. More work needs to be done on this form of print but it would seem that there is not very much material for such a study in European collections.

NOTES ON CHAPTER XVII

[1] *Ouwehand, C.: Surimono uit het bezit van leden van de Vereeninging voor Japansche Grafiek en Kleinkunst.* Museum Boymans, Rotterdam, 1953. This is a splendid guide to the subject with some interesting illustrations. The whole text is in Dutch.

[2] *Tsichold, Jan.: Hu Cheng-Yen, a Chinese Wood Engraver and Picture Printer,* Basle, 1943.

³ *Strange, E. F.: Japanese Colour Prints.* Victoria and Albert Museum, London, 6th edition, 1931.

There is a chapter in this book devoted to *Surimono* as there is in this author's earlier book: *Japanese Illustration*: London, 1897. A further article on the *surimono* by the same author is 'The surimono in Japan'; *The Connoisseur*, August 1904, vol. 9, No. 36, pp. 41–46.

CHAPTER XVIII

The Japanese Illustrated Book and the Collector

FOR THOSE who wish to collect the illustrated books of Japan, a few words about their format, characteristics and kinds may be helpful and may even be expected in a work such as the present one. The fact that some artists did their best work in book illustration rather than for single sheet prints makes some knowledge of these books almost essential for the serious collector and student. However, a few preliminary remarks must be made and such a serious collector must take them seriously: firstly, it is essential that he should be able to consult, on occasion, two basic works[1] both alas! out of print, rare and consequently expensive; secondly, he must read Dr C. Ouwehand's most erudite and unique essay[2] which, in the space of little more than a dozen pages, will not only show him how, ideally, his collection should be catalogued but, even more to the point, will prepare him for the intricate, baffling and even exhausting study of the vexed question of editions, lacking the awareness of which he will be very seriously handicapped; thirdly, he must own and learn to use that magistral and canonical work on reading Japanese names and inscriptions[3] without which no student of Japanese arts can move far or accomplish anything. Yet to use it will require much earnest study and many disappointments although something may be done to lessen both of these by consulting as an adjunct the most useful and little known Russian work by Dr E. A. Folkman[4] which, with the very minimum knowledge of Russian, can be used with advantage.

There is yet another preliminary matter which, although not perhaps essential, needs to be emphasized and which probably cannot be better done than in the words of Mrs Louise Norton Brown, herself the person who had possibly the greatest knowledge of the Japanese illustrated book ever acquired by a European collector: she writes, 'The effort and study spent in learning a little of the language and enough of the Chinese characters to read signatures and dates is

21. Torii Kiyotada (*fl.* 1716–45). Yaoya Ō Shichi standing before a kyōdai and looking over her shoulder at her reflection in a mirror. *Hoso-ban* coloured by hand. Signed: Torii Kiyotada. Publisher: Tzumiya. (See page 128.)

22. A *mitate* subject by Hiroshige. A woman outside a house in the evening, carrying a present likened to the poetess and diarist, Murasaki Shikibu (10th to 11th centuries), in an *uchiwa*-shaped cartouche above. Plate No. 60 of the series *Ogura magai hyakunin isshu* (The Ogura Collection of the Hundred Poets). With the seal of Nanushi censor reading 'Hama'. Publisher: Ibaya Senzaburō (Dansendō). Date of series: 1844. Engraver: Komindō.

so small in proportion to the immense interest and delight one will gain by having this knowledge, that the time given to acquiring it is more than well spent.'

Yet given all this knowledge, if it is to be put to the best use then some facts about the Japanese book must be known. It will appear to be unnecessary to say that Japanese books commence on what, to one knowing only European languages, would be the last page and are consequently read 'backwards'. But, commenced in the right way, it will yet be found that very few of the old Japanese books have title pages and even where these are present, it is only very exceptionally that they will contain the information which we expect to see on the title page of a European book. As a general rule the title of the work will be on a label pasted on the front cover or—and often as well—on the top right-hand corner of the preliminary table of contents. Labels however are often missing or, if present, quite frequently are in the almost indecipherable form of a cursive or semi-cursive script which may add to the formidable difficulty that this presents by writing one or more characters in an abbreviated or lesser known alternative form. For this reason it is best to turn to the inside pages which list the contents where, if one is fortunate, the title will be in the ordinary printed script given in reference books.

The signatures of artists on book illustrations can be a complicated matter. Sometimes one comes across instances where the artist's name has been cancelled and it may be that this practice was followed when an edition was issued by a publisher other than the original, one, or perhaps by an associate provincial publisher.

Having read the title, which in many illustrated books may include the artist's name (in this case it will commonly be the first characters of the title), one will usually find the names of artist, publisher and date of publication given in a colophon; these may be found by the help of the 'key characters' given here (Appendixes III and VII). But besides the colophon many of the old Japanese books have some final notes, called *obugaki* (Chinese *po*) and these often contain most useful information. As is well known, the sheets of paper on which the printing is done are folded into two and bound on their free edges: it is these sheets that are numbered and not the pages, thus 29 will refer to the two pages made out of the twenty-ninth bound sheet; these numbers, together with the repeated title of the book, often come on the crease and may therefore be difficult to see;

16

moreover, in a few works the numbers may be printed at the lower right or left corner of the sheet and may then be concealed by the binding. Nor is this the only difficulty since in some, mostly seventeenth and earlier eighteenth century books, the sheets will be numbered with combined numbers which makes the counting of the leaves extremely complicated, a matter which can be one degree further confused by the custom shown in some old books of counting the illustrated leaves as extra ones.

Early Buddhist books are printed on a heavy, thick coarse paper but these are rarely offered in European salerooms, a fact which applies with even more force to the beautiful *Saga-bon* and *Koetsu-bon* (see page 38) which were printed on a special and very beautiful paper. From the Kwanei era to the middle eighteenth century books, with but few exceptions, were printed on a fine thin paper but with the advent of colour printing, an absorbent, soft and thicker paper was used.

The covers of books are important since they often provide valuable evidence for bibliographical expertise. Early Buddhist books were either in the form of scrolls or mounted as *orihon* (i.e. with the sheets joined edge to edge and made to fold into covers which might be of paper or of wood). Commentaries on religious works or explanations of ritual as well as other kinds of early books were mounted in dark red-brown leathery paper covers and these are quite characteristic of the books produced in the fifteenth and sixteenth centuries. For the first six decades of the seventeenth century, books were bound in paper covers having extremely refined designs stamped upon them, the colours commonly being red, dark blue, black, brown and dark green. This practice seems to have continued with the Kyōto publishers, with whom it originated, but the Edo publishing firms favoured simple paper covers in light brown. From about 1675 to 1715 books produced in Edo had their title slips pasted on the middle of the cover rather than at the top left-hand side and although there are exceptions to this, it may be taken as a characteristic of this period and may be used, with some validity, to date such works.

Much knowledge has to go to the study of the various editions of a book and for this the publisher's name is extremely important and should always be compared with those given by Kenji Toda in his great catalogue (l.c.). Also, where possible, one should compare the date given in the colophon with the date given for the writing of the preface; where these differ by more than a year or so, one may well be dealing with a later edition. The dates at which a publishing house is known to have been active are also an important adjunct to the study of editions and these will be found in the list of publishers given in the present volume.

'Remainders' of a given work (Dr Lane in *Ukiyo-e* Art, No. 10, p. 14, mentions a collection of Saikaku's stories) were sometimes re-issued under a completely new title. The old title was cut out and new title slips pasted over afterwards. In my own collection is a book of designs with just such a slip pasted on the cover but the old title still remains inside.

Not infrequently one may find charming single volumes of some work which the main references will show to have been in more than one volume and it is therefore useful to know how the volumes were numbered. Usually, but only if the total number of volumes in a set was more than four, they are numbered with numerals. If of two only, they are marked *Ken* (above) and *Kon* (below), or *Jō* (upper) and *Ge* (bottom) whilst if there are three volumes the two latter characters are used together with *Chu* (middle). Three-volume editions are also sometimes marked, *Ten*, *Chi*, *Jin* (Heaven, Earth and Man). Four-volume editions may be marked in one of two ways, *viz*. Spring, Summer, Autumn, Winter (*Haru*, *Natsu*, *Aki*, *Fuyu*) or by the points of the compass, North, South, East, West (*Kita*, *Minami*, *Higashi* and *Nishi*).

There is no doubt but that the subject of covers and bindings of old Japanese books will come to take on greater significance as more detailed study is given to it. Some of the papers used for these covers are extremely beautiful and not a few are quite exceptional examples of 'blind printing'. Moreover, some of those used for works of the *ukiyo-e* school are beginning to attract the attention of Japanese scholars: Mr Juzō Suzuki[5] has recently published a short study of the illustrated covers of the *Gokan-bon* or story books which from 1803 to about 1835 were issued in sets of from five to ten booklets bound up together in one case which often had a *ukiyo-e* print design on it. Mr Suzuki mentions one such in which Hokusai and Kuniyoshi collaborated together.

It is the albums of coloured prints in notable series by famous *ukiyo-e* artists that demand large prices in western salerooms today.

More often these works are known only as single sheet prints, because in many instances, the original books have been broken up and the prints sold separately. For this reason it is worth collecting the title-pages of such albums which, in the past, have been largely disregarded. These often contain beautifully coloured abstract designs as a background to the detailed listing of the plates in the album. Such a one is the title page from Sugakudo's *KwaChō* album (see Plate 17). Many of the great *uikyo-e* artists drew illustrations for the trifling novelettes which appeared in such numbers in the late eighteenth and nineteenth centuries and which, since they are bound in yellow covers, are known as *kibyoshi*. These are still fairly common and do not demand any great expenditure to acquire them, yet they may in some instances contain designs of considerable merit. The *meishō-ki* or guide books have already been mentioned (page 181) and although few of these have illustrations of any great merit, yet here and there some of considerable charm may be found.

During the nineteenth and the latter part of the eighteenth centuries, several of the Kyōto publishers issued collections of Kanō and Kōrin school paintings which were reproduced as wood-block prints. These are mostly disappointing and boring but occasionally one finds a volume with something worthwhile in it. Albums devoted to reproductions of paintings, or of original designs for woodcuts, by artists of the Shijō and Maruyama schools are as a rule more worth obtaining although some tastes may tire of the rather facile 'naturalism' which these sometimes but not always, show. Among the best of these works are the albums of such artists as Seiyō Gassō, Kikuchi Yōsai, Keichurō Hakuyei and all the work in this style by Yamaguchi Soken.

The years 1880 to about 1905 saw many famous books reprinted, particularly those of the *ukiyo-e* school, and some of these reprints have great charm. However, only the most naïve or the most sanguine collector will make the mistake of supposing them to be the originals. Again in 1915 and 1916 many famous old works in the *ukiyo-e* style were published by Yoshikawa Kobunkan and Zuga Keikokan of Tōkyō. These reprints are very beautiful indeed and well worth obtaining. The greater number of books which will be encountered by the collector in the shops of smaller dealers will prove to be woodcut reproductions of paintings by artists of various schools living in the four decades from 1860 to 1900 or else reproductions of the older books mentioned above. Of the former there are few that do not possess a facile charm but the period was not one that was conducive to work rising above a competent mediocrity: with the latter, one might well confuse re-issues from old blocks, already often badly worn, with the original books, the first editions of which won great fame. Of such re-issues it is impossible to make any general statement: some are worth acquiring if only for one or two plates that still hold something of their original quality; others, e.g. Hokusai's *Mangwa*, may be worth having to complete a series. They may be held until the opportunity occurs to replace such a volume with an earlier and less worn edition.

There are many other kinds of old book well worth the study of the collector and student. Early works on flower arrangement may sometimes be found in the hands of dealers but curiously enough these are seldom found in the salerooms. Reprints of early works on the tea ceremony, often dating from the Meiji era, may sometimes be found in the catalogues of Japanese booksellers, as may one or other of the many works on gardens and garden-making. Perhaps even more delightful to the average collector are the little books of designs for textiles, metal work and other such arts: at the very lowest level these show unending ingenuity and most of them contain work in which this is combined with a sense of placing and spacing that is never at fault and a power of abstraction and of the happy combination of motifs that puts even the most insignificant of these booklets among the greatest books of design in the world.

There are still many of these works available to the western collector and the comparatively small prices for which they can be obtained should not cause them to be disregarded. Some of these books of design are not woodcuts at all but engravings on copper plates (see Plate 4), of which many are works of great beauty, showing powers of engraving and printing beyond all but the very greatest of the European work in this technique. Most of these copper-engraved books date from the last half of the nineteenth century and one of the best of them is *Karakusa Moya Hinagata*, published by Matsuzaki Nakaba in 1885. It was compiled by Takizawa Sei and engraved on copper by Yasudō Yanagi Tarō; it is in five volumes. Another technique of reproduction, rarely to be met with but which yet produced works of much elegance and surprising harmony, is that of *Kappazuri*. This consisted of block-printing the outlines of the design in the normal way and then colouring the areas so contained by means of stencils. This seems to have been used for a short time from the sixth to the eighth decades of the eighteenth century to provide a relatively cheap means of printing in colour. Possibly the most famous book in *kappazuri* is Tachibana Minkō's *Saigwa Shokunin Burui* ('The Classes of Artisans in Coloured Pictures') published in 1770, with a second edition in 1784. The technique of *kappazuri* was continued in the later eighteenth century by a few artists in Kyōto and Ōsaka of whom the most important were Yanagawa Shunsui, Chōshiu and Harukawa.

A special study might be made of the so-called 'smallpox' books that were printed in red and were thought to have a curative effect. These books are called variously *hōsō-e*, *yōkō-e bon* and *aka-hon*. Several noted artists designed for such works including Shunchō and Eisen but they are not at all common. Perhaps conveniently to be classified with these, although the subject matter is quite different, since that of the former is mostly in the form of illustrations of old romances, are the *hashika-e* or pictures illustrating measures to be taken against measles. These are all in Kamigata *ukiyo-e* style and mostly date from 1862 when there was a serious epidemic in Kyōto and Ōsaka. The prints show guardian deities, medicines and hygienic measures to be taken against the disease. The only work known to me on this subject is that edited by Mr H. Muneta.[6]

Finally, of slightly earlier date than the last, are the so-called *namazu-e*. Although wood-block prints, these are really a true folk art, believed to have amuletic properties guarding against earthquakes and producing treasures. Some are in black and white but, more usually, they are coloured. The *namazu* (also called, *jishinuwo*) is the giant catfish which, lying under the earth, is believed to cause earthquakes by its movements when angered. Pictures for its propitiation and co-operation also exist in the form of paintings on paper or wood. All of the known *namazu-e* prints seem to date from just after the great earthquake of 1855. Dr C. Ouwehand is the author of the only authoritative European work on these pictures. (Ouwehand, C. '*Namazu-e* and their themes'. Leiden, 1964. None of these prints bear a publisher's seal and very few are signed by the artist. Among the few artists that have left their signatures on them are Ichiyusai Kuniteru and Ichieisai Yoshitsuya, the first a pupil of Kunisada, the latter of Kuniyoshi. A few of the *namazu-e* bear art names like 'Kindō' (Golden Hall) and 'Enju' (Extended Longevity) but nothing whatever is known of the individuals who bore them.

NOTES ON CHAPTER XVIII

[1] *Brown, L. N.* (Mrs): *Block Printing and Book Illustration in Japan from the earliest period to the twentieth century*: London and New York, 1924. The death of the authoress before its publication prevented the book having any final revision. It is a vast storehouse of facts, some of them quite out of the way ones, but it needs to be used with *Kenji Toda's: Descriptive Catalogue of Chinese and Japanese illustrated books in the Ryerson Library of the Art Institute of Chicago*, Chicago, 1931. Mr Ryerson bought the whole of Mrs Brown's collection of books and a feature of this catalogue is that it gives a valuable guide to the contents of almost all the works mentioned.

[2] *Ouwehand, C.*: 'An Annotated Description of Hokusai's *Shuga Ichiran*' in 'The Wonder of Man's Ingenuity'; *Mededlingen van het Rijksmuseum voor Volkenkunde*, No. 15. Leiden (1962), pp. 110–121.

[3] *Koop and Inada: Japanese Names and How to Read them*, London, 1923, n.ed., 1963.

[4] *Folkman, E. A.: Slovar Yaponski Imen I Familieye*, Moscow, 1958.

[5] *Juzo Suzuki*: 'Ukiyo-e Bookcovers in the early nineteenth century'. *Ukiyo-e Art*, No. 2 (1963), pp. 31–32.

[6] *Muneta, H.*: ed., 'Collection of Colour prints depicting sanitation for Measles', Kyōto (1963), privately printed. 100 copies only.

CHAPTER XIX

Miscellaneous Notes on Prints and Books

'STATES' AND EDITIONS

IN A SENSE, it is not possible to talk of the 'states' of a Japanese print in the way in which that term is applied to western engravings. In these latter the word 'state' distinguishes an alteration made to the plate by the artist himself or under his immediate supervision and, for this reason, a second state might be an improvement on the first as in some of the engravings of Turner's *Liber Studiorum*. We know from some extant letters of Hokusai that the artist sometimes wrote instructions to his publisher as to what he wished done and even what engraver he wanted to work for him but it seems that he could rarely have supervised a printing and what has been written to the contrary is largely a European invention. As we now know, the publisher almost always had absolute powers to control the production of the prints and quite certainly not all publishers exercised these to the same advantage. Some like the gifted Tsutaya Juzaburō, himself a highly successful man of business, went to great trouble and expense to get fine work but many blocks, once used, were sold to other publishers who produced other editions of the same work and usually with progressive deterioration.

Of the existence of different editions of a print or book there can be no doubt whatsoever since we have the evidence of the publishers' names, of dates, and often of alterations wrought in the blocks themselves, even to the extent of erasing the name of the original artist and substituting another, although this is rare. Sometimes a successful design may be copied line for line, with or without the most minor alterations, and the new blocks so produced have inserted on them the name of a different and, sometimes, more fashionable artist. It is indeed difficult to know whether to call these reproductions, reprints or editions and one has the feeling that the western terms for such do not really apply to these woodcuts.

If various 'editions' are matters of fact, the question of 'states' is far from being so and the simple affirmation that this or that print is in the 'first' or 'earlier' state is seldom little more than an expression of the opinion that the writer happens to prefer one colouring to another or, more crudely, possesses one so coloured rather than the other. In the past, the question of 'states' has given rise to some extremely acrimonious discussion and even vitriolic abuse; yet the *proven* facts are relatively simple: 1. By reason of the technique of production (see page 60) no two copies of a print will be *exactly* alike. 2. That where the tool marks on a block can be seen on a print, such a print must be an early impression. 3. That where a block is obviously unworn, as shown by sharpness of line and by the exactitude of register and without the smudging of the colours, such a print will, other things being equal, be earlier than one that shows these defects. 4. That where an important feature of a design is lacking in some impressions, e.g. the slight cloud over the face of the moon in some prints of No. 32 of Hiroshige's *Kisokaidō* series (see page 185), it is a reasonable assumption that those with the feature in question are earlier than those without. 5. That most so-called 'states' differ only in the manner of colouring and this may exist as *a.* a difference in actual colours used, *b.* a difference in the intensity or shading of a colour, or *c.* a combination of both.

In those instances where different colours are used, one or two points may be considered. Firstly, there are prints of equally good register, colouring and impression in which one or more colours differ. This is so in plate 27 of Hiroshige's 'Hundred Views of Edo' (*Kabata, Ume Yashiki*) where, apart from other differences, the foreground may be of a strong, dark green or of a much lighter and softer green. Lacking any other evidence, either could be the first 'state'; having noted the different printings of the design there is probably little point in refining on this. There exist instances, however, where certain colours are entirely lacking in some impressions: this is so in some of the more notable sheets of Utamaro where a certain light cadmium yellow and lilac, keys to new, vivid colour harmonies, are entirely replaced by other and more usual colours. Since the lilac appears to have been produced by overprinting or, more likely, by mixing colours on the block, and the yellow derived from the tuberous roots of turmeric, these would have been more costly in both material and labour and it is reasonable to suppose that only the earlier impressions, made when the blocks were quite fresh, would have been used for such printings. Therefore the strong possibility is that such colours mark earlier 'states' but there is inherently no impossibility in these impressions having been made at any time. There is in fact no *decisive* evidence.

Differences of the kinds mentioned in the last paragraph together with a difference in the manner of shading or the intensity of printing are to be seen in such a print as the famous 52nd. of Hiroshige's 'Hundred Views of Edo', the *Ō-Hashi no Yudachi* (Sudden Rain Storm on the Great Bridge). Here the sky may be black or blue and either colour finely or sharply graded; the piers of the bridge grey or black and, more telling than anything else, there are prints, the impressions of which are so carefully and delicately taken that the details of the houses on the opposite shore show through the curtain of rain whilst in still other impressions there are small areas of light yellow in the water that convey with extraordinary vividness the electrified atmosphere of a thunderstorm in midsummer. One has the impression that these are the work of different printers trying out different effects, perhaps under the direction of the publisher himself. There is no evidence to suppose that any one of these is earlier than another and to call one of them 'the correct state', as Stewart does, is, one supposes, merely a method of designating what is deemed to be the most effective to the writer or owner.

FORGERIES, REPRODUCTIONS, IMITATIONS AND REPRINTS

Much has from time to time been written on these matters and it is not necessary to use much space in the present book to deal with them. It may be said at once that for the most part these terms have to be rather carefully defined in order to make them applicable to the Japanese woodcut. Moreover, the rather distasteful emotional overtones which, rightly or wrongly, are called up when any of these categories are invoked for a product of western art, are somewhat misconceived when applied to Japanese books and prints.

Deliberate forgeries do certainly exist and a few are extremely difficult to detect but they are very few indeed and confined, as one would expect, to the prints that fetch great prices in the salerooms. The majority of the later forgeries can be detected by the stiffer, harder and often less translucent paper on which they are printed and by the absence of the rarer colours of the original as well as a marked difference in the colour quality itself, a matter which can possibly best be seen in the lighter blues, greens and yellows. Contemporary, or near contemporary forgeries were often achieved merely by adding the name of an artist whose prints were in good demand to a design provided by another artist. Shiba Kōkan's 'confession' of his part in thus forging the prints of Harunobu is well known and indeed the larger sheets of Harunobu seem to have attracted the attention of forgers from his own day almost to the present. Utamaro is another artist who has suffered in this way but usually the forgeries of his work are more easily detected, at least the later ones. When a print in the style of some master is issued without a signature or an illustrated book is published without the name of the artist being given these, if actually drawn by another hand, need not necessarily be intended as forgeries; they are better termed imitations. Such imitations are extremely difficult to detect on occasion and this is especially so with many of the early illustrated seventeenth-century books. For example, several artists engaged in this work seem almost certainly to have imitated the designs of Moronobu.

Reprints are made when a work is re-issued from old and worn blocks. Perhaps no work suffered from this practice so much as Hokusai's *Mangwa*. There are copies of this to be found where the thick, blotched, broken lines and small puddles of ink all combine to suggest a block on which very little of the original design remains above the general surface of the wood. Not infrequently—in both prints and books—this condition was remedied by recutting the block. An expert engraver, taking plenty of time, could do this exceedingly well and some very fine works have been re-issued in this way but they are not many. In later times, expert engravers were few, informed connoisseurs not much more numerous and for the most part, publishers, lacking incentive, were content to take something much less perfect. The thicker lines, the imperfect register in colour work and sometimes the change of paper, all make the reprint in this sense fairly easily detectable.

Little need be said of reproductions. Produced for the most part by the old methods and called into being by publishers who are both scholars and artists, they are themselves well worth the attention of those collectors whose purse is restricted. Reproductions issued, often from unique copies of an original, by Mr Toyohisa Adachi are superb things of their kind, the worth and beauty of which must be apparent to all but the exceedingly rich who can own originals or the excessively snobbish who are denied sight by a mock purism. Very fine wood-block reproductions are also produced by S. Watanabe as, in an earlier day, they were by the late Mr Enji Takamizawa. With almost all these reproductions the wood-engraving and the printing are little short of miraculous but the old *hōsho* paper still seems, alas, to defy all attempts to make similar papers today.

SEALS ON PRINTS

Half a century ago the nature of some of the seals found on prints was not understood and it was only with the first discoveries of the late Mr Happer who investigated certain of the seals on the prints of Hiroshige, that it began to be seen that a study of them might help very much in the dating of a print. The work of the late Major J. J. O'Brien Sexton in this field put the whole matter on a workable basis and made it applicable to a considerable period of time. Finally, in 1932 Mr Ishii Kendō, in a now very rare little book,[1] published a very thorough full length study of censor seals on colour prints and this remains the definitive account of the matter.

The often repeated attempt of the government to censor and sometimes to prohibit the publication of single sheet prints was probably first made at least as early as the beginning of the eighteenth century. Binyon and Sexton quote an edict of 1721 and there seems evidence that this was not the first. Control of publication and the enforcement of a kind of copyright law was vested in the City Magistrates (*Machibugyō*) but usually these only passed judgment on doubtful cases. Most of the designs were passed for publication by censors who originally were very influential members of the Guild of Wholesale Publishers and were called *Gyōji*. As in other countries and times, under similar systems, abuses of one sort or another continued to develop and more edicts were issued, usually with only temporary effect. Artists, engravers, printers and publishers were all held to be responsible for any infringement of the law and punishment was scaled from a mere reprimand to banishment. Censors too were not considered above the law in this respect and for a dereliction of duty could, at least in theory, suffer similarly. Later *Nanushi*, the headmen of the wards of the city, could also act as censors and all such censors were appointed on a roster, each serving for one or two months at a time although the roster was not regularly kept over the whole period. Monthly rosters by three pairs of censors were started in 1847 and by 1849 four pairs of censors were acting, Watanbe replacing Yoshimura in that year.

After a modification of a previous edict of the same year (1790), in the ninth month of Kwansei 2, the censors began the custom of affixing a seal signifying that the design had their approval: this seal reads '*kiwame*' and was in use, either by itself or combined with, or accompanied by, certain other seals until a little after 1845 and it probably signifies 'investigated' or 'decided' (i.e. in favour?). On many prints published between 1790 and 1800, it is absent altogether but the reason for this is in doubt. In many instances it almost certainly indicates an infringement of copyright, which occurred from time to time, and a document dated 1840 and cited by Binyon and Sexton (l.c.) makes especial mention of pirated editions put on the market by engravers, a practice which was again forbidden at that time, publication being restricted to the wholesale booksellers.

Mr Kendō made an extended investigation of the seals on fan prints, nearly a third of his essay being given up to these. In the first years of the nineteenth century these fan prints (*uchiwa-e*) were sealed with characters which combined the year with the character '*aratame*' (approved) and later this last word was used on ordinary prints, firstly in an oval form (white on black) from 1848 to 1851 and then in a circular form from December 1853 to 1857 inclusive. Date seals in various forms appear in 1805 and later the censors themselves signed with the character for a part of their name—usually the first syllable. In various ways the '*kiwame*' seal too, became combined with date seals which give valuable evidence for the dating of prints. For one year after 1857 the *aratame* seal was discontinued, the prints for 1858 having the date seal only. However, from 1859 it is incorporated, in various ways, with the date seal itself in a single circular outline. Prints carry separate censor seals, either one or two, between the years 1842 and 1853 inclusive and these too are valuable clues in dating prints. In 1859 and subsequently, prints have a combined three character date and '*aratame*' seal and this marks the final stage in the practice of putting the seal of official approval upon prints. The way in which these various seals are used is perhaps best shown by the classification used by Mr Kendō in his essay. It is as follows:

1. Period of the *Kiwame* seal.
    A. Period of separate *Kiwame* seal (1790–1842).
    B. Period of subsidiary and accompanying seals.
        a. With accompanying year and month seals.
        b. With accompanying seals of *gyōgi* censors, i.e. ones who were publishers.
    C. Later period of separate *Kiwame* seals.
2. Period of the *Nanushi* censors' separate seals used singly (July 1842 to end of 1846).
3. Period of paired *Nanushi* seals. 1847–1853 (1848 with three pairs of censors; 1849–1853 with four pairs of censors).
4. Period of three seals; paired *Nanushi* seals and the year date seal. (Introduced 1852).
5. Period of the revised year date and paired seals.
6. Period of the simple month-and-year date seals.
7. Period of the three character single date seal (1859–1870).

Examples of all these seals and of some fan seals will be found in Appendix VI.

More than forty years ago it was proved, by investigations which checked the date seal on a theatrical print with the known date of the first performance of the drama in which the depicted role occurs, that prints of theatrical scenes were designed and published at about the same date as the first production of the play concerned. On the assumption that this generally holds good for plays which were performed before the use of date seals on prints, such a print may often be fairly accurately dated by turning up in one of the books of reference the recorded date of the first performance of the play in question.

SIZES OF PRINTS AND GLOSSARY OF TECHNICAL TERMS USED IN PRINTING

The sizes in which prints were issued were not chosen at random: they depend on the stock sizes of the papers used for printing and this is basically so even for *surimono* where the variation in the size is very large. Unusual papers were very occasionally chosen and this goes some way to account for the many different dimensions given to the prints at various periods. However, there were other factors which accounted for this too; obviously sheets could be folded and cut in different ways so creating prints of different sizes even when on the same paper but, more difficult to detect unless one knows the sizes, is the fact that large numbers of prints have been trimmed and it is always to be commended when cataloguers give the exact dimensions of any given print since comparison between different copies is much facilitated.

Aiban 34·5 × 22·6 cm. (syn. *ainishiki*). The half of a *hōsho* sheet—*kōbosho*.

Aka-hon Books printed in red and given to smallpox patients (syn. *Hōsōye-bon* and *Yoko-ye bon*).

Atenashi-to bokashi. Irregular shading produced by floating the colour on to a damp block.

Bai-ōban 45·7 × 34·5 cm. A full size sheet. Probably most frequently found in the sheets of primitives.

Beni-girai Prints in very restricted colour range. Most notable designers of this type of print were Shunchō and Shunman.

Benizuri-e Prints in two colours. Almost always this is rose pink and green but the latter might have yellow or, more rarely, blue substituted.

Chuban 25·5 × 19 cm. One quarter of an *ōbosho* sheet. Much used by eighteenth-century artists such as Harunobu and Kiyonaga.

Chu-tanzaku 38 × 12·7 cm. Half *ōban* cut lengthwise.

Ebankiri 19 × 51·5 cm. (syn. *Naga-gurimono*).

Edori-bon Early printed books with illustrations coloured by hand.

E-Zōshiya Illustrated novels.

Fuki-bokashi Graded shading produced by wiping the colour from the block with a cloth.

Hakkake Double or overprinting. Most frequently used to deepen a colour but sometimes for grading it.

Han A wood-block on which the design is engraved.

Hashira A printed *reserved* field on the outer edges of the pages of a book which contains the title. More rarely it was placed at the top of the page thus indicating that the book was intended to be mounted *orihon* fashion.

Hashira-e 73 × 12 cm. So called 'pillar prints' made by pasting two sheets together (see Plate 6).

Hosoban 33 × 14·3 cm. Nearly all the many prints of actors by artists of the Katsukawa school are this size.

Hoso-e A rather indefinite and somewhat erroneous term used by British and French cataloguers as a synonym of *Hosoban*.

Hotoke-bon Sacred books.

Ichimai-e A single sheet print.

Ishizuri-e 'Stone printed pictures', i.e. ones made to imitate the Chinese ones which were from *intaglio* designs. The effect was to give a print of white on black.

Jōruri-bon Books containing the texts of ballad dramas, usually illustrated.

Kaku-surimono 21·3 × 18 cm. (syn. *shikishiban*) used for the common square-shaped *surimono*.

Kakemono-e A term rather loosely applied to prints of the shape of *hashira-e* but very much wider.

Kamban Posters.

Kappazuri-e Pictures produced by stencilling. Either the whole design was so produced or the colours were applied by stencils, within a block printed outline.

Katsura no tsuyazuri The printing of black on black to give a shining surface.

Kimekomi Blind or gauffrage printing by which figures were outlined.

Kirara-e Prints with a mica background.

Kizuri-e Prints with a yellow background.

Koban 22·8 × 17·2 cm. Half *aiban* size, the two halves being printed at the same time.

Ko-yotsugiri 17·2 × 11·4 cm. An *aiban* cut into quarter sheets.

Ko-tanzaku 34·5 × 7·6 cm. An *aiban* sheet cut into three longitudinally.

Kubari-hon Privately printed works.

Kusa-zuri-e (*rokushō-e*) Prints in grass green and yellow.

Mameban A term applied to any sheet smaller than *ko-yotsugiri*.

Mitzugiri 22·5 × 12·8 cm. An *ōban* sheet cut into three horizontally.

Mokuroku A list or catalogue.

Naga-ōban 60·5 × 30·2 cm. A rare size used mostly by a few primitives of the early Torii school.

Naga-ban 51·5 × 23 cm. A rather rare size used very occasionally by Hokusai, Utamaro and Toyokuni.

Nishiki-e (Brocade Prints) A term applied to polychrome prints in which all the colours are printed from wood-blocks.

23 A. *Above:* Hiroshige Ichiryusai (1797–1858). Half sheet Tokaidō series No. 19. Yejiri. Travellers crossing the bridge called Koyoshida. Signed: Hiroshige *gwa*. Publisher: Tsutaya Kichizō. Seals of Nanushi censors: Murata and Mera. Probably 1848 or 1849. 23 B. *Below:* Eisen and Hiroshige. Kisokaidō series No. 20. Katsukake. Rain on Hiratsuka Moor, *yoko-e*. Signed Eisen *gwa*. Publisher Hoeidō. (See page 185.)

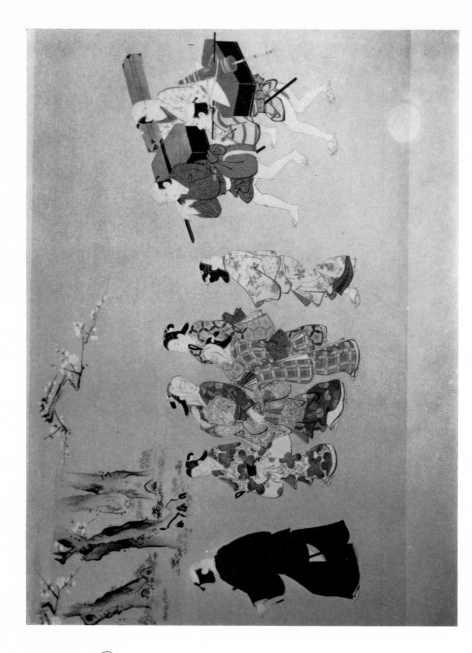

24. *Ukiyo-e* painting,
Plum Blossom Viewing
Party by Chōsun
Miyagawa (1682–1752).
From a wood-cut
reproduction by Shimbi
Shōin Co. (See page 41.)

Ōban 38·2 × 23 cm. The commonest of all sizes for both horizontal and vertical prints. It is half of the sheet called *ō-bōsho*. Usually this was cut before the prints were made.

Ō-bōsho 51·2 × 23 cm. A rare size mostly used for some early illustrated books.

Ōgata-chuban 28·3 × 21·7 cm. A quarter of the sheet size called *ōbiro-bōsho*. A favourite size of Harunobu's.

Ō-hosoban 38 × 17 cm. A rather rare size mostly used for early hand-coloured prints (syn. *Ō-tanzaku*).

Ō-tanzaku 38 × 17 cm. Same size as *Ō-hosoban* but used by cata-loguers for the Hiroshige bird and flower prints and a few others. Perhaps worth keeping to designate these later prints.

Ryōmen Gwajō A folding album with the illustrations on both sides of the paper.

Sanchō-gake An *ōban* sheet divided into three longitudinally. Used rarely for some later books of patterns.

Shichōgake. An *ōban* sheet divided into four longitudinally.

Shomotsu-bon The usual kind of sewn binding for books.

Shō-tanzaku 25·5 × 9·5 cm. An *ōban* divided into four vertically.

Shozuri The earliest edition of a book.

Sumi-e Prints (or brush paintings) in black and white only. Un-coloured.

Tan-e Hand-coloured prints using *tan* (see page 65).

Tate-e A vertical composition.

Tembokashi Printing the sky in such a way that the upper part is darker than the lower. Much used by Hiroshige but also in other landscape prints.

Tsuya-zuri A gauffrage printing used in such a way that the face of the paper on which is the outlined design, is burnished.

Uchiwa-e Fan prints.

Uki-e Pictures showing some use of European perspective.

Urushi-e The so-called 'lacquer' prints (see page 57).

Yoko-e Horizontal compositions.

Yotsugiri 19 × 12·5 cm. An *ōban* quarter sheet, all the four prints being printed at once from an *ōban* size block; hence often used for a series of small prints.

Zōho A supplement to a work.

NOTES ON CHAPTER XIX

[1] *Ishii Kendō: Nishiki-e no aratame-in no kosho* ('Investigation of Censor Seals on Brocade Prints'), Tōkyō, 1932. A limited edition of only 300 copies was made of this book which is now, unfortunately, very rare in the stock of Japanese booksellers. It is the most complete account that exists of these seals and is an invaluable aid to the serious collector. Much of the book deals with a unique investigation of fan prints and their seals— a subject which it would be nearly impossible to study in Europe. An excellent article on the subject, in English, is that by B. W. Robinson in the *Burlington Magazine*, vol. XCVIII (1956), pp. 54ff.

Appendixes

Japanese Year Dates and Chronology arranged for dating Prints either by Date Seal or other Evidence

Year A.D.	Japanese Period (nengō)	Year of the Cycle	Zodiacal Name of the Year	Intercalary Month	Short Months*
1744	Yenkiō	1	Rat		1, 3, 5, 6, 8, 9, 12
5		2	Ox		4, 6, 7, 9, 10, 12 I
6		3	Tiger	Jan./Feb.	3, 5, 7, 9, 10
7		4	Hare		1, 3, 6, 8, 10, 12
8	Kwanyen	5	Dragon	Nov./Dec.	1, 4, 6, 9, 10 I, 12
9		6	Snake		2, 3, 5, 8, 11
1750		7	Horse		1, 3, 4, 6, 8, 12
1	Hōreki	8	Sheep	July/Aug.	2, 4, 5, 6I, 8, 11
2		9	Monkey		2, 4, 5, 7, 8, 11
3		10	Cock		3, 4, 5, 6, 8, 9, 12
4		11	Dog	March/April	2I, 5, 6, 8, 9, 11
5		12	Wild Boar		3, 5, 7, 9, 10, 12
6		13	Rat	Dec./Jan.	3, 5, 8, 10, 11I, 12
7		14	Ox		2, 5, 7, 10, 12
8		15	Tiger		2, 3, 5, 7, 11
9		16	Hare	Aug./Sept.	1, 3, 4, 6, 7I, 10
1760		17	Dragon		1, 3, 4, 6, 7, 10
1		18	Snake		2, 4, 5, 7, 8, 10
2		19	Horse	May/June	3, 4I, 5, 7, 8, 10
3		20	Sheep		2, 4, 6, 8, 9, 11
4	Meiwa	21	Monkey		2, 5, 7, 9, 10, 12
5		22	Cock	Jan./Feb.	1, 4, 7, 9, 11, 12
6		23	Dog		2, 4, 7, 10, 12
7		24	Wild Boar	Oct./Nov.	1, 3, 5, 7, 9I, 12
8		25	Rat		2, 3, 5, 6, 9
9		26	Ox		1, 3, 4, 6, 7, 9
1770		27	Tiger	July/Aug.	2, 4, 5, 6I, 7, 9
1		28	Hare		1, 3, 5, 7, 8, 10

Year A.D.	Japanese Period (nengō)	Year of the Cycle	Zodiacal Name of the Year	Intercalary Month	Short Months*
1772	Anyei	29	Dragon	July/Aug.	1, 4, 6, 8, 9, 11
3		30	Snake	April/May	1, 3I, 6, 8, 9, 11
4		31	Horse		1, 4, 6, 8, 10, 12
5		32	Sheep		2, 4, 6, 9, 12, 12I
6		33	Monkey	Jan./Feb.	2, 4, 6, 8, 12
7		34	Cock		2, 3, 5, 6, 8, 12
8		35	Dog	Aug./Sept.	3, 4, 6, 7, 8, 12
9		36	Wild Boar		2, 4, 6, 7, 9, 12
1780		37	Rat		3, 5, 7, 8, 10, 12
1	Temmei	38	Ox	June/July	4, 5I, 7, 8, 10, 12
2		39	Tiger		3, 5, 7, 9, 11
3		40	Hare		1, 3, 6, 8, 10, 12
4		41	Dragon	Feb./March	1I, 3, 5, 8, 10, 12
5		42	Snake		2, 4, 5, 8, 11
6		43	Horse	Nov./Dec.	1, 3, 5, 6, 8, 11
7		44	Sheep		2, 3, 5, 6, 8, 11
8		45	Monkey		2, 4, 6, 7, 9, 11
9	Kwansei	46	Cock	July/Aug.	3, 5, 6I, 7, 9, 11
1790		47	Dog		2, 5, 7, 8, 10, 12
1		48	Wild Boar		2, 5, 7, 9, 11
2		49	Rat	March/April	1, 2I, 4, 7, 9, 11
3		50	Ox		1, 3, 5, 7, 10, 12
4		51	Tiger	Dec./Jan.	2, 4, 5, 7, 11, 12
5		52	Hare		2, 4, 5, 7, 10
6		53	Dragon		1, 3, 5, 6, 8, 10
7		54	Snake	Aug./Sept.	2, 4, 6, 7, 7I, 9
8		55	Horse		1, 4, 6, 7, 9, 10
9		56	Sheep		1, 5, 6, 8, 10, 11
1800		57	Monkey	May/June	2, 4I, 6, 8, 10, 12
1		58	Cock		2, 4, 6, 9, 11
2	Kiowa	59	Dog		1, 3, 4, 6, 10, 12
3		60	Wild Boar	Feb./March	1I, 3, 4, 6, 9, 12
4	Bunkwa	1	Rat		2, 4, 5, 7, 9
5		2	Ox	Sept./Oct.	1, 3, 5, 6, 7, 8I, 12
6		3	Tiger		3, 5, 6, 7, 9, 12
7		4	Hare		4, 6, 7, 9, 10
8		5	Dragon	July/Aug.	1, 4, 6, 7, 9, 10, 12

Year A.D.	Japanese Period (nengō)	Year of the Cycle	Zodiacal Name of the Year	Intercalary Month	Short Months*
1809	Bunkwa	6	Snake	July/Aug.	3, 6, 8, 10, 12
1810		7	Horse		1, 3, 6, 9, 11
I		8	Sheep	March/April	1, 2, 3, 5, 8, 11
2		9	Monkey		1, 3, 4, 6, 8, 12
3		10	Cock	Dec./Jan.	2, 4, 5, 6, 8, 11I
4		11	Dog		2, 4, 5, 6, 8, 11
5		12	Wild Boar		3, 5, 6, 7, 9, 11
6		13	Rat	Sept./Oct.	3, 5, 7, 8I, 9, 11
7		14	Ox		2, 5, 7, 9, 10, 12
8	Bunsei	15	Tiger		3, 5, 8, 10, 11
9		16	Hare	May/June	1, 3, 4I, 7, 10, 12
1820		17	Dragon		1, 3, 5, 7, 11
I		18	Snake		1, 3, 4, 6, 8, 11
2		19	Horse	Feb./March	1I, 3, 4, 5, 7, 10
3		20	Sheep		2, 4, 5, 6, 8, 10
4		21	Monkey	Sept./Oct.	3, 4, 6, 7, 8I, 10
5		22	Cock		2, 4, 6, 8, 9, 11
6		23	Dog		2, 5, 7, 9, 10, 12
7		24	Wild Boar	July/Aug.	2, 5, 6I, 9, 10, 12
8		25	Rat		2, 4, 7, 9, 12
9		26	Ox		1, 3, 5, 7, 10
1830	Tempo	27	Tiger	April/May	1, 2, 3I, 5, 6, 9
I		28	Hare		1, 3, 4, 5, 7, 9
2		29	Dragon	Dec./Jan.	2, 4, 5, 6, 8, 10
3		30	Snake		1, 3, 5, 6, 8, 10
4		31	Horse		1, 4, 6, 7, 9, 11
5		32	Sheep	Aug./Sept.	1, 4, 7, 7I, 9, 11
6		33	Monkey		1, 3, 6, 8, 10, 12
7		34	Cock		2, 4, 6, 9, 11
8		35	Dog	May/June	1, 3, 4I, 5, 6, 8, 11
9		36	Wild Boar		1, 3, 4, 6, 8, 12
1840		37	Rat		3, 4, 5, 7, 9
I		38	Ox	Feb./March	1, 2, 4, 5, 7, 9, 12
2		39	Tiger		3, 5, 6, 8, 10, 12
3		40	Hare	Oct./Nov.	4, 6, 7, 9, 10, 12
4		41	Dragon		3, 5, 7, 9, 11
5		42	Snake		1, 3, 6, 8, 10, 12

Year A.D.	Japanese Period (*nengō*)	Year of the Cycle	Zodiacal Name of the Year	Intercalary Month	Short Months*
1846	Tempo	43	Horse	Oct./Nov.	2, 4, 5I, 8, 10, 12
7		44	Sheep		2, 4, 5, 8, 11
8	Kayei	45	Monkey	April/May	1, 3, 4, 6, 8, 12
9		46	Cock		2, 4, 4I, 6, 8, 11
1850		47	Dog		2, 4, 5, 7, 9, 11
1		48	Wild Boar		3, 5, 6, 8, 10, 12
2		49	Rat	March/April	2I, 5, 6, 8, 10, 12
3		50	Ox		2, 5, 7, 9, 11
4	Ansei	51	Tiger	Aug./Sept.	1, 3, 5, 7I, 9, 11
5		52	Hare		1, 3, 4, 7, 10, 12
6		53	Dragon		2, 3, 5, 7, 11
7		54	Snake	June/July	1, 3, 4, 5I, 7, 10
8		55	Horse		1, 3, 4, 6, 7, 10
9		56	Sheep		2, 4, 5, 7, 8, 10
1860	Mangen	57	Monkey	April/May	2, 4, 5, 7, 8, 10
1	Bunkiū	58	Cock		1, 4, 6, 8, 10, 11
2		59	Dog		2, 5, 7, 8I, 10, 12
3		60	Wild Boar		1, 4, 6, 9, 11
4	Genji	1	Rat		1, 2, 4, 6, 10, 12
5	Keiō	2	Ox	June/July	2, 3, 5, 6, 9, 12
6		3	Tiger		2, 4, 5, 6, 9
7		4	Hare		1, 3, 5, 6, 7, 9
8	Meiji	5	Dragon	May/June	1, 4, 4I, 6, 7, 9, 12

* I following a number denotes the inter-calary month of the year.

YOKOHAMA ARTISTS

OSAKA SCHOOL

SOME UKIYO–E ARTISTS AND THEIR SIGNATURES: I

A list of some *ukiyo-e* Artists and their Signatures

THE grouping of the artists into schools has a varying validity at different times and for different names. One must not expect too great an exactitude in this respect nor that considerable anomalies will not be met with; in part this is because the group classification applies rather more to painting than to print production but also in part, because the style of certain artists may often change to bring it into line with the prevailing taste of the public at the time. Shikitei Samba (1775–1822) says that in the early days of the school all *ukiyo-e* were done in the Torii style; if this is true, it is equally certain that, in the last days, all artists were more or less tainted with the decadence of the Utagawa and therefore, even though an artist may have been trained in the canons of another school, yet almost always one can find in his work the influence of the Utagawa. It is in the light of this that the grouping given here must be viewed.

Most liable to confusion is the group loosely listed here as 'Primitives'. Some cannot really be considered primitive in the more restricted sense and the title must be taken to mean simply that such artists are fairly early designers of the *ukiyo-e* print. The addition of the names of several artists of great rarity would have much extended the list but added little to its usefulness. Sukenobu himself engendered a whole school—the Terai— but to list its members separately would have been to small purpose. Mostly book illustrators and painters, it included such artists as Shigefusa, Naofusa and Hasegawa Mitsunobu and they can be thought of as representing a *ukiyo-e* school of Kyōto and Ōsaka. In the third quarter of the eighteenth century this school was supplanted by another, the Settei, founded by Tsukioka Settei, characterized by designs of greater vigour. Their sheets prints are excessively rare and their book illustrations not much more common.

The Ōsaka School
1. ASHIHIRO. Portraits of actors, 1820–1830.
2. ASHIYUKI actor portraits and *surimono*, 1820–1830.
3. ASHIKIYO. Portraits of actors, about 1825.
4. ASHIMARO. Portraits of actors, about 1825.
5. ASHIKUNI. Perhaps the same as Shunshi and a little earlier than the others. Actors.

6. HOKUJU, 1748–1815, real name Asai Shōtei. Pupil of Hokusai. Also in Edo.

7. HOKUTSUI. Worked about 1810–1820.

8. HOKUEI. Earlier signature 'Shunkō'. Worked 1825–1849 approx. Actors, *surimono* and illustrations to editions of *kabuki* dramas.

9. Shunshōsai HOKUCHŌ. Actors. Pupil of Hokushu.

10. Sekkotei HOKUMIŌ. Actors and rare *surimono*.

11. HOKUGA.

12. HOKUI no fude. Mostly book illustrations, *c.* 1830–1850.

13. Seiyōsai SHUNSHI. Actor portraits, 1820–1830. Perhaps the same as Ashikuni.

14. SHUNYŌ. Perhaps pupil of Hokushu. Actors and dramatic scenes.

15. Shummansai HOKKAKU. Said to have been an actor. Prints of actors 1835 onwards.

16. ENJAKU. Perhaps an actor. Very fine dramatic prints, *c.* 1850. Rare.

17. BAIKA.

18. KUNIHIRO. Many actor portraits, *c.* 1820–1840.

19. MASUNOBU. Rare actor portraits, *c.* 1850.

20. SADAHIRO. Actors and illustrations, about 1830.

21. Gochōtei SADAMASU (= Kunimasu). Actors, *c.* 1830–1850.

22. HIROSADA. Many portraits of actors, some of great merit, during the period 1835–1845.

23. HIRONOBU. Rare portraits.

24. SADAHIRO.

25. SADAKAGE. Actors, *bijin-e* (rare in this school) and *surimono*, *c.* 1840.

26. SADANOBU. Portraits, illustrations and landscapes (some good but derivative), *c.* 1835–1855.

27. SHIGEHARU. Actors and illustrations of some merit in certain instances; born 1802, died 1853.

28. SADAFUSA. Portraits of actors, *c.* 1830.

29. NIHŌ. Landscapes (very rare) and *surimono* of good quality, *c.* 1850.

30. NOBUHIRO. Rare actor portraits.

31. KUNIKAZU. Actors and dramatic scenes from contemporary theatre, *c.* 1845.

32. KUNIHARU.

33. MITSUNOBU. Rare portraits of actors, *c.* 1850. Usually of sombre colour and striking pose.

34. YOSHIUME. Pupil of Kuniyoshi. Actors, *c.* 1850–1860.

35. NAGAHIDE (So read by Kurth and also Hajek but there is some doubt) see 135.

36. YOSHICHIKA. Actors, *c.* 1850.

37. Jukōdō YOSHIKUNI. Actors, *c.* 1850.

38. YOSHISHIGE. Book illustrations, *c.* 1850.
39. YOSHITAKI. Actors and landscapes, 1840–1899.
40. 'Sadayoshi's pupil YOSHITSUGU'.
41. YOSHIYUKI. Actors and landscapes in the 1860s.
42. YOSHITOYO. Actor portraits, *c.* 1850.
43. SHUNTEI. Illustrations—a few of some merit, *c.* 1800–1810.

Artists of the Yokohama-e

Most of these artists of course produced other kinds of print as well and the very short note of themes given here refers only to their work in this *genre*.

44. Sensai EITAKU. Figures.
45. YOSHIKAZU. Figures.
46. NAOMASA *gwa*. Figures.
47. YOSHIIKU *gwa*. Figures.
48. YOSHITOMI. Figures.
49. YOSHIMORI. Figures.
50. SHŌZAN. Views, figures and scenes in both the European and Chinese quarters. An interesting artist perhaps influenced by the Nagasaki-e and active about 1875.
51. TOYOSHIGE II. Views especially with trains (Not Toyoshige I = Gosotei Toyokuni).
52. Utagawa KUNITSURU. Street scenes, etc.
53. KUNIMATSU. Scenes.
54. KUNITOSHI. Scenes.
55. Baiju KUNITOSHI. Views; perhaps not same as 54.
56. KUNIMASA. Views.
57. IKKEI. Views.
58. KUNITERU. Views.
59. KUNIMARU. Figures in scenes. Often several sheet prints.
60. KUNIAKI. Figures in scenes.
61. UTATORA. Figures in views.
62. HIROSHIGE III. Street scenes and figures; often with trains and western buildings.
63. SADAHIDE. Certainly the best and most experienced of these artists. Figures, views, shipping, etc. Some interiors. Book illustrations, 1850s and 1860s.
64. HIROSHIGE II. Figures, views and imported animals.
65. YOSHITOSHI. Figures.
66. YOSHICHIKA. Figures.
67. YOSHITSUYA. Figures.
68. YOSHITORA. Figures and scenes in European countries and America.

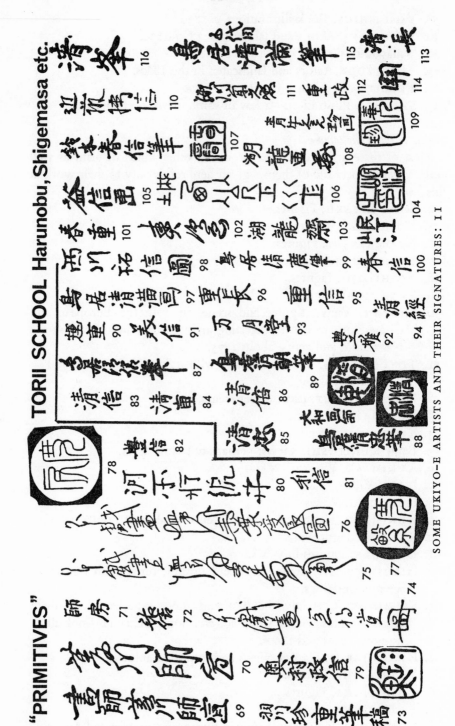

'*Primitives*'. Used here in a loose sense and mainly for those not so obviously in the Torii traditions.

69. Gwashi Hishikawa MORONOBU (?–1694) *Bijin-e*, Interiors of Yoshiwara. *Ichimai-e*, very rare.
70. Hishikawa MORONOBU (cursive style).
71. MOROFUSA, fl. 1685–1703. Several books and half a dozen single sheets.
72. SUKENOBU (1671–1751). Many books which inspired several later artists. Sheet prints very rare. He influenced at least two generations.
73. Hanegawa CHINCHŌ hikko with seal 'Chinchō' (1679–1754). A samurai. Work rare.
74. Kumeidō SHINSHI.
75. Ando KWAIGETSUDŌ, active 1710–1725. Courtesans. The wonderful prints of the Kwaigetsudō are the most sought after of all— as they are the rarest. Only thirty-nine are known to exist today.
76. Doshu KWAIGETSUDŌ.
77. Seal of Dohan KWAIGETSUDŌ.
78. Seal of Doshin KWAIGETSUDŌ.
79. Okumura MASANOBU (1686–1764). Prolific artist, publisher and bookseller. Figures, interiors, courtesans, actors and *shunga*.
80. Ishikawa RYUSEN, fl. 1680–1710s. Book illustrations and rare single sheets.
81. TOSHINOBU, fl. 1717 to about 1745. Fine *urushi-e* in *hoso-ban* format.
82. TOYONOBU (1711–1785). One of the finest *ukiyo-e* artists especially of *benizuri-e*.

Torii School

83. KIYONOBU I (1664–1729). Founder of this school which is noted for actor prints of great power, delineated in highly calligraphic line. A poster artist, his prints are very rare. The *kabuki* handbills designed by him and others of this school are distinguished by a swirling heavy script.
84. KIYOSHIGE (worked a little before 1725 to a little after 1760). Rare.
85. KIYOTADA (about 1718–1748).
86. KIYOMASU. Two artists of this name, the first worked from 1696 to early 1720s, whilst the second seems to have died in 1763. Both did fine work but also both were responsible for rather more mediocre prints.
87. Torii KIYONOBU fude.
88. 'Yamato gwashi Torii KIYOTADA' and seal KIYOTADA.

89. Torii KIYOTOMO fude and seal (fl. 1720–1745 approx.). Mostly *urushi-e*.

90. TERUSHIGE. Pupil of Kiyonobu, worked approx. 1725–1735.

91. YOSHINOBU. Illustrated books of plays and made some rare *benizuri-e*, c. 1740s.

92. TOYOMASA. Designed early *nishiki-e* between 1767 and 1773.

93. MANGETSUDŌ. Pupil of Masanobu working 1740s.

94. KIYOTSUNE, active 1760s and 1770s. Mostly actors.

95. SHIGENOBU. An early name and signature of 82.

96. SHIGENAGA (1697–1756). Interiors, figures and fine bird prints.

97. Torii KIYOMITSU gwa (1735–1785). Produced much work including some very fine *hashirakake-e*. Many *bijin-e* and some of the finest nudes in Japanese art.

98. Nishikawa Sukenobu zu (see No. 72).

99. Torii KIYOHIRO fude (active 1750s and 1760s). Mostly actors in *benizuri-e*.

(*Kawamata School* Nos. 100–109)

100. HARUNOBU (1725–1771). One of the most important artists of the *ukiyo-e* style. Nearly all his prints were of courtesans or *bijin-e*. The best of his prints were probably produced for limited circles of art connoisseurs and other highly refined and literate Edo citizens. Almost all of his work has a persuasive charm and innocence.

101. HARUSHIGE. This used to be thought an earlier art name of Shiba Kokan but is now believed to be that of a separate artist, see No. 186. Copied Harunobu's work.

102. HARUTSUGU (also read HARUJI) fl. 1760s. Pupil of Harunobu; work rare.

103. KORIUSAI (fl. 1760–1784). A samurai and friend of Harunobu. Earlier signature Haruhiro. His subjects are similar to those of his friend with the addition of children—to which several of his prints are devoted—and a fine series of birds. He excelled in the form of the pillar-print. His colour range is darker than that of Harunobu and his work has a greater expanse of rust red. In the *hosoban* prints his figures are often clustered nearer together and make his designs seem more static than Harunobu's. The work of both, however, is very similar.

104. MINKŌ (fl. about one decade from 1762). Work resembles Harunobu's. His *Saigwa shokunin burui* was produced with stencils and is very fine.

105. KUNINOBU. Pupil of Masunobu. Produced *urushi-e* 1734.

106. Jōsei Sanjin KYŌSEN kō. (fl. 1760s). His signature on prints has

long puzzled scholars. He was the chairman of one of the chief literary clubs which commissioned prints from Harunobu and others. He may himself have designed some of the prints so signed but more likely he devised what others executed.

107. Sukuki Harunobu fude with seal. See No. 100.
108. Koriusai gwa with a *kakihan* (written seal). See No. 103.
109. Seigyō GYŌCHIN gwa with seal 'gyōchin'. (Also transliterated KYŌCHIN) (fl. 1740s?)
110. Kondō KATSUNOBU (fl. 1720) son of Kiyoharu who was noted for his *Kompira-bon*, he produced some rare but meritorious *urushi-e*.
111. Nishimura MAGOSABURŌ (Shigenobu). Earlier name of Ishikawa Shuha Toyonobu.
112. SHIGEMASA (1739–1820). Founder of Kitao School. Calligrapher and book illustrator. His scarce prints are unsigned.
113. KIYONAGA (Torii IV) (1752–1815). His work shows several influences besides Torii traditions. Very notable prints in the 1780s but the earlier work is but mediocre.
114. 'Seki' sig. of Kiyonaga (No. 113).
115. 'The 5th Torii KIYOMITSU fude' = Kiyomitsu II (1787–1869) sig. after 1815 of Kiyonaga's pupil, Kiyomine, see No. 116.
116. KIYOMINE. Early name of Kiyomitsu II.

Hanabusa School
117. Hanabusa ITCHŌ (1652–1724) an unorthodox Kanō school painter whose subjects, often humorous, were drawn from plebeian life. His sketches were extensively published throughout the eighteenth century and reprinted many times in the nineteenth. They were a constant influence on *ukiyo-e* but in general show a wider and deeper sympathy than anything in *ukiyo-e* itself. He founded the Hanabusa school.

Miyagawa-Katsukawa Schools
118. TOMINOBU Miyagawa School. Prints very rare but of some grace and marked by boldness of design.
119. SHUNSHŌ (1726–1792). Pupil of Miyagawa Shunsui and founder of the Katsukawa school. Noted for theatrical prints and a prolific producer of them in the two decades from 1770.
120. SHUNSEN (fl. 1800–1820 approx.). Mostly *bijin-e* in landscape.
121. SHUNDŌ (fl. 1780–1792). Actors in dramatic roles in *hosoban* format.
122. SHUNJŌ (died Aug. 1787). All his single sheet prints seem to date from the last two years of his life; previously he illustrated *kibyoshi*.

MIYAGAWA–KATSUKAWA & KITAO KITAGAWA & SCHOOL OF EISHI

SOME UKIYO-E ARTISTS AND THEIR SIGNATURES: III

123. SHUNKŌ (1743–1812). Produced some outstanding prints and is credited with the invention of the 'large head' portrait which, however, seems to have been earlier than his time.

124. SHUNCHŌ (fl. 1778–1795 approx.). Pupil of Shunshō; almost all his great prints are in the style of Kiyonaga whom he surpasses in the best of his work.

125. SHUNTEI (1770–1820). Some early actor prints but most commonly met with are prints of warriors, battles, etc. Some interesting landscapes in European manner.

126. SHUNYEI (1762–1819). Some actor prints of great merit. May have influenced Sharaku.

127. SHUNZAN (fl. 1782–1798). Actor prints but later influenced by Kiyonaga.

128. SHUNKYŌ produced a few rare prints about 1810.

129. Katsukawa SHUNSHŌ with kakihan (1726–1792) see No. 119.

130. Vase seal of Shunshō.

131. Vase seal of Shunkō.

132. SHUNTŌ. Pupil of Shunyei. Produced a few rare but fine prints in the first years of the nineteenth century. Some *mitate* themes are known by him in which young women play analogues of the main acts in theatrical productions.

133. SHUNKŌ (II) Shunsen's signature after 1812. See No. 120.

134. Yanagawa SHUNSUI. Worked in Kyōto during the last quarter of the eighteenth century and produced some good stencil prints. Relations with the Miyagawa school are problematical.

135. CHOSHU. This name is also read Nagahide by Kurth who says that he produced colour prints using also mica and metal powders. Further, Professor Kurth claimed that there were two artists of this name and that this one was a pupil of Chōki—a view now discredited. Choshdu produced stencil prints in both Kyōto and Ōsaka at the same time as the last.

Kitao School (Founder Shigemasa see No. 112).

136. MASAYOSHI (1764–1824). Pupil of Masanobu. His early work was in pure *ukiyo-e* style but later he worked in other styles, some highly individualistic such as that of the rapid sketches called *ryaku-gwa-shiki*.

137. MASANOBU (Kitao) (1761–1816). All his sheet prints—mostly *bijin-e*—were done in his early life. In middle age he became famous as the novelist Santo Kyoden.

138. Kubo SHUNMAN gwa (1757–1820). A very individualistic artist drawing his primary inspiration from Kiyonaga rather than from

his master, Shigemasa. Most of his single sheet prints are *bijin-e* of women of noble presence and reposeful gesture. He is also one of the great masters of the *surimono* using, quite frequently, 'still-life' themes.

139. Seals of SHUNMAN occurring on *surimono*.

Kitagawa School.

140. 'UTAMARO fude' signature of 1794.

141. 'UTAMARO fude' signature of 1804.

142. 'Kitagawa' (UTAMARO) sig. on the Shell Book. Utamaro (1754–1808) is considered by some to be the greatest of all the *ukiyo-e* artists and, in so far as such a generalization can have any meaning, this may be true. He was undoubtedly limited in his themes, the work of his maturity being almost restricted to *bijin-e*. That he had great gifts in other directions is attested by the Shell Book ('Gifts of the Ebb Tide'), the 'Insect Book' (*Mushi Erabi*) and the work on birds (*Momoshidori awase*) but these remain somewhat isolated in his output. His influence dominated *ukiyo-e* for the last twenty years of his life.

143. TOYOAKI. Early name of Utamaro.

144. Seal UTAMARO.

145. UTAMARO (II) fude (fl. 1800–1810). With very few exceptions his work is not impressive.

146. KIKUMARO (I) fude. Best of Utamaro's pupils. Signed thus, 1795–1805.

147. TSUKIMARO fude. Signature of No. 146, from 1805 to 1820.

148. 'Kwanunsai TSUKIMARO fude'. A late signature of 147.

149. SENKWA.

150. 'KIKUMARO II fude' pupil of Kikumaro I, worked in the 1830s. Does not appear to be the same as Yukimaro, son of Kikumaro I.

151. HIDEMARO. Pupil of Utamaro I. Active during Bunkwa (1804–1817).

152. SHIKIMARO. Contemporary of last.

153. YOSHIMARO. Pupil of Kikumaro I. Active 1810s. About 1819 took the name of Kitao Shigemasa III. Sometimes signed Yoshimarō. Active until 1840.

154. SHUCHŌ gwa. Active c. 1795–1800. Study of his rather rare prints gives him an increasing reputation. *Bijin-e*, fine *surimono*, *kwa-chō* and European influenced *uki-e*.

155. Angyusai YENSHI (active 1787–1793). Rare *bijin-e* and actors (=? Angyusai Shudō).

156. BUNKYŌ (1767–1830). Is the novelist Sakuragawa Jihinari. Very rare prints.
157. SORAKU. Pupil of Yeishi. Portrait busts of young women but his work in prints is rare. Was a noted *kyōka* poet.
158. RYUKOKU (active *c.* 1808–1816?). Work in style of Utamaro.
159. BANKI fude (=BANKI II) Worked at same period and in similar style to 158.
160. BANKI (I). Seems to have been influenced by Utamaro, Shunshō and Kiyonaga. His prints are rare but represent a rather wide range of subjects. He designed at least one successful *hashirakake-e* of half length figures in the style of Utamaro.
161. BANRI. Rare artist. Work shows influence both of Kiyonaga and early Utamaro.
162. SHUCHŌ. Another signature of 154.
163. BUNRŌ (active 1795–1800) pupil of Tamagawa Shuchō.
164. RYUNSAI. Some fine figure studies, somewhat in the manner of Kiyonaga but with a certain resemblance to early Utamaro. Dates unknown.
165. SEKIJŌ (active *c.* 1798–1807). Pupil of Sekiyen.
166. SEKIHŌ. Same master and same period of activity as last.

School of Eishi (the so-called 'Hosoda School').
167. EISHI gwa. An early signature.
168. EISHI gwa. A later signature (1756–1829). A highly individual artist of very great talent. His restrained and rather low colouring and the unusually perfect placing of accessories combine to give an impressively aristocratic atmosphere to his work.
169. CHŌBUN gwa. In seal script. A signature of Chōbunsai Eishi (No. 168).
170. EISHŌ gwa (active 1790s–1810). Pupil of 168 but influenced also by 142. Mostly designed pictures of courtesans.
171. Chōkōsai EISHŌ gwa. Signature of 170.
172. Shōeido EISHŌ gwa. Another signature of No. 170.
173. Chōensai EISHIN fude (active *c.* 1793–1805) variously stated to be the pupil of 168 and of EIZAN but the former is certainly correct.
174. GOKYŌ (active around 1795). Pupil of 168 whose style he followed with great exactitude. Prints by him are very rare but of high quality.
175. EIRI (active 1788–1805). Designed but few prints in manner of Eishi. He also illustrated some *kibyoshi* with a certain success.
176. EISUI (active 1795 to about 1801). Responsible for some rather individualistic designs in the style of his master, Eishi.

INDEPENDENT ARTISTS   UTAGAWA SCHOOL

SCHOOL OF HOKUSAI

SOME UKIYO-E ARTISTS AND THEIR SIGNATURES: IV

177. EIJU. Active about same time as last. Probably an amateur.
178. EIKŌ. Known only as a painter of *ukiyo-e* and not as print designer. Some of his work has been illustrated however in later block printed illustrated books.
179. EITOKU. A rare artist active about 1800. Designed very few prints.

Independent Artists.

180. Tōshusai SHARAKU (worked 1794 and 1795). One of the most highly valued artists of *ukiyo-e* school. Nothing is known for certain of his life although there is perhaps some slight evidence that he was a Nō actor of this name. He designed prints for Tsutaya but being unsuccessful at this time disappeared the following year. All his work concerns people of the *kabuki* theatre except for one portrait of a wrestler.
181. Ichijusai KUNIMASA (1773–1810). Pupil of Toyokuni whose style he followed in some early prints but later did some impressive actor portraits much influenced by Sharaku yet with individual characteristics of his own. His work is perhaps even rarer than Sharaku's.
182. 'Kabukidō'. Signature of Kabukidō ENKYŌ (worked 1796). An amateur who designed a few actor portraits very much in the style of Sharaku. These are highly prized but very rare.
183. BUNCHŌ (active 1760s and 1770s). Work for all its high individuality shows the influence of Harunobu. Portraits of actors. Thought by some to be among the greatest artists of the school. His work is rare and not easily assessed. (See Plate 13).
184. HANZAN (active 1840s–1860s). An Ōsaka artist most noted for his *surimono* which are in an exceptional, broad, sketchy style.
185. SUGAKUDŌ (Worked 1859–1860). A native of Ōsaka whose Kwachō prints are sometimes of quite exceptional merit.
186. KOKAN SHIBA (1747–1818). Pupil of Harunobu. Much influenced by western art which he studied at Nagasaki. Worked also with oil painting, copper-plate engraving and lithography as well as a few *ukiyo-e* style woodcuts. Also used the name Harushige, see No. 101.
187. (Kōno) BAIREI (1844–1895). Studied Shijō school methods but produced some woodcuts of merit although of somewhat garish colour. Noted mostly for volumes of bird and flower studies produced in the 1880s and 1890s. Signed also Chōkuho and Shijun.
188. ZESSHIN (1807–1891). Noted painter and lacquerer. Specialized in

birds and flowers. Produced a few very noteworthy and individual *surimono*.

School of Hokusai.

189. HOKUSAI Tatsumasa (1760–1849) signature of about 1800. Perhaps the most prolific of all *ukiyo-e* artists and certainly the most experimental. His work is very uneven in quality. He used more than twenty other names, many for quite short periods in the different stages of his career. He did work in all the subjects known to *ukiyo-e* art and to some other schools as well. The best of his work is now rather hard to come by although late reprints of his books are not uncommon.

190. Katsu (shika) SHUNRŌ. Name given to him by Shunshō whose pupil he was. Hokusai used the name at various times until 1796. This signature dates from 1786.

191. Hishikawa SŌRI. A signature used by Hokusai about 1797 and found in his *kibyōshi* and *surimono* of this period. He was, in fact, Sōri IV. The first two of the name were painters only, the first (early eighteenth century) studied both Sumiyoshi and Korin schools. The third was the illustrator of Kyosen's 'Segen Jui'.

192. Gwakyōjin HOKUSAI. A signature adopted about 1800.

193. Zen Hokusai Iitsu.

194. HOKUSAI. Name in seal script from the 'Mangwa'.

196. HOKUSAI. With phonetic reading in *kana* script.

196. 'Gwakyō rōjin manji HOKUSAI' signature from 1838.

197. TAITŌ (II) Hokusai himself was Taito I. This pupil was active from 1821 to about 1853. He was given the name in 1820 when Hokusai took the name Iitsu (No. 193). He was earlier known as Hokusen. Because he copied the master's prints without authority, he was known as 'Dog Hokusai'.

198. HOKUJU (active *c.* 1802–1834). Book illustrations and some meritorious *surimono*.

199. HOKUI (active *c.* 1830–1840).

200. HOKUEI. An Ōsaka artist (see No. 8), pupil of Hokusai.

201. HOKUBA (1770–1844). Pupil of Hokusai. Noted for book illustrations, some humorous single sheets and certain exquisitely detailed *surimono*.

202. HOKKEI (worked 1810–1856). Perhaps the best of the master's pupils. He was responsible for some very fine *surimono*, a few Ōsaka school prints and several illustrated books.

203. Kikō KEISEI. A pupil of the last. Perhaps an amateur: he produced a few rare *surimono*.

204. SHINSAI (active 1803 to about 1815). Several books, some good *surimono* and some rare and interesting landscape prints. Hokusai gave him the name in 1800.
205. HOKUSHU. A pupil of Hokusai's active in the Ōsaka school about 1830–1840.
206. GAKUTEI (active 1800 to about 1840) pupil of Hokkei and of Hokusai. A good book illustrator, he also produced some rare and effective landscape sheets but is mostly remembered as one of the masters of the *surimono*. These last are rich and detailed and usually with all the refinements of printing reserved for this kind of work.
207. SŌRI gwa. A signature of Hokusai's from 1798.
208. Yanagawa SHIGENOBU (1784–1832). Pupil of Hokusai and later son-in-law. Worked in Ōsaka and Edo. Known for a few interesting prints of Nō actors.
209. HOKUGA. A pupil of Hokusai. His work is of poor quality but he is said to have been expert at mixing colours.
210. HOKUSUI. A member of this school who, about 1850, was responsible for some small landscape sheets which have a surprising charm and are drawn and printed with considerable care. He had a rather restrained colouring.

Utagawa School.
211. Utagawa TOYOHARU gwa. An early signature (1735–1814). Founder of the school. His work is lacking in power and his early landscapes are little more than topographical essays. His *uki-e* and battle scenes were very important historical developments in *ukiyo-e*.
212. Ichirysai Utagawa TOYOHARU gwa. A later signature.
213. Seal of TOYOHARU.
214. TOYOHIRO (1763–1828). Essayed almost all subjects but remains a *petit maître* of charming atmosphere and gentleness—characteristics apparent in his *surimono* particularly.
215. TOYOHISA (active 1808–1818?). Made a few actor prints.
216. TOYOHIDE. An Ōsaka artist.
217. YEIZAN (1787–1867). Founder of the Kikugawa school. Produced many prints, some in style of Utamaro. He also copied Toyokuni. Figure subjects.
218. YEISEN (1790–1848). Prolific designer of prints of women.
219. TOYOKUNI (I) (1769–1825). An influential artist who, although prolific, has claim to only a few really great works. The name was also used by Toyokuni II, Toyoshige and Toyokuni III (Kunisada).
220. TOYOKUNI II (Toyoshige) (1777–1835). Signs also Gōsotei, Ichiyeisai and Ichiryusai Toyokuni.

221. TOYOKUNI (III) (Kunisada) (1786–1865). Produced an enormous quantity of work usually of negligible quality but among it probably more fine prints than are usually accredited to him.
222. KUNISADA, see 221.
223. KUNIHISA. Three of this name; two women pupils of Toyokuni I and II and a man signing Ichiryusai, Ippōsai, and Ichiunsai Toyokuni.
224. KUNIHIKO (Kokkisha).
225. KUNITSUNA (Ichiransai and Ichirantei).
226. KUNITOMO. Pupil of Toyokuni II.
227. KUNINAO. Two artists of this name, the first a pupil of Toyokuni I (1793–1854).
228. KUNINAGA. Ichiunsai (active 1801–1829).
229. KUNIMORI. Ippōsai, Kōchōrō, pupil of Toyokuni II.
230. KUNIYOSHI (1797–1861). Known for his *musha-e* (pictures of heroes) but was responsible for some fine landscape, *shunga* and pictures of cats.
231. KUNIYASU (1794–1834) Ippōsai. Fellow student with 230 under Toyokuni I.
232. KUNIMITSU (active 1802–1810s) Ichiōsai.
233. KUNICHIKA. Pupil of Toyokuni I: Ichiyosai, Ikkeisai and Keseisha.
234. KEISAI (Yeisen).
235. YOSHIMARU (active 1807–1840). Pupil of Tsukimaro but did not escape Utagawa influence.
236. YOSHIKUNI. Pupil of Kuniyoshi, worked in Ōsaka. Signed Jukōdō, Shunkōdō, Toyokawa.
237. YOSHIHARU.
238. YOSHITORA (active 1850–1880). Ichimōsai, Kinchōrō and Mōsai. Some satirically humorous work of slight interest among much rubbish.
239. KUNIMUNE. Student of Toyokuni I.
240. KUNITERU. Pupil of Toyokuni I. Used name Issai. A KUNITERU II, pupil of Kunisada.
241. KUNIKIYO. Pupil of Toyokuni I.
242. HIROSHIGE I (1797–1858). Artist with enormous output. Noted for some of the finest atmospheric landscape prints especially those depicting snow and rain.
243. HIROKAGE (worked 1851–1866). Pupil of Hiroshige I.
244. Kwaisai YOSHITOSHI (died 1892). His best work was worthy of a better place in history.
245. FUSATANE (worked 1849–1859) Isshōsai.

246. HISANOBU (worked 1800 to about 1820) of uncertain affinities.

247. GOSHICHI (worked around 1802). Pupil of Yeizan. His *surimono* are often excellent.

248. KYŌSAI (1831–1889). Pupil of Kuniyoshi. Had individual style. Often humorous.

249. SHIGENOBU (1826–1869) was Hiroshige II and the son-in-law of Hiroshige I.

250. ŌSENCHO. A pupil of Yeisen, No. 218.

251. YOSHITSUNA. A pupil of Kuniyoshi, No. 230.

252. Utagawa SADASHIGE (1830–1874) was Kuniteru II and of some merit.

253. SADATORA (worked 1830s and 1840s). Pupil of Kunisada. Some interesting prints.

254. CHIKAMARO. A name used by Kyōsai, No. 248.

Japanese Chronology

1	2	3	4	5	6	7	8	9	10
一	二	三	四	五	六	七	八	九	十

NUMERALS

Rat	Ox	Tiger	Hare	Dragon	Snake	Horse	Goat	Ape	Cock	Dog	Boar
子	丑	寅	卯	辰	巳	午	未	申	酉	戌	亥

YEAR NAMES

Hōei	Shōtoku	Kōhō	Gembun	Kwampō	Enkō	Kwanen	Hōreki
宝永	正徳	享保	元文	寛保	延享	寛延	宝暦
1704	1711	1716	1736	1741	1744	1748	1751

Meiwa	Anei	Temmei	Kwansei	Kôwa	Bunkwa	Bunsei	Tempō
明和	安永	天明	寛政	享和	文化	文政	天保
1764	1772	1781	1789	1801	1804	1818	1830

Kōkwa	Kaei	Ansei	Man-en	Bunkyu	Genji	Kei-ō	Meiji
弘化	嘉永	安政	萬延	文久	元治	慶應	明治
1844	1848	1854	1860	1861	1864	1865	1868

NENGŌ

Agemaki

1

Anekawa

2

Arashi

3

4

5

6

Bandō

7

8

9

10

11

Fujimura

12

Hayakawa

13

Ichikawa

14

15

16

17

18

19

20

21

22

23

24

25

26

27

28

29

30

31

Ichimura

32

33

34

Iwai

35

36

ACTORS' MON

APPENDIX IV

A LIST OF ACTORS' MON

The name of an actor usually found upon a print is his professional name or *geimei*, e.g. Sawamura Sojurō, and occasionally there will be added his number in the line of succession which, in this instance, might be the third. Sometimes he may be cited on the print only by his literary name or *haimyō* which, for the present example, was *Tosshi*. More rarely in the earlier prints but more frequently in later ones, will be found only his *ya-go* which here, as for most of the Sawamura, was *Kinokuniya*. The first word of the *geimei* is that of the '*ke*' or line (family ?—into which he was certainly adopted in most instances), the second word is the name which, either he has initiated himself—as with the first of any *Ke*—or which has been given to him when he attained a certain proficiency in the art. It makes for confusion in identifying the actors on prints, that this second name may be changed more than once and that some actors, although not very frequently, might pass from one *Ke* to another; thus Morita Kanya VIth whose *haimyō* was *Zankyō*, became successively Takinaka Shigenei, Sawamura Shigenei and Sawamura Kodenji and all of these, of course, refer to the same man.

Members of the *ke* or 'school' of acting tended, in practice, to share the same badge or, at least, the same motif for the badge or *mon* and such a badge was called their *jō-mon*. Most actors had in addition a more personal *mon* called the *kae-mon* which was frequently used by the actor in private life but not when in character on the stage although, very exceptionally, both may be found on a print. Most of the *mon* in the present list are *jō-mon* but some *kae-mon* are also given when these are known to occur on prints of any kind. It will be seen therefore that, in the absence of the ability to read the Japanese name of the actor or, if this *is* possible, to identify him from his *haimyō* if only that should be given on the print, it is often possible to name him, or at least the school to which he belongs, by being able to identify his *mon*. Hence the importance of the present list. (Considerably more biographical detail is available for some of these actors and will be found in Binyon and Sexton's *Japanese Colour Prints*, London 1923, 2nd ed. 1960).

1. Agemaki Rinza but before 1756 was Azuma.
2. Anekawa Shinshirō (1690–1749) but *jō-mon* of the whole school.
3. Arashi *jō-mon*
4. Arashi Sangorō (1726–1729).
5. Arashi Wakano.
6. Arashi Ōtohachi (1732–1768).
7. Bandō *jō-mon*.
8. Bandō Hikosaburō II.
9. Bandō Mitsugorō I *jō-mon*.
10. Bandō Mitsugorō II *kae-mon*: *jō-mon* as 9.
11. Bandō Hikosaburō III, 1759–1803/1806–1811.
12. Fujimura Hantayu *jō-mon*.
13. Hayakawa Shinkatsu, 1703–1711/1712–1738.
14. Ichikawa Danjurō II and the *mon* of the Naritaya and Kuraiya.

15. The *jō-mon* of the Osaka branch of the Naritaya. Sumizō Ichikawa occurs in late prints.
16. Ichikawa Danzō I, 1695–1740 (after 1731 he removed the character '*ichi*').
17. Ichikawa Sōsaburō, 1731–1753.
18. Ichikawa Raizō I (*kaemon*)—his *jō-mon* was 14—and Ichikawa Monnosuke II, 1756–1794.
19. Ichikawa Masugorō, 1727–1741.
20. Ichikawa. *Jō-mon* of the *ke* Omodokaya.
21. Ichikawa Danzō III, 1739–1772 intermittently.
22. Ichikawa Ōmezō, 1776–1800/1804–1824.
23. Ichikawa Danjurō VI, 1782–1799.
24. Ichikawa Kōmazō II, 1770–1801.

25. Ichikawa Yaōzō II, 1751–1777. *Kae-mon*. For *jō-mon* he used No. 27.
26. Ichikawa Monnosuke, 1700–1727.
27. Ichikawa Yaōzō I, 1747–1759.
28. Ichikawa Kōmazō.
29. Ichikawa Ōmezō.
30. Ichikawa Monnosuke III?
31. Ichikawa Danzō who also used No. 16.
32. Ichimura Uzayemon VIII.
33. Ichimura Uzayemon IX, 1731–1785.
34. Ichimura Uzayemon XII for whose successors it became the *jō-mon*. Also used by Kakitsu.
35. Iwai Sagenda (1700–1718).
36. Iwai Hanshiro II (1700–1710) and Hanshiro III (1722–1756).

Iwai
continued

37

38

Kametani

39

Kamimura

40

Katsuyama

41

Kirinami

42

Matsumoto

43

44

45

Matsushima

46

Morita

47

48

Nakajima

49

50

Nakamura

51

52

53

54

55 上

56

57

58

59

60

61

62

63

64

65

66

67

68

69

70

71

72

73

74

ACTORS' MON

37 and 38. *Jō-* and *kae-mon* of Iyai Hanshiro IV, 1753–1800 intermittently.

39. Kametani Kikusan *jō-mon.*

40. Kamimura Kichisaburō, 1700–1708.

41. Katsuyama Matsugorō, 1707–1723.

42. Kirinami Onoe (*kae-mon*).

43. Matsumoto Koshirō, 1700–1729.

44. Matsumoto Kōshirō II, 1719–1776. Took No. 45 as *kae-mon.*

45. Matsumoto Kōshirō IV, 1754–1800 intermittently. *Kae-mon.* Took No. 44 as his *jō-mon.*

46. Matsushima Hyōtarō, 1700–1725 intermittently.

47. Morita Kanya became the *jō-mon* used by most of the *ke.*

48. Morita Kanya VI, 1736–1770.

49. Nakajima Kanzayemon, 1700–1710. *Jō-mon* also of Miyoyemon I, 1714–1762, and Miyoyemon II, 1755–1782.

50. Nakajima Sambōzō and several others of the *ke.*

51. Nakamura Senza, 1716–1718.

52. Nakamura Takesburō, 1700–1720.

53. Nakamura Shichisaburō I, 1700–1713 and *jō-mon* of Shichisaburo II who used No. 56 for his *kae-mon.*

54. Nakamura Denjuro I, 1700–1713.

55. Nakamura Kichibei, 1716–1739.

56. Nakamura Shichisaburō I and II.

57. Nakamura Sukegorō, 1725–1763.

58. Nakamura Utayemon I, 1757–1770.

59. Nakamura Denkurō II, 1733–1755.

60. Nakamura Tomijurō I, 1731–1778 intermittently and Noshi I, 1770–1777.

61. Nakamura Kiyosaburō, 1749–1758.

62. Nakamura Kumetarō I, 1748–1755.

63. Nakamura Nakazō I Kaemon. Acted intermittently with several changes of *mon*, 1745–1786. Used No. 54 as *jō-mon.*

64. Nakamura Nakazō II, 1778–1796.

65. Nakamura Matsue, 1761–1785. Used No. 66 as the *jō-mon.*

66. Jo-mon of No. 65.

67. Nakamura Sukegorō II, 1761–1798. *kae-mon.* Used 68 for *jō-mon.*

68. Nakamura Sukegorō I, 1725–1763.

69. Nakamura Nakazō. It is as No. 64 without the '*oni*' character in the centre and was used as a *jō-mon* by several later actors of the school.

70. Used by an Ōsaka Branch of the Nakamura (Tennōjiya ?).

71. Used by Baigyoku I and Fukusake I and found on some Ōsaka prints.

72. Used as *jō-mon* in this school by the long line of actors with the name Kanzaburō.

73. Used by the later actors of the Nakamura, with the name Utayemon and by the family Shikan.

74. A common *mon* in the school in later times and found on a late print of the actor Shibajaku (?III). Note differences from other butterfly *mon.*

Nakayama

75

Nishikawa

76

Ogawa

77

Ogino

78

79

Onoe

80

81

82

Osagawa

83

Ōtani

84

85

86

Sakata

87

88

Sanjō

89

90

Sanokawa

91

92

Sawamura

93

94

95

Segawa

96

97

98

99

Sodeoka

100

Sodezaki

101

102

103

Takenaka

104

Tomizawa

105

106

Tamazawa

107

Tsuruya

108

Yamashina

109

Yamashita

110

Yoshizawa

111

ACTORS' MON

75. Nakayama Raisuke *jō-mon*.
76. Nishikawa Kōnosuke, 1700–1702.
77. Ogawa Zengorō, ?1711–1732.
78. Ogino Isaburō, 1724–1747 *Kae-mon*.
79. Ogino Daikichi. Probably a *jō-mon* derived from the Onoe.
80. Onoe Kikugoro I, 1742–1766/1769–1773. *Kae-mon*.
81. Onoe Kikugoro I jō-mon and also the mon of later actors of this name.
82. Onoe Matsusuke, 1756–1814 intermittently. Sometimes used 81 as a *jō-mon*.
83. Osagawa Tsuneo I, 1750–1766.
84. Ōtani Hirōji III, 1755–1798 *jō-mon*.
85. Ōtani Hirōji I, 1701–1743 intermittently. Also used as a *jō-mon* by Hirōji II.
86. Ōtani Oniji *Kae-mon*.
87. Sakata Hangoro II, 1742–1782, and of Hangorō III (Hanjurō), 1756–1795. *Jō-mon*.
88. Sakata Hangorō II. *Kae-mon*.

89. Sanjō Kantarō, 1714–1749.
90. Sanjō actors. A later form of the butterfly of the *jō-mon*; also used as *kae-mon* by Segawa Kikunojo III.
91. Sanokawa Mangiku, 1718–1743 intermittently. *Kae-mon*.
92. *Jō-mon* of the Sanokawa.
93. Sawamura Kodenji, 1700–1702.
94. Sawamura Sōjuro, 1718 – 1755 intermittently. It is the *jō-mon* of almost all the actors of this *ke*.
95. Sawamura Sōjurō III, 1759–1800 intermittently. *Kae-mon*.
96. Segawa Kikunojō I, 1730–1748, intermittently.
97. Segawa Kikujirō, 1731–1773 intermittently.
98. Segawa Yujirō, 1764–1808. He changed his name a bewildering number of times and his *mon* with each. This is his *mon* as Yujirō; as Yaozo he used No. 99 and as Yaozō the same *mon* as No. 98.

100. Sodeoka Shōtarō, 1716–1733.
101. Sodezaki Nuinosuke, 1702–1711.
102. Sodezaki Miwano, 1725–1735.
103. Sodezaki Iseno, 1726–1745.
104. Takenake Kasen, 1734–1769.
105. Tomizawa Hansaburō, 1710–1718.
106. Tomizawa Montarō, 1730–1749.
107. Tamazawa Saijirō, 1733–1751.
108. Tsuruya Namboku, 1732–1752.
109. Yamashina Shirojurō.
110. Yamashita Kinsaka I, 1711 – 1742 intermittently. The actor Kinsaku II, 1752–1794, used this *mon* in a white outer circle. With some individual variations this was the *jō-mon* of the school.
111. Yoshizawa Ayame II, 1745–1752. Ayame I had the same *mon* but in black on white. Ayame IV had a similar mon which was *jō-mon* of the school.

In the study of these *mon* and of the actors who used them, the most useful references are 'Shoku Kabuki Nendaiki' ed. by Hiroya Yutarō (Tōkyō, 1925) and 'Kinsei Nippon Yengeki-shi' by Ihara Tōshirō (Tōkyō, 1913). These give portraits and short biographies of all the principal actors. Unfortunately only the second of these was available to me when writing the present work.

一筆 1　八重桐 2　十返 3　人里 4　九重 5

千石 6　三洲 7　春千 8　鳥馬千 9　歳川 10

春 11　太夫千 12　中紬 13　山夕 14　川小千 15

川 16　王ノ 17　江 18　墨夕 19　菊王 20

琴 21　玉裁 22　玉床 23　玉富 24　玉 25

白今 26　白炒 27　昭照 28　高白緑 29　物 30

半 31　露路 38　大 39　江 40　末 41　姫 42

俊絹 48　原衣 44　木炒 45　門地 46　夫川 47

川炒 53　在 58　川 59　大町 60　五部 61　妻 62　小 63

俳 49　衣笠 50　衣救 51　吉野 52　保 57

THE NAMES OF FAMOUS COURTESANS

APPENDIX V

THE NAMES OF FAMOUS COURTESANS

The rather lengthy tables of these names are necessitated by the fact that there are somewhat few characters shared in common among many names. There are also two further difficulties: the same character may have very different readings in different names and some of these readings will be found to be distinctly unusual ones. For this reason each name has been recorded separately. Exigencies of space have made it necessary for the columns to run on continuously so that one character of a name may be at the foot of one column and the other at the head of the next: this must be kept in mind when hunting for a particular name found on a print. Some names occur in these tables which are not in the accompanying lists and this is to be explained by the fact that it has proved impossible to locate a reference giving the house in which the owner of the name was an inmate. The names are arranged, as far as spacing has allowed, in order of the increasing complexity, *i.e.* the number of strokes, of the first character of each name. From the readings of these characters given here it should be possible to read the names of other courtesans that are not given in the accompanying list.

1. Hitofude (also a locution used in letters written by women and meaning 'just a line' or 'a few lines')
2. Yayegiri
3. Tokayeri
4. Nanasato
5. Kokonoye
6. Kawanoto
7. Sanshu
8. Mitsuharu
9. Chidori
10. Chitose
11. Chiharu
12. Chibune
13. Yugiri
14. Yubaye
15. Kumegawa
16. Kodayu
17. Nakayama
18. Ōi
19. Shirosumi
20. Shiroharu
21. Tamagawa
22. Tamanoye
23. Tamatoko
24. Tamashō
25. Tamagiku
26. Tamagoto
27. Tamahagi
28. Tamateru
29. Tamakadzura
30. Shiramono
31. Shirakawa
32. Shiro
33. Shirotaye
34. Shirotama
35. Shiroito
36. Shirabei
37. Shiragiku
38. Shiratsuya
39. Uriuno
40. Motosuye
41. Suyehiro (lit. a type of folding fan)
42. Takehime
43. Yegawa
44. Handayu
45. Taye
46. Yemon
47. Jigoku-dayu
48. Sayoginu
49. Koromode
50. Kinugasa
51. Yemon
52. Yoshino
53. Yoshikawa
54. Ariwara
55. Koshikibu
56. Sata
57. Sakao
58. Taye
59. Somakawa
60. Ōmachi
61. Adzuma
62. Kuretake
63. Oguruma

梅[117]　倭[123]

虎　枝[106]　泉　御[101]

武[90]　花　町[91]　花

妻[80]　琴　巷[75]

尾　村[69]　石[74]

尾山[64]　泊　瀬[65]　松　阿[71]　古　許[66]

THE NAMES OF FAMOUS COURTESANS

64. Ōyama
65. Hatsuse
66. Koya
67. Koya
68. Matsuyama
69. Matsumura
70. Matsukaze
71. Matsundo
72. Matsuhana
73. Matsumagi
74. Akashi
75. Nagato
76. Nagao
77. Nagohama
78. Chōtō
79. Nagaho
80. Tsumagōto
81. Makinoto
82. Ōmaki
83. Toriwa
84. Hanasaki
85. Kwachō

86. Hanayanagi
87. Kwayu
88. Hanandō
89. Hananoto
90. Hanagōromo
91. Hanamachi
92. Hananowatashi
93. Hanateru
94. Hanatsuma
95. Hanazome
96. Hanamurasaki
97. Hanaōgi
98. Hanamado
99. Hanatsuya
100. Hanatsuru
101. Toragozen
102. Otobane
103. Shinateru
104. Shigeoka
105. Shigemoto
106. Shigeririye
107. Senju

108. Harushiba
109. Haruno
110. Yoshito
111. Mitsuma
112. Wakamatsu
113. Wakana
114. Wakana
115. Wakataye
116. Wakaura
117. Wakaume
118. Wakamurasaki
119. Wakaba
120. Minadzuru
121. Somekawa
122. Somenosuke
123. Yamato
124. Suzunami
125. Ukishima
126. Ukifume (this is also the title of chapter 51 of the *Genji Monogatari*).
127. Kuranosuke

誰袖182　津美176　槙紀162　雲雅147　助筆　　高城川128

睽177　　羶祭　　尾助167　照然163　川173　大司178

尾183　繪春179　妙168　大勢169　姫善174　彈琴180

山184　歌172　歌　滿洲170　加滿166　昭萬171　稻壽186

高雄129　唐師137　山142　野扇133　瀧鳥143

高木130　撰の139　石岩134　常夏　津陸145

梅木146　唐崎136　菊宮141　山152　井157

揚場150　巻雲151　勝木　都路156　長盛161

橋185　小岡175　袖乙　　鴨186

THE NAMES OF FAMOUS COURTESANS

128. Takagi
129. Takao
130. Takamura
131. Takamadodayu
132. Miyagawa
133. Miyagi
134. Makinoto
135. Morokoshi
136. Karagiku
137. Morokoshi (this name seems originally to have been taken by prostitutes from the Ryu Kyu Islands)
138. Ōgino
139. Asaju
140. Michinoku
141. Umegaye
142. Onoyama
143. Onodaki
144. Toriiwa

145. Tokidzu
146. Tokigi
147. Tokiyoshi
148. Komurasaki
149. Renzan
150. Sushore
151. Agemaki
152. Katsuyama
153. Utanosuke
154. Yosogi
155. Asadzuma
156. Miyakoji
157. Kumoi
158. Kumodori
159. Tomikawa
160. Kisegawa
161. Kichō
162. Morinosuke
163. Hanaōgi
164. Sugawara
165. Suganosuke

166. Nioteru
167. Makinosuke
168. Terutaye
169. Daisei
170. Manshu
171. Mitsusode
172. Makino-ō
173. Kasen
174. Utahime
175. Sugaoka
176. Katsumi
177. Kawasemi
178. Yeishi
179. Masuharu
180. Kotobiki
181. Koine
182. Tagasode
183. Shidzu-no-ō
184. Misayama
185. Ōhashi
186. Ainare

THE NAMES OF FAMOUS COURTESANS

187. Nishikinokōji
188. Shinoura
189. Hamamurasaki
190. Ōiso
191. Agemaki
192. Kasumino
193. Usugumo
194. Yenishi
195. Shigeteru
196. Kaoi
197. Kayede

198. Toyoōka
199. Toyohara
200. Toyoteru
201. Segawa
202. Seyama
203. Takigawa
204. Takahashi
205. Tsuyazumi
206. Fujiwara
207. Kozakura

LOCUTIONS USED IN PRINTS OF WOMEN

1. Bijin (a Beauty)
2. Biyo (a Beauty)
3. Waka (young)
4. Yuri (a prostitute quarter)
5. Musume nana Komachi (Girls as the Seven Komachi)
6. Go (Shichi) kenjin. Five (Seven) courtesans from as many houses
7. Seirō meikun (Famous courtesans)
8. Yoshiwara
9. Jorō (a prostitute—in the Edo dialect)
10. Seirō bijin (Beauties of the Pleasure Quarters)
11. Ōiran (a prostitute of the highest class).
12. Ōidan (Literally, 'a flower bed'—a euphemism for a brothel)
13. Hanaguruma (Literally, 'a flower chariot', a cant name given to a serving maid in a brothel but in this sense it is read 'kwasha')
14. Ōgi (a prostitute, a substitution for the next . . .)
15. Ōgi (a fan, see No. 14)
16. Haru (read thus as 'Spring' but read 'Shun' it means 'erotic')
17. Ten (Den). (A shop. Usually one dealing in dried goods is understood. It is found on prints depicting lovely shop assistants)
18. Shōka (a brothel)
19. Kuruwa no naka or kuruwa no uchi. (Literally 'within the quarter'. It is said of inmates of the Yoshiwara)
20. Yugeijō (courtesans)
21. Jōshi (Lovers' Double Suicide)
22. Yukun (a courtesan)
23. Yujo (a courtesan)
24. Keisei (a courtesan)
25. Ageya (a brothel)

APPENDIX VI

EXAMPLES OF CENSORS' SEALS

The seal forms of numerals and zodiacal animals (*Junishi*) which are given in the table of dates will be found of great use in reading the majority of these censor seals found on prints. However, minor variations in the seal and also the particular way in which two or more seals are grouped together, are themselves of significance: the only full treatment of this is in the work of Mr Ishii Kendō (l.c.).

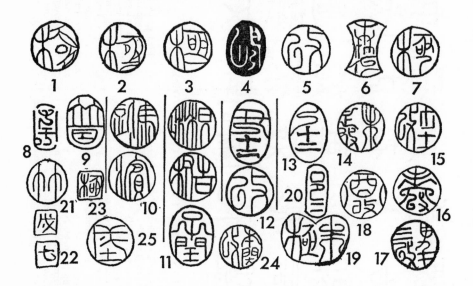

1, 2, 3. Three seals reading *kiwame* (investigated). No. 1 is the earliest and No. 3 the latest: there were other variants of this. These seals were used, either by themselves or with others from 1790 to 1845.

4. Oval seal reading *aratame* (examined) used from 1848 to 1851.

5. Round *aratame* seal, used December 1853 to 1857 inclusive.

6. A seal of a kind showing that the usual formalities had been complied with. It reads *Mori-ji*, i.e. Morijiya Jihei, the publisher who acted for a time as a censor (*gyōji*) of the Guild of Wholesale Publishers. Such seals are found in several very unusual shapes, only one round one—that of Tsuruya Kinsuke—being known. These seals were used with the *kiwame* seal from 1812 to 1815.

7. A type of *Kiwame* seal used, with minor variations from 1804 onwards.

8. A seal denoting the month. This one reads *juni* (twelve). This type of seal was used alone in 1805 and 1806 and with No. 7 from

February 1805 to December 1810 inclusive.

9. A type of seal used from 30th January, 1843 to February 1848. These are the seals of *Nanushi* censors and show one syllable of their name. This one reads *Fu* but the identity of the owner is uncertain.

10. A two-seal arrangement used from January 1847 to February 1853. Lower reads *Hama*, a *nanushi*. Upper *Tanaka* also a *nanushi*. This was the period of two *nanushi* seals on each print.

11. Three-seal period from February/April 1852 to December 1853. Top: a *nanushi*, Muramatsu. Middle: a *nanushi*, Yoshimura. Bottom: *Ne roku*, i.e. Rat Year, intercalary month=March/April 1852.

12. Two-seal period from January 1854 to December 1857. Top and bottom seals read, *Ushi* (Ox year) 12th (month)=January 1854, and *Aratame*.

13. Used singly from January 1858 to January 1859. Reads Snake 11th month=November 1859.

14. From 1860 to 1876. Reads Goat year 1,

incorporated with *aratame*. Nos. 14 to 19 inclusive show way 's' in which the two were combined.

15. Horse 11 *aratame* (1870).
16. Goat 1 *aratame* (1871).
17. Monkey 3 *aratame* (1860).
18. Cock 8 *aratame* (1861).
19. Goat *aratame* (1859).
20. Muraji=Murataya Jirobei, *gyōji* censor.
21. *Take*=Takeguchi Shoyemon. This type of seal used 1840 to 1853.
22. Dog (year) 7th (month)=1814 (August/September) only.
23. *Kiwame* ona *bijin-e* fan print by Kunisada.
24. Horse, intercalary month=November/December 1870.
25. Dog 11=October/November 1874.

CHARACTERS USED IN PUBLISHERS' NAMES

APPENDIX VII

CHARACTERS USED IN PUBLISHERS' NAMES

This table is designed to provide help in reading the names of publishers and, to a lesser extent, of engravers and printers. It must be used in conjunction with the 'table of characters used in the names of artists of the *ukiyo-e* school' (Appendix IX) which contains a number of characters also occurring in the names of publishers. The characters in the accompanying table include those commonly found in the 'personal' or 'fore-' names of the publishers listed in the text. Many of them are linked together by braces and these must be read *as a whole* although any particular character may be given an unusual or abnormal reading by so doing. The numbers 3 to 23 inclusive are common terminations of personal names and so may serve as 'keys' to these names when occurring in the colophons of books. Numbers 24 to 40 inclusive are added to such endings as *hei, bei, suke*, etc. to complete the 'personal' name whilst numbers 41 to 46 are some less common endings of 'art' names which, although used by a few publishers will probably be found more commonly in the names of engravers. The remaining characters, with the exception of numbers 1 and 2 are those commonly used in the *ya-go* or *dō-go* of publishers, those given unusual readings in such names and certain characters which, although not of common occurrence in such a context, are not included in the list of those used in the names of *ukiyo-e* artists. Once again the readings of those linked by braces are the readings given to the two characters taken together.

Numbers 1 and 2 are key characters by the presence of which the name of a publisher may be located in the colophon of a book. They represent the terminating suffix of the *dō-* and *ya-go* respectively. In such a position they should be read with the preceding two (rarely, one or three) characters which, if transliterated in accordance with the readings given here, will usually be found to give one of the names in the accompanying list of publishers.

1. Dō a hall	40. Yao	74. -shirō, ki
2. Ya denotes a shop or place of business.	41. Sai	75. -saki, -zaki
	42. Ken	76. -saka, -zaka
3. -hei, -bei	43. Sha	77. -shita, -noshita
4. -yemon, but read Uyemon when alone.	44. Tei	78. -nami, -ba, -wa
	45. Yen	79. -tsuki (-dzuki)
5. -zayemon, but read Sayemon when alone.	46. Kwan	80. Adzuma
	47. Sō, Shō, ai or Ō	81. Tsutsu
6, 7, 8, 9, 10, and 11. all read, -suke.	48. Boku (Ura)	82. Kwan, Maru
	49. Ari	83. Kyu, Ku
12. Tarō	50. Ta (Da)	84. Mori, Shun
13. Ichirō	51. Kin, Kon, Kane	85. Sa, Suke
14. Saburō	52. Kō (Gu)	86. Tsuta, Chō
15. Hikisaburō	53. Yei	87. Waka (Jaka)
16. Kichirō	54. Hon	88. Sei, Shō, Kiyo
17. Koshirō	55. Tō, Tsu	89. Sei, Si
18. Heisakurō	56. Sho	90. To, Ko, iye
19. Toshirō	57. Yei	91. Kin, Kon
20. Jurō	58. Yetsu, Koshi	92. Kichi, Ki, Kitsu, Ye, yoshi
21. Shōyemon	59. Fuji (Tō)	
22. Gennosuke	60. Take	93. Chu, Tada
23. Tokubei	61. Kawa, Gawa, Sen	94. Suwara
24. Ta	62. Yama	95. Ki, Yoshi
25, and 26. Ichi or I	63. Gen, Gwan	96. Kwaka (Toshi)
27, 28 and 29. Ji	64. Hō	97. Idzumi, Sen
30. San	65. Yei	98. So. But in the combination shown in the following it is read as indicated.
31. Shi	66. Rin, h(b) ayashi	
32. Go	67. Sei, Shō, I	
33. Roku	68. -uchi, -nouchi	
34. Shichi	69. -mura	99. Kadzusa
35. Hachi	70. Hei	100. Gio, Go, Na, Uo (uwo)
36. Ku	71. -kuchi, guchi	101. Ye, Kō
37 and 38. Ju	72. -matsu, Shō	102. Kane, Ken
39. Yaso	73. -shirō	

LOCUTIONS USED IN CONNEXION WITH BOOKS

紅墁 103　治之 104　伊 105　仙場 106　衛 107　和口 108　墁崎 109　銀 110　和 111　崎 112

若 113　市 115　萬 117　魚 119　居 121　劣 123　基 125
藏 116　滇越 118　兼帯 120　鶴 122　地 124　126

撰者 1　輯者 5　韋韋 9　繪 20　黃畫 38　紙 41　冊 39　十 42　襪 40

書賈 2　絹編 10　應 6　兄 16　新本 21　通 35　由 36　式 34　大和 31

書肆 3　者 7　畫 13　墨畫 14　版 23　彫 25　版考 29　新 22　刻 26　撥 44

寫 4　曆 8　好 11　版 12　繪 18　噸 19　和 43

103. Ko
104. Masu, Sō (Zō).
105. Ji, Chi.
106. Shi, Shiba.
107. I, Kore.
108. Ba, Jō.
109. Sen, nori, hito.
110. Kwa. Wa, Kazu.
111. Yei (ei), e. Also used as an alternative form of

the character in 3, 4 and 5.
112. Ki
113. Iwa, Gan.
114. Gin
115. Shi, Chi, ichi.
116. Su, Shu.
117. Ta
118. So (Zo) jura, masa.
119. Gio, Go, Na, uo (uwo).

A contracted form of No. 100.
120. Koshi, Koye, Yetsu.
121. Tsuru, Kaku (Kwaku).
122. Kane, Ken.
123. Iwa.
124. Ji.
125. Ise.
126. Jin.

LOCUTIONS USED IN CONNEXION WITH BOOKS

This list is a collection of words and phrases used in the titles or colophons of books, in connexion with signatures on prints or in native writings about illustrated books. It should be used together with the special tables on pages 310–313.

1. Senshu. Author (the first character is sometimes used by itself after an author's name and is then read 'sensa'.)
2. Shoku. A bookseller.
3. Honya. A bookseller.
4. Utushi. A copy.
5. Henshu. Compiled or edited by.
6. Hensha. Compiler or editor.
7. Hompon. A new edition.
8. Goyomi. An almanac.
9. Utsushi. A copy.
10. Moyō. A pattern or design.
11. Niōjite or Niōzu. Before a signature it signifies 'by special request'.
12. Utsusa. To copy.
13. Senkengwa. Fashionable illustrations.
14. Hankoku. A reprint.
15. Zōhan. A publisher.
16. Yekiōdai. 'Paired illustrations', i.e. one with another inset or in a reserve panel.
17. Sumi-e. A black and white sketch.
18. E. A drawing or design.
19. Hanashi. A story.
20. Nazoraye. 'A comparison'; a word found in print titles.
21. Tojihon. A bound book.
22. Jōshi. Published or publishing.
23. Jōhan. Published or publishing.
24. Jōboku. Published or publishing.
25. Shinchō. A new work.
26. Shinkoku. A new edition.
27. Shi. So read after the name of a publisher in which position it means 'Published by'.
28. Shōcha. A manual.
29. Kaihan. First issued.

30. Shimpan. A new work.
31. Owari. In colophons it means 'the end'.
32. Surimono (see chapter on these).
33. Dzukō. An illustrated treatise.
34. Dzushiki. A method of drawing.
35. Dzu-i. An illustrated series of books or prints.
36. Dzu-kai. Illustrations.
37. Gwasen. A collection of pictures.
38. Gwatsu. A series of drawings.
39. Engi. An historical work dealing with the foundation of temples or shrines.
40. Aohon. Cheap books in green or blue covers. They were designed for a popular market and dealt with historical incidents, plays, songs and popular dances and festivals.
41. Kibyoshi. Cheap, illustrated fiction of the 'Shilling shocker' kind. They were successors to the *ukiyo-zoshi*. Literally 'Yellow backs'.
42. Sasshi. A pamphlet, leaflet or brochure.
43. Fukuro Toji.
44. Yamato Toji.
These were two styles of binding which supplanted earlier ones used in medieval times. The first (43) means 'pouch binding' and originated in China. In this the leaves and covers were sewn together through five pierced holes. The second was a native style binding (44) utilizing four pierced holes—two at the top and two at the bottom—the threads being passed through these and tied separately. In cataloguing books the style of binding should always be recorded.

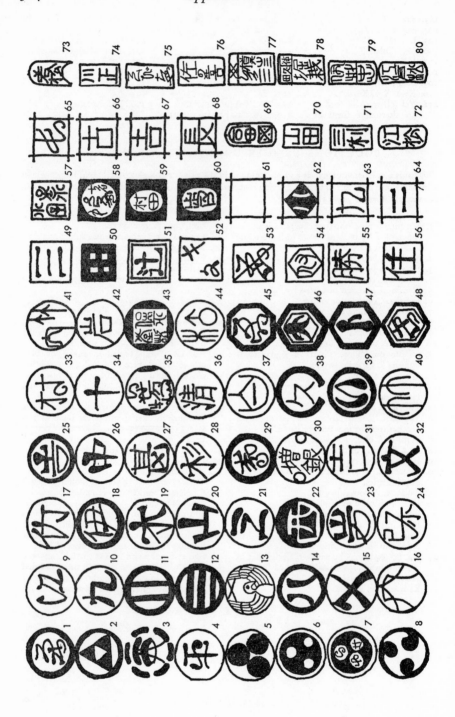

THE TRADE MARKS OF SOME EDO PUBLISHERS

APPENDIX VIII

THE TRADE MARKS OF SOME EDO PUBLISHERS

The majority of *ukiyo-e* colour prints have the publisher's trade-mark on them, sometimes accompanied by his seal. Quite often only the latter appears and, with the help of Koop and Inada's work on Japanese names, it presents little difficulty in reading especially if the possible readings given in that work are compared with the list of publishers in the foregoing pages. However, the unusual variants in which some characters are written and one or other of the types of seal character occasionally employed create special difficulties for the beginner: for these reasons it is sometimes easier to identify the publisher by his sign (*iye no shirushi*). Many of the latter however have not yet been identified and the following list gives most of those known to date. Identification of such a sign depends on finding it on a print—or more likely the colophon of a book—together with a readable seal of the publisher who was concerned in its production. It should be remarked here that the seal is generally composed of two characters each of which is the first syllable of the first and second name respectively, viz. 'Maruko'=Maruya Kohei.

The trade marks given here are arranged in accordance with a scheme first used by Mr B. W. Robinson in his monograph on Kuniyoshi—a scheme which in practice has proved to be very useful indeed. In the present list the marks are grouped into the following categories: 1. Within a circle. 2. Within an hexagon or octagon. 3. Within a square—including those with produced corners. 4. Within a rectangle. 5. Within a fan shape. 6. Within an angle. 7. Within a lozenge or diamond. 8. Within a triangle. 9. Under a single 'mountain' (the term is Mr Robinson's). 10. Under a double 'mountain'. 11. Under a triple 'mountain'. 12. Under crossed 'hockey sticks'. 13. In a vase, gourd or bag. 14. Single unenclosed characters or signs. 15. Miscellaneous.

1. Komatsuya Dembei
2. Urokogataya
3. Nakajimaya Risuke
4. Hiranoya Kichibei
5. Iseya Sanjirō
6. Iseya Kimbei
7. Iseya ?
8. Kiyomidzuya
9. Yedoya
10. Maruya Kuzayemon
11. Yezakiya Kichibei
12. Ibaya Sensaburō
13. Tsuruya Kihei
14. Yamaguchiya Kihei
15. Ibaya Kyubei
16. Kawaguchiya Chōzō
17. Takenouchi Magahachi
18. ? Maruya Tetsujirō (f. Robinson)
19. Iseya Tōkichi
20. Maruya Kohei
21. Mikawaya Rihei
22. Nishimuraya Genroku
23. Iwatoya Kisaburō
24. Matsumura Yahei
25. Yoshimaya Sonokichi
26. Tambaya
27. Maruya Jimpachi
28. Sugiwaraya ?

29. Tsuruya Ume?
30. Masuya Jimpachi
31. Yemiya Kichiyemon
32. Maruya Bunyemon
33. Murataya Jirōbei
34. Nishimaya Shinroku
35. Iseya Sōyemon
36. Maruya Seijirō
37. Ōsakaya Shōsuke
38. Ibaya Kyubei
39. Sawamuraya Rihei
40. Takenouchi Magohachi
41. Takenouchi Kikwakudo. (Perhaps this marks an amalgamation of the two firms.)
42. Iwatoya Yamagata, cf. No. 23!
43. Hoyeidō
44. Wakamatsuya Gensuke
45. Yamatoya
46. Daikokuya Kinnosuke
47. Yenshuya Hikobei
48. Igaya Kanyemon
49. Shimidzuya
50. Kagiya Shōjirō
51. Tsujiya Yasubei
52. Aritaya Kiyoyemon
53. Masuya ?

54. Izutsuya Kanyemon II
55. Nakamuraya Katsugorō
56. Sumimaruya Jinsuke
57. Hoyeidō
58. Sakaiya
59. Murataya
60. Nakajimaya
61. Omiya Yohei
62. Kogaya Katsugorō
63. Sakaiya Kurobei
64. Kawaguchiya Chōzō
65. Aridaya Seiyemon
66. Kogaya Kitsugorō
67. Sumiyoshiya Masagorō
68. Aritaya Kiyoyemon
69. Tomitaya ?
70. Yamadaya Sanshirō
71. Mikawaya Rihei II
72. Yedoya Matsugorō
73. Wakamatsuya Yoshirō
74. Kawaguchiya Shōhei
75. Ebisuya ?
76. Sanoya Kihei
77. 'Idzusan'
78. Horikoshi ?
79. Iseya Chusei
80. Yedoya Matsugorō

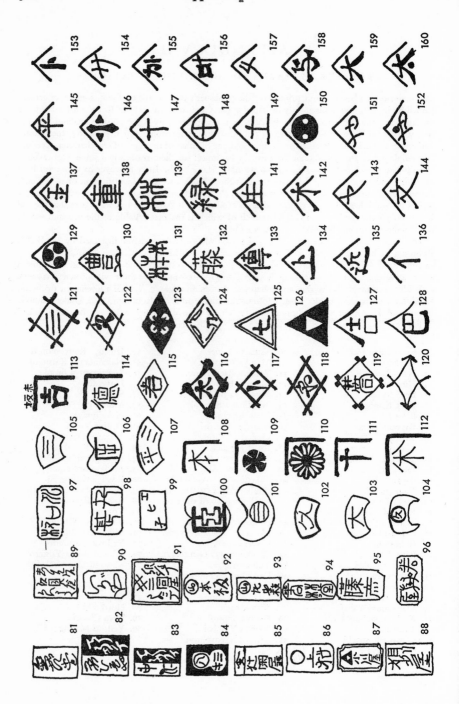

THE TRADE MARKS OF SOME EDO PUBLISHERS

81. Yenkakudō
82. Yebisuya Shōshichi
83. Kinshōdō
84. Mitaye Kihachi
85. Tsujiokaya Bunsuke
86. Uemuraya
87. Urokogataya
88. Sagamiya
89. Emiya
90. Igaya
91. Igaya
92. Yamamoto = Maruya Kohei
93. Maruya
94. Jakurindō = Yokasaya Yoichi
95. Fujiokaya Hikotarō
96. Wakasaya Yoichi
97. Isekane ? Kawaguchi
98. Maruya Jimpachi
99. Ebiya (ne ? 'moto', i.e. 'the original' ?).
100. Hirabashiya Shōgorō
101. Ibaya Sensaburō
102. Ibaya Kyubei = Kinseidō
103. Omiya Kuhei
104. Ibaya Kyubei
105. 'San'=? Sanmaidō

106. Rinshōdō
107. Sankindō
108. Daikokuya Heikichi
109. Azumaya Daisuke
110. Kikuya Ichibei
111. Kojimaya ?
112. Idzusan ?
113. Iseya Kanekichi
114. Hamadaya Tokubei
115. Wakasaya Yoichi
116. Ningyoya Takichi
117. Ebiya Rinnosuke
118. Izutsuya Chuzayemon
119. Izutsuya Sanyemon
120. Sagamiya
121. Yenami
122. Marukyudō
123. Uyedaya Kyujirō
124. Fujiwaraya Bunjirō
125. Ogawa Shichirōbei and Yenomoto Kichibei
126. Urokogataya
127. Yamashirōya (Shōk-wakudō) and Izudtsuya
128. Iwaiya
129. Nishimuraya Yohachi
130. Toyojimaya Bunjiye-mon
131. Mariya Jihei

132. Yamashirōya Tōkei
133. Yamaden
134. Kawaguchiya Uhei
135. Soshuya Yohei
136. Sanoya Kihei
137. Yamazakiya Kimbei
138. Joshuya Juzō
139. Iseya Rihei
140. Echizenya Heisaburō
141. Yamadaya Shōbei
142. Echigoya Chōhachi
143. Fujiokaya Hikotarō
144. Tsujiokaya Bunsuke
145. Omiya Heihachi
146. Shin Iseya Kohei
147. Yamadaya Juhei
148. Daikokuya Kyubei
149. Maruya Kyushirō
150. Daikokuya Kinjirō
151. Fujiokaya Hikotarō
152. Fujiokaya Keijirō
153. Yenshuya Matabei
154. Ōdaya Takichi
155. Tsuruya Kiyemon
156. Gusokya Kahei
157. Tajimaya Yahei
158. Hori Takichi
159. Joshuya Kinzō
160. Ningyōya Takichi

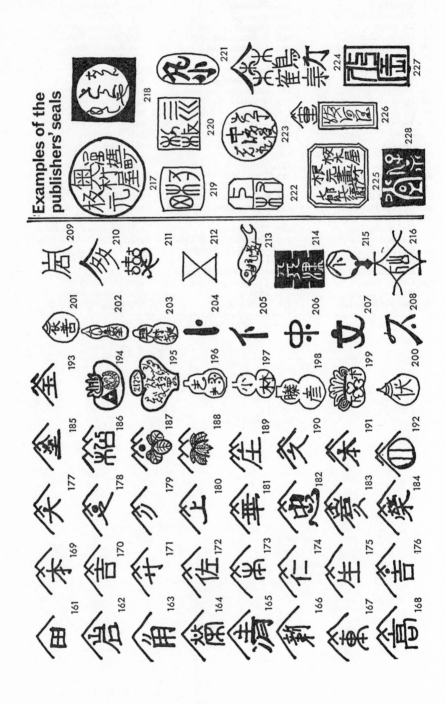

THE TRADE MARKS OF SOME EDO PUBLISHERS

161. Yamaden ?
162. Katoya
163. Kadomaruya
164. Takahashiya
165. Kiyomidzuya
166. Shinsenyendō
167. Surugaya
168. Takasu Shōshichi
169. Iwatoya Gempachi and Izumiya Ichibei
170. Kagaya Kichibei
171. Matsumoto Sahei
172. Yamadaya Sasuke
173. Takatsuya Isuke
174. Kinshodō (NOT Kinshōdō!)
175. Yebisuya Shōshichi = Kinshōdō
176. Yorozuya Kichibei
177. Jōshuya Kinzo
178. Fujiokaya Keijirō
179. ? Kuwagataya
180. Iseya Sōyemon
181. ? Herindō
182. Chusuke ?
183. Iwamoto Kyubei
184. Takahashiya
185. Mikawaya
186. Matsumura Yahei
187. Tsutaya Kichizō

188. Tsutaya Jusaburō
189. Ebisuya Shōshichi
190. Yamamotoya Heikichi
191. Kawaguchiya Shōzō
192. Yezakiya Tatsukura
193. Moritaya Hanjirō
194. Tsuruya and Urokogataya together
195. Izumiya
196. Reads 'Mitsuoki' the gourd seal of Okumuraya (Masunobu)
197. Kobayashiya Matsugorō
198. Fujihiko
199. Kinoshita Jinyemon
200. Fushimiya Genroku
201. Fushimiya Genroku as 200
202. Shiōya Shōsaburō
203. Okumuraya Genroku
204. Yamaguchiya Tōbei
205. Yamaguchiya Chusuke
206. Akamatsuya Shōtarō
207. Shiuwaya Bunshichi
208. Nishikiya Takemura
209. Kadzusaya Iwakichi
210. Ningyōya Takichi
211. Kiriya
212. Iseya Heibei
213. Ebisuya

214. Amamatsuya Hosuke
215. Yenshuya Matabei
216. 'Senichi'—see list
The following publishers' seals are chosen only as examples. When the publisher's name is printed in full the seal often follows it. A seal under the artist's name on a print is most frequently that of the artist himself and not the publisher.
217. Reads 'Tōri shio chō Okumuraya Hammoto' i.e. the publisher Okumuraya in Tori shio street.
218. Sakaiya hammoto
219. Murata han
220. Mikawaya Ai (hei) han
221. Maruko
222. Uemura
223. Nakajimaya
224. Tsurushin—later used by Moriji
225. Hangiya Shichirōbei
226. Surugaya
227. Ezakiya Tatsukura
228. Hoyeidō

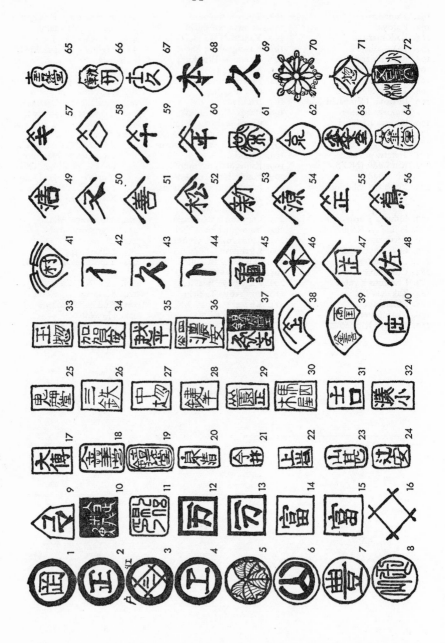

SUPPLEMENTARY LIST OF PUBLISHERS' TRADE MARKS

APPENDIX IX

SUPPLEMENTARY LIST OF PUBLISHERS' TRADE MARKS

These marks have accumulated whilst the present book was printing. They have been re-drawn from the *Jihon zōshi tonya mei zenchō* (Register of the addresses of the Former Wholesalers of Story Books), a rare work reproduced in facsimile by Juzō Suzuki in his *Nippon Hangwa benran*.

1. Okanoya Manjirō
2. Hirabayashiya Shōgorō
3. Musashiya Isaburō
4. Echizenya Hachiyemon
5. Okanaya Taheiji
6. Iseya Tokubei
7. Futaya Takekichi
8. Tomaya Senzaburō
9. Iseya Komatarō
10. Owariya Kiyoshichi
11. Kamiya Gorōbei
12. Miyoshiya Sōbei
13. Matsuya Shinzō
14. Sanoya Tomigorō
15. Sanoya Sadakichi
16. Izuya Sankichi
17. Ōshimaya Sayemon
18. Suwaraya Sasuke
19. Toganeya Niisaburō
20. Izumiya Kiyoshichi
21. Imaiya Sōbei
22. Kazusaya Iwazo
23. Yamashiroya Kambei
24. Tsujiya Yasubei

25. Honya Shōsuke
26. Mikawaya Tetsugorō
27. Nakajimaya Sōsuke
28. Kenya Shōgorō
29. Sonoharaya Shōsuke
30. Kiya Sōjirō
31. Masuya Kichigorō
32. Minatoya Kohei
33. Tamaya Sōkichi
34. Kagaya Yasubei
35. Koshimuraya Heisuke
36. Nōshuya Yasubei
37. Ebijuya Shōshichi
38. Iseya Uyemon
39. Kamaya Kihei
40. Hayashiya Shōgorō
41. Sawamuraya Rihei
42. Iseya Tokubei
43. Iseya Isaburō
44. Fujiya Munesuke
45. Kameya Iwakichi
46. Fukitaya Takichi
47. Okazakiya Mohei
48. Mikawaya Sahei

49. Shimidzuya Naojirō
50. Sasaya Matabei
51. Riuya Zembei
52. Matsuzakaya Kinnosuke
53. Yamashirōya Niiroku
54. Kamiya Gembei
55. Shiya Kihei
56. Murataya Ichigorō
57. Matsuzakaya Kikujirō
58. Hishiya Tomoshichi
59. Okazuya Jubei
60. Yamashirōya Heisuke
61. Yamatoya Shōbei
62. Miyakoya Kohei
63. Kikuya Kosaburō
64. Shioya Mosaburō
65. Shimaya Tetsuya
66. Surugaya Sabujirō
67. Honya Kiubei
68. Ohashiya Yashichi
69. Takadaya Takemasa
70. Chōjiya Heibei
71. Mikuraya Sōkichi
72. Kobayashiya Matsugorō

	A	B	C	D	E	F	G	H	I	J	K	L	M	N	O
1	安	近	菫	川	画	氏	北	治	藍	鈴	紅	麿	所	杭	柒
2	芦	設	田	下	嵯	畎	畑	壽	筆	溪	京	尢	明		
3	朋	鳥	傳	文	八	秀	一	常	兼	軒	與	政	峯	本	
4	馬	朝	藤	源	語	彦	偉	香	高	氣	塾	江	升	尢	宗
5	邊	長	風	月	伯	廣	井	雲	旦	景	喬	好	雅	滴	村
6	墨	調	房	玉	花	之	爲	段	罷	幾	琶	水	倍	宮	妙
7	ト	兆	牛	宇	牛	麦	衛	兼	河	枝	清	好	妖	門	南
8	文	蝶	雄	江	原	芳	意	景	川	木	公	花	眞	檻	年
9	地	藤	盂	口	抱	居	春	吾	員	菊	香	國	麿	寺	止
10	國	呈	嵩	都	与	鳥	石	上	王	尢	乇	松		盤	野

TABLE OF CHARACTERS USED IN THE NAMES OF THE
ARTISTS OF THE UKIYO-E SCHOOL

APPENDIX X

TABLE OF CHARACTERS USED IN THE NAMES OF THE ARTISTS OF THE UKIYO-E SCHOOL

These characters are arranged in the alphabetical order of their transliterated readings. As is well known, Japanese characters may be read in at least two ways and often more than two. In the following list, where the alternative reading is restricted to only one or two instances among the names of the artists, it is given in brackets after the common reading but where its alternative readings are fairly common the character is given in alphabetical order, two or three times. The table should be of use in turning the Japanese into the English transliteration and may also be of use in turning the English back into the Japanese character but in this it will obviously not be immediately apparent which of two or more characters with the same reading should be used and a choice will have to be made on other evidence in this instance. It is thought that the names of all known artists of this school are covered by the characters of the present table.

A. 1. An
2. Ashi
3. Aki
4. Ba
5. Be
6. Boku
7. Boku
8. Bun
9. Chi
10. Chika
B.1. Chika
2. Chika
3. Chō
4. Chō
5. Chō
6. Chō
7. Chō
8. Chō
9. Dō
10. Dō
C.1. Dō
2. Da
3. Den
4. Fuji
5. Fu
6. Fusa
7. Fusa
8. Ga
9. Gaku
10. Gaku
D.1. Gawa
2. Ge
3. Gen
4. Gen
5. Getsu or Ges
6. Gioku
7. Go
8. Gō
9. Guchi
10. Gun
E.1. Gwa
2. Gwa
3. Hachi
4. Haku
5. Haku
6. Hana

7. Han
8. Hara
9. Haru
10. Ha
F.1. He
2. Hide
3. Hide
4. Hiko
5. Hiro
6. Hisa
7. Hishi
8. Hō
9. Hō
10. Hō
G.1. Hoku or Hok
2. Hoso
3. and 4. Ichi (Ik, Ip, It, Itsu or Kadzu)
5, 6, 7, 8, 9, all I
10. Ishi
H.1. Ji
2. Jui
3. Jō
4. Ka
5. Ka
6. Ka
7. Kado
8. Kage
9. Kage
10. Kami
I.1. Kan
2. Kane
3. Katsu
4. Katsu
5. Katsu
6. Ki
7. Kawa
8. Kawa
9. Kazu
10. Kei
J.1. Kei
2. Kei
3. Ken
4, 5, 6, 7, 8, all Ki
9. Kiku
10. Kichi

K.1. Kin
2. Kio
3. Kio]
4. Kiō
5. Kiō
6. Kita
7. Kiyo
8. Kō
9 and 10, Kō
L.1, 2, 3, 4, 5, all Kō
6. Ko
7. Ko
8. Kwa
9. Kuni (Koku)
10. Man
M.1. Maru
2. Maru
3. Masa
4. Masa
5. Masa
6. Masu
7. Masu
8. Ma
9. Maro
10. Matsu
N.1. Matsu
2. Mei
3. Mine
4. Mitsu
5. Mitsu
6. Miya
7. Mon
8. Mo
9. Mori
10. Mori
O.1. Mori
2. Moro
3. Moto
4. Mune
5. Mura
6. Myō
7. Nan
8. Nen (Toshi)
9. No
10. No

	P	Q	R	S	T	U	V	W	X	Y	Z	Aa	Bb	Cc	Dd
1	鍋	漢	峰	柳	齋	杲	飾	嵩	田	且	留	洞	洞	尾	夫
2	長	宣	樂	龍	方	仙	嶋	宗	大	種	富	顧	厳	給	柴
3	水	完	蘭	龕	谷	鮮	圭	齋	收	凡	虵	敀	谷	谷	江
4	中	周	園	春	鴈	信	倍	春	竹	谷	虎	到	山	山	園
5	直	大	韻	柳	清	流	而	焦	松	鳥	亭	藤	雲	豊	豊
6	三	應	嶺	蓮	而	囘	焦	翠	罹	亭	利	虎	虎	遠	遠
7	日	櫻	運	即	成	乙	雪	洲	而	爲	俊	年	笑	燕	燕
8	西	奥	理	六	石	之	焦	鈴	尺	輝	草	若	安	右	谷
9	信	肇	珋	貞	川	重	忠	丹	披	東	月	月	原	右	褥
10	延	鳳	立	戴	扇	千	蛋	迂	探	時	等	經	渡	水	搗

TABLE OF CHARACTERS USED IN THE NAMES OF THE
ARTISTS OF THE UKIYO-E SCHOOL

P.1. Nabe
2. Naga
3. Naga
4. Naka
5. Nawo
6. Ni
7. Nichi
8. Nishi
9. Nobu
10. Nobu
Q.1. Nobu
2. Nobu
3. Nori
4. Nori
5. Ō
6. Ō
7. Ō
8. Oku
9. Pitsu
10. Pō
R.1. Pō
2. Raku
3. Ran
4. Ran
5. Rei
6. Ren
7. Ren
8. Ri
9. Rin
10. Ritsu (Riu)
S.1. Riu
2. Riu
3. Rō
4. Riyo
5. Rō
6. Rō
7. Rō
8. Roku
9. Sada
10. Sai
T.1. Sai
2. Sato
3. Sei
4. Sei
5. Sei
6. Sei
7. Sek (Sess) (Set)
8. Seki
9. Sen

10. Sen
U.1. Sen
2. Sen
3. Sen
4. Shu
5. Shi
6. Shi
7. Shi
8. Shiba
9. Shige
10. Shikō
V.1. Shika
2. Shima
3. Shin
4. Shin
5. Shiu
6. Shiu
7. Shō
8. Shō
9. Shō
10. Sho
W.1. Sō
2. Sō
3. Sō
4. Shun
5. Sugi
6. Sui
7. Suke
8. Suzu
9. Tada
10. Tada
X.1. Ta
2. Ta
3. Taka
4. Take
5. Taki
6. Taku
7. Tame
8. Tami
9. Tan
10. Tan
Y.1. Tan
2. Tane
3. Tani
4. Tei
5. Tei
6. Tei
7. Teru
8. Teru

9. Tō
10. Toki
Z.1. Tome
2. Tomi
3. Tomo
4. Tora
5. Tori
6. Toshi
7. Toshi
8. Toshi
9. Tō or To
10. Tō
Aa.1, 2, 3, 4, 5, all Tō
6. Tora
7. Toshi
8. Tsui
9. Tsuki
10. Tsune
Bb.1. Tsuna
2. Tsura
3. Tsuya
4. Toyo
5. Um (Un)
6. Uta
7. Uta
8. Uye
9. Wara
10. Watana
Cc.1. Wo
2. Wō
3. Ya
4. Yama
5. Ya
6. Yama
7. Yasu
8. Yasu
9. Ye
10. Yei
Dd.1. Yei
2. Yei
3. Ye
4. Yen
5. Yen
6. Yen
7. Yen
8. Yō
9. Yō
10. Yu

	Ee	Ff	Gg	Hh	Ii
1	勇	芦	氣	辛	山
2	幽	義	雪	善	尤
3	芳	湯	之	三	藏

Ee.1. Yu
2. Yu
3. Yoshi
Ff.1. Yoshi
2. Yoshi

3. Yuki
Gg.1. Yuki
2. Yuki
3. Yuki
Hh.1. Yuki

2. Zen
3. Zabu
Ii.1. Zan
2. Zaye
3. Zō

NAMES OF THE ARTISTS OF THE CLASSICAL SCHOOL

竹洞 ₁ 鵬齋 ₂ 文鳳 ₃ 古秀 ₄ 眞虎 ₅ 梅亭 ₆ 文村 ₇ 墨僊 ₈

楠亭 ₉ 月樵 ₁₀ 等溪 ₁₁ 椿年 ₁₂ 素絢 ₁₃ 琦鳳 ₁₄ 吳春 ₁₅ 水石 ₁₆

芳中 ₁₇ 蕙齋 ₁₈ 南岳 ₁₉ 琳和 ₂₀ 嘉言 ₂₁ 公朝 ₂₂ 雲窒 ₂₃ 紫石 ₂₄ 大雅堂 ₂₅ 墨 ₂₉ 任原文庫 ₂₆ 夷葉齋青 ₂₇ 名家画譜 ₂₈ 洋 ₃₀

耳鳥齋 ₃₁

1. Chikudo	15. Goshun	published in five volumes (1810?).
2. Bōsai	16. Suiseki	27. Kanyōsai
3. Bumpō	17. Hōchu	28. Meika Gafu: title of another collection of paintings which were reproduced as wood-blocks and published in three volumes (1814).
4. Koshu	18. Keisai	
5. Matora	19. Nangaku	
6. Baitei	20. Minwa	
7. Buson	21. Kagen	
8. Bokusen	22. Kōchō	
9. Nantei	23. Umshitsu	
10. Gesshō	24. Shiseki	29. Umboku
11. Tokei	25. Taigadō	30. Seiyō
12. Chinnen	26. Ariwara Bunko: the title	31. Nichōsai
13. Sōken	of a famous collection of	
14. Kihō	designs of this school	

屋尾[1] 竹角[24] 田[41] 美岡[和] 田[52] 絵[67]

樓[2] 西[海老] 泉[35] 渡濃[47] 稻島[53] 桐[67]

文字[3] 矢田[25] 全品[36] 若[48] 木[60] [巴]檜[59]

宇[8] 佐[野松] 東川[42] 松[48] 鳥[61] 山[69]

久喜[18] 立[五] 局扇[37] 姿海老[49] 殿歌[62] 本[60]

喜[13] 花[松][26] 玄[之] 桐巣[44] 鷦[63] 吉[70]

一扇[14] 明樓[15] 浦筒[43] 菊[63] 村[70]

卍[5] 出[21] 小屋[38] 本菱[50] 圓南[64] 歌[71]

山口[10] 大[27] 近松[39] 時[45] 假名[65] 南[71]

カ[6] 戸四目[28] 江[39] 筑本[56] 興[72]

三[三浦][7] 日角[28] 玉葉宗[29] 州渡濃[40] 御[住][72]

澤文字[11] 井大[16]

筒井[12] 玉[17]

浦海[12] 江[23]

APPENDIX XII

NAMES OF HOUSES IN THE YOSHIWARA

More houses will be found in this table than in the accompanying list (pages 147–156) because many of these, although shown in prints and more particularly in books, have not been found by me in contexts which name any of the inmates. Some of these brothels seem to have existed only in earlier or later times than those of the true colour print of *ukiyo-e style*. If I have come across them in illustrated books of any date, I have entered them in the list in the hope that further research will enable at least one or two of the inmates to be identified.

The first two characters in the table may be taken as 'key' characters and either of them is frequently a sign of the name of a brothel. In any context which is suspected to contain the name of one of the houses of the Yoshiwara these characters should be the ones to be looked for first: the preceding one to three characters will be the name of the brothel in question. In most instances these two suffixes are interchangeable but sometimes the 'ro-name' is quite different from that of the more commonly used 'ya-name'. All the characters given in this list should be understood to have the suffix ya following them although it is not repeated beyond No. 1.

1. Ya, a brothel
2. Rō, a brothel
3. Monjiya
4. Ichimonji-ya
5. Riki-ya
6. Chōji-ya
7. Sagami ya (Miura-ya)
8. Manji-ya
9. Kukimanji-ya
10. Yamaguchi-ya
11. Tozawa-ya
12. Idzutsu-ya
13. Maruebi-ya
14. Ōgi-ya
15. Gōmei-rō (another name for the Ōgi-ya)
16. Daimonji-ya
17. Tama-ya
18. Yeiki-ya
19. Yada-ya
20. Tachibana-ya
21. Idzu-ya
22. Yotsume-ya
23. Ōye-ya
24. Take-ya
25. Nishida-ya
26. Sanomatsu-ya
27. Hiōgo-ya
28. Sumi-ya
29. Kadotama-ya
30. Kadoebi-ya
31. Akatsuta-ya
32. Owari-ya
33. Komatsu-ya
34. Matsuba-ya
35. Idzuma-ya
36. Kane–ya
37. Higashi-ōgi-ya (this was one of the chief brothels in Ōsaka)
38. Shibaura-ya
39. Omi-ya
40. Shinano-ya
41. Okada-ya
42. Shinagawa-ya
43. Shige-idzutsu-ya
44. Idzumi-ya
45. Harumoto-ya
46. Ebi-ya
47. Mino-ya
48. Wakamatsu-ya
49. Sugata-Ebi-ya (i.e. the fashionable Ebi-ya)
50. Kiribishi-ya
51. Tokiuta-ya
52. Kurada-ya
53. Takashima-ya
54. Ibaraki-ya
55. Hishi-ya
56. Kikumoto-ya
57. Chikuzen-ya
58. Tomoe-ya (see following)
59. The Tomoe character used for the house of that name.
60. Inamotō-ya
61. Tsuta-ya
62. Ebi-ya
63. Tsuru-ya
64. Maru-ya
65. Kana-ya
66. Mame-ya
67. Kiri-ya
68. Kashiwa-ya
69. Yamamoto-ya
70. Yoshimura-ya
71. Utamina-ya
72. Yogo-ya

曾¹ 叢⁴ 小⁶ 艸⁸ 画¹⁰ 圖¹² 画¹⁵ 漢¹⁷ 畫¹⁹ 畫²¹
我 畫 畫 筆 譜 解 鑑 画 史 會
鹿² 祖⁵ 草⁷ 漢⁹ 圖¹¹ 畫¹³ 畫¹⁶ 畫¹⁸ 畫²⁰ 鑑²²
畫 畫 筆 画 會 傳 式 本 苑 鏡²³
達³ 筆 祖 畫 画¹⁴ 法 筆 訣 碩²⁴

CLASSICAL SCHOOL

繪¹ 江³ 俳⁵ 和⁸ 首¹² 山¹⁴ 源¹⁷ 曾²⁰ 和²³ 花
本 戸 諧 漢 東¹⁰ 水 氏 我 歌 鳥
名² 六⁴ 狂⁶ 百⁹ 海¹³ 拓 伊¹⁵ 物¹⁸ 漫²¹ 美²⁴
所 歌 歌 人 道 世 勢 語 畫 人
記 傴 合⁷ 一 盡¹¹ 繪 筆¹⁶ 帖¹⁹ 女²² の²⁵

UKIYO-E SCHOOL AND OTHERS

KEY CHARACTERS FOR READING BOOK TITLES

APPENDIX XIII

KEY CHARACTERS FOR READING BOOK TITLES

CLASSICAL SCHOOL

The table of characters will show, even on cursory examination, how a single character may be differently combined in a title and also how a character may take either of two readings. The two forms of 'GWA' should also be noted: these are quite interchangeable in titles of books, as elsewhere. It will also be readily apparent that different combinations of characters may have the same reading, i.e. Sōgwa (Nos. 5 and 6).

1. Sōga	9. Kangwa	17. Kangwa
2. Sogwa	10. Gwafu	18. Gwahon
3. Umpitsu Sogwa	11. Dzu-e	19. Gwashi
4. Sōgwa	12. Dzu-kai	20. Gwayen
5. Sōgwa	13. Gwaden	21. Gwaye
6. Shogwa	14. Gwahō Hikketsu	22. Kagami
7. Sōhitsu	15. Gwakan	23. Kagami
8. Sōhitsu	16. Gwashiki	24. Kagami

UKIYO-E SCHOOL AND OTHERS

1. Ehon	10. Tokaidō	19. Jo
2. Meisho-ki	11. Dzukushi	20. Waka
3. Edo	12. Sansui	21. Mangwa
4. Rok'kasen	13. Ukiyo-e	22. Onna
5. Haikai	14. Genji	23. Kwachō
6. Kyoka	15. Ise	24. Bijin
7. Awase	16. Hitsu	25. No
8. Wakan	17. Sōga (Brothers)	
9. Hiakunin Isshiu	18. Monogatari	

CHARACTERS USED ON COVERS AND IN COLOPHONS OF BOOKS

A	B	C	D	E	F	G	H	I	J
版	上	孩	冊	帙	冤	樣	名	天	秋
元	中	編	卷	第	寫	編	朿	地	冬
板	下	初	七	箒	寫	輯	抄	人	漫
元	全	物	之	一	寫	景	冬	春	画
梓	終	冊	上	覽	摹	像	丈	夏	圖

A.1, 2. *Hammoto* (publisher, i.e. one who owned the blocks).

A.3, 4. *Hammoto* (publisher, an alternative written form).

A.5. *Shinzu* (publisher. A new character sometimes found on western style printings of early Meiji times).

B.1. *Jo* (Upper). 2. *Chu* (Middle). 3. *Ge* (Lower) used to denote first, second and third volumes of a three-volume work.

B.4. *Zen* (to denote a single volume work).

B.5. *Owari* (denoting the last or final volume).

C.1. *Owari* (as B.5 but cursive style).

C.2. *Hen* (a part).

C.3. *Sho* (first).

C.4. (as C.3 but cursive style) so, *Shohen* (first part).

C.5. *Satsu* (a volume) usually found on older works.

D.1. *Satsu* (as C.5 but cursive style).

D.2. *Maki* (a volume).

D.3, 4, 5, reading *Hichi no jo*, i.e. first volume of seven and so for other numbers.

E.1. *Chitsu* (a case or portfolio) volumes are sometimes fitted into folding cases and so *shō chitsu*=first case, etc.

E.2. *Dai* a number, so *dai ni*=number two, etc.

E.3. *Dai* (as E.2 but cursive style).

E.4, 5. *Ichiran* (a synopsis) occurs on books of views of provinces, roads, rivers, etc.

F.1. *Ichiran* (a cursive version of E.4 and 5, together).

F.2, 3, 4. All forms of *utsusu* (copied in the sense of copied from Nature).

F.5. *Bosu* (copied) used in copying the works of another artist.

G.1. With F.5 read *Moyo* (Patterns) on books of designs.

G.2, 3. *Henshu*. (Collected or arranged.)

G.4. *Kei* (Views).

G.5. *Zō* (Portraits).

H.1, 2. *Meishō* (Famous places).

H.3, 4, 5. (Actually only two characters). *Monogatari* (cursive style). Tales.

I.1, 2, 3. *Ten, Chi, Jin.* (Heaven, Earth, Man) used to number three volumes.

I.4, 5, and J.1, 2. *Shun, Ka, Shu, Tō* (Spring, Summer, Autumn, Winter) used to number four volume works.

J.3, 4. *Manga* (Rough Sketches) in seal characters.

J.5. *Dzu* (Pictures) in seal characters.

A GENERAL BIBLIOGRAPHY OF WORKS
ON JAPANESE PRINTS
AND
ILLUSTRATED BOOKS

GENERAL WORKS ON JAPANESE PRINTS AND ILLUSTRATED BOOKS

AMSDEN, D.: *Impressions of Ukiyo-e.* San Francisco and New York 1905.

ANDERSON, W.: *Japanese wood engravings; their history, technique and character.* London and N.Y. 1908.

AUBERT, L.: *Les Maîtres de l'estampe Japonaise.* Paris 1914.

AZECHI, U.: Japanese Woodblock Prints: their techniques and Appreciation. Tōkyō 1963.

BACHOFER, L.: *Die Kunst der Japanischen Holzschnittmeister.* Munchen 1922.

BENESCH, O.: *Die Spätmeister des Japanischen Holzschnitts.* Wien, n.d.

BING, S.: *Exposition de gravure japonaise.* Paris 1890.

BINYON, L.: *A Catalogue of the Japanese and Chinese Woodcuts in the British Museum.* London 1916.

BINYON, L. and SEXTON, J. J. O'BRIEN: *Japanese Colour Prints.* London 1923.

BLUNT, W.: *Japanese Colour Prints from Harunobu to Utamaro.* London 1952.

BOLLER, W.: *Masterpieces of the Japanese Color Woodcut.* Boston, n.d. London 1957.

BROWN, L. N.: *Japanese Wood Engraving From the Earliest Times to the Present Day.* London 1921.

BROWN, L. N.: *Block Printing and Book Illustration in Japan.* London 1924.

CHIBA, REIKO: *The Making of a Japanese Print.* Tōkyō 1964.

'C.O.': *Japanse Penseel-Tekeningen:* Rijksmuseum voor Volkenkunde. Leiden, n.d. (*c.* 1960).

DARMON, J. E.: *Répertoire des estampes Japonaises. Les artistes et leur signatures, les procédés, etc.* Paris 1922.

DOUGLAS, K. R.: 'Japanese Illustrated Books'. *Bibliographica.* Vol. III. London 1897.

EDMUNDS, WILL H.: The Identification of Japanese Colour Prints. *Burlington Magazine.* January, March, April, September 1922.

EINSTEIN, K.: *Der Fruhere Japanische Holzschnitt.* Berlin 1922.

FENELLOSA, E. F.: *The Masters of Ukiyo-e.* N.Y. 1896.

FENELLOSA, E. F.: *An Outline History of the Ukiyo-e.* Tōkyō and Braunschweig 1901.

FICKE, A. D.: *Chats on Japanese Colour Prints.* London 1915.

FREITAS, JORDAO DE: *A Imprensa de tipos móveis em Macau e no Japao nos fins do seculo XVI.* Coimbra 1916.

FUJIKAKE SHIZUYA: *Ukiyo-e no Kenkyu:* 3 vols. Tōkyō 1943.

FUJIKAKE, S.: *Japanese Woodblock Prints.* Tōkyō 1953.

GOOKIN, F. W.: *Japanese Colour Prints and their Designers.* N.Y. 1913.

GOOKIN, F. W.: *Descriptive Catalogue of Japanese Colour Prints; The Collection of Alexander G. Mosle.* Leipzig 1927.

GOOKIN, F. W.: *Catalogue of Japanese Colour Prints in the Collection of the late Alexis Rouart.* Paris 1922.

GUNSAULUS, HELEN C.: *The Clarence Buckingham Collection of Japanese Prints. The Primitives.* Vol. I. Portland Maine. U.S.A. 1955.

HAJEK, L.: *The Osaka Woodcuts.* London, n.d. (1950s).

HAJEK, L.: *Harunobu.* London, n.d. (1950s).

HAJEK, L.: *Utamaro.* London, n.d. (1950s).

HAJEK, L.: *Japanese Woodcuts; the Primitives.* London, n.d. (1950s).

HAJEK, L.: *Hokusai.* London, n.d. (1950s).

(All the above volumes by Dr L. Hajek deal with many more artists than those of their titles which merely designate a period or school and since they are more general they are listed in this section.)

HEMPEL, R.: *Okubi-e Porträts in Japanischen Farbenholzschnitt,* Stuttgart 1964.

HILLIER, J.: *Japanese Masters of the Colour Print.* London 1954.

HILLIER, J.: *The Japanese Print; a New Approach.* London 1960.

HIYAMA, Y.: *Gyotaku: The Art and Technique of the Japanese Fish Print.* New York 1964.

HOLLOWAY, O. E.: *The Graphic Art of Japan.* London 1957.

IIJIMA, K.: *Ukiyo-e-shi Utagawa Retsuden* (Lives of the Utagawa Masters of the Genre Print).

INOUE, W.: *Ukiyo-e Shiden* (Biographies of masters of the Ukiyo-e school). Tōkyō 1931.

ISHIDA, M.: *Japanese Buddhist Prints.* Tōkyō 1964.

JOOP, G.: *Japanische Farbenholzschnitte.* Braunschweig 1964.

KONDO, I.: Japanese Genre Painting. Rutland, U.S.A. 1961.

KURTH, J.: *Der Japanische Holzschnitt.* Munich 1911.

KURTH, J.: *Die Primitiven des Japanholzschnitts.* Dresden 1922.

KURTH, J.: *Die Geschichte des Japanischen Holzschnitts.* 3 vols. Leipzig 1925–1930.

LANE, R.: *Masters of the Japanese Print.* London 1962.

LEDOUX, L. V.: *The Japanese Prints of the Ledoux Collection.* 5 vols. N.Y. 1942–1951.

LEMOISNE, P. A.: *L'Estampe Japonaise.* Paris 1914.

LÖWENSTEIN, F. E.: *Die Handzeichnungen der Japanischen Holzschnittmeister* Plauern. 1923.

MATSUKATA, S.: *Catalogue of Ukiyo-e Prints in the Collection of Mr K. Matsukata*. Ōsaka 1925.

Metropolitan Museum of Art Miniatures. Japanese Prints N.Y. 1952.

METZGAR, J. D.: *Adventure in Japanese Prints*. Los Angeles, n.d.

MICHENER, J.: *The Floating World*. N.Y. 1952.

MICHENER, J.: *Japanese Prints: from Early Masters to Modern*. N.Y. 1959.

MORRISON, A.: *Painters of Japan* (Vol. 2, chapter on Ukiyo-e painters).

NARAZAKI, M. and KONDO, I.: *Critical History of Japanese Landscape Woodprints*. Tōkyō 1951.

PERZYNSKI, F.: *Der Japanische Farbenholzschnitt*. Berlin 1922.

ROBINSON, B. W.: *Japanese Landscape Prints of the Nineteenth Century*. London 1957.

RUFFY, A. W.: *Japanese Colour Prints*. London 1952.

RUMPF, F.: *Meister des Japanischen Farbenholzschnittes*. Berlin 1924.

RUMPF, F.: *Die Anfänge des Japanischen Holzschnittes in Edo. Ostasiatische Zeitsch*. N.F. 7. 1924.

RUMPF, F.: *Die Anfänge des Farbenholzschnitts in China and Japan*. Dresden 1897, rev. ed. in English 1910.

SEIDLITZ, W. VON: *Geschichte des Japanischen Farbenholzschnitts*. Dresden 1897 and 1910. (French and English translations of this work were published.)

SERVOLINI, L.: *La Xilografia Giapponese*. Milan. 1950.

SEXTON, J. J. O'BRIEN: 'Illustrated Books of Japan, I–IV.' *Burlington Magazine*. November 1917, March 1918, October 1918 and March 1919. (Deals with some books of Shigenobu and Utamaro.)

SHIMIDZU, F.: *Ukiyo-e jin mei Jiten oyobi gendai hangaku mei kan*. Tōkyō 1955 (a dictionary of print artists).

STERN, H.P.: *Figure Prints of Old Japan*. San Francisco 1959.

STEWART, B.: *On Collecting Japanese Colour Prints*. London 1917.

STEWART, B.: *Japanese Colour Prints and the subjects they Illustrate*. London 1920.

STEWART, B.: *Subjects Portrayed in Japanese Colour Prints*. London 1922.

STRANGE, E. F.: *Tools and Materials Illustrating the Japanese Methods of Colour Printing*. London 1924.

STRANGE, E. F.: *Japanese Illustration*. London 1897.

STRANGE, E. F.: *The New Year's Card of Japan* (The Ludgate, n.s. Vol. 5.) London 1898.

STRANGE, E. F.: *The Colour Prints of Japan: an appreciation*. London 1895.

STRANGE, E. F.: *The Colour Prints of Japan*. London 1904. American edition. N.Y. 1904.

STRANGE, E. F.: *Japanese Colour Prints*. London 1907, and many later reprints and editions.

SUZUKI, J.: *Nippon hangwa benran* (Kodansha, Tokyo 1962) an encyclopaedic companion to the study of Japanese prints.

TAJIMA, S.: *Masterpieces Selected from the Ukiyo-e School.* Tokyo, 5 vols. 1906–1909.

TAKAHASHI, S.: *The Evolution of Ukiyo-e.* Yokohama 1955.

TAKAHASHI, S.: *The Japanese Wood-Block Prints through two hundred and fifty years.* Tōkyō 1965.

TOKUNO, T.: 'Japanese Woodcutting and Woodcut Printing.' *Rep. U.S. Nat. Mus. for* 1891/92. Wash.

TRESSAN, LE MARQUIS DE: 'Documents Japonais relatifs à histoire de l'estampe.' *Bull. de la Société Franco-Japonaise de Paris.* Paris, January 1914.

TODA, K.: Descriptive Catalogue of Japanese and Chinese Illustrated Books in the Ryerson Library of the Art Institute of Chicago. Chicago 1931.

UKIYO-E. A full colour book of the Ukiyo-e taken from the Hiraki collection. Rep. in original sizes. Vol. I: *Beautiful Women.* U.S.A. 1964 to be completed in 5 vols.

UKIYO-E TAIKA SHUSEI: Tokyo 1931–1932.

VIGNIER, M. and INADA, H.: *Estampes Japonaises.* 5 vols. Paris 1909.

VOLKER, T.: *Ukiyo-e Quartet. Publisher, Designer, Engraver and Printer.* Leiden 1949 and reprint.

MONOGRAPHS ON INDIVIDUAL ARTISTS

HARUNOBU

KONDO, I.: *Suzuki Harunobu.* Kodansha: Lib. of Art. Vol. 7. U.S.A. and Tōkyō 1956.

KURTH, J.: *Suzuki Harunobu:* Munich 1922.

WATERHOUSE, D. B.: *Harunobu and his Age.* London 1964.

YOSHIDA, T.: *Harunobu Zenshu.* Tōkyō 1942.

HIROSHIGE

AMSDEN, D. and HAPPER, J. S.: *The Heritage of Hiroshige.* San Francisco 1912.

CHIBA, R.: *Hiroshige's Tōkaidō in prints and poetry.* Tōkyō 1963.

EXNER, W.: *Hiroshige.* London 1960.

NOGUCHI, Y.: *Hiroshige.* N. Y. 1921.

ROBINSON, B.W.: *Hiroshige.* London 1963.

STRANGE, E. F.: *The Colour Prints of Hiroshige.* London 1925.

TAKAHASHI, S.: *Ando Hiroshige.* Tōkyō and U.S.A. Kodansha Lib. Art. Vol. 6.

TAMBA, T.: *The Art of Hiroshige,* Tōkyō 1965.

TAMBA, T.: *Works of Hiroshige in the Tamba Collection.* Ōsaka 1965.

(VOLKER, T.): *Hiroshige. Herinnerringstentoonstelling 1858–1958. Ver voor Japanse Grafisk en Kleinkunst 1938–1958.* Rotterdam 1958.

HOKUSAI

BOWIE, T. R.: *The Drawings of Hokusai.* U.S.A. 1964.
GONCOURT, E. DE: *Hokusai.* Paris 1896.
GRAY, B.: *Hokusai 1760–1849.* Cat. Mem. Exhibition. London 1948.
HILLIER, J.: *Hokusai, Paintings, Drawings and Woodcuts.* London 1955.
HOLMES, C. J.: *Hokusai.* N.Y. and London 1901.
KONDO, I.: *Katsushika Hokusai.* Kodansha Lib. of Art. Vol. 1. Vermont and Tokyo 1955.
PERZYNSKI, F.: *Hokusai.* Leipzig 1904.
REVON, H.: *Étude sur Hokusai.* Paris 1898.
WINZINGER, F.: *Hokusai.* Müchen 1964.

KAIGETSUDO

FICKE, A. D.: 'The Prints of the Kwaigetsudo.' *The Arts.* Vol. 4. No. 2. N.Y. 1923.
LANE, R., *Kaigetsudō.* U.S.A. 1959.

KIYONAGA (see also under erotic prints).
HIRANO, C.: *Kiyonaga: A Study of his Life and Works.* Boston 1939. 2 vols.
TAKAHASHI, S.: *Torii Kiyonaga:* Kodansha Lib. of Art. Vol. 8. Vermont and Tokyo 1956.
SHIBUI, K.: *Ukiyo-e Hanga.* Series 5 (Kiyonaga). Tōkyō 1964.

KUNIYOSHI

ROBINSON, B. W.: *Kuniyoshi.* London 1961.
SPEISER, W. *Kuniyoshi; ein Meister des japanischen Farbholzschnitts.* Essen 1963.

SHARAKU

ADACHI, T., ed.: *Sharaku* (a complete collection of fascimile prints). Text by Yoshida Teruji. Tokyo 1952.
GRILLI, E.: *Sharaku.* London 1959.
HENDERSON, H. G. and LEDOUX, L. V.: *The Surviving Works of Sharaku.* N. Y. 1939.
KONDI, I.: *Toshusai Sharaku.* Kodansha Lib. of Art. Vol. 2. Vermont and Tokyo 1952.
KURTH, J.: *Sharaku.* Munich 1922.
RUMPF, F.: *Sharaku.* Berlin 1932.

SHUNSHŌ
GOOKIN, F.: *Katsukawa Shunshō 1726–1793.* Art Institute, Chicago 1931. Mimeographed only.
SUCCO, F.: *Katsukawa Shunshō:* Dresden 1922.

TOYOKUNI
KIKUCHI, S.: *Utagawa Toyokuni.* Kodansha Library of Art. Vol. 9. Vermont and Tokyo 1957.
SUCCO, F.: *Utagawa Toyokuni und seine Zeit:* Munich 1913–1914.
FUJIKAKE SHIZUYA: *Toyokuni Ukiyo-e Shu.* Tōkyō 1926.

UTAMARO
GONCOURT, E. DE: *Outamaro. Le Peintre des Maisons Vertes.* Paris 1891.
HILLIER, J.: *Utamaro.* London 1961.
INOUE, W.: Utamaro Memorial Exhibition. Tōkyō 1926.
KURTH, J.: *Utamaro.* Leipzig 1907.
SHIBUI KIYOSHI: *Utamaro.* Tōkyō 1952.
YOSHIDA, T.: *Utamaro Zenshu.* Tōkyō 1941.

SHUNGA (EROTIC WORKS)
ANON: *Hihan Kiyonaga.* Tōkyō 1953.
ANON: *Japanische Erotik. Sechsunddreissig Holzschnitts von Moronobu, Harunobu, Utamaro.* Munchen 1907.
DENSMORE, M.: *Les Estampes érotiques japonaises.* Paris 1961.
GROSBOIS, C.: *Shunga, Bilder des Fruhlings.* Berlin 1964.
HAYASHI, Y.: *A Study of Erotic Books illustrated by Harunobu.* Tōkyō 1964.
HAYASHI, Y.: *A Study of the Erotic Books of Toyokuni I.* Tōkyō 1964.
Nippon Empon Dai-Shusei (Bibliography of Japanese Erotic Books) edited by the Research Society of Erotic Books. Tōkyō 1960. (Gives title, story and illustrative contents of each work listed.)
PONCETTON, F.: *Les érotiques Japonais, recueil d'estampes du 16me. au 19me, siècle tirées des grandes collections Parisiennes.* Paris 1925.
SHIBUI, K.: *Genroku ko-hanga shuei. Estampes Érotiques Primitives du Japon.* 2 vols. Tōkyō 1926–1928.
SHIBUI, K.: *Yoshiwara-bon.* Tōkyō 1936.
SHIBUI, K.: *The Primitives.* Tōkyō 1954.
SHIBUI, K.: *Utamaro.* Tōkyō 1952. (Deals with the life and work of this artist but illustrates and gives a large amount of space to the Shunga.)
SHIBUI, K.: *Koryusai no makura-e. Nagoya Shōka Daigaku Ronshu. No. 6.* (Nagoya 1961).
TAKAHASHI, T.: *Eros Japan,* Tōkyō, 1964. Ltd. ed. vol. I only. A most important and erudite study of Asian eroticism.

YOSHIDA, E.: *Kiyonaga.* Tokyo 1953. (Deals largely with this artist's *shunga.*)

CATALOGUES OF PRIVATE AND PUBLIC
COLLECTIONS OF JAPANESE PRINTS

(Large catalogues with extensive general notes are listed in the section on General Works on Japanese Prints. See above.)

BJURSTRÖM, P.: *Japanska Träsnitt.* Japanese colour prints in the National Museum. Stockholm 1958.

Catalogue of Fukuba's collection of Ukiyo-e paintings to be shown at the Japan British Exhibition. London 1910.

Catalogues van voorwerpen en boekwerken betreffende de Japansche prentkunst uit's Rijks Ethnografisch Museum. Tentoonstelling gehouden in het Leidsch Volkshuis van 15–20 January, 1906.

'C.O.': *Japanse Penseel-Tekeningen.* Rijksmuseum voor Volkenkunde. Leiden, n.d. 1960 (an exhibition of interesting *ukiyo-e* sketches from the Lieftinck collection).

Die Sammlung japanischer Farbenholzschnitte des Kaiser-Wilhelm-museums zu Cranefeld, Deneken. Cranefeld 1922.

FONTEIN, J.: *Japanse grafiek. 4 Juli–27 Augustus, 1962.* Gools Museum. Hilversum 1962.

'G.H.': An Exhibition of Japanese Prints by Suzuki Harunobu. *Art Inst. Bull.* (Chicago). Vol. 20 (1926).

GOOKIN, F. W.: *Catalogue of a Loan Exhibition of Japanese Colour Prints.* Chicago 1908.

GOOKIN, F. W.: *Catalogue of a memorial exhibition of Japanese Colour Prints from the Clarence Buckingham Collection.* Chicago 1915.

GOOKIN, F. W.: Descriptive Catalogue of Japanese Colour Prints, the Collection of Alexander G. Mosle. Leipzig 1927.

GRAY, B.: 'Japanese Prints from the Tuke Collection. The Kō Signature.' *British Museum Quarterly, XII, No.* 3 (1938) pp. 96–99.

HEMPEL, R.: *Sammlung Theodor Scheiwe.* Munster 1957–1959 (2 vols.).

HEMPEL, R.: *Holzschnittkunst Japans: Landschaft, Mimen, Kurtisanen.* Stuttgart 1963.

Illustrated Catalogue of the Ukiyo-e Prints in the Tōkyō National Museum. 1962–1964. 3 vols.–3,000 illustrations.

KAWAURA, K.: *Album of Old Japanese Prints of the Ukiyo-e School.* Tokyo 1919.

KOECHLIN, R.: Exposition d'Estampes Japonaises Primitives. *Bull. d.l. Soc. Franco–Japon. No. 14.* Paris 1909.

KOECHLIN, R.: 'Troisième Exposition d'estampes Japonaises au Musée des

Arts Décoratifs. Kiyonaga, Sharaku, Buncho.' *Bull. d.l. Soc. Franco–Japon. No. 21.* Paris 1911.

KOECHLIN, R.: 'Sixième Exposition d'Estampes Japonaises.' *Bull. d.l. Soc. Franco–Japon. No. 34/35.* Paris 1915.

KURTH, J.: *Japanische Holzschnitte aus der Sammlung Straus–Negbauer in Frankfurt a.M. Ausgestellt im Stadelschen Institut Nov. bis. Dez. 1909.* Frankfurt 1909.

'L.J.E.': 'An Introduction to the Special Exhibition of the Art of the Ukiyo-e School.' *Mus. Fine Arts. Bull.* Boston February 1914.

'L.J.E.': 'A Special Exhibition of Japanese Prints by Kiyonaga, Buncho and Utamaro.' *Mus. Fine Arts Bull.* Boston December 1916.

LEDOUX, L. V.: *A Descriptive Catalogue of an Exhibition of Japanese Land-scape, Bird and Flower Prints and Surimono from Hokusai to Hiroshige.* 2 vols. N.Y. 1924.

LEDOUX, L. V.: *Exhibition of Japanese Figure Prints from Moronobu to Toyo-kuni.* The Grolier Club. N.Y. 1923.

LEDOUX, L. V.: *Japanese Figure Prints, 1775–1800.* N.Y. 1936.

MORRISON, A.: *Exhibition of Japanese Prints.* The Fine Art Soc. London 1909 and 1910. 2 vols.

MATSUKATA, K.: *Catalogue of the Ukiyo-e Prints in the Collection of Mr Kojiro Matsukata.* Ōsaka 1925.

PRIEST, A.: *Japanese Prints from the Henry L. Phillips Collection.* N. Y. 1947.

PUNNETT, R. C., PROFESSOR: *Loan Exhibition of Japanese Prints from the Collection of Professor R. C. Punnett.* Roy. Albert Mem. Mus. Exeter 1960. (Professor Punnett (*in litt.* 24. vi. 63) informs me that his collection of Japanese prints is now in the Bristol City Art Gallery.)

STRANGE, E. F.: *Japanese Colour Prints lent by R. Leicester, Harmsworth.* Victoria and Albert Museum. London 1913.

TAKAHASHI, S. and KONDA, I. et al.: *Colour Prints published by the Tōkyō National Museum,* 1956–1958, 6 vols.

TAKAHASHI, S.: *Ukiyo-e. Prints from the Hiraki Collection,* 1964–1966, 5 vols. Tōkyō.

(TIEDEMANN, H.): *Japanese Colour Prints.* Collection formed by Mrs. T. Straus–Negbauer. Berlin, n.d. ?1925.

UKIYO-E ZENSHU: *Mus. Ueno.* Japan 1958.

VIGNIER, M.: *Estampes Japonaises primitives exposées au Musée des Arts Décoratifs en Février 1909.* Paris 1909.

VISSER, M. W. DE: *Japansche Kleurendrukken in het Rijks Ethnographisch Museum to Leiden.* Amsterdam 1911–1915 (16 parts).

YAMANAKA: *Exhibition of Japanese Prints.* 1926.

CATALOGUES OF AUCTION SALES OF JAPANESE PRINTS

AMSTERDAM
Cock-Blomhoff 1907; Lieftinck 1935. Various Collections (Brandt) 1964.

BERLIN
Perl 1913; Bondy 1927; Straus-Negbauer 1928; Solf 1936.

BRUSSELS
Massart 1962.

COLOGNE
Bretschneider 1908.

HAMBURG
Behrens, Saenger, Smidt 1909.

KYŌTO
Otani 1909.

LEIPZIG
Mosle 1927.

MUNCHEN
Kropp 1910.

LONDON
Happer, Salt Webster and Scantlebury 1909; Anon. Barclay, Blondeau, Appleton, Gookin, van Heymel, Ritchie, Swettenham 1910; 'An Importer of Japanese Products' 1911; Anon. Tuke, Miller, Satow, Foxwell, Blow, Orange and Thorneycroft, Swettenham 1912; 'A Gentleman Residing in Paris', Tebbs, 1913; Dauckwerts 1914; Genthe 1915; Kington, Baker, Hilditch 1916; 'A Parisian Collector', Hall, Reuben and Evans, Wilson 1918; Crewdson 1919; Getting 1920; Thatcher Clarke 1921; Sexton 1923; Crzellitzer, Mienzil 1925; Hall, Harmsworth 1938; McNair Scott 1960; Foster, Leckell, Mitchell, Mitchell and Epstein, Meade 1961; Darby, Dening, Sands, Kitson, Oppenheimer, Mitchell, Hart, Kingston, Wilkinson 1962; Mellor 1963; Little, Coyne, Kurtz, Mitchell and Carter 1964.

NEW YORK
Bunkyo Matsuki 1907–1908; Blanchard, Metzgar 1916; Hirakawa,

Genthe 1917; May 1918; Hunter, Metzgar 1919; Hoyt, Ficke 1920; Ficke, Spaulding, 'French Connoisseur', Shraubstadter, van Caneghen, 'A Distinguished French Connoisseur' (Jacquin), 1921; Rouart, The Bremen Art Museum, Hamilton, Easter, Field 1922; A Collection from Berlin 1923; 'A New York Collector' 1924; Ficke, Kawaura 1925; Mori 1926; Wright 1927; Fuller, Garland 1945; Church 1946; Phillips 1947; Morse 1957.

PARIS
Hayashi 1902; Gillot, Barboutau 1904; 'S. L. de Londres', 'Un Amateur de l'Étranger' 1909; Ikeda, Barboutau 1910; 'M.A.D.', 'Mme. L.', Morita 1912; Bermond, Manos 1913; Manzi 1920; Barnes 1921; Haviland, Gonse, Charvarse, Saloman 1922; Haviland, Gonse, Sarda 1923; Haviland, Gonse 1924; Isaac 1925; Javal, Corbin 1926; Haviland, Haase 1927; Migeon 1931; Portier 1933; Chausson 1936.

SCARBOROUGH
Holtby 1958.

ENCYCLOPAEDIAS AND DICTIONARIES OF UKIYO-E

Suzuki Juzō. Nippon Hangwa Benran. Kodansha, Tōkyō. 1962. It is regretted that this work was not known to me when writing the present book. Not only would it have lightened the labours of research but it would have enabled the lists in my own work to be more complete. It is a truly encyclopaedic companion to the study of the Japanese print although it does not cover the subjects that were illustrated. A very lavish use of abbreviated characters in the text may make difficulties for some occidental students of the written language. As a guide to publishers, printers and engravers this erudite little work is without equal.
Yoshida, T. Ukiyo-e Jiten. Tōkyō 1965, 3 vols.

PERIODICALS AND COLLECTIONS OF PRINTS
PUBLISHED SERIALLY

Nihon Fuzuoka Zu-e. Tōkyō 1914–1915. 12 vols.
Nippon Hangwa Bijutsu Zenshu. Tōkyō 1960–1962. 9 vols.
Shibui, K. Ukiyo-e Zuten. Tōkyō 1964 et seq. 24 vols.
Ukiyo-e Taika Shushei. Tōkyō 1931—1932. 20 vols. with a supplementary 6 vols. published in 1933.
Ukiyo-e Taisei. Tōkyō 1930–1931. 12 vols.

Ukiyo-e no Kenkyu. Tōkyō 1921–1928. The Magazine of the old Ukiyo-e
society.

Ukiyo-e Zenshu. Tōkyō 1952–1957.

Ukiyo-e Art. Tōkyō 1962 et seq. The journal of the new Japan Ukiyo-e
Society. Ten issues to date.

Nippon Ukiyo-e Kyōkai Kaihō. Tōkyō 1962 et seq. The Bulletin of the
Japan Ukiyo-e Society. Fourteen issues to date.

SOME JAPANESE WORKS NOT MENTIONED IN THE TEXT

Fujikake, Shizuya: *Ukiyo-e Taika Gashu.* Tōkyō 1915.

Fujikake, Shizuya: *Matsukata Ukiyo-e Hanga-shu Kassetsu.* Tōkyō 1915.

Goya Hachiguchi: *Yamato Nishiki-e.* 12 vols. Tōkyō 1918.

Kishida Ryusai: *Shōki Nikuhitsu Ukiyo-e.* Tōkyō 1926.

Nakata Tsunosuke: *Ukiyo-e Shuki.* Tōkyō 1944.

Yoshida Teruji: *Ukiyo-e Taisei,* 4 vols. Tōkyō 1930.

Toyonari Yamamura: *Shibai Nishiki-e Shusei.* Tōkyō 1919. (A useful
reference for theatrical colour prints.)

Ushiyama, J.: *Ukiyo-e Kyōen Gashu.* Tōkyō 1931. (An important study
of the nude in Japanese art.)

SOME JAPANESE ILLUSTRATED SALE CATALOGUES OF PRINTS

Kimbei Murata 1913 to 1920; Shōbisha 1926; Shōbisha, Shimizu Gensendō, Owari-kai 1927; Owari-kai 1928; Owari-kai, Shōbisha, Shimizu,
Fujiwara 1929; Kyōto Nishiki-e 1930; Shimizu Gensendō 1931; Kinko-
kai 1933.

NOTE: *Douglas, R. K.* Catalogue of Japanese Printed Books and Manu-
scripts in the Library of the British Museum. London 1898 and *Douglas,
R. K.* Catalogue of Japanese Printed Books and Manuscripts in the
British Museum acquired during the years 1899–1903. London 1904.
This large work is still useful to the student of the Japanese illustrated
book but it cannot be used by anyone without some knowledge of the
Japanese language since all the titles are romanized in sinico-Japanese
readings and are therefore mostly quite unrecognizable. However,
Chinese and Japanese characters are also given and these make it still a
valuable and easily obtained reference. Prof. Twitchett is perhaps rather
too severe in his castigation of this work.

INDEX